Head First Ruby

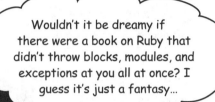

Wouldn't it be dreamy if there were a book on Ruby that didn't throw blocks, modules, and exceptions at you all at once? I guess it's just a fantasy...

Jay McGavren

Damian,
Great to
meet you!
#oscon

Beijing · Boston · Farnham · Sebastopol · Tokyo

O'REILLY®

Head First Ruby

by Jay McGavren

Printed in the United States of America.

Published by O'Reilly Media, Inc., 1005 Gravenstein Highway North, Sebastopol, CA 95472.

O'Reilly Media books may be purchased for educational, business, or sales promotional use. Online editions are also available for most titles (*http://safaribooksonline.com*). For more information, contact our corporate/institutional sales department: (800) 998-9938 or *corporate@oreilly.com*.

Series Creators:	Kathy Sierra, Bert Bates
Editors:	Meghan Blanchette, Courtney Nash
Cover Designer:	Ellie Volkhausen
Production Editor:	Melanie Yarbrough
Production Services:	Rachel Monaghan
Indexer:	Bob Pfahler

Printing History:

November 2015: First Edition.

Code for this book was developed using 100% recycled electrons.

ISBN: 978-1-449-37265-1

[M]

To open source software creators everywhere.
You make all of our lives better.

Author of Head First Ruby

Jay McGavren

Jay McGavren was working on automation for a hotel services company when a colleague introduced him to *Programming Perl* (a.k.a. the Camel Book). It made him an instant Perl convert, as he liked actually writing code instead of waiting for a 10-person development team to configure a build system. It also gave him the crazy idea to write a technical book someday.

In 2007, with Perl sputtering, Jay was looking for a new interpreted language. With its strong object orientation, excellent library support, and incredible flexibility, Ruby won him over. He's since used Ruby for two game libraries, for a generative art project, and as a Ruby on Rails freelancer. He's been working in the online developer education space since 2011.

You can follow Jay on Twitter at *https://twitter.com/jaymcgavren*, or visit his personal website at *http://jay.mcgavren.com*.

Table of Contents (Summary)

Table of Contents (the real thing)

Intro

Your brain on Ruby. Here *you* are trying to *learn* something, while here your *brain* is, doing you a favor by making sure the learning doesn't *stick*. Your brain's thinking, "Better leave room for more important things, like which wild animals to avoid and whether naked snowboarding is a bad idea." So how *do* you trick your brain into thinking that your life depends on knowing how to program in Ruby?

1

more with less

Code the Way You Want

You're wondering what this crazy Ruby language is all about,

and if it's right for you. Let us ask you this: ***Do you like being productive?*** Do you feel like all those extra compilers and libraries and class files and keystrokes in your other language bring you closer to a **finished product**, **admiring coworkers**, and **happy customers**? Would you like a language that **takes care of the details** for you? If you sometimes wish you could stop maintaining boilerplate code and *get to work on your problem*, then Ruby is for you. Ruby lets you **get more done with less code.**

Source code

my_program.rb

The Ruby interpreter

The computer executes your program.

methods and classes
Getting Organized

2

You've been missing out. You've been calling methods and creating objects like a pro. But the only methods you could call, and the only kinds of objects you could create, were the ones that Ruby defined for you. Now, it's your turn. You're going to learn to create your *own* methods. You'll also create your own **classes**—templates for new objects. *You'll decide* what objects based on your class will be like. You'll use **instance variables** to define what those objects *know*, and **instance methods** to define what they *do*. And most importantly, you'll discover how defining your own classes can make your code *easier to read and maintain*.

Objects

Class

inheritance

Relying on Your Parents

3

So much repetition! Your new classes representing the different types of vehicles and animals are awesome, it's true. But you're having to *copy instance methods from class to class*. And the copies are starting to fall out of sync—some are fine, while others have bugs. Weren't classes supposed to make code *easier* to maintain?

In this chapter, we'll learn how to use **inheritance** to let your classes *share* methods. Fewer copies means fewer maintenance headaches!

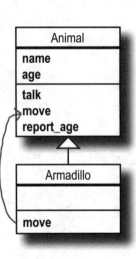

initializing instances

Off to a Great Start

Right now, your class is a time bomb.
Every instance you create starts out as a clean slate. If you call certain instance methods before adding data, an error will be raised that will bring your whole program to a screeching halt.

In this chapter, we're going to show you a couple of ways to create objects that are safe to use right away. We'll start with the `initialize` method, which lets you pass in a bunch of arguments to set up an object's data *at the time you create it*. Then we'll show you how to write **class methods**, which you can use to create and set up an object even **more** easily.

No more blank names and negative salaries for our new employees? And it won't delay the payroll project? Nice job!

arrays and blocks

Better Than Loops

A whole lot of programming deals with lists of things. Lists of

addresses. Lists of phone numbers. Lists of products. Matz, the creator of Ruby, knew this. So he worked *really hard* to make sure that working with lists in Ruby is *really easy*. First, he ensured that **arrays**, which keep track of lists in Ruby, have lots of *powerful methods* to do almost anything you might need with a list. Second, he realized that writing code to *loop over a list* to do something with each item, although tedious, is something developers were doing *a lot*. So he added **blocks** to the language, and removed the need for all that looping code. What is a block, exactly? Read on to find out…

Code from the method stays the same.

```
puts "We're in the method, about to invoke your block!"
puts "We're in the block!"
puts "We're back in the method!"
```

Block code changes!

block return values

How Should I Handle This?

You've seen only a fraction of the power of blocks. Up until now, the *methods* have just been handing data off to a *block*, and expecting the block to handle everything. But a *block* can also return data to the *method*. This feature lets the method get *directions* from the block, allowing it to do more of the work.

In this chapter, we'll show you some methods that will let you take a *big, complicated* collection, and use **block return values** to cut it down to size.

6

```
        [2, 3, 4]
    number ** 2
        [4, 9, 16]
```

```
["...Truncated is amazing...",
 "...Truncated is funny...",
 "...Truncated is astounding..."]
        find_adjective(review)
        [ amazing",
            "funny",
        "astounding"]
```

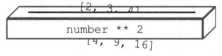

hashes

Labeling Data

7

Throwing things in piles is fine, until you need to find something again. You've already seen how to create a collection of objects using an *array*. You've seen how to process *each item* in an array, and how to *find items* you want. In both cases, you start at the beginning of the array, and *look through Every. Single. Object.* You've also seen methods that take big collections of parameters. You've seen the problems this causes: method calls require a big, *confusing collection of arguments* that you have to remember the exact order for.

What if there were a kind of collection where *all the data had labels* on it? You could *quickly find the elements* you needed! In this chapter, we'll learn about Ruby **hashes**, which do just that.

Start at the top; search the whole pile.

Array

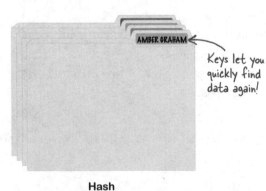

AMBER GRAHAM

Keys let you quickly find data again!

Hash

references

Crossed Signals

8

Ever sent an email to the wrong contact? You probably had a hard time sorting out the confusion that ensued. Well, *Ruby objects* are *just like those contacts* in your address book, and *calling methods* on them is like *sending messages* to them. If your address book gets *mixed up*, it's possible to send messages to the *wrong object*. This chapter will help you *recognize the signs* that this is happening, and help you *get your programs running smoothly* again.

Oak Street in reality

Oak Street according to Andy's address book

9

mixins

Mix It Up

Inheritance has its limitations. You can only inherit methods from one class. But what if you need to share *several sets of behavior* across several classes? Like methods for starting a battery charge cycle and reporting its charge level—you might need those methods on phones, power drills, and electric cars. Are you going to create a *single* superclass for all of *those*? (It won't end well if you try.) Or methods for starting and stopping a motor. Sure, the drill and the car might need those, but the phone won't!

In this chapter, we'll learn about **modules** and **mixins**, a powerful way to *group methods together* and then share them *only with particular classes that need them*.

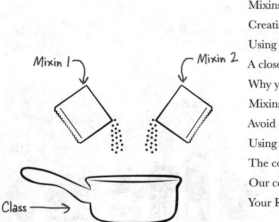

10

comparable and enumerable
Ready-Made Mixes

You've seen that mixins can be useful. But you haven't seen their full power yet. The Ruby core library includes two mixins that will *blow your mind*. The first, `Comparable`, is used for comparing objects. You've used operators like <, >, and == on numbers and strings, but `Comparable` will let you use them on *your* classes. The second mixin, `Enumerable`, is used for working with collections. Remember those super-useful `find_all`, `reject`, and `map` methods that you used on arrays before? Those came from `Enumerable`. But that's a tiny fraction of what `Enumerable` can do. And again, you can mix it into *your* classes. Read on to see how!

I'll take this one!

Choice   Prime   Select

11

documentation
Read the Manual

There isn't enough room in this book to teach you <u>all</u> of Ruby.

There's an old saying: "Give someone a fish, and you feed them for a day. Teach them how to fish, and you feed them for a lifetime." We've been *giving you fish* so far. We've shown you how to use a few of Ruby's classes and modules. But there are dozens more, some of them applicable to your problems, that we don't have room to cover. So it's time to *teach you how to fish*. There's excellent **documentation** freely available on all of Ruby's classes, modules, and methods. You just have to know where to find it, and how to interpret it. That's what this chapter will show you.

We only know the things we've learned from this book. How do we look up classes, modules, and methods **for ourselves**?

Documentation for the "today" class method →

```
.today([start = Date::ITALY]) ⇒ Object

Date.today #=> #<Date: 2011-06-11 ..>

Creates a date object denoting the present day.
```

```
#year ⇒ Integer

Returns the year.
```

← Documentation for the "year" instance method

exceptions

Handling the Unexpected

12

In the real world, the unexpected happens. Someone could

delete the file your program is trying to load, or the server your program is trying to
contact could go down. Your code could check for these exceptional situations, but
those checks would be mixed in with the code that handles normal operation. (And
that would be a big, unreadable mess.)

This chapter will teach you all about Ruby's exception handling, which lets you write
code to handle the unexpected, and keep it separate from your regular code.

unit testing

Code Quality Assurance

13

Are you sure your software is working right now? Really sure?

Before you sent that new version to your users, you presumably tried out the new features to ensure they all worked. But did you try the *old* features to ensure you didn't break any of them? *All* the old features? If that question makes you worry, your program needs automated testing. Automated tests ensure your program's components work correctly, even after you change your code.

Unit tests are the most common, most important type of automated test. And Ruby includes **MiniTest**, a library devoted to unit testing. This chapter will teach you everything you need to know about it!

ListWithCommas
items
join

Pass.

☑ If items is set to ['apple', 'orange', 'pear'], then join should return "apple, orange, and pear".

Fail!

☒ If items is set to ['apple', 'orange'], then join should return "apple and orange".

14

web apps

Serving HTML

This is the 21st century. Users want web apps. Ruby's got you covered there, too! Libraries are available to help you host your own web applications and make them accessible from any web browser. So we're going to spend these final two chapters of the book showing you how to build a full web app.

To get started, you're going to need **Sinatra**, a third-party library for writing web applications. But don't worry, we'll show you how to use the **RubyGems** tool (included with Ruby) to download and install libraries automatically! Then we'll show you just enough HTML to create your own web pages. And of course, we'll show you how to serve those pages to a browser!

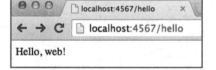

saving and loading data
Keep It Around

15

Your web app is just throwing users' data away. You've set up a form for users to *enter* data into. They're expecting that you'll *save* it, so that it can be *retrieved* and *displayed* to others later. But that's not happening right now! Anything they submit just *disappears*.

In this, our final chapter, we'll prepare your app to save user submissions. We'll show you how to set it up to accept form data. We'll show you how to convert that data to Ruby objects, how to save those objects to a file, and how to retrieve the right object again when a user wants to see it. Are you ready? Let's finish this app!

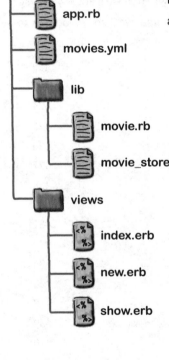

← → C ⬜ localhost:4567/form ☆

Degrees Fahrenheit: 75   [Submit]

← → C ⬜ localhost:4567/convert ☆

75.0 degrees Fahrenheit is 23.9 degrees Celsius.

leftovers

The Top Ten Topics (We Didn't Cover)

We've covered a lot of ground, and you're almost finished with this book.

We'll miss you, but before we let you go, we wouldn't feel right about sending you out into the world without a *little* more preparation. We can't possibly fit everything you'll need to know about Ruby into these few pages… (Actually, we *did* include everything originally, by reducing the type point size to .00004. It all fit, but nobody could read it. So we threw most of it away.) But we've kept all the best bits for this Top Ten appendix.

This really *is* the end of the book. Except for the index, of course. (A must-read!)

A CSV file

```
Associate,Sale Count,Sales Total
"Boone, Agnes",127,1710.26
"Howell, Marvin",196,2245.19
"Rodgers, Tonya",400,3032.48
```

sales.csv

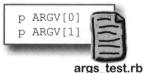

```
p ARGV[0]
p ARGV[1]
```

args_test.rb

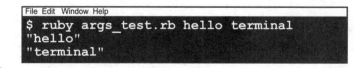

```
File Edit Window Help
$ ruby args_test.rb hello terminal
"hello"
"terminal"
```

how to use this book

Intro

*I can't believe they put **that** in a Ruby book.*

In this section, we answer the burning question: "So why DID they put that in a book on Ruby?"

Who is this book for?

If you can answer "yes" to **all** of these:

 Do you have access to a computer with a text editor?

 Do you want to learn a programming language that makes development **easy** and **productive**?

 Do you prefer **stimulating dinner-party conversation** to **dry, dull, academic lectures**?

this book is for you.

Who should probably back away from this book?

If you can answer "yes" to any **one** of these:

 Are you <u>completely</u> new to computers?

(You don't need to be advanced, but you should understand folders and files, how to open a terminal app, and how to use a simple text editor.)

 Are you a ninja rockstar developer looking for a **reference** book?

 Are you **afraid to try something new**? Would you rather have a root canal than mix stripes with plaid? Do you believe that a technical book can't be serious if it describes class inheritance using armadillos?

this book is *not* for you.

[Note from Marketing: this book is for anyone with a valid credit card.]

We know what you're thinking

"How can *this* be a serious book on developing in Ruby?"

"What's with all the graphics?"

"Can I actually *learn* it this way?"

We know what your *brain* is thinking

Your brain craves novelty. It's always searching, scanning, *waiting* for something unusual. It was built that way, and it helps you stay alive.

So what does your brain do with all the routine, ordinary, normal things you encounter? Everything it *can* to stop them from interfering with the brain's *real* job—recording things that *matter*. It doesn't bother saving the boring things; they never make it past the "this is obviously not important" filter.

How does your brain *know* what's important? Suppose you're out for a day hike and a tiger jumps in front of you—what happens inside your head and body?

Neurons fire. Emotions crank up. *Chemicals surge*.

And that's how your brain knows…

This must be important! Don't forget it!

But imagine you're at home or in a library. It's a safe, warm, tiger-free zone. You're studying. Getting ready for an exam. Or trying to learn some tough technical topic your boss thinks will take a week, 10 days at the most.

Just one problem. Your brain's trying to do you a big favor. It's trying to make sure that this *obviously* unimportant content doesn't clutter up scarce resources. Resources that are better spent storing the really *big* things. Like tigers. Like the danger of fire. Like how you should never have posted those party photos on your Facebook page. And there's no simple way to tell your brain, "Hey, brain, thank you very much, but no matter how dull this book is, and how little I'm registering on the emotional Richter scale right now, I really *do* want you to keep this stuff around."

Your brain thinks THIS is important.

Great. Only 545 more dull, dry, boring pages.

Your brain thinks THIS isn't worth saving.

We think of a "Head First" reader as a <u>learner</u>.

So what does it take to *learn* something? First, you have to *get* it, then make sure you don't *forget* it. It's not about pushing facts into your head. Based on the latest research in cognitive science, neurobiology, and educational psychology, *learning* takes a lot more than text on a page. We know what turns your brain on.

Some of the Head First learning principles:

Make it visual. Images are far more memorable than words alone, and make learning much more effective (up to 89% improvement in recall and transfer studies). It also makes things more understandable. **Put the words within or near the graphics** they relate to, rather than on the bottom or on another page, and learners will be up to *twice* as likely to solve problems related to the content.

Use a conversational and personalized style. In recent studies, students performed up to 40% better on post-learning tests if the content spoke directly to the reader, using a first-person, conversational style rather than taking a formal tone. Tell stories instead of lecturing. Use casual language. Don't take yourself too seriously. Which would *you* pay more attention to: a stimulating dinner-party companion, or a lecture?

Get the learner to think more deeply. In other words, unless you actively flex your neurons, nothing much happens in your head. A reader has to be motivated, engaged, curious, and inspired to solve problems, draw conclusions, and generate new knowledge. And for that, you need challenges, exercises, and thought-provoking questions, and activities that involve both sides of the brain and multiple senses.

Get—and keep—the reader's attention. We've all had the "I really want to learn this, but I can't stay awake past page one" experience. Your brain pays attention to things that are out of the ordinary, interesting, strange, eye-catching, unexpected. Learning a new, tough, technical topic doesn't have to be boring. Your brain will learn much more quickly if it's not.

Touch their emotions. We now know that your ability to remember something is largely dependent on its emotional content. You remember what you care about. You remember when you *feel* something. No, we're not talking heart-wrenching stories about a boy and his dog. We're talking emotions like surprise, curiosity, fun, "what the…?", and the feeling of "I rule!" that comes when you solve a puzzle, learn something everybody else thinks is hard, or realize you know something that "I'm more technical than thou" Bob from Engineering *doesn't*.

Metacognition: thinking about thinking

If you really want to learn, and you want to learn more quickly and more deeply, pay attention to how you pay attention. Think about how you think. Learn how you learn.

Most of us did not take courses on metacognition or learning theory when we were growing up. We were *expected* to learn, but rarely *taught* to learn.

But we assume that if you're holding this book, you really want to learn how to develop Ruby apps. And you probably don't want to spend a lot of time. If you want to use what you read in this book, you need to *remember* what you read. And for that, you've got to *understand* it. To get the most from this book, or *any* book or learning experience, take responsibility for your brain. Your brain on *this* content.

The trick is to get your brain to see the new material you're learning as Really Important. Crucial to your well-being. As important as a tiger. Otherwise, you're in for a constant battle, with your brain doing its best to keep the new content from sticking.

I wonder how I can trick my brain into remembering this stuff...

So just how *DO* you get your brain to treat programming like it was a hungry tiger?

There's the slow, tedious way, or the faster, more effective way. The slow way is about sheer repetition. You obviously know that you *are* able to learn and remember even the dullest of topics if you keep pounding the same thing into your brain. With enough repetition, your brain says, "This doesn't *feel* important to him, but he keeps looking at the same thing *over* and *over* and *over*, so I suppose it must be."

The faster way is to do **anything that increases brain activity,** especially different *types* of brain activity. The things on the previous page are a big part of the solution, and they're all things that have been proven to help your brain work in your favor. For example, studies show that putting words *within* the pictures they describe (as opposed to somewhere else in the page, like a caption or in the body text) causes your brain to try to makes sense of how the words and picture relate, and this causes more neurons to fire. More neurons firing = more chances for your brain to *get* that this is something worth paying attention to, and possibly recording.

A conversational style helps because people tend to pay more attention when they perceive that they're in a conversation, since they're expected to follow along and hold up their end. The amazing thing is, your brain doesn't necessarily *care* that the "conversation" is between you and a book! On the other hand, if the writing style is formal and dry, your brain perceives it the same way you experience being lectured to while sitting in a roomful of passive attendees. No need to stay awake.

But pictures and conversational style are just the beginning...

Here's what WE did

We used ***pictures***, because your brain is tuned for visuals, not text. As far as your brain's concerned, a picture really *is* worth a thousand words. And when text and pictures work together, we embedded the text *in* the pictures because your brain works more effectively when the text is *within* the thing it refers to, as opposed to in a caption or buried in the body text somewhere.

We used ***redundancy***, saying the same thing in *different* ways and with different media types, and *multiple senses*, to increase the chance that the content gets coded into more than one area of your brain.

We used concepts and pictures in ***unexpected*** ways because your brain is tuned for novelty, and we used pictures and ideas with at least *some **emotional*** *content*, because your brain is tuned to pay attention to the biochemistry of emotions. That which causes you to *feel* something is more likely to be remembered, even if that feeling is nothing more than a little ***humor***, ***surprise***, or ***interest***.

We used a personalized, ***conversational style***, because your brain is tuned to pay more attention when it believes you're in a conversation than if it thinks you're passively listening to a presentation. Your brain does this even when you're *reading*.

We included ***activities***, because your brain is tuned to learn and remember more when you ***do*** things than when you *read* about things. And we made the exercises challenging-yet-doable, because that's what most people prefer.

We used ***multiple learning styles***, because *you* might prefer step-by-step procedures, while someone else wants to understand the big picture first, and someone else just wants to see an example. But regardless of your own learning preference, *everyone* benefits from seeing the same content represented in multiple ways.

We include content for ***both sides of your brain***, because the more of your brain you engage, the more likely you are to learn and remember, and the longer you can stay focused. Since working one side of the brain often means giving the other side a chance to rest, you can be more productive at learning for a longer period of time.

And we included ***stories*** and exercises that present ***more than one point of view,*** because your brain is tuned to learn more deeply when it's forced to make evaluations and judgments.

We included ***challenges***, with exercises, and by asking ***questions*** that don't always have a straight answer, because your brain is tuned to learn and remember when it has to *work* at something. Think about it—you can't get your *body* in shape just by *watching* people at the gym. But we did our best to make sure that when you're working hard, it's on the *right* things. That ***you're not spending one extra dendrite*** processing a hard-to-understand example, or parsing difficult, jargon-laden, or overly terse text.

We used ***people***. In stories, examples, pictures, etc., because, well, *you're* a person. And your brain pays more attention to *people* than it does to *things*.

Here's what YOU can do to bend your brain into submission

So, we did our part. The rest is up to you. These tips are a starting point; listen to your brain and figure out what works for you and what doesn't. Try new things.

Cut this out and stick it on your refrigerator.

---

1 Slow down. The more you understand, the less you have to memorize.

Don't just *read*. Stop and think. When the book asks you a question, don't just skip to the answer. Imagine that someone really *is* asking the question. The more deeply you force your brain to think, the better chance you have of learning and remembering.

2 Do the exercises. Write your own notes.

We put them in, but if we did them for you, that would be like having someone else do your workouts for you. And don't just *look* at the exercises. **Use a pencil.** There's plenty of evidence that physical activity *while* learning can increase the learning.

3 Read "There Are No Dumb Questions."

That means all of them. They're not optional sidebars, ***they're part of the core content!*** Don't skip them.

4 Make this the last thing you read before bed. Or at least the last challenging thing.

Part of the learning (especially the transfer to long-term memory) happens *after* you put the book down. Your brain needs time on its own, to do more processing. If you put in something new during that processing time, some of what you just learned will be lost.

5 Talk about it. Out loud.

Speaking activates a different part of the brain. If you're trying to understand something, or increase your chance of remembering it later, say it out loud. Better still, try to explain it out loud to someone else. You'll learn more quickly, and you might uncover ideas you hadn't known were there when you were reading about it.

6 Drink water. Lots of it.

Your brain works best in a nice bath of fluid. Dehydration (which can happen before you ever feel thirsty) decreases cognitive function.

7 Listen to your brain.

Pay attention to whether your brain is getting overloaded. If you find yourself starting to skim the surface or forget what you just read, it's time for a break. Once you go past a certain point, you won't learn faster by trying to shove more in, and you might even hurt the process.

8 Feel something.

Your brain needs to know that this *matters*. Get involved with the stories. Make up your own captions for the photos. Groaning over a bad joke is *still* better than feeling nothing at all.

9 Write a lot of code!

There's only one way to learn to develop Ruby apps: **write a lot of code**. And that's what you're going to do throughout this book. Coding is a skill, and the only way to get good at it is to practice. We're going to give you a lot of practice: every chapter has exercises that pose a problem for you to solve. Don't just skip over them—a lot of the learning happens when you solve the exercises. We included a solution to each exercise—don't be afraid to **peek at the solution** if you get stuck! (It's easy to get snagged on something small.) But try to solve the problem before you look at the solution. And definitely get it working before you move on to the next part of the book.

Read me

This is a learning experience, not a reference book. We deliberately stripped out everything that might get in the way of learning whatever it is we're working on at that point in the book. And the first time through, you need to begin at the beginning, because the book makes assumptions about what you've already seen and learned.

It helps if you've done a *little* programming in some other language.

Most developers discover Ruby *after* they've learned some other programming language. (They often come seeking refuge from that other language.) We touch on the basics enough that a complete beginner can get by, but we don't go into great detail on what a variable is, or how an `if` statement works. You'll have an easier time if you've done at least a *little* of this before.

We don't cover every single class, library, and method ever created.

Ruby comes with a *lot* of classes and methods built in. Sure, they're all interesting, but we couldn't cover them all if this book was *twice* as long. Our focus is on the core classes and methods that *matter* to you, the beginner. We make sure you have a deep understanding of them, and confidence that you know how and when to use them. In any case, once you're done with *Head First Ruby*, you'll be able to pick up any reference book and get up to speed quickly on the classes and methods we left out.

The activities are NOT optional.

The exercises and activities are not add-ons; they're part of the core content of the book. Some of them are to help with memory, some are for understanding, and some will help you apply what you've learned. ***Don't skip the exercises.***

The redundancy is intentional and important.

One distinct difference in a Head First book is that we want you to *really* get it. And we want you to finish the book remembering what you've learned. Most reference books don't have retention and recall as a goal, but this book is about *learning*, so you'll see some of the same concepts come up more than once.

The code examples are as lean as possible.

It's frustrating to wade through 200 lines of code looking for the two lines you need to understand. Most examples in this book are shown in the smallest possible context, so that the part you're trying to learn is clear and simple. So don't expect the code to be robust, or even complete. That's *your* assignment after you finish the book. The book examples are written specifically for *learning*, and aren't always fully functional.

We've placed all the example files on the Web so you can download them. You'll find them at *http://headfirstruby.com/*.

Acknowledgments

Series Founders:

Huge thanks need to go first to the Head First founders, **Kathy Sierra** and **Bert Bates**. I loved the series when I encountered it a decade ago, but never imagined I might be writing for it. Thank you for creating this amazing style of teaching!

Bert deserves double credit, for offering extensive feedback on the early drafts, when I hadn't quite mastered the Head First Way. Because of you, ***Head First Ruby*** is a better book, and I am a better author!

At O'Reilly:

My eternal gratitude to my editor, **Meghan Blanchette**. She has an unwavering commitment to make books the best they can be, resolve that sustained me through those grueling second (and third) revisions. Thanks to **Mike Loukides** for helping me get on O'Reilly's radar in the first place, and to **Courtney Nash** for getting the project set up.

Thanks also to everyone else at O'Reilly who made this happen, particularly **Rachel Monaghan**, **Melanie Yarbrough**, and the rest of the production team.

Technical Reviewers:

Everyone makes mistakes, but luckily I have tech reviewers **Avdi Grimm**, **Sonda Sengupta**, **Edward Yue Shung Wong**, and **Olivier Lacan** to catch all of mine. You will never know how many problems they found, because I swiftly destroyed all the evidence. But their help and feedback were definitely necessary and are forever appreciated!

And More Thanks:

Ryan Benedetti, for helping get the project unstuck when it was mired in the early chapters. **Deborah Robinson** for typesetting help. **Janet McGavren** and **John McGavren** for proofreading. **Lenny McGavren** for photography. Readers of the Early Release, especially **Ed Fresco** and **John Larkin**, for catching typos and other glitches. Members of the **Ruby Rogues Parley** forum for feedback on code samples.

Perhaps most importantly, thanks to **Christine**, **Courtney**, **Bryan**, **Lenny**, and **Jeremy** for their patience and support. It's good to be back!

This book uses the Ruby logo, Copyright © 2006, **Yukihiro Matsumoto**. It's licensed under the terms of the Creative Commons Attribution-ShareAlike 2.5 License agreement, at *http://creativecommons.org/licenses/by-sa/2.5/*.

Safari® Books Online

Safari Books Online (*www.safaribooksonline.com*) is an on-demand digital library that delivers expert content in both book and video form from the world's leading authors in technology and business. Technology professionals, software developers, web designers, and business and creative professionals use Safari Books Online as their primary resource for research, problem solving, learning, and certification training.

Safari Books Online offers a range of product mixes and pricing programs for organizations, government agencies, and individuals. Subscribers have access to thousands of books, training videos, and prepublication manuscripts in one fully searchable database from publishers like O'Reilly Media, Prentice Hall Professional, Addison-Wesley Professional, Microsoft Press, Sams, Que, Peachpit Press, Focal Press, Cisco Press, John Wiley & Sons, Syngress, Morgan Kaufmann, IBM Redbooks, Packt, Adobe Press, FT Press, Apress, Manning, New Riders, McGraw-Hill, Jones & Bartlett, Course Technology, and dozens more. For more information about Safari Books Online, please visit us online.

1 more with less

Code the Way You Want

Come see how awesome Ruby is! We'll learn about variables, strings, conditionals, and loops. Best of all, you'll have a working game by the end of the chapter!

You're wondering what this crazy Ruby language is all about,

and if it's right for you. Let us ask you this: *Do you like being productive?* Do you feel like all those extra compilers and libraries and class files and keystrokes in your other language bring you closer to a **finished product**, **admiring coworkers**, and **happy customers**? Would you like a language that **takes care of the details** for you? If you sometimes wish you could stop maintaining boilerplate code and *get to work on your problem*, then Ruby is for you. Ruby lets you **get more done with less code.**

The Ruby philosophy

Back in the 1990s in Japan, a programmer named Yukihiro Matsumoto ("Matz" for short) was dreaming about his ideal programming language. He wanted something that:

*   Was easy to learn and use

*   Was flexible enough to handle any programming task

*   Let the programmer concentrate on the problem they were trying to solve

*   Gave the programmer less stress

*   Was object-oriented

He looked at the languages that were available, but felt that none of them was exactly what he wanted. So he set out to make his own. He called it Ruby.

After tinkering around with Ruby for his own work for a while, Matz released it to the public in 1995. Since then, the Ruby community has done some amazing things:

*   Built out a vast collection of Ruby libraries that can help you do anything from reading CSV (comma-separated value) files to controlling objects over a network

*   Written alternate interpreters that can run your Ruby code faster or integrate it with other languages

*   Created Ruby on Rails, a hugely popular framework for web applications

This explosion of creativity and productivity was enabled by the Ruby language itself. Flexibility and ease of use are core principles of the language, meaning you can use Ruby to accomplish any programming task, in fewer lines of code than other languages.

Once you've got the basics down, you'll agree: Ruby is a joy to use!

Flexibility and ease of use are core principles of Ruby.

Get Ruby

First things first: you can *write* Ruby code all day, but it won't do you much good if you can't *run* it. Let's make sure you have a working Ruby **interpreter** installed. We want version 2.0 or later. Open up a new terminal window (also known as a *command-line prompt*) and type:

Adding "-v" makes Ruby show the version number.

```
ruby -v
```

"ruby" by itself launches a Ruby interpreter.

Press Ctrl-C to exit the interpreter and return to your OS prompt.

```
File Edit Window Help
$ ruby -v
ruby 2.0.0p0 (2013-02-24 revision 39474) [x86_64-darwin11.4.2]
$ ruby
^Cruby: Interrupt

$
```

When you type **ruby -v** at a prompt, if you see a response like this, you're in business:

```
ruby 2.0.0p0 (2013-02-24 revision 39474) [x86_64-darwin11.4.2]
```

We don't care about the other stuff in this output, as long as it says "ruby 2.0" or later.

Do this!

If you don't have Ruby 2.0 or later, visit *www.ruby-lang.org* and download a copy for your favorite OS.

By the way, if you accidentally type ruby by itself (without the -v), Ruby will wait for you to enter some code. To exit this mode, just hold the Control key and press the C key on your keyboard. You can do this any time you need Ruby to exit immediately.

Use Ruby

Ruby source files that you can execute are referred to as **scripts**, but they're really just plain-text files. To run a Ruby script, you simply save your Ruby code in a file, and run that file with the Ruby interpreter.

You may be used to other languages (like C++, C#, or Java) where you have to manually compile your code to a binary format that a CPU or virtual machine can understand. In these languages, your code can't be executed before you compile it.

Other languages:

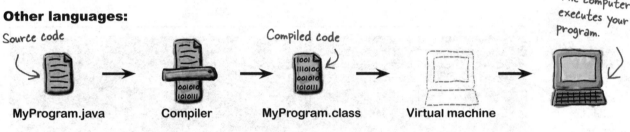

With Ruby, *you skip that step*. Ruby instantly and automatically compiles the source code in your script. This means *less time* between writing your code and trying it out!

The Ruby way:

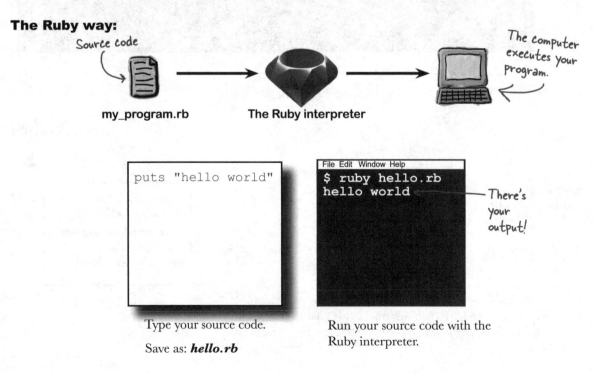

```
puts "hello world"
```

Type your source code.

Save as: **hello.rb**

```
File Edit Window Help
$ ruby hello.rb
hello world
```

There's your output!

Run your source code with the Ruby interpreter.

Use Ruby—interactively

There's another big benefit to using a language like Ruby. Not only do you not have to run a compiler each time you want to try out your code, but you don't even have to put it in a script first.

Ruby comes with a separate program, called **irb** (for **I**nteractive **R**u**b**y). The irb shell lets you type any Ruby expression, which it will then immediately evaluate and show you the results. It's a great way to learn the language, because you get immediate feedback. But even Ruby professionals use irb to try out new ideas.

Throughout the book, we'll be writing lots of scripts to be run via the Ruby interpreter. But any time you're testing out a new concept, it's a great idea to launch irb and experiment a bit.

So what are we waiting for? Let's get into irb now and play around with some Ruby expressions.

Using the irb shell

Open a terminal window, and type **irb**. This will launch the interactive Ruby interpreter. (You'll know it's running because the prompt will change, although it may not match exactly what you see here.)

From there, you can type any expression you want, followed by the Enter/Return key. Ruby will instantly evaluate it and show you the result.

When you're done with irb, type **exit** at the prompt, and you'll be returned to your OS's prompt.

Type "irb" at the system prompt and press the Return key.

irb will launch and show the irb prompt.

irb evaluates the expression and shows you the result (marked with "=>").

```
File Edit Window Help
$ irb
irb(main):001:0> 1 + 2
=> 3
irb(main):002:0> "Hello".upcase
=> "HELLO"
irb(main):003:0> exit
$
```

Now you can type any Ruby expression you want, then press the Return key.

When you're ready to exit irb, type "exit" and press Return.

Your first Ruby expressions

Now that you know how to launch irb, let's try out a few expressions and see what results we get!

Type the following at the prompt, then press Return:

```
1 + 2
```

You'll be shown the result:

```
=> 3
```

Math operations and comparisons

Ruby's basic math operators work just like they do in most other languages. The + symbol is for addition, − for subtraction, * for multiplication, / for division, and ** for exponentiation.

You can use < and > to compare two values and see if one is less than or greater than another. You can also use == (that's *two* equals signs) to see if two values are equal.

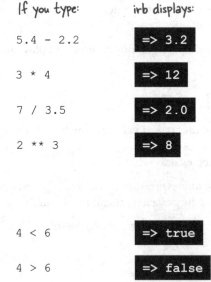

If you type:	irb displays:
5.4 - 2.2	=> 3.2
3 * 4	=> 12
7 / 3.5	=> 2.0
2 ** 3	=> 8
4 < 6	=> true
4 > 6	=> false
2 + 2 == 5	=> false

Strings

A **string** is a series of text characters. You can use strings to hold names, email addresses, phone numbers, and a million other things. Ruby's strings are special because even very large strings are highly efficient to work with (this isn't true in many other languages).

The easiest way to specify a string is to surround it either with double quotes (") or single quotes ('). The two types of quotes work a little differently; we'll cover that later in the chapter.

```
"Hello"          => "Hello"

'world'          => "world"
```

Variables

Ruby lets us create **variables**—names that refer to values.

You don't have to declare variables in Ruby; assigning to them creates them. You assign to a variable with the = symbol (that's a *single* equals sign).

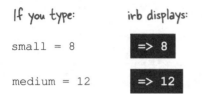

If you type: irb displays:

```
small = 8        => 8

medium = 12      => 12
```

A variable name starts with a lowercase letter, and can contain letters, numbers, and underscores.

Once you've assigned to variables, you can access their values whenever you need, in any context where you might use the original value.

```
small + medium    => 20
```

Variables don't have types in Ruby; they can hold any value you want. You can assign a string to a variable, then immediately assign a floating-point number to the same variable, and it's perfectly legal.

```
pie = "Lemon"     => "Lemon"

pie = 3.14        => 3.14
```

The += operator lets you add on to the existing value of a variable.

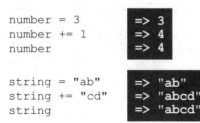

```
number = 3        => 3
number += 1       => 4
number            => 4

string = "ab"     => "ab"
string += "cd"    => "abcd"
string            => "abcd"
```

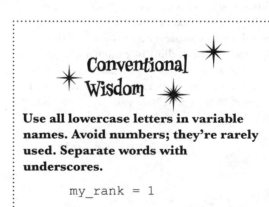

Conventional Wisdom

Use all lowercase letters in variable names. Avoid numbers; they're rarely used. Separate words with underscores.

```
my_rank = 1
```

This style is sometimes called "snake case," because the underscores make the name look like it's crawling on the ground.

Everything is an object!

Ruby is an *object-oriented* language. That means your data has useful **methods** (fragments of code that you can execute on demand) attached directly to it.

In modern languages, it's pretty common for something like a string to be a full-fledged object, so of course strings have methods to call:

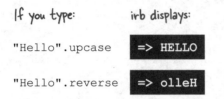

If you type: irb displays:

`"Hello".upcase`   `=> HELLO`

`"Hello".reverse`   `=> olleH`

What's cool about Ruby, though, is that *everything* is an object. Even something as simple as a number is an object. That means numbers have useful methods, too.

`42.even?`   `=> true`

`-32.abs`   `=> 32`

Calling a method on an object

When you make a call like this, the object you're calling the method on is known as the method **receiver**. It's whatever is to the left of the dot operator. You can think of calling a method on an object as *passing it a message*—like a note saying, "Hey, can you send me back an uppercase version of yourself?" or "Can I have your absolute value?"

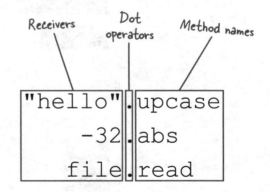

Exercise

Open a new terminal window, type **irb**, and hit the Enter/Return key. For each of the Ruby expressions below, write your guess for what the result will be on the line below it. Then try typing the expression into irb, and hit Enter. See if your guess matches what irb returns!

```
42 / 6
```

....

```
name = "Zaphod"
```

....

```
name.upcase
```

....

```
"Zaphod".upcase
```

....

```
name.reverse
```

....

```
name.upcase.reverse
```

....

```
name.class
```

....

```
name * 3
```

....

```
5 > 4
```

....

```
number = -32
```

....

```
number.abs
```

....

```
-32.abs
```

....

```
number += 10
```

....

```
rand(25)
```

....

```
number.class
```

....

Exercise Solution

Open a new terminal window, type `irb`, and hit the Enter/Return key. For each of the Ruby expressions below, write your guess for what the result will be on the line below it. Then try typing the expression into irb, and hit Enter. See if your guess matches what irb returns!

42 / 6

7

5 > 4

true

Assigning to a variable returns whatever value is assigned.

name = "Zaphod"

"Zaphod"

number = -32

-32

name.upcase

"ZAPHOD"

You can call methods on an object stored in a variable...

number.abs

32

"Zaphod".upcase

"ZAPHOD"

But you don't even have to store it in a variable first!

-32.abs

32

This adds 10 to the value in the variable, then assigns the result back to the variable.

You can call a method on the value returned from a method.

name.reverse

"dohpaZ"

number += 10

-22

name.upcase.reverse

"DOHPAZ"

The answer will vary (it really is random)

rand(25)

A random number

Yes, this IS a method call, we just don't specify a receiver. More about this soon!

An object's class decides what kind of object it is.

name.class

String

number.class

Fixnum

A Fixnum is a kind of integer.

name * 3

"ZaphodZaphodZaphod"

You can "multiply" strings!

Let's build a game

In this first chapter, we're going to build a simple game. If that sounds daunting, don't worry; it's easy when you're using Ruby!

Let's look at what we'll need to do:

I've put together this list of eight requirements for you. Can you handle it?

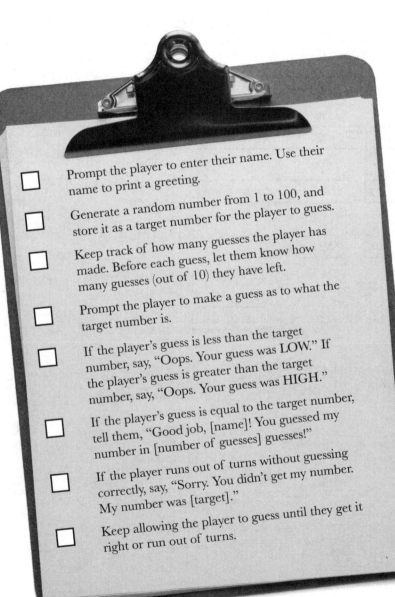

- [ ] Prompt the player to enter their name. Use their name to print a greeting.

- [ ] Generate a random number from 1 to 100, and store it as a target number for the player to guess.

- [ ] Keep track of how many guesses the player has made. Before each guess, let them know how many guesses (out of 10) they have left.

- [ ] Prompt the player to make a guess as to what the target number is.

- [ ] If the player's guess is less than the target number, say, "Oops. Your guess was LOW." If the player's guess is greater than the target number, say, "Oops. Your guess was HIGH."

- [ ] If the player's guess is equal to the target number, tell them, "Good job, [name]! You guessed my number in [number of guesses] guesses!"

- [ ] If the player runs out of turns without guessing correctly, say, "Sorry. You didn't get my number. My number was [target]."

- [ ] Keep allowing the player to guess until they get it right or run out of turns.

Gary Richardott
Game Designer

Input, storage, and output

Our first requirement is to greet the user by name. To accomplish that, we'll need to write a script that *gets input* from the user, *stores* that input, and then uses that stored value to *create some output*.

We can do all this in just a few lines of Ruby code:

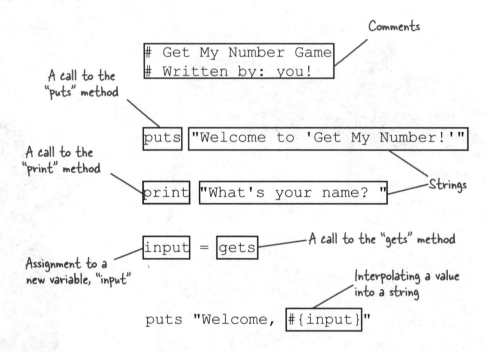

We'll go into detail on each component of this script over the next few pages. But first, let's give it a try!

Running scripts

We've written a simple script that fulfills our first requirement: to greet the player by name. Now, you'll learn how to execute the script so you can see what you've created.

Do this!

Step One:

Open a new document in your favorite text editor, and type in the following code.

```
# Get My Number Game
# Written by: you!

puts "Welcome to 'Get My Number!'"
print "What's your name? "

input = gets

puts "Welcome, #{input}"
```

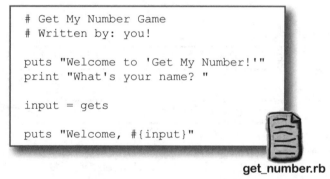

get_number.rb

Step Two:

Save the file as *get_number.rb*.

Step Three:

Open up a terminal window and change into the directory where you saved your program.

Step Four:

Run the program by typing **ruby get_number.rb**.

Step Five:

You'll see a greeting and a prompt. Type your name and hit the Enter/Return key. You'll then see a message that welcomes you by name.

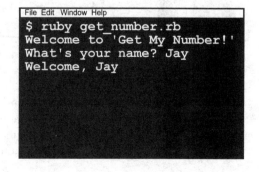

```
File Edit Window Help
$ ruby get_number.rb
Welcome to 'Get My Number!'
What's your name? Jay
Welcome, Jay
```

Let's take a few pages to look at each part of this code in more detail.

Comments

Our source file starts out with a couple of comments. Ruby ignores everything from a hash mark (#) up until the end of the line, so that you can leave instructions or notes for yourself and your fellow developers.

If you place a # in your code, then everything from that point until the end of the line will be treated as a comment. This works just like the double-slash (//) marker in Java or JavaScript.

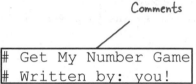

```
# Get My Number Game
# Written by: you!
```

Comments

```
i_am = "executed" # I'm not.
# Me neither.
```

"puts" and "print"

The actual code starts with a call to the puts method ("puts" is short for "**put s**tring"), which displays text on standard output (usually the terminal). We pass puts a string containing the text to display.

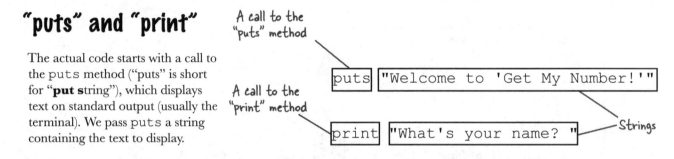

A call to the "puts" method

A call to the "print" method

```
puts "Welcome to 'Get My Number!'"

print "What's your name? "
```

Strings

We pass another string to the print method on the following line, to ask the user their name. The print method works just like puts, except that puts adds a newline character at the end of the string (if it doesn't already have one) to skip to the following line, whereas print doesn't. For cosmetic reasons, we end the string that we pass to print with a space, so that our text doesn't run up against the area where the user types their name.

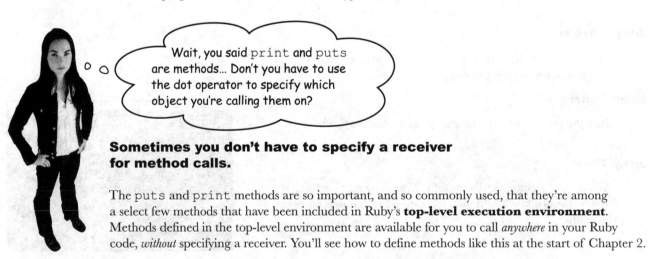

Wait, you said print and puts are methods... Don't you have to use the dot operator to specify which object you're calling them on?

Sometimes you don't have to specify a receiver for method calls.

The puts and print methods are so important, and so commonly used, that they're among a select few methods that have been included in Ruby's **top-level execution environment**. Methods defined in the top-level environment are available for you to call *anywhere* in your Ruby code, *without* specifying a receiver. You'll see how to define methods like this at the start of Chapter 2.

Method arguments

The `puts` method takes a string and prints it to standard output (your terminal window).

```
puts "first line"
```

The string passed to the `puts` method is known as the method **argument**.

The `puts` method can take more than one argument; just separate the arguments with commas. Each argument gets printed on its own line.

```
puts "second line", "third line", "fourth line"
```

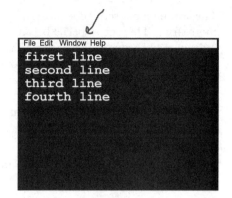

What it looks like in your terminal

"gets"

The `gets` method (short for "**get s**tring") reads a line from standard input (characters typed in the terminal window). When you call `gets`, it causes the program to halt until the user types their name and presses the Enter key. It returns the user's text to the program as another string.

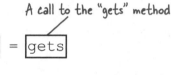

A call to the "gets" method

Assignment to a new variable, "input"

As with `puts` and `print`, you can call the `gets` method from anywhere in your code without specifying a receiver.

Parentheses are optional on method calls

Method arguments *can* be surrounded with parentheses in Ruby:

```
puts("one", "two")
```

But the parentheses are optional, and in the case of `puts`, most Rubyists prefer to leave them off.

```
puts "one", "two"
```

As noted above, the `gets` method reads a line from standard input. It doesn't (usually) need any arguments:

```
gets
```

Rubyists are *adamant* that parentheses *not* be used if a method takes *no* arguments. So please, don't do this, even though it's valid code:

```
gets()
```
No!

✳ Conventional ✳ Wisdom ✳

Leave parentheses off of a method call if there are no arguments. You can leave them off for method calls where there *are* arguments as well, but this can make some code more difficult to read. When in doubt, use parentheses!

String interpolation

The last thing our script does is to call `puts` with one more string. This one is special because we **interpolate** (substitute) the value in the `name` variable into the string. Whenever you include the `#{...}` notation *inside* a double-quoted string, Ruby uses the value in the curly braces to "fill in the blank." The `#{...}` markers can occur anywhere in the string: the beginning, end, or somewhere in the middle.

Interpolating a value into a string

```
puts "Welcome, #{input}"
```

Output ──➤ `Welcome, Jay`

You're not limited to using variables within the `#{...}` marker—you can use any Ruby expression.

```
puts "The answer is #{6 * 7}."
```

Output ──➤ `The answer is 42.`

Note that Ruby applies interpolation only in *double*-quoted strings. If you include a `#{...}` marker in a *single*-quoted string, it will be taken literally.

```
puts 'Welcome, #{input}'
```

Output ──➤ `Welcome, #{input}`

there are no Dumb Questions

Q: Where are the semicolons?

A: In Ruby, you *can* use semicolons to separate statements, but you generally *shouldn't*. (It's harder to read.)

```
puts "Hello";  ⟵ No!
puts "World";
```

Ruby treats separate lines as separate statements, making semicolons unnecessary.

```
puts "Hello"
puts "World"
```

Q: My other language would require me to put this script in a class with a "main" method. Doesn't Ruby?

A: No! That's one of the great things about Ruby—it doesn't require a bunch of ceremony for simple programs. Just write a few statements, and you're done!

Ruby doesn't require a bunch of ceremony for simple programs.

What's in that string?

```
File Edit Window Help
$ ruby get_number.rb
Welcome to 'Get My Number!'
What's your name? Jay
Welcome, Jay
```

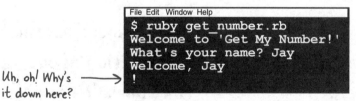

What kind of welcome is that? Let's show our users a little enthusiasm! At least put an exclamation point at the end of that greeting!

Well, that's easy enough to add. Let's throw an exclamation point on the end of the greeting string, after the interpolated value.

```ruby
puts "Welcome to 'Get My Number!'"
print "What's your name? "

input = gets

puts "Welcome, #{input}!"
```

Just this one little character added!

But if we try running the program again, we'll see that rather than appearing immediately after the user's name, the exclamation point jumps down to the next line!

Uh, oh! Why's it down here? ⟶

```
File Edit Window Help
$ ruby get_number.rb
Welcome to 'Get My Number!'
What's your name? Jay
Welcome, Jay
!
```

Why is this happening? Maybe there's something going on within that `input` variable...

Printing it via the `puts` method doesn't reveal anything special about it, though. If we append this line to the code above, we'd see this output:

```ruby
puts input
```

Inspecting objects with the "inspect" and "p" methods

Now let's try again, using a method meant especially for troubleshooting Ruby programs. The `inspect` method is available on any Ruby object. It converts the object to a string representation that's suitable for debugging. That is, it will reveal aspects of the object that don't normally show up in program output.

Here's the result of calling `inspect` on our string:

```
puts input.inspect
```
 ←——— A-HA!

What's that \n at the end of the string? We'll solve that mystery on the next page…

Printing the result of `inspect` is so common that Ruby offers another shortcut: the p method. It works just like `puts`, except that it calls `inspect` on each argument before printing it.

This call to p is effectively identical to the previous code:

```
p input
```

Remember the p method; we'll be using it in later chapters to help debug Ruby code!

> The "inspect" method reveals information about an object that doesn't normally show up in program output.

Escape sequences in strings

Our use of the p method has revealed some unexpected data at the end of the user's input:

```
p input
```

These two characters, the backslash (\\) and the n that follows it, actually represent a single character: a newline character. (The newline character is named thus because it makes terminal output jump down to a *new line*.) There's a newline at the end of the user input because when the user hits the Return key to indicate their entry is done, that gets recorded as an extra character. That newline is then included in the return value of the gets method.

The backslash character (\\) and the n that follows it are an **escape sequence**—a portion of a string that represents characters that can't normally be represented in source code.

The most commonly used escape sequences are \\n (newline, as we've seen) and \\t (a tab character, for indentation).

```
puts "First line\nSecond line\nThird line"
puts "\tIndented line"
```

```
First line
Second line
Third line
        Indented line
```

Commonly used escape sequences

If you include this in a double-quoted string...	...you get this character...
\n	newline
\t	tab
\"	double-quotes
\'	single-quote
\\	backslash

Normally, when you try to include a double-quotation mark (") in a double-quoted string, it gets treated as the end of the string, leading to errors:

```
puts ""It's okay," he said."
```
Error ⟶
```
syntax error, unexpected
tCONSTANT
```

If you escape the double-quotation marks by placing a backslash before each, you can place them in the middle of a double-quoted string without causing an error.

```
puts "\"It's okay,\" he said."
```
```
"It's okay," he said.
```

Lastly, because \\ marks the start of an escape sequence, we also need a way to represent a backlash character that *isn't* part of an escape sequence. Using \\\\ will give us a literal backslash.

```
puts "One backslash: \\"
```
```
One backslash: \
```

Bear in mind that most of these escape sequences apply only in *double*-quoted strings. In *single*-quoted strings, most escape sequences are treated literally.

```
puts '\n\t\"'
```
```
\n\t\"
```

Calling "chomp" on the string object

```
File Edit  Window Help
$ ruby get_number.rb
Welcome to 'Get My Number!'
What's your name? Jay
Welcome, Jay
!
```

Okay, so the output is messed up because the user input string has a newline character at the end of it. What can we do about that?

We can use the chomp method to remove the newline character.

If the last character of a string is a newline, the chomp method will remove it. It's great for things like cleaning up strings returned from gets.

The chomp method is more specialized than print, puts, and gets, so it's available only on individual string objects. That means we need to specify that the string referenced by the input variable is the *receiver* of the chomp method. We need to use the dot operator on input.

```
# Get My Number Game
# Written by: you!

puts "Welcome to 'Get My Number!'"
print "What's your name? "

input = gets

name = input.chomp

puts "Welcome, #{name}!"
```

We'll store the return value of "chomp" in a new variable, "name".

Calling the "chomp" method

The dot operator

The string in "input" is the receiver of the "chomp" method.

We'll use "name" in the greeting, instead of "input".

The chomp method returns the same string, but without the newline character at the end. We store this in a new variable, name, which we then print as part of our welcome message.

If we try running the program again, we'll see that our new, emphatic greeting is working properly now!

```
File Edit  Window Help
$ ruby get_number.rb
Welcome to 'Get My Number!'
What's your name? Jay
Welcome, Jay!
```

What methods are available on an object?

You can't call just any method on just any object. If you try something like this, you'll get an error:

```
puts 42.upcase
```
Error → `undefined method `upcase' for 42:Fixnum (NoMethodError)`

Which, if you think about it, isn't so wrong. After all, it doesn't make a lot of sense to capitalize a number, does it?

But, then, what methods *can* you call on a number? That question can be answered with a method called `methods`:

```
puts 42.methods
```

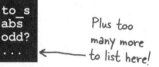
```
to_s
abs
odd?
...
```
Plus too many more to list here!

If you call `methods` on a string, you'll get a different list:

```
puts "hello".methods
```
```
to_i
length
upcase
...
```
Plus too many more to list here!

Why the difference? It has to do with the object's class. A **class** is a blueprint for making new objects, and it decides, among other things, what methods you can call on the object.

There's another method that lets objects tell us what their class is. It's called, sensibly enough, `class`. Let's try it out on a few objects.

```
puts 42.class
puts "hello".class
puts true.class
```
```
Fixnum
String
TrueClass
```

We'll be talking more about classes in the next chapter, so stay tuned!

there are no
Dumb Questions

Q: How do I find out what all these methods do?

A: We cover how to look up documentation on a class's methods in Chapter 11. But for right now, you don't need to know about the majority of these methods. (And you may *never* need to.) Don't worry: if a method is important, we'll go over how to use it!

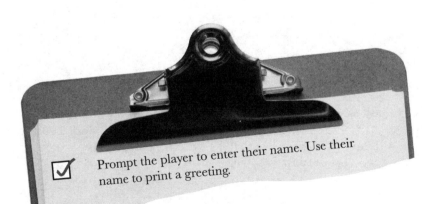

 Prompt the player to enter their name. Use their name to print a greeting.

That's all the code for our first requirement. You can check it off the list!

Generating a random number

Our player greeting is done. Let's look at our next requirement.

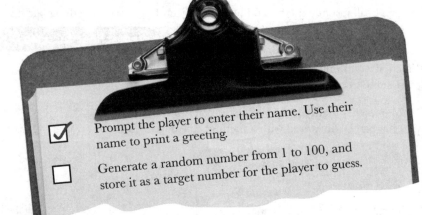

☑ Prompt the player to enter their name. Use their name to print a greeting.

☐ Generate a random number from 1 to 100, and store it as a target number for the player to guess.

The `rand` method will generate a random number within a given range. It should be able to create a target number for us.

We need to pass an argument to `rand` with the number that will be at the upper end of our range (100). Let's try it out a couple of times:

```
puts rand(100)
puts rand(100)
```

```
67
25
```

Looks good, but there's one problem: `rand` generates numbers between *zero* and *just below* the maximum value you specify. That means we'll be getting random numbers in the range 0–99, not 1–100 like we need.

That's easy to fix, though. We'll just add 1 to whatever value we get back from `rand`. That will put us back in the range of 1–100!

```
rand(100) + 1
```

We'll store the result in a new variable, named `target`.

```
# Get My Number Game
# Written by: you!

puts "Welcome to 'Get My Number!'"

# Get the player's name, and greet them.
print "What's your name? "
input = gets
name = input.chomp
puts "Welcome, #{name}!"
```

Our new code!

```
# Store a random number for the player to guess.
puts "I've got a random number between 1 and 100."
puts "Can you guess it?"
target = rand(100) + 1
```

Converting to strings

That's another requirement down! Let's look at the next one...

☑ Generate a random number from 1 to 100, and store it as a target number for the player to guess.

☐ Keep track of how many guesses the player has made. Before each guess, let them know how many guesses (out of 10) they have left.

"Keep track of how many guesses the player has made..." Looks like we'll need a variable for the number of guesses. Obviously, when the player first starts, they haven't made any guesses, so we'll create a variable named `num_guesses` that's set to 0 initially.

```ruby
num_guesses = 0
```

Now, the first thing you might attempt to do in order to display the number of guesses remaining is to concatenate (join) the strings together using the plus sign (+), as many other languages do. Something like this *won't work*, however:

```ruby
remaining_guesses = 10 - num_guesses
puts remaining_guesses + " guesses left."
```
⟵ Gives an error!

The + operator is used to *add numbers* as well as to *concatenate strings*, and since `remaining_guesses` contains a number, this plus sign looks like an attempt to add numbers.

What's the solution? You need to convert the number to a string. Almost all Ruby objects have a `to_s` method you can call to do this conversion; let's try that now.

```ruby
remaining_guesses = 10 - num_guesses
puts remaining_guesses.to_s + " guesses left."
```

`10 guesses left.`

That works! Converting the number to a string first makes it clear to Ruby that you're doing concatenation, not addition.

Ruby provides an easier way to handle this, though. Read on...

Ruby makes working with strings easy

Instead of calling `to_s`, we could save ourselves the effort of explicitly converting a number to a string by using string interpolation. As you saw in our code to greet the user, when you include `#{...}` in a double-quoted string, code within the curly braces is evaluated, converted to a string if necessary, and interpolated (substituted) into the longer string.

The automatic string conversion means we can get rid of the `to_s` call.

```ruby
remaining_guesses = 10 - num_guesses
puts "#{remaining_guesses} guesses left."
```

```
10 guesses left.
```

Ruby lets us do operations directly within the curly braces, so we can also get rid of the `remaining_guesses` variable.

```ruby
puts "#{10 - num_guesses} guesses left."
```

```
10 guesses left.
```

The `#{...}` can occur anywhere within the string, so it's easy to make the output a little more user-friendly, too.

```ruby
puts "You've got #{10 - num_guesses} guesses left."
```

```
You've got 10 guesses left.
```

Now the player will know how many guesses they have left. We can check another requirement off our list!

```ruby
# Get My Number Game
# Written by: you!

puts "Welcome to 'Get My Number!'"

# Get the player's name, and greet them.
print "What's your name? "
input = gets
name = input.chomp
puts "Welcome, #{name}!"

# Store a random number for the player to guess.
puts "I've got a random number between 1 and 100."
puts "Can you guess it?"
target = rand(100) + 1
```

Our new code! {
```ruby
# Track how many guesses the player has made.
num_guesses = 0

puts "You've got #{10 - num_guesses} guesses left."
```

Converting strings to numbers

☑ Keep track of how many guesses the player has made. Before each guess, let them know how many guesses (out of 10) they have left.

☐ Prompt the player to make a guess as to what the target number is.

Our next requirement is to prompt the player to guess the target number. So we need to print a prompt, then record the user's input as their guess. The `gets` method, as you may recall, retrieves input from the user. (We already used it to get the player's name.) Unfortunately, we can't just use `gets` by itself to get a number from the user, because it returns a string. The problem will arise later, when we try to compare the player's guess with the target number using the > and < operators.

```
print "Make a guess: "
guess = gets
guess < target  ←——┐ Either of these will
guess > target  ←——┘ result in an error!
```

We need to convert the string returned from the `gets` method to a number so that we can compare the guess to our target number. No problem! Strings have a `to_i` method to do the conversion for us.

This code will call `to_i` on the string returned from `gets`. We don't even need to put the string in a variable first; we'll just use the dot operator to call the method directly on the return value.

```
guess = gets.to_i
```

When you call `to_i` on a string, it ignores any non-numeric characters that follow the number. So we don't even need to remove the newline character left by `gets`.

Common conversions

If you call this method on an object...	...you get this kind of object back.
to_s	string
to_i	integer
to_f	floating-point number

If we want to test our changes, we can print out the result of a comparison.

```
puts guess < target
```

`true`

Much better—we have a guess that we can compare to the target. That's another requirement done!

```
. . .
# Store a random number for the player to guess.
puts "I've got a random number between 1 and 100."
puts "Can you guess it?"
target = rand(100) + 1

# Track how many guesses the player has made.
num_guesses = 0

puts "You've got #{10 - num_guesses} guesses left."
print "Make a guess: "
guess = gets.to_i
```

Our new code!

Conditionals

Two more requirements for our game down,
four to go! Let's look at the next batch.

☑ Prompt the player to make a guess as to what the target number is.

☐ If the player's guess is less than the target number, say, "Oops. Your guess was LOW." If the player's guess is greater than the target number, say, "Oops. Your guess was HIGH."

☐ If the player's guess is equal to the target number, tell them, "Good job, [name]! You guessed my number in [number of guesses] guesses!"

☐ If the player runs out of turns without guessing correctly, say, "Sorry. You didn't get my number. My number was [target]."

Now, we need to compare the player's guess with the target. *If* it's too high, we print a message saying so. *Otherwise, if* it's too low, we print a message to that effect, and so on... Looks like we need the ability to execute portions of our code only under certain *conditions*.

Like most languages, Ruby has **conditional** statements: statements that cause code to be executed only if a condition is met. An expression is evaluated, and if its result is true, the code in the conditional body is executed. If not, it's skipped.

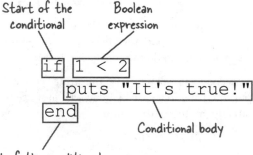

Start of the conditional · Boolean expression

```
if 1 < 2
    puts "It's true!"
end
```

End of the conditional · Conditional body

As with most other languages, Ruby supports multiple branches in the condition. These statements take the form if/elsif/else.

Note that there's no "e" in the middle of "elsif"!

```
if score == 100
    puts "Perfect!"
elsif score >= 70
    puts "You pass!"
else
    puts "Summer school time!"
end
```

Conditionals rely on a **Boolean** expression (one with a true or false value) to decide whether the code they contain should be executed. Ruby has constants representing the two Boolean values, true and false.

```
if true
    puts "I'll be printed!"
end
```

```
if false
    puts "I won't!"
end
```

Conditionals (continued)

Ruby also has all the comparison operators you're used to.

```ruby
if 1 == 1
  puts "I'll be printed!"
end
```

```ruby
if 1 > 2
  puts "I won't!"
end
```

```ruby
if 1 < 2
  puts "I'll be printed!"
end
```

```ruby
if 1 >= 2
  puts "I won't!"
end
```

```ruby
if 2 <= 2
  puts "I'll be printed!"
end
```

```ruby
if 2 != 2
  puts "I won't!"
end
```

Said aloud as "not equal to"

It has the Boolean negation operator, !, which lets you take a true value and make it false, or a false value and make it true. It also has the more-readable keyword not, which does basically the same thing.

```ruby
if ! true
  puts "I won't be printed!"
end
```

```ruby
if ! false
  puts "I will!"
end
```

```ruby
if not true
  puts "I won't be printed!"
end
```

```ruby
if not false
  puts "I will!"
end
```

If you need to ensure that two conditions are *both* true, you can use the && ("and") operator. If you need to ensure that *either* of two conditions is true, you can use the || ("or") operator.

```ruby
if true && true
  puts "I'll be printed!"
end
```

```ruby
if true && false
  puts "I won't!"
end
```

```ruby
if false || true
  puts "I'll be printed!"
end
```

```ruby
if false || false
  puts "I won't!"
end
```

I notice that you're indenting the code between the if and the end. Is that required?

Indented two spaces!

```ruby
if true
  puts "I'll be printed!"
end
```

No, Ruby doesn't treat indentation as significant to the meaning of the program (unlike some other languages, such as Python).

But indenting code within if statements, loops, methods, classes, and the like is just good coding style. It helps make the structure of your code clear to your fellow developers (and even to yourself).

We need to compare the player's guess to the random target number. Let's use everything we've learned about conditionals to implement this batch of requirements.

We add this variable to track whether we should print the "you lost" message. We'll also use it later to halt the game on a correct guess.

Here are our "if" statements!

We'll see a cleaner way to write this in a moment.

get_number.rb

```ruby
# Get My Number Game
# Written by: you!

puts "Welcome to 'Get My Number!'"

# Get the player's name, and greet them.
print "What's your name? "
input = gets
name = input.chomp
puts "Welcome, #{name}!"

# Store a random number for the player to guess.
puts "I've got a random number between 1 and 100."
puts "Can you guess it?"
target = rand(100) + 1

# Track how many guesses the player has made.
num_guesses = 0

# Track whether the player has guessed correctly.
guessed_it = false

puts "You've got #{10 - num_guesses} guesses left."
print "Make a guess: "
guess = gets.to_i

# Compare the guess to the target.
# Print the appropriate message.
if guess < target
  puts "Oops. Your guess was LOW."
elsif guess > target
  puts "Oops. Your guess was HIGH."
elsif guess == target
  puts "Good job, #{name}!"
  puts "You guessed my number in #{num_guesses} guesses!"
  guessed_it = true
end

# If player ran out of turns, tell them what the number was.
if not guessed_it
  puts "Sorry. You didn't get my number. (It was #{target}.)"
end
```

The opposite of "if" is "unless"

This statement works, but it's a little awkward to read:

```
if not guessed_it
  puts "Sorry. You didn't get my number. (It was #{target}.)"
end
```

In most respects, Ruby's conditional statements are just like most other languages. Ruby has an additional keyword, though: `unless`.

Code within an `if` statement executes only if a condition is *true*, but code within an `unless` statement executes only if the condition is *false*.

```
unless true                      unless false
  puts "I won't be printed!"       puts "I will!"
end                              end
```

The `unless` keyword is an example of how Ruby works hard to make your code a little easier to read. You can use `unless` in situations where a negation operator would be awkward. So instead of this:

```
if ! (light == "red")
  puts "Go!"
end
```

You can write this:

```
unless light == "red"
  puts "Go!"
end
```

We can use `unless` to clean up that last conditional.

```
unless guessed_it
  puts "Sorry. You didn't get my number. (It was #{target}.)"
end
```

Much more legible! And our conditional statements are working great!

You'll see something like this if you run get_number.rb now...

As it stands right now, though, the player gets only one guess—they're supposed to get 10. We'll fix that next...

Conventional Wisdom

It's <u>valid</u> to use `else` and `elsif` together with `unless` in Ruby:

```
unless light == "red"
  puts "Go!"
else          ←——Confusing!
  puts "Stop!"
end
```

But it's very hard to read. If you need an `else` clause, use `if` for the main clause instead!

```
if light == "red"
  puts "Stop!"←
else                Moved
  puts "Go!"        up here
end
```

```
File Edit  Window Help
$ ruby get_number.rb
Welcome to 'Get My Number!'
What's your name? Jay
Welcome, Jay!
I've got a random number between 1 and 100.
Can you guess it?
You've got 10 guesses left.
Make a guess: 50
Oops. Your guess was HIGH.
Sorry. You didn't get my number. (It was 34.)
```

Loops

Great work so far! We have just one more requirement to go for our guessing game!

☑ If the player's guess is less than the target number, say, "Oops. Your guess was LOW." If the player's guess is greater than the target number, say, "Oops. Your guess was HIGH."

☑ If the player's guess is equal to the target number, tell them, "Good job, [name]! You guessed my number in [number of guesses] guesses!"

☑ If the player runs out of turns without guessing correctly, say, "Sorry. You didn't get my number. My number was [target]."

☐ Keep allowing the player to guess until they get it right or run out of turns.

Currently, the player gets one guess. Since there's 100 possible target numbers, those don't seem like very fair odds. We need to keep asking the player 10 times, or until they get the right answer, whichever comes first.

The code to prompt for a guess is already in place, so we just need to run it *more than once*. We can use a **loop** to execute a segment of code repeatedly. You've probably encountered loops in other languages. When you need one or more statements to be executed over and over, you place them inside a loop.

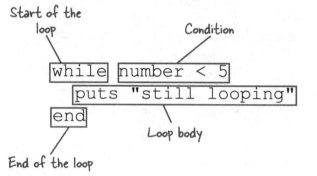

A `while` loop consists of the word `while`, a Boolean expression (just like in `if` or `unless` statements), the code you want to repeat, and the word `end`. The code within the loop body repeats *while* the condition is true.

Here's a simple example that uses a loop for counting.

```
number = 1
while number <= 5
  puts number
  number += 1
end
```

```
1
2
3
4
5
```

Just as `unless` is the counterpart to `if`, Ruby offers an `until` loop as a counterpart to `while`. An `until` loop repeats *until* the condition is true (that is, it loops while it's false).

Here's a similar example, using `until`.

```
number = 1
until number > 5
  puts number
  number += 1
end
```

```
1
2
3
4
5
```

Here's our conditional code again, updated to run within a `while` loop:

The loop will stop after the player's 10th guess, or when they guess correctly, whichever comes first.

```ruby
# Track how many guesses the player has made.
num_guesses = 0

# Track whether the player has guessed correctly.
guessed_it = false

while num_guesses < 10 && guessed_it == false
```

This code is exactly the same; we've just nested it inside the loop.

```ruby
  puts "You've got #{10 - num_guesses} guesses left."
  print "Make a guess: "
  guess = gets.to_i
```

We need to add 1 to the guess count each loop, so we don't loop forever.

```ruby
  num_guesses += 1
```

No changes here, either.

```ruby
  # Compare the guess to the target.
  # Print the appropriate message.
  if guess < target
    puts "Oops. Your guess was LOW."
  elsif guess > target
    puts "Oops. Your guess was HIGH."
  elsif guess == target
    puts "Good job, #{name}!"
    puts "You guessed my number in #{num_guesses} guesses!"
    guessed_it = true
  end
```

This marks the end of the code that will loop.

```ruby
end

unless guessed_it
  puts "Sorry. You didn't get my number. (It was #{target}.)"
end
```

There's one more readability improvement we can make. As with the `if` statement that we replaced with an `unless`, we can make this `while` loop read more clearly by replacing it with an `until`.

Before:
```ruby
while num_guesses < 10 && guessed_it == false
  ...
end
```

After:
```ruby
until num_guesses == 10 || guessed_it
  ...
end
```

Here's our complete code listing.

get_number.rb

```ruby
# Get My Number Game
# Written by: you!

puts "Welcome to 'Get My Number!'"

# Get the player's name, and greet them.
print "What's your name? "
input = gets
name = input.chomp
puts "Welcome, #{name}!"

# Store a random number for the player to guess.
puts "I've got a random number between 1 and 100."
puts "Can you guess it?"
target = rand(100) + 1

# Track how many guesses the player has made.
num_guesses = 0

# Track whether the player has guessed correctly.
guessed_it = false

until num_guesses == 10 || guessed_it

  puts "You've got #{10 - num_guesses} guesses left."
  print "Make a guess: "
  guess = gets.to_i

  num_guesses += 1

  # Compare the guess to the target.
  # Print the appropriate message.
  if guess < target
    puts "Oops. Your guess was LOW."
  elsif guess > target
    puts "Oops. Your guess was HIGH."
  elsif guess == target
    puts "Good job, #{name}!"
    puts "You guessed my number in #{num_guesses} guesses!"
    guessed_it = true
  end

end

# If the player didn't guess in time, show the target number.
unless guessed_it
  puts "Sorry. You didn't get my number. (It was #{target}.)"
end
```

Let's try running our game!

Our loop is in place—that's the last requirement! Let's open a terminal window and try running the program!

 Keep allowing the player to guess until they get it right or run out of turns.

```
File Edit Window Help Cheats
$ ruby get_number.rb
Welcome to 'Get My Number!'
What's your name? Gary
Welcome, Gary!
I've got a random number between 1 and 100.
Can you guess it?
You've got 10 guesses left.
Make a guess: 50
Oops. Your guess was LOW.
You've got 9 guesses left.
Make a guess: 75
Oops. Your guess was HIGH.
You've got 8 guesses left.
Make a guess: 62
Oops. Your guess was HIGH.
You've got 7 guesses left.
Make a guess: 56
Oops. Your guess was HIGH.
You've got 6 guesses left.
Make a guess: 53
Good job, Gary!
You guessed my number in 5 guesses!
$
```

Our players will love this! You implemented everything we needed, and you did it on time, too!

Using variables, strings, method calls, conditionals, and loops, you've written a complete game in Ruby! Better yet, it took fewer than 30 lines of code! Pour yourself a cold drink—you've earned it!

Your Ruby Toolbox

You've got Chapter 1 under your belt and now you've added method calls, conditionals, and loops to your toolbox.

Statements

Conditional statements execute the code they enclose if a condition is met.

Loops execute the code they enclose repeatedly. They exit when a condition is met.

Up Next...

All your code is in one big lump right now. In the next chapter, you'll learn how to break your code into easily maintainable chunks, using classes and methods.

BULLET POINTS

- Ruby is an interpreted language. You don't have to compile Ruby code before executing it.

- You don't need to declare variables before assigning to them. You also don't have to specify a type.

- Ruby treats everything from a # to the end of the line as a comment—and ignores it.

- Text within quotation marks is treated as a string—a series of characters.

- If you include # { . . . } in a Ruby string, the expression within the braces is interpolated into the string.

- Method calls *may* need one or more arguments, separated by commas.

- Parentheses are optional around method arguments. Leave them off if you're not passing any arguments.

- Use the `inspect` and `p` methods to view debug output for Ruby objects.

- You can include special characters within double-quoted strings by using escape sequences like `\n` and `\t`.

- You can use the interactive Ruby interpreter, or irb, to quickly test out the result of Ruby expressions.

- Call `to_s` on almost any object to convert it to a string. Call `to_i` on a string to convert it to an integer.

- `unless` is the opposite of `if`; its code won't execute *unless* a statement is *false*.

- `until` is the opposite of `while`; it executes repeatedly *until* a condition is true.

2 methods and classes

Getting Organized

How am I supposed to find anything in all this code? I wish the developers had split it up into methods and classes...

You've been missing out. You've been calling methods and creating objects like a pro. But the only methods you could call, and the only kinds of objects you could create, were the ones that Ruby defined for you. Now, it's your turn. You're going to learn to create your *own* methods. You'll also create your own **classes**—templates for new objects. *You'll decide* what objects based on your class will be like. You'll use **instance variables** to define what those objects *know*, and **instance methods** to define what they *do*. And most importantly, you'll discover how defining your own classes can make your code *easier to read and maintain*.

Defining methods

Got-A-Motor, Inc., is working on their "virtual test-drive" app, which lets their customers try vehicles out on their computers without needing to visit a showroom. For this first version, they need methods to let users step on the virtual gas, sound the virtual horn, and turn on the virtual headlights in low-beam or high-beam mode.

Method definitions look like this in Ruby:

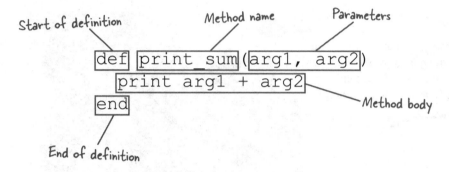

Start of definition   Method name   Parameters

```
def print_sum(arg1, arg2)
  print arg1 + arg2
end
```

Method body

End of definition

If you want calls to your method to include arguments, you'll need to add **parameters** to the method definition. Parameters appear after the method name, within parentheses. (You should leave off the parentheses if there are no parameters.) Each argument on the method call gets stored in one of the parameters within the method.

The method body consists of one or more Ruby statements that are executed when the method is called.

Let's create our very own methods to represent the actions in the test-drive app.

Here are two methods for accelerating and sounding the horn. They're about as simple as Ruby methods can be; each method body has a pair of statements that print strings.

These statements will be run when the method is called.
   — Method takes no parameters.

```
def accelerate
  puts "Stepping on the gas"
  puts "Speeding up"
end
```

These statements will be run when the method is called.
   — Method takes no parameters.

```
def sound_horn
  puts "Pressing the horn button"
  puts "Beep beep!"
end
```

The `use_headlights` method is only slightly more complex; it takes a single parameter, which is interpolated into one of the output strings.

One method parameter

```
def use_headlights(brightness)
  puts "Turning on #{brightness} headlights"
  puts "Watch out for deer!"
end
```

Parameter is used in the output.

That's all it takes! With these method definitions in place, we're ready to make calls to them.

Calling methods you've defined

You can call methods you've defined just like any other. Let's try out our new vehicle simulator methods.

Ruby lets you put calls to your methods anywhere—even within the same source file where you defined them. Since this is such a simple program at this point, we'll do that, just for convenience. We'll just stick the method calls right after the method declarations.

```ruby
def accelerate
  puts "Stepping on the gas"
  puts "Speeding up"
end

def sound_horn
  puts "Pressing the horn button"
  puts "Beep beep!"
end

def use_headlights(brightness)
  puts "Turning on #{brightness} headlights"
  puts "Watch out for deer!"
end

sound_horn
accelerate
use_headlights("high-beam")
```

Calls without arguments

This is used as the "brightness" argument.

vehicle_methods.rb

When we run the source file from the terminal, we'll see the result of our method calls!

```
File Edit Window Help
$ ruby vehicle_methods.rb
Pressing the horn button
Beep beep!
Stepping on the gas
Speeding up
Turning on high-beam headlights
Watch out for deer!
$
```

I notice you didn't use the dot operator to specify a receiver for those method calls, just like when we call the `puts` and `print` methods.

That's right. Like `puts` and `print`, these methods are included in the top-level execution environment.

Methods that are defined outside of any class (like these examples) are included in the top-level execution environment. Like we saw back in Chapter 1, you can call them anywhere in your code, *without* using the dot operator to specify a receiver.

Method names

The method name can be one or more lowercase words, separated by underscores. (This is just like the convention for variable names.) Numbers are legal, but rarely used.

It's also legal for a method name to end in a question mark (?) or exclamation point (!). These endings have no special meaning to Ruby. But by convention, methods that return a Boolean (true/false) value are given names that end in ?, and methods that have potentially surprising side effects are given names that end in !.

Lastly, it's legal for a method name to end in an equals sign (=). Methods ending in this character are used as attribute writers, which we'll be looking at in the upcoming section on classes. Ruby *does* treat this ending specially, so don't use it for a regular method, or you may find it acts strangely!

Parameters

If you need to pass data into your method, you can include one or more parameters after the method name, separated by commas. In your method body, parameters can be accessed just like any variable.

```ruby
def print_area(length, width)
  puts length * width
end
```

Optional parameters

Got-A-Motor's developers are happy with our work on the virtual test-drive system...mostly.

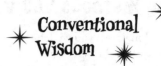

Conventional Wisdom

Method names should be in "snake case": one or more lowercase words, separated by underscores, just like variable names.

```ruby
def bark
end

def wag_tail
end
```

As with method calls, you should leave parentheses off the method definition if there are no parameters. Please don't do this, even though it's legal:

```ruby
def no_args()
  puts "Bad Rubyist!"
end
```

But if there are parameters, you should always include parentheses. (Back in Chapter 1, we saw some tasteful exceptions when we were making method calls, but there are no exceptions when we're declaring methods.) Leaving them off is legal, but again, don't do it:

```ruby
def with_args first, second
  puts "No! Bad!"
end
```

> Do we **have** to specify an argument on this `use_headlights` method? We almost always use `"low-beam"`, and we're copying that string everywhere in our code!

```ruby
use_headlights("low-beam")
stop_engine
buy_coffee
start_engine
use_headlights("low-beam")
accelerate
create_obstacle("deer")
use_headlights("high-beam")
```

Optional parameters (continued)

This scenario is pretty common—you use one particular argument 90% of the time, and you're tired of repeating it everywhere. But you can't just take the parameter out, because 10% of the time you need a different value.

There's an easy solution, though: *make the parameter optional*. You can provide a default value in the method declaration.

Here's an example of a method that uses default values for some of its parameters:

```ruby
def order_soda(flavor, size = "medium", quantity = 1)
  if quantity == 1
    plural = "soda"
  else
    plural = "sodas"
  end
  puts "#{quantity} #{size} #{flavor} #{plural}, coming right up!"
end
```

Default value for size

Default value for quantity

Now, if you want to override the default, just provide an argument with the value you want. And if you're happy with the default, you can skip the argument altogether.

Specify flavor; use default for size and quantity.

```ruby
order_soda("orange")
order_soda("lemon-lime", "small", 2)
order_soda("grape", "large")
```

Specify everything.

Specify flavor and size; use default for quantity.

```
1 medium orange soda, coming right up!
2 small lemon-lime sodas, coming right up!
1 large grape soda, coming right up!
```

There is one requirement to be aware of with optional parameters: they need to appear *after* any other parameters you intend to use. If you make a required parameter following an optional parameter, you won't be able to leave the optional parameter off:

```ruby
def order_soda(flavor, size = "medium", quantity)
  ...
end

order_soda("grape")
```

Don't place an optional parameter before a required one!

Error →

```
wrong number of
arguments (1 for 2..3)
```

there are no Dumb Questions

Q: What's the difference between an argument and a parameter?

A: You define and use *parameters* within a method *definition*. You provide *arguments* with method *calls*.

Parameter

```ruby
def say_hello(name)
  puts "Hello, #{name}!"
end
```

Parameter

```ruby
say_hello("Marcy")
```

Argument

Each argument you pass with the method call gets stored in a method parameter.

The two terms mostly serve to distinguish whether you're talking about a method *definition* or a method *call*.

Optional parameters (continued)

Let's make that `use_headlights` parameter optional, to earn some goodwill with the developers using our methods.

```ruby
def use_headlights(brightness = "low-beam")
  puts "Turning on #{brightness} headlights"
  puts "Watch out for deer!"
end
```

Now, they won't have to specify the brightness, unless they want the high beams.

```ruby
use_headlights          ← Uses the default, "low-beam"
use_headlights("high-beam")  ← Overrides the
                                default
```

```
Turning on low-beam headlights
Watch out for deer!
Turning on high-beam headlights
Watch out for deer!
```

```ruby
use_headlights          ←
stop_engine                 No argument
start_engine                needed!
use_headlights          ←
accelerate
use_headlights("high-beam")
```

Yeah, this will make scripting our test drives a **lot** easier! Thanks!

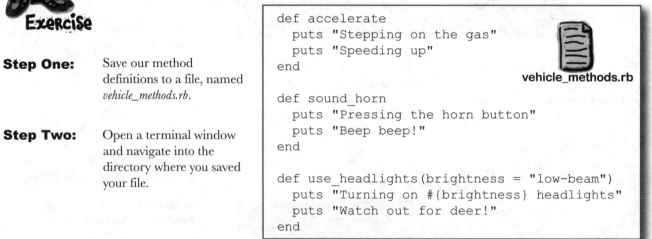

We've finished up our methods for Got-A-Motor's virtual test-drive app. Let's try loading them up in irb, and take them for a spin.

Exercise

Step One: Save our method definitions to a file, named *vehicle_methods.rb*.

Step Two: Open a terminal window and navigate into the directory where you saved your file.

vehicle_methods.rb

```ruby
def accelerate
  puts "Stepping on the gas"
  puts "Speeding up"
end

def sound_horn
  puts "Pressing the horn button"
  puts "Beep beep!"
end

def use_headlights(brightness = "low-beam")
  puts "Turning on #{brightness} headlights"
  puts "Watch out for deer!"
end
```

Exercise (Continued)

Step Three: Since we're loading code from a file into irb, we want to be able to load Ruby files from the current directory. So we're going to invoke irb a little differently this time.

In the terminal, type this and press Enter:

```
irb -I .
```
A flag that means "search the current directory for files to load."

The `-I` is a *command-line flag*, a string that you add on to a command to change how it operates. In this case, `-I` alters the set of directories that Ruby searches for files to load. And the dot (`.`) represents the current directory.

Step Four: Now, irb should be loaded, and we should be able to load the file with our methods. Type this line:

```
require "vehicle_methods"
```

Ruby knows to search in *.rb* files by default, so you can leave the extension off. If you see the result `true`, it means your file was loaded successfully.

Now, you can type in a call to any of our methods, and they'll be run!

Here's a sample session:

```
$ irb -I .
irb(main):001:0> require "vehicle_methods"
 => true
irb(main):002:0> sound_horn
Pressing the horn button
Beep beep!
 => nil
irb(main):003:0> use_headlights
Turning on low-beam headlights
Watch out for deer!
 => nil
irb(main):004:0> use_headlights("high-beam")
Turning on high-beam headlights
Watch out for deer!
 => nil
irb(main):005:0> exit
$
```

Return values

Got-A-Motor wants the test-drive app to highlight how fuel-efficient their cars are. They want to be able to display the mileage a car got on its most recent trip, as well as lifetime average mileage.

In the first scenario, you're dividing the mileage from the car's trip odometer by the number of gallons from your last fill-up, and in the second you're dividing the main odometer's value by the car's lifetime fuel use. But in both cases, you're taking a number of miles and dividing it by a number of gallons of fuel. So do you still have to write two methods?

Nope! As in most languages, Ruby methods have a **return value**, a value that they send back to the code that called them. A Ruby method can return a value to its caller using the `return` keyword.

You can write a single `mileage` method and use its return value in your output.

```
def mileage(miles_driven, gas_used)
  return miles_driven / gas_used
end
```

Then, you can use the same method to calculate both types of mileage.

```
trip_mileage = mileage(400, 12)
puts "You got #{trip_mileage} MPG on this trip."

lifetime_mileage = mileage(11432, 366)
puts "This car averages #{lifetime_mileage} MPG."
```

```
You got 33 MPG on this trip.
This car averages 31 MPG.
```

Implicit return values

You don't actually need the `return` keyword in the above method. The value of the last expression evaluated within a method automatically becomes that method's return value. So our `mileage` method could be rewritten without an explicit `return`:

```
def mileage(miles_driven, gas_used)
  miles_driven / gas_used
end
```

It will still work in exactly the same way.

```
puts mileage(400, 12)
```

33

Methods <u>return</u> a value to the code that called them.

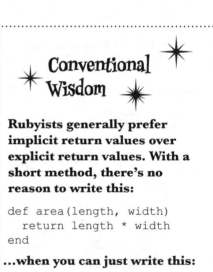

✳ Conventional ✳
Wisdom ✳

Rubyists generally prefer implicit return values over explicit return values. With a short method, there's no reason to write this:

```
def area(length, width)
  return length * width
end
```

...when you can just write this:

```
def area(length, width)
  length * width
end
```

Returning from a method early

> So why does Ruby even have a `return` keyword, if it's usually unnecessary?

There are still some circumstances where the `return` keyword is useful.

The `return` keyword causes the method to exit, without running the lines of code that follow it. This is useful in situations where running that code would be pointless, or even harmful.

For example, consider the case where a car is brand-new and hasn't been driven anywhere yet. The miles driven and the gas used would both be zero. What happens if you call the `mileage` method for such a car?

Well, `mileage` works by dividing `miles_driven` by `gas_used`... And, as you may have learned in your other programming language, dividing anything by zero is an error!

```
puts mileage(0, 0)
```
Error ⟶
```
in `/': divided by 0
(ZeroDivisionError)
```

We can fix this by testing whether `gas_used` is zero, and if so, returning from the method early.

```
def mileage(miles_driven, gas_used)
  if gas_used == 0          ⟵── If no gas has been used...
    return 0.0              ⟵── ...return zero.
  end
  miles_driven / gas_used  ⟵── This code won't be run
end                              if "gas_used" is zero.
```

If we try the same code again, we'll see that it returns `0.0`, without attempting the division operation. Problem solved!

```
puts mileage(0, 0)
```

Methods are a great way to reduce duplication, and keep your code organized. But sometimes methods by themselves aren't enough. Let's leave our friends at Got-A-Motor for now, to look at a somewhat fuzzier problem...

Some messy methods

The folks at Fuzzy Friends Animal Rescue are in the middle of a fundraising drive, and are creating an interactive storybook application to raise awareness. They've approached your company for help. They need many different types of animals, each of which has its own sounds and actions.

They've created some methods that simulate movement and animal noises. They call these methods by specifying the animal type as the first argument, followed by any additional arguments that are needed.

Here's what they have so far:

```ruby
def talk(animal_type, name)
  if animal_type == "bird"
    puts "#{name} says Chirp! Chirp!"
  elsif animal_type == "dog"
    puts "#{name} says Bark!"
  elsif animal_type == "cat"
    puts "#{name} says Meow!"
  end
end
```

The animal type parameter is used to select which string is printed.

```ruby
def move(animal_type, name, destination)
  if animal_type == "bird"
    puts "#{name} flies to the #{destination}."
  elsif animal_type == "dog"
    puts "#{name} runs to the #{destination}."
  elsif animal_type == "cat"
    puts "#{name} runs to the #{destination}."
  end
end

def report_age(name, age)
  puts "#{name} is #{age} years old."
end
```

This method is the same for all animal types, so there's no animal type parameter.

And here are some typical calls to those methods:

```ruby
move("bird", "Whistler", "tree")
talk("dog", "Sadie")
talk("bird", "Whistler")
move("cat", "Smudge", "house")
report_age("Smudge", 6)
```

```
Whistler flies to the tree.
Sadie says Bark!
Whistler says Chirp! Chirp!
Smudge runs to the house.
Smudge is 6 years old.
```

Fuzzy Friends just needs you to add 10 more animal types and 30 more actions, and version 1.0 will be done!

Too many arguments

> That's looking pretty messy with just **three** animal types and **two** actions. Those "if" and "elsif" statements are long already, and look at all those method arguments! Isn't there a better way to organize this code?

Part of the problem with the virtual storybook methods is that we're having to pass around too much data. Look at these calls to the move method, for example:

We need the destination argument...

```
move("bird", "Whistler", "tree")
move("cat", "Smudge", "house")
```

...but do we really have to pass these each time?

The destination argument belongs there, sure. It doesn't make sense to move without a destination. But do we really have to keep track of values for the animal_type and name arguments, so that we can include them each time? It's also becoming hard to tell which argument is which!

Too many "if" statements

The problem isn't just with the method arguments, either—things are messy *inside* the methods. Consider what the talk method would look like if we added 10 more animal types, for example...

Each time you want to change the sound an animal makes (and you *will* be asked to change the sounds; you can count on it), you'll have to search through all those elsif clauses to find the right animal type... What happens when the code for talk becomes more complex, adding things like animations and sound file playback? What happens when *all* of the action methods are like that?

What we need is a better way to represent which animal type we're working with. We need a better way to break all that code up by animal type, so that we can maintain it more easily. And we need a better way to store the attributes for each individual animal, like their name and their age, so we don't have to pass so many arguments around.

We need to keep the animals' data, and the code that operates on that data, in one place. We need *classes* and *objects*.

```ruby
def talk(animal_type, name)
  if animal_type == "bird"
    puts "#{name} says Chirp! Chirp!"
  elsif animal_type == "dog"
    puts "#{name} says Bark!"
  elsif animal_type == "cat"
    puts "#{name} says Meow!"
  elsif animal_type == "lion"
    puts "#{name} says Roar!"
  elsif animal_type == "cow"
    puts "#{name} says Moo."
  elsif animal_type == "bob"
    puts "#{name} says Hello."
  elsif animal_type == "duck"
    puts "#{name} says Quack."
  ...
  end
end
```

We don't even have room to print all this...

Designing a class

The benefit of using objects is that they keep a set of data, and the methods that operate on that data, in one place. We want those benefits in the Fuzzy Friends app.

To start creating your own objects, though, you're going to need classes. A **class** is a blueprint for making objects. When you use a class to make an object, the class describes what that object *knows* about itself, as well as what that object *does*.

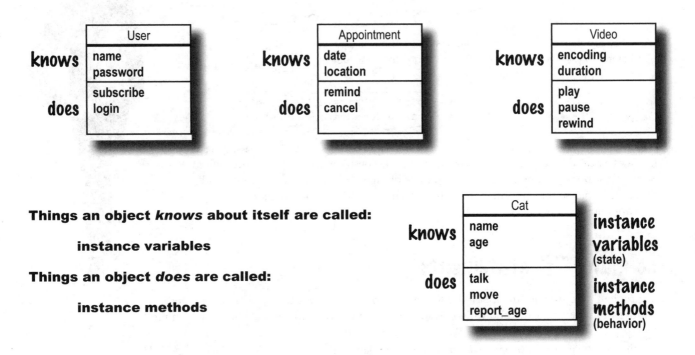

Things an object *knows* about itself are called:

> **instance variables**

Things an object *does* are called:

> **instance methods**

An **instance** of a class is an object that was made using that class. You only have to write *one* class, but you can make *many* instances of that class.

Think of "instance" as another way of saying "object."

Instance variables are variables that belong to one object. They comprise everything the object **knows** about itself. They represent the object's state (its data), and they can have different values for each instance of the class.

Instance methods are methods that you can call directly on that object. They comprise what the object **does**. They have access to the object's instance variables, and can use them to change their behavior based on the values in those variables.

What's the difference between a class and an object?

A class is a blueprint for an object. The class tells Ruby how to make an object of that particular type. Objects have instance variables and instance methods, but those variables and methods are *designed* as part of the class.

Objects

If <u>classes</u> are cookie cutters, <u>objects</u> are the cookies they make.

Class

Each instance of a class can have its own values for the instance variables used within that class's methods. For example, you'll define the Dog class only once. Within that Dog class's methods, you'll specify only once that Dog instances should have name and age instance variables. But each Dog *object* will have its own name and age, distinct from all the other Dog instances.

Dog class:

Dog
name age
talk move report_age

instance variables (state)

instance methods (behavior)

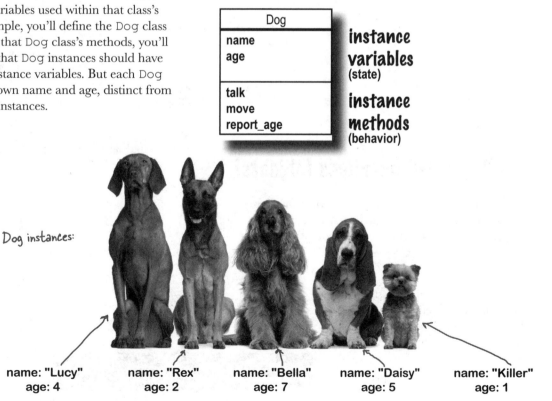

Dog instances:

name: "Lucy"
age: 4

name: "Rex"
age: 2

name: "Bella"
age: 7

name: "Daisy"
age: 5

name: "Killer"
age: 1

Your first class

Here's an example of a class we could use in our interactive storybook:
a Dog class.

We use the `class` keyword
to start a new class definition,
followed by the name of our
new class.

Within the class definition,
we can include method
definitions. Any method we
define here will be available
as an instance method on
instances of the class.

We mark the end of the
class definition with the `end`
keyword.

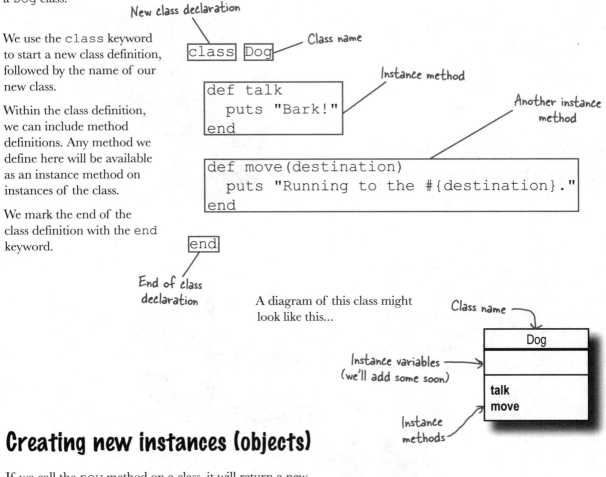

A diagram of this class might
look like this...

Creating new instances (objects)

If we call the `new` method on a class, it will return a new
instance of that class. We can then assign that instance to a
variable, or do whatever else we need to do with it.

```
fido = Dog.new
rex = Dog.new
```

Once we have one or more instances of the class, we can
call their instance methods. We do it in the same way we've
called all other methods on objects so far: we use the dot
operator to specify which instance is the method's receiver.

```
fido.talk
rex.move("food bowl")
```

```
Bark!
Running to the food bowl.
```

Breaking up our giant methods into classes

The animal rescue's solution uses strings to track what type of animal they're dealing with. Also, all knowledge of the different ways that different animals should respond is embedded in giant `if`/`else` statements. Their approach is unwieldy, at best.

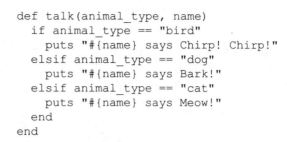

```ruby
def talk(animal_type, name)
  if animal_type == "bird"
    puts "#{name} says Chirp! Chirp!"
  elsif animal_type == "dog"
    puts "#{name} says Bark!"
  elsif animal_type == "cat"
    puts "#{name} says Meow!"
  end
end
```

The object-oriented approach

Now that you know how to create classes, we can take an *object-oriented* approach to the problem. We can create a *class* to represent each *type* of animal. Then, instead of one *big* method that contains behavior for *all* the animal types, we can put *little* methods in *each* class, methods that define behavior specific to that type of animal.

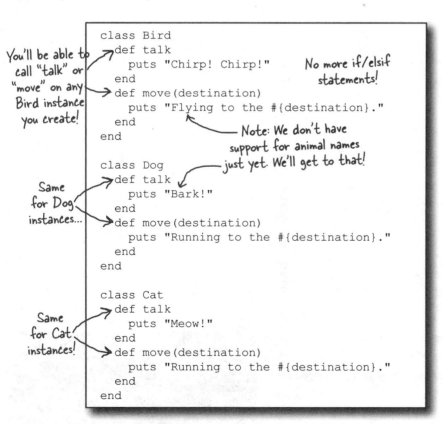

You'll be able to call "talk" or "move" on any Bird instance you create!

No more if/elsif statements!

Note: We don't have support for animal names just yet. We'll get to that!

Same for Dog instances...

Same for Cat instances!

```ruby
class Bird
  def talk
    puts "Chirp! Chirp!"
  end
  def move(destination)
    puts "Flying to the #{destination}."
  end
end

class Dog
  def talk
    puts "Bark!"
  end
  def move(destination)
    puts "Running to the #{destination}."
  end
end

class Cat
  def talk
    puts "Meow!"
  end
  def move(destination)
    puts "Running to the #{destination}."
  end
end
```

Conventional Wisdom

Ruby class names must begin with a capital letter. Letters after the first should be lowercase.

```ruby
class Appointment
  ...
end
```

If there's more than one word in the name, the first letter of each word should also be capitalized.

```ruby
class AddressBook
  ...
end

class PhoneNumber
  ...
end
```

Remember how the convention for variable names (with underscores separating words) is called "snake case"? The style for class names is called "camel case," because the capital letters look like the humps on a camel.

Creating instances of our new animal classes

With these classes defined, we can create new instances of them (new objects based on the classes) and call methods on them.

Just as with methods, Ruby lets us create instances of classes right in the same file where we declared them. You probably won't want to organize your code this way in larger applications, but since this is such a simple app right now, we can go ahead and create some new instances right below the class declarations.

```ruby
class Bird
  def talk
    puts "Chirp! Chirp!"
  end
  def move(destination)
    puts "Flying to the #{destination}."
  end
end

class Dog
  def talk
    puts "Bark!"
  end
  def move(destination)
    puts "Running to the #{destination}."
  end
end

class Cat
  def talk
    puts "Meow!"
  end
  def move(destination)
    puts "Running to the #{destination}."
  end
end

bird = Bird.new
dog = Dog.new
cat = Cat.new

bird.move("tree")
dog.talk
bird.talk
cat.move("house")
```

animals.rb

} Create new instances
   of our classes.

} Call some methods on
   the instances.

```
File Edit Window Help
$ ruby animals.rb
Flying to the tree.
Bark!
Chirp! Chirp!
Running to the house.
$
```

If we save all this to a file named *animals.rb*, then run `ruby animals.rb` from a terminal, we'll see the output of our instance methods!

Updating our class diagram with instance methods

If we were to draw a
diagram of our new
classes, they'd look
something like this:

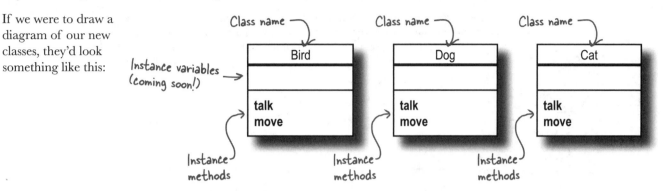

At this point, instances of our classes have two instance methods (things they can *do*): `talk` and `move`.
They don't yet have any instance variables (things they *know*), however. We'll be looking at that next.

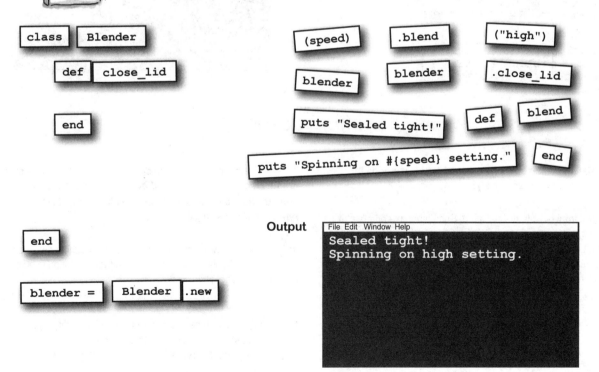

Code Magnets

A working Ruby program is scrambled up on the fridge. Some of the code snippets are in the correct places, but others have been moved around randomly. Can you rearrange the code snippets to make a working program that produces the output listed below?

```
class     Blender

    def   close_lid

    end


end

blender =    Blender  .new
```

```
(speed)        .blend        ("high")

blender        blender       .close_lid

      puts "Sealed tight!"        def    blend

puts "Spinning on #{speed} setting."        end
```

Output

```
File Edit Window Help
Sealed tight!
Spinning on high setting.
```

Code Magnets Solution

A working Ruby program is scrambled up on the fridge. Some of the code snippets are in the correct places, but others have been moved around randomly. Can you rearrange the code snippets to make a working program that produces the output listed below?

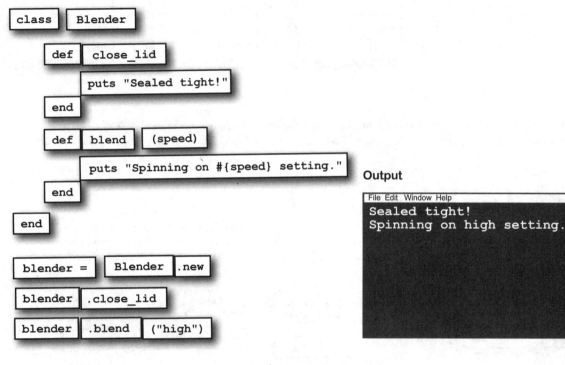

```ruby
class Blender

  def close_lid
    puts "Sealed tight!"
  end

  def blend (speed)
    puts "Spinning on #{speed} setting."
  end

end

blender = Blender .new
blender .close_lid
blender .blend ("high")
```

Output

```
File Edit Window Help
Sealed tight!
Spinning on high setting.
```

there are no Dumb Questions

Q: Can I call these new `move` and `talk` methods by themselves (without an object)?

A: Not from outside the class, no. Remember, the purpose of specifying a receiver is to tell Ruby which object a method is being called on. The `move` and `talk` methods are *instance methods*; it doesn't make sense to call them without stating which instance of the class you're calling them on. If you try, you'll get an error, like this:

```
move("food bowl")

undefined method `move' for
main:Object (NoMethodError)
```

Q: You say that we have to call the `new` method on a class to create an object. You also said back in Chapter 1 that numbers and strings are objects. Why don't we have to call `new` to get a new number or string?

A: Creating new numbers and strings is something developers need to do so frequently that special shorthand notation is built right into the language: string and number *literals*.

```
new_string = "Hello!"
new_float = 4.2
```

Doing the same for other classes would require modifying the Ruby language itself, so most classes just rely on `new` to create new instances. (There are exceptions; we'll get to those in later chapters.)

Our objects don't "know" their names or ages!

The animal rescue's lead developer points out a couple of details we forgot to address with our class-based solution:

> We're supposed to see the animal's name when we call these methods! And where is the `report_age` **method?**

```
Flying to the tree.
Bark!
Chirp! Chirp!
Running to the house.
```

She has a point; we're missing a couple of features from the original program.

Let's start by readding the `name` parameter to the `talk` and `move` methods:

A name will have to be provided when we call these methods, like before.

```ruby
class Bird
  def talk(name)
    puts "#{name} says Chirp! Chirp!"
  end
  def move(name, destination)
    puts "#{name} flies to the #{destination}."
  end
end
```

And like before, we'll use the names in the output.

```ruby
class Dog
  def talk(name)
    puts "#{name} says Bark!"
  end
  def move(name, destination)
    puts "#{name} runs to the #{destination}."
  end
end

class Cat
  def talk(name)
    puts "#{name} says Meow!"
  end
  def move(name, destination)
    puts "#{name} runs to the #{destination}."
  end
end
```

Too many arguments (again)

Now that we've readded the name parameter to the talk and move methods, we can once again pass in the animal's name to be printed.

```
dog = Dog.new
dog_name = "Lucy"
dog.talk(dog_name)
dog.move(dog_name, "fence")

cat = Cat.new
cat_name = "Fluffy"
cat.talk(cat_name)
cat.move(cat_name, "litter box")
```

```
Lucy says Bark!
Lucy runs to the fence.
Fluffy says Meow!
Fluffy runs to the litter box.
```

Come on. We already have a variable to hold the animal object. You really want us to pass a **second** variable with the animal's name everywhere? What a pain!

```
dog = Dog.new
dog_name = "Lucy"
cat = Cat.new
cat_name = "Fluffy"
```

Actually, we <u>can</u> do better. We can use instance variables to store data <u>inside</u> the object.

One of the key benefits of object-oriented programming is that it keeps data, and the methods that operate on that data, in the same place. Let's try storing the names *in* the animal objects so that we don't have to pass so many arguments to our instance methods.

Local variables live until the method ends

So far, we've been working with **local variables**—variables that are *local* to the current scope (usually the current method). When the current scope ends, local variables cease to exist, so they *won't* work for storing our animals' names, as you'll see below.

Here's a new version of the Dog class with an additional method, make_up_name. When we call make_up_name, it stores a name for the dog, for later access by the talk method.

```ruby
class Dog

  def make_up_name
    name = "Sandy"         ←——— Store a name.
  end

  def talk
    puts "#{name} says Bark!"
  end                          ⤷ Attempt to access
                                  the stored name.
end
```

The moment we call the talk method, however, we get an error, saying the name variable doesn't exist:

```ruby
dog = Dog.new
dog.make_up_name
dog.talk
```

Error
↓

```
in `talk': undefined local
variable or method `name' for
#<Dog:0x007fa3188ae428>
```

What happened? We *did* define a name variable, back in the make_up_name method!

The problem, though, is that we used a *local* variable. Local variables live only as long as the method in which they were created. In this case, the name variable ceases to exist as soon as make_up_name ends.

```ruby
class Dog

  def make_up_name
    name = "Sandy"
  end  ←——————————— "name" drops out of scope
                      as soon as the method ends.
  def talk
    puts "#{name} says Bark!"
  end
                     ⤷ This variable no
end                    longer exists here!
```

Trust us, the short life of local variables is a *good* thing. If *any* variable was accessible *anywhere* in your program, you'd be accidentally referencing the wrong variables *all the time*! Like most languages, Ruby limits the scope of variables in order to prevent this sort of mistake.

Just imagine if this local variable... →

```ruby
def alert_ceo
  message = "Sell your stock."
  email(ceo, message)
end

email(shareholders, message)
```

...were accessible here...

Whew! Close one.

Error →
```
undefined local variable
or method `message'
```

Instance variables live as long as the instance does

Any local variable we create disappears as soon as its scope ends. If that's true, though, how can we store a `Dog`'s name together with the object? We're going to need a new kind of variable.

An object can store data in **instance variables**: variables that are tied to a particular object instance. Data written to an object's instance variables stays with that object, getting removed from memory only when the object is removed.

An instance variable looks just like a regular variable, and follows all the same naming conventions. The only difference in syntax is that its name begins with an "at" symbol (@).

> **An object's instance variables are kept around as long as the object is.**

```
my_variable        @my_variable
```

Local variable　　　**Instance variable**

Here's that `Dog` class again. It's identical to the previous one, except that we added two little @ symbols to convert the *two* local variables to *one* instance variable.

```
class Dog

  def make_up_name
    @name = "Sandy"
  end

  def talk
    puts "#{@name} says Bark!"
  end

end
```

Store a value in an instance variable. →

⌐ Access the instance variable.

Now, we can make the exact same call to `talk` that we did before, and the code will work! The `@name` instance variable that we create in the `make_up_name` method is still accessible in the `talk` method.

```
dog = Dog.new
dog.make_up_name
dog.talk
```

```
Sandy says Bark!
```

Instance variables live as long as the instance does (continued)

With instance variables at our disposal, it's easy to add the `move` and `report_age` methods back in as well...

```ruby
class Dog

  def make_up_name
    @name = "Sandy"
  end

  def talk
    puts "#{@name} says Bark!"
  end

  def move(destination)
    puts "#{@name} runs to the #{destination}."
  end

  def make_up_age
    @age = 5
  end

  def report_age
    puts "#{@name} is #{@age} years old."
  end

end

dog = Dog.new
dog.make_up_name
dog.move("yard")
dog.make_up_age
dog.report_age
```

Our new code!

```
Sandy runs to the yard.
Sandy is 5 years old.
```

And now that we have instance variables, we can finally fill in that hole in the class diagram for Dog!

Instance variables →

Instance methods →

Dog
name
age
talk
move

That's an improvement. But this class only lets us make 5-year-old dogs named Sandy!

That's true. Up next, we'll discuss a way to set a dog's name and age to other values.

57

Encapsulation

Thanks to instance variables, we now have a way to store names and ages for our animals. But our `make_up_name` and `make_up_age` methods only allow us to use hardcoded values (we can't change them when the program's running). We need a way for our program to set any values we want.

```ruby
class Dog

  def make_up_name
    @name = "Sandy"
  end

  def make_up_age
    @age = 5
  end
  ...
end
```

Code like this *won't* work, though:

```ruby
fido = Dog.new
fido.@age = 3
```

Error

```
syntax error, unexpected tIVAR
```

Ruby never allows us to access instance variables directly from outside our class. This isn't due to some authoritarian agenda; it's to keep other programs and classes from modifying your instance variables willy-nilly.

Let's suppose that you *could* update instance variables directly. What's to prevent other portions of the program from setting the variables to invalid values?

This is invalid code!

```ruby
fido = Dog.new
fido.@name = ""
fido.@age = -1
fido.report_age
```

If you COULD do that, the output would be...

```
is -1 years old.
```

Who is *how* old? This object's data is clearly invalid, and the user can see it in the program output!

Blank names and negative ages are just the start. Imagine someone accidentally replacing the value in an `Appointment` object's `@date` instance variable with a phone number. Or setting the `@sales_tax` on all their `Invoice` objects to zero. All kinds of things could go wrong!

To help avoid exposing an object's data to malicious (or clumsy) users, most object-oriented languages encourage the concept of **encapsulation**: preventing other parts of the program from directly accessing or changing an object's instance variables.

Attribute accessor methods

To encourage encapsulation and protect your instances from invalid data, Ruby doesn't allow you to access or change instance variables from outside the class. Instead, you can create **accessor methods**, which will write values to the instance variables and read them back out again for you. Once you're accessing your data through accessor methods, it's easy to extend those methods to *validate* your data—to reject any bad values that get passed in.

Ruby has two kinds of accessor methods: *attribute writers* and *attribute readers*. (An *attribute* is another name for a piece of data regarding an object.) Attribute *writer* methods *set* an instance variable, and attribute *reader* methods *get* the value of an instance variable back.

Here's a simple class with writer and reader methods for an attribute named `my_attribute`:

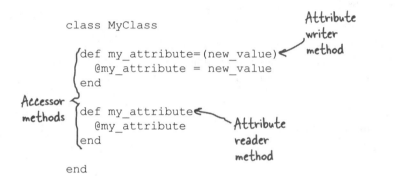

```
class MyClass

    def my_attribute=(new_value)          Attribute
        @my_attribute = new_value         writer
    end                                   method

    def my_attribute                      Attribute
        @my_attribute                     reader
    end                                   method

end
```

Accessor methods

If we create a new instance of the above class…   `my_instance = MyClass.new`

…we can set the attribute like this…   `my_instance.my_attribute = "a value"`

…and read the attribute like this.   `puts my_instance.my_attribute`

Accessor methods are just ordinary instance methods; we only refer to them as "accessor methods" because their primary purpose is to access an instance variable.

Look at the attribute reader method, for example; it's a perfectly ordinary method that simply returns the current value of `@my_attribute`.

```
def my_attribute          Nothing magic about the reader!
    @my_attribute         It just returns the current value.
end
```

Attribute accessor methods (continued)

Like attribute *reader* methods, an attribute *writer* method is a perfectly ordinary instance method. We just call it an "attribute writer" method because the primary thing it does is to update an instance variable.

```
class MyClass

  def my_attribute=(new_value)
    @my_attribute = new_value
  end

  ...

end
```

Attribute writer method

It may be a perfectly ordinary method, but *calls* to it are treated somewhat specially.

Remember that earlier in the chapter, we said that Ruby method names could end in = (an equals sign)? Ruby allows that equals-sign ending so that it can be used in the names of attribute writer methods.

```
def my_attribute=(new_value)
  ...
end
```

Part of the method name!

When Ruby sees something like this in your code:

```
my_instance.my_attribute = "a value"
```

…it translates that into a call to the `my_attribute=` instance method. The value to the right of the = is passed as an argument to the method:

A method call ↓   The method argument ↓

```
my_instance.my_attribute=("a value")
```

The above code is valid Ruby, and you can try it yourself if you like:

```
class MyClass
  def my_attribute=(new_value)
    @my_attribute = new_value
  end
  def my_attribute
    @my_attribute
  end
end

my_instance = MyClass.new
my_instance.my_attribute = "assigned via method call"
puts my_instance.my_attribute
my_instance.my_attribute=("same here")
puts my_instance.my_attribute
```

A call to "my_attribute=", disguised as assignment

A call to "my_attribute=" that actually looks like one!

✳ Conventional Wisdom ✳

This alternate way of calling attribute writer methods is shown only so that you can understand what's going on behind the scenes. In your actual Ruby programs, you should only use the assignment syntax!

```
assigned via method call
same here
```

Using accessor methods

Now we're ready to use what we've learned in the Fuzzy Friends application. As a first step, let's update the Dog class with methods that will let us read and write @name and @age instance variables. We'll also use @name and @age in the report_age method. We'll look at adding data validation later.

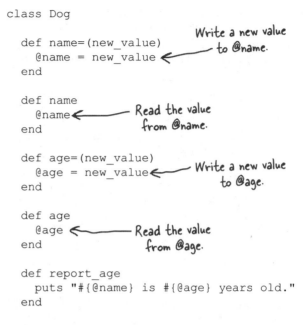

```
class Dog

  def name=(new_value)          Write a new value
    @name = new_value              to @name.
  end

  def name                 Read the value
    @name                    from @name.
  end

  def age=(new_value)          Write a new value
    @age = new_value               to @age.
  end

  def age                 Read the value
    @age                    from @age.
  end

  def report_age
    puts "#{@name} is #{@age} years old."
  end

end
```

With accessor methods in place, we can (indirectly) set and use the @name and @age instance variables from outside the Dog class!

```
fido = Dog.new
fido.name = "Fido"      Set @name for Fido.
fido.age = 2            Set @age for Fido.
rex = Dog.new
rex.name = "Rex"        Set @name for Rex.
rex.age = 3            Set @age for Rex.
fido.report_age
rex.report_age
```

```
Fido is 2 years old.
Rex is 3 years old.
```

Writing a reader and writer method by hand for each attribute can get tedious, though. Next, we'll look at an easier way...

Conventional Wisdom

The name of an attribute reader method should usually match the name of the instance variable it reads from (without the @ symbol, of course).

```
def tail_length
  @tail_length
end
```

The same is true for attribute writer methods, but you should add an = symbol on to the end of the name.

```
def tail_length=(value)
  @tail_length = value
end
```

Attribute writers and readers

Creating this pair of accessor methods for an attribute is so common that Ruby offers us shortcuts—methods named `attr_writer`, `attr_reader`, and `attr_accessor`. Calling these three methods within your class definition will automatically define new accessor methods for you:

Write this within your class definition...

...and Ruby will automatically define these methods:

Write this within your class definition...	...and Ruby will automatically define these methods:	
`attr_writer :name`	```def name=(new_value) @name = new_value end```	Just like our old definition!
`attr_reader :name`	```def name @name end```	Just like our old definition!
`attr_accessor :name`	```def name=(new_value) @name = new_value end def name @name end```	Defines two methods at once!

All three of these methods can take multiple arguments, specifying multiple attributes that you want to define accessors for.

`attr_accessor :name, :age`

Defines FOUR methods at once!

Symbols

In case you're wondering, those `:name` and `:age` things are symbols. A Ruby **symbol** is a series of characters, like a string. Unlike a string, though, a symbol's value can't be changed later. That makes symbols perfect for use inside Ruby programs, to refer to anything whose name doesn't (usually) change, like a method. For example, if you call the method named `methods` on an object in irb, you'll see that it returns a list of symbols.

`:hello`

Ruby symbols ⟶ `:over_easy`

`:east`

```
> Object.new.methods
=> [:class, :singleton_class, :clone, ...]
```

A symbol reference in Ruby code always begins with a colon (`:`). A symbol should be in all lowercase, with words separated by underscores, just like a variable name.

Attribute writers and readers in action

The Dog class currently devotes 12 lines of code to accessor methods. With the `attr_accessor` method, we can shrink that down to 1 line!

It will let us reduce our Dog class's size...

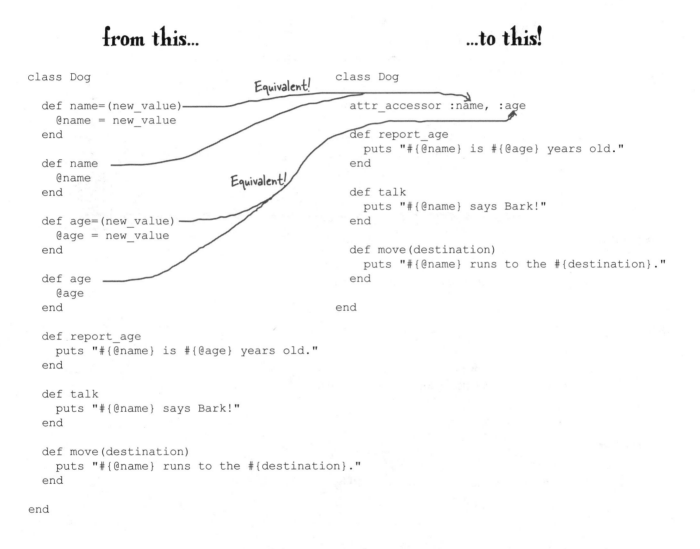

from this...

```
class Dog

  def name=(new_value)
    @name = new_value
  end

  def name
    @name
  end

  def age=(new_value)
    @age = new_value
  end

  def age
    @age
  end

  def report_age
    puts "#{@name} is #{@age} years old."
  end

  def talk
    puts "#{@name} says Bark!"
  end

  def move(destination)
    puts "#{@name} runs to the #{destination}."
  end

end
```

Equivalent!

Equivalent!

...to this!

```
class Dog

  attr_accessor :name, :age

  def report_age
    puts "#{@name} is #{@age} years old."
  end

  def talk
    puts "#{@name} says Bark!"
  end

  def move(destination)
    puts "#{@name} runs to the #{destination}."
  end

end
```

How's *that* for efficiency? It's a lot easier to read, too!

Let's not forget why we're writing accessor methods in the first place, though. We need to *protect* our instance variables from invalid data. Right now, these methods don't do that... We'll see how to fix this in a few pages!

We haven't really gotten to play around with classes and objects much yet. Let's try another irb session. We'll load up a simple class so we can create some instances of it interactively.

Step One:

Save this class definition to a file, named *mage.rb*.

```ruby
class Mage

  attr_accessor :name, :spell

  def enchant(target)
    puts "#{@name} casts #{@spell} on #{target.name}!"
  end

end
```

mage.rb

Step Two:

In a terminal window, navigate into the directory where you saved your file.

Step Three:

We want to be able to load Ruby files from the current directory, so as in the previous exercise, type the following to launch irb:

```
irb -I .
```

Step Four:

As before, we need to load the file with our saved Ruby code. Type this line:

```
require "mage"
```

Exercise (Continued)

Here's a sample session:

With our `Mage` class's code loaded, you can try creating as many instances as you like, set their attributes, and have them cast spells at each other! Try the following for starters:

```
merlin = Mage.new
merlin.name = "Merlin"
morgana = Mage.new
morgana.name = "Morgana"
morgana.spell = "Shrink"
morgana.enchant(merlin)
```

```
File  Edit  Window  Help
$ irb -I .
irb(main):001:0> require 'mage'
 => true
irb(main):002:0> merlin = Mage.new
 => #<Mage:0x007fd432082308>
irb(main):003:0> merlin.name = "Merlin"
 => "Merlin"
irb(main):004:0> morgana = Mage.new
 => #<Mage:0x007fd43206b310>
irb(main):005:0> morgana.name = "Morgana"
 => "Morgana"
irb(main):006:0> morgana.spell = "Shrink"
 => "Shrink"
irb(main):007:0> morgana.enchant(merlin)
Morgana casts Shrink on Merlin!
 => nil
irb(main):008:0>
```

Who am I?

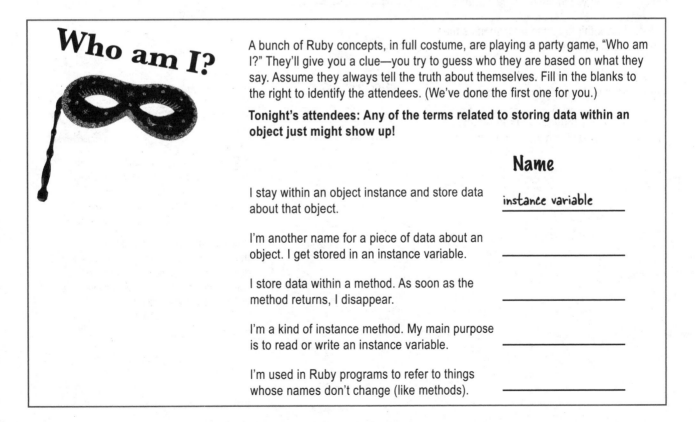

A bunch of Ruby concepts, in full costume, are playing a party game, "Who am I?" They'll give you a clue—you try to guess who they are based on what they say. Assume they always tell the truth about themselves. Fill in the blanks to the right to identify the attendees. (We've done the first one for you.)

Tonight's attendees: Any of the terms related to storing data within an object just might show up!

Name

Clue	Name
I stay within an object instance and store data about that object.	*instance variable*
I'm another name for a piece of data about an object. I get stored in an instance variable.	_____
I store data within a method. As soon as the method returns, I disappear.	_____
I'm a kind of instance method. My main purpose is to read or write an instance variable.	_____
I'm used in Ruby programs to refer to things whose names don't change (like methods).	_____

Who am I? Solution

	Name
I stay within an object instance and store data about that object.	instance variable
I'm another name for a piece of data about an object. I get stored in an instance variable.	attribute
I store data within a method. As soon as the method returns, I disappear.	local variable
I'm a kind of instance method. My main purpose is to read or write an instance variable.	accessor method
I'm used in Ruby programs to refer to things whose names don't change (like methods).	symbol

there are no Dumb Questions

Q: What's the difference between an accessor method and an instance method?

A: "Accessor method" is just a way of describing one particular *kind* of instance method, one whose primary purpose is to get or set the value of an instance variable. In all other respects, accessor methods are ordinary instance methods.

Q: I set up an instance variable outside an instance method, but it's not there when I try to access it. Why?

```
class Widget
  @size = 'large'
  def show_size
    puts "Size: #{@size}"
  end
end

widget = Widget.new
widget.show_size
```

Empty!

`Size:`

A: When you use instance variables outside of an instance method, you're actually creating an instance variable *on the class object*. (That's right, even classes are themselves objects in Ruby.)

While there are potential uses for this, they're beyond the scope of this book. For now, this is almost certainly not what you want. Instead, set up the instance variable within an instance method:

```
class Widget
  def set_size
    @size = 'large'
  end
  ...
end
```

Pool Puzzle

Your **job** is to take code snippets from the pool and place them into the blank lines in the code. **Don't** use the same snippet more than once, and you won't need to use all the snippets. Your **goal** is to make code that will run and produce the output shown.

```ruby
class Robot

  def _____
    @head
  end

  def _____(value)
    @arms = value
  end

  _____ :legs, :body

  attr_writer _____

  _____ :feet

  def assemble
    @legs = "RubyTek Walkers"
    @body = "BurlyBot Frame"
    _____ = "SuperAI 9000"
  end

  def diagnostic
    puts _____
    puts @eyes
  end

end
```

```ruby
robot = Robot.new

robot.assemble

robot.arms = "MagGrip Claws"
robot.eyes = "X-Ray Scopes"
robot.feet = "MagGrip Boots"

puts robot.head
puts robot.legs
puts robot.body
puts robot.feet
robot.diagnostic
```

Output

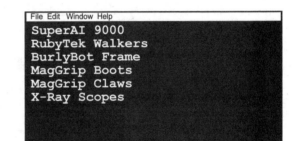

```
File Edit Window Help
SuperAI 9000
RubyTek Walkers
BurlyBot Frame
MagGrip Boots
MagGrip Claws
X-Ray Scopes
```

Note: each thing from the pool can only be used once!

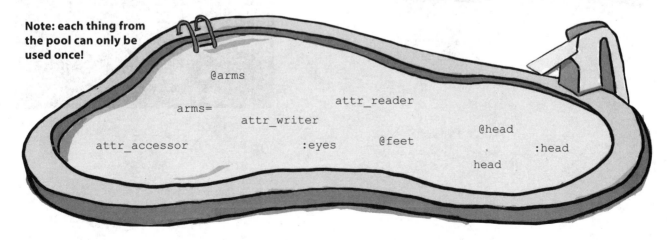

```
@arms

arms=                    attr_reader

        attr_writer

attr_accessor    :eyes    @feet    @head

                                   :head

                        head
```

Pool Puzzle Solution

Your **job** is to take code snippets from the pool and place them into the blank lines in the code. **Don't** use the same snippet more than once, and you won't need to use all the snippets. Your **goal** is to make code that will run and produce the output shown.

```ruby
class Robot

  def head
    @head
  end

  def arms=(value)
    @arms = value
  end

  attr_reader :legs, :body

  attr_writer :eyes

  attr_accessor :feet

  def assemble
    @legs = "RubyTek Walkers"
    @body = "BurlyBot Frame"
    @head = "SuperAI 9000"
  end

  def diagnostic
    puts @arms
    puts @eyes
  end

end
```

```ruby
robot = Robot.new

robot.assemble

robot.arms = "MagGrip Claws"
robot.eyes = "X-Ray Scopes"
robot.feet = "MagGrip Boots"

puts robot.head
puts robot.legs
puts robot.body
puts robot.feet
robot.diagnostic
```

Output

```
File Edit Window Help Lasers
SuperAI 9000
RubyTek Walkers
BurlyBot Frame
MagGrip Boots
MagGrip Claws
X-Ray Scopes
```

Ensuring data is valid with accessors

Remember our scenario from a nightmare world where Ruby let programs access instance variables directly, and someone gave your Dog instances *blank* names and *negative* ages? Bad news: now that you've added attribute writer methods to your Dog class, someone actually *could*!

```ruby
joey = Dog.new
joey.name = ""
joey.age = -1
joey.report_age
```

`is -1 years old.`

Don't panic! Those same writer methods are going to help us prevent this from happening in the future. We're going to add some simple data *validation* to the methods, which will give an error any time an invalid value is passed in.

Since `name=` and `age=` are just ordinary Ruby methods, adding the validation is really easy; we'll use ordinary `if` statements to look for an empty string (for `name=`) or a negative number (for `age=`). If we encounter an invalid value, we'll print an error message. Only if the value is valid will we actually set the `@name` or `@age` instance variables.

We only define the reader methods automatically, since we're defining writer methods ourselves.

```ruby
class Dog

  attr_reader :name, :age

  def name=(value)
    if value == ""
      puts "Name can't be blank!"
    else
      @name = value
    end
  end

  def age=(value)
    if value < 0
      puts "An age of #{value} isn't valid!"
    else
      @age = value
    end
  end

  def report_age
    puts "#{@name} is #{@age} years old."
  end

end
```

If the name is blank, print an error message.

Set the instance variable only if the name is valid.

If the age is negative, print an error message.

Set the instance variable only if the age is valid.

Errors—the "emergency stop" button

> So now we get a warning if an invalid name or age is set. Great. But then the program goes right on to call `report_age` anyway, and the name and age are blank!

```
glitch = Dog.new
glitch.name = ""
glitch.age = -256
glitch.report_age
```

```
Name can't be blank!
An age of -256 isn't valid!
 is  years old.
```

Blank!

Instead of just *printing* a message, we need to deal with invalid parameters in the `name=` and `age=` accessor methods in a more meaningful way. Let's change the validation code in our `name=` and `age=` methods to use Ruby's built-in `raise` method to report any errors.

```
raise "Something bad happened!"
```

That's `raise` as in "raise an issue." Your program is bringing a problem to your attention.

You call `raise` with a string describing what's wrong. When Ruby encounters the call, it stops what it's doing and prints your error message. Since this program doesn't do anything to handle the error, it will exit immediately.

Using "raise" in our attribute writer methods

Here's our updated code for the Dog class...

Now that we're using `raise` in both of our writer methods, we don't need to use an `else` clause on the `if` statements. If the new value is invalid and the `raise` statement is executed, the program will halt. The statement that assigns to the instance variable will never be reached.

If "value" is invalid...

...execution will halt here.

```ruby
class Dog

  attr_reader :name, :age

  def name=(value)
    if value == ""
      raise "Name can't be blank!"
    end
    @name = value
  end

  def age=(value)
    if value < 0
      raise "An age of #{value} isn't valid!"
    end
    @age = value
  end

  def report_age
    puts "#{@name} is #{@age} years old."
  end

end
```

This statement won't be reached if "raise" is called.

If "value" is invalid...

...execution will halt here.

This statement won't be reached if "raise" is called.

Now, if a blank name is passed in to `name=`, Ruby will report an error, and the entire program will exit.

```ruby
anonymous = Dog.new
anonymous.name = ""
```

Error →
```
in `name=': Name
can't be blank!
(RuntimeError)
```

You'll get another error message if someone tries to set the age to a number less than zero.

```ruby
joey = Dog.new
joey.age = -1
```

Error →
```
in `age=': An age
of -1 isn't valid!
(RuntimeError)
```

In Chapter 12, we'll see that errors can also be handled by other parts of your program, so that it can continue running. But for now, naughty developers that try to give your Dog instance a blank name or a negative age will know immediately that they have to rewrite their code.

> Awesome! Now if there's an error in a developer's code, it'll be brought to their attention before a user sees it. Nice work!

Our complete Dog class

Here's a file with our complete Dog class, plus some code to create a Dog instance.

```ruby
class Dog                              Setting up "name"
                                       and "age" attribute
  attr_reader :name, :age        ← reader methods

  def name=(value)         ← Attribute writer
    if value == ""           method for "@name"
      raise "Name can't be blank!"
    end                ←       Data validation
    @name = value
  end

  def age=(value)          ← Attribute writer
    if value < 0             method for "@age"
      raise "An age of #{value} isn't valid!"
    end          ←         Data validation
    @age = value
  end

  def move(destination)  ← Instance method
    puts "#{@name} runs to the #{destination}."
  end              ← Using an instance variable

  def talk    ← Instance method.
    puts "#{@name} says Bark!"
  end          ← Using an instance variable

  def report_age  ← Instance method
    puts "#{@name} is #{@age} years old."
  end                    ← Using instance variables

end

dog = Dog.new        ← Creating a new Dog instance
dog.name = "Daisy"   ← Initializing attributes
dog.age = 3       ←
dog.report_age  ←
dog.talk   ←           Calling instance methods
dog.move("bed")  ←
```

dog.rb

Do this! ↙

Type the above code into a file named
dog.rb. Try adding more Dog instances! Then run
ruby dog.rb from a terminal.

Dog
name
age
move
talk
report_age

instance variables (state)

instance methods (behavior)

We have instance methods that act as *attribute accessors*, letting us get and set the contents of our instance variables.

```ruby
puts dog.name
dog.age = 3
puts dog.age
```

```
Daisy
3
```

We have instance methods that let our dog object do things, like move, make noise, and report its age. The instance methods can make use of the data in the object's instance variables.

```ruby
dog.report_age
dog.talk
dog.move("bed")
```

```
Daisy is 3 years old.
Daisy says Bark!
Daisy runs to the bed.
```

And we've set up our attribute writer methods to *validate* the data passed to them, raising an error if the values are invalid.

```ruby
dog.name = ""
```

Error →

```
in `name=': Name
can't be blank!
(RuntimeError)
```

Your Ruby Toolbox

That's it for Chapter 2! You've added methods and classes to your toolbox.

Statements

Con
the
is m

Loo
enc
a cc

Methods

You can make method parameters optional by providing default values.

It's legal for a method name to end in ?, !, or =.

Methods return the value of their last expression to their caller. You can also specify a method's return value with a `return` statement.

Classes

A class is a template for creating object instances.

An object's class defines its instance methods (what it DOES).

Within instance methods, you can create instance variables (what the object KNOWS about itself).

BULLET POINTS

- A method body consists of one or more Ruby statements that will be executed when the method is called.

- Parentheses should be left off of a method definition if (and only if) you're not defining any parameters.

- If you don't specify a return value, methods will return the value of the last expression evaluated.

- Method definitions that appear within a class definition are treated as instance methods for that class.

- Outside a class definition, instance variables can only be accessed via accessor methods.

- You can call the `attr_writer`, `attr_reader`, and `attr_accessor` methods within your class definition as a shortcut for defining accessor methods.

- Accessor methods can be used to ensure data is valid before it's stored in instance variables.

- The `raise` method can be called to report an error in your program.

Up Next...

You've created a complete `Dog` class. Now we just need to add all the same features to the `Cat` and `Bird` classes!

Not excited by the prospect of duplicating all that code? Don't worry! The next chapter is all about inheritance, which will make the task easy!

3 inheritance

Relying on Your Parents

My siblings and I used to quarrel over our inheritance. But now that we've learned how to share everything, things are working out great!

So much repetition! Your new classes representing the different types of vehicles and animals are awesome, it's true. But you're having to *copy instance methods from class to class*. And the copies are starting to fall out of sync—some are fine, while others have bugs. Weren't classes supposed to make code *easier* to maintain?

In this chapter, we'll learn how to use **inheritance** to let your classes *share* methods. Fewer copies means fewer maintenance headaches!

Copy, paste... Such a waste...

Back at Got-A-Motor, Inc., the development team wants to try this "object-oriented programming" thing out for themselves. They've converted their old virtual test-drive app to use classes for each vehicle type. They have classes representing cars, trucks, and motorcycles.

Here's what their class structure looks like right now:

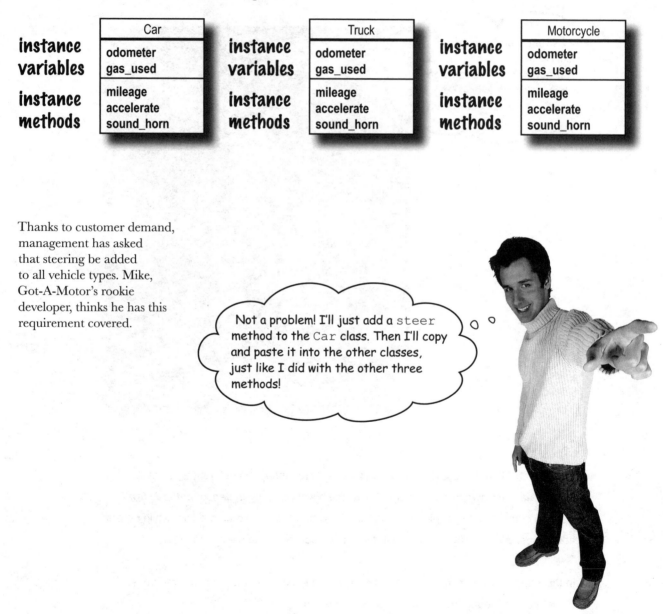

Car
odometer
gas_used
mileage
accelerate
sound_horn

instance variables

instance methods

Truck
odometer
gas_used
mileage
accelerate
sound_horn

instance variables

instance methods

Motorcycle
odometer
gas_used
mileage
accelerate
sound_horn

instance variables

instance methods

Thanks to customer demand, management has asked that steering be added to all vehicle types. Mike, Got-A-Motor's rookie developer, thinks he has this requirement covered.

Not a problem! I'll just add a `steer` method to the `Car` class. Then I'll copy and paste it into the other classes, just like I did with the other three methods!

Mike's code for the virtual test-drive classes

```ruby
class Car

  attr_accessor :odometer
  attr_accessor :gas_used

  def mileage
    @odometer / @gas_used
  end

  def accelerate
    puts "Floor it!"
  end

  def sound_horn
    puts "Beep! Beep!"
  end

  def steer          ← Copy!
    puts "Turn front 2 wheels."
  end

end
```

```ruby
class Truck

  attr_accessor :odometer
  attr_accessor :gas_used

  def mileage
    @odometer / @gas_used
  end

  def accelerate
    puts "Floor it!"
  end

  def sound_horn
    puts "Beep! Beep!"
  end

  def steer          ← Paste!
    puts "Turn front 2 wheels."
  end

end
```

```ruby
class Motorcycle

  attr_accessor :odometer
  attr_accessor :gas_used

  def mileage
    @odometer / @gas_used
  end

  def accelerate
    puts "Floor it!"
  end

  def sound_horn
    puts "Beep! Beep!"
  end

  def steer    ← Paste!
    puts "Turn front 2 wheels."
  end

end
```

But Marcy, the team's experienced object-oriented developer, has some reservations about this approach.

> This copy-pasting is a bad idea. What if we needed to change a method? We'd have to change it in every class! And look at the Motorcycle class—motorcycles don't **have** two front wheels!

Marcy is right; this is a maintenance nightmare waiting to happen. First, let's figure out how to address the duplication. Then we'll fix the steer instance method for Motorcycle objects.

Inheritance to the rescue!

Fortunately, like most object-oriented languages, Ruby includes the concept of **inheritance**, which allows classes to inherit methods from one another. If one class has some functionality, classes that inherit from it can get that functionality *automatically*.

Instead of repeating method definitions across many similar classes, inheritance lets you move the common methods to a single class. You can then specify that other classes inherit from this class. The class with the common methods is referred to as the **superclass**, and the classes that inherit those methods are known as **subclasses**.

If a superclass has instance methods, then its subclasses automatically inherit those methods. You can get access to all the methods you need from the superclass, without having to duplicate the methods' code in each subclass.

Here's how we might use inheritance to get rid of the repetition in the virtual test-drive app…

> Inheritance allows multiple subclasses to inherit methods from a single superclass.

1 We see that the `Car`, `Truck`, and `Motorcycle` classes have several instance methods and attributes in common.

Car
odometer gas_used
mileage accelerate sound_horn steer

Truck
odometer gas_used
mileage accelerate sound_horn steer

Motorcycle
odometer gas_used
mileage accelerate sound_horn steer

2 Each one of these classes is a type of vehicle. So we can create a new class, which we'll choose to call `Vehicle`, and move the common methods and attributes there.

Vehicle
odometer gas_used
mileage accelerate sound_horn steer

Inheritance to the rescue! (continued)

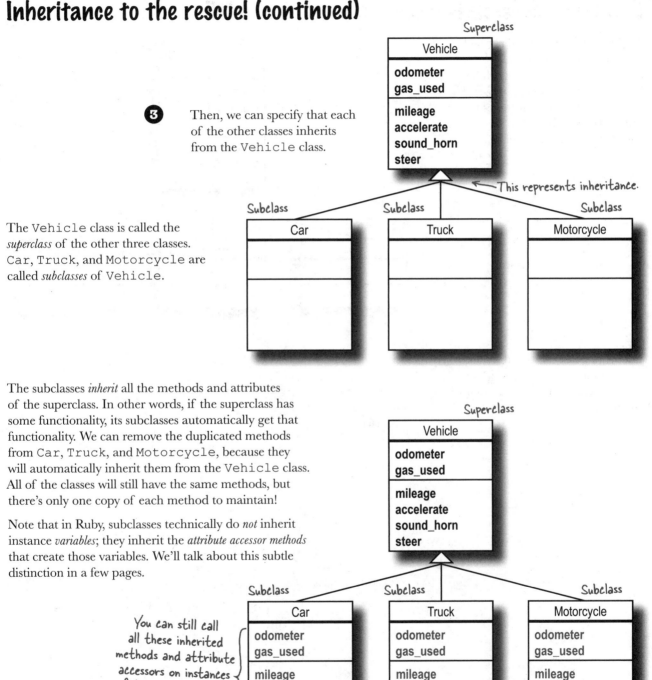

3 Then, we can specify that each of the other classes inherits from the `Vehicle` class.

The `Vehicle` class is called the *superclass* of the other three classes. `Car`, `Truck`, and `Motorcycle` are called *subclasses* of `Vehicle`.

The subclasses *inherit* all the methods and attributes of the superclass. In other words, if the superclass has some functionality, its subclasses automatically get that functionality. We can remove the duplicated methods from `Car`, `Truck`, and `Motorcycle`, because they will automatically inherit them from the `Vehicle` class. All of the classes will still have the same methods, but there's only one copy of each method to maintain!

Note that in Ruby, subclasses technically do *not* inherit instance *variables*; they inherit the *attribute accessor methods* that create those variables. We'll talk about this subtle distinction in a few pages.

Defining a superclass (requires nothing special)

To eliminate the repeated methods and attributes in our `Car`, `Truck`, and `Motorcycle` classes, Marcy has created this design. It moves the shared methods and attributes to a `Vehicle` *superclass*. `Car`, `Truck`, and `Motorcycle` are all *subclasses* of `Vehicle`, and they *inherit* all of `Vehicle`'s methods.

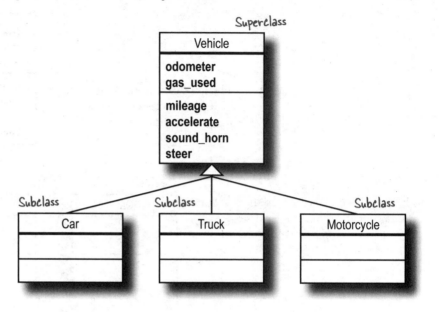

There's actually no special syntax to define a superclass in Ruby; it's just an ordinary class. (Most object-oriented languages are like this.)

All attributes will be inherited when we declare a subclass.

So will all instance methods.

```ruby
class Vehicle

  attr_accessor :odometer
  attr_accessor :gas_used

  def accelerate
    puts "Floor it!"
  end

  def sound_horn
    puts "Beep! Beep!"
  end

  def steer
    puts "Turn front 2 wheels."
  end

  def mileage
    return @odometer / @gas_used
  end

end
```

Defining a subclass (is really easy)

The syntax for subclasses isn't much more complicated. A subclass definition looks just like an ordinary class definition, except that you specify the superclass it will inherit from.

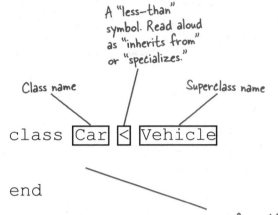

A "less-than" symbol. Read aloud as "inherits from" or "specializes."

Class name

Superclass name

```
class Car < Vehicle

end
```

We can define additional methods and attributes here, but for now we'll just use the inherited ones.

Ruby uses a less-than (<) symbol because the subclass is a *subset* of the superclass. (All cars are vehicles, but not all vehicles are cars.) You can think of the subclass as being *lesser than* the superclass.

So here's all we have to write in order to specify that Car, Truck, and Motorcycle are subclasses of Vehicle:

```
class Car < Vehicle
end

class Truck < Vehicle
end

class Motorcycle < Vehicle
end
```

As soon as you define them as subclasses, Car, Truck, and Motorcycle inherit all the attributes and instance methods of Vehicle. Even though the subclasses don't contain any code of their own, any instances we create will have access to all of the superclass's functionality!

```
truck = Truck.new
truck.accelerate
truck.steer

car = Car.new
car.odometer = 11432
car.gas_used = 366

puts "Lifetime MPG:"
puts car.mileage
```

```
Floor it!
Turn front 2 wheels.
Lifetime MPG:
31
```

Our Car, Truck, and Motorcycle classes have all the same functionality they used to, without all the duplicated code. Using inheritance will save us a lot of maintenance headaches!

Adding methods to subclasses

As it stands, there's no difference between our `Truck` class and the `Car` or `Motorcycle` classes. But what good is a truck, if not for hauling cargo? Got-A-Motor wants to add a `load_bed` method for `Truck` instances, as well as a `cargo` attribute to access the bed contents.

It won't do to add `cargo` and `load_bed` to the `Vehicle` class, though. The `Truck` class would inherit them, yes, but so would `Car` and `Motorcycle`. Cars and motorcycles don't *have* cargo beds!

So instead, we can define a `cargo` attribute and a `load_bed` method *directly on the* `Truck` *class.*

```ruby
class Truck < Vehicle

  attr_accessor :cargo

  def load_bed(contents)
    puts "Securing #{contents} in the truck bed."
    @cargo = contents
  end

end
```

If we were to draw the diagram of `Vehicle` and its subclasses again now, it would look like this:

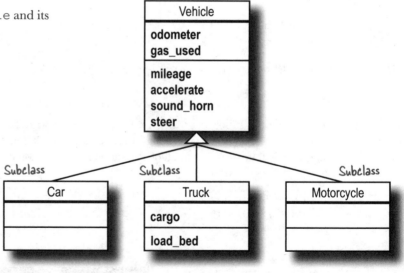

With these code changes in place, we can create a new `Truck` instance, then load and access its cargo.

```ruby
truck = Truck.new
truck.load_bed("259 bouncy balls")
puts "The truck is carrying #{truck.cargo}."
```

```
Securing 259 bouncy balls in the truck bed.
The truck is carrying 259 bouncy balls.
```

Subclasses keep inherited methods alongside new ones

A subclass that defines its own methods doesn't lose the ones it inherits from its superclass, though. `Truck` will still have all the attributes and methods it inherits from `Vehicle`, but `cargo` and `load_bed` will be added alongside them.

If we redrew our diagram with the inherited attributes and methods included, it would look like this:

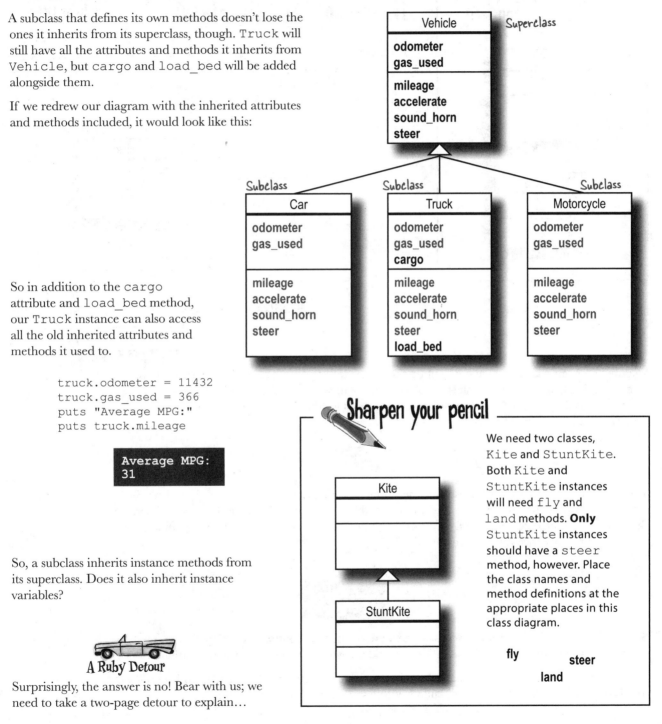

So in addition to the `cargo` attribute and `load_bed` method, our `Truck` instance can also access all the old inherited attributes and methods it used to.

```
truck.odometer = 11432
truck.gas_used = 366
puts "Average MPG:"
puts truck.mileage
```

```
Average MPG:
31
```

So, a subclass inherits instance methods from its superclass. Does it also inherit instance variables?

A Ruby Detour

Surprisingly, the answer is no! Bear with us; we need to take a two-page detour to explain…

Sharpen your pencil

We need two classes, `Kite` and `StuntKite`. Both `Kite` and `StuntKite` instances will need `fly` and `land` methods. **Only** `StuntKite` instances should have a `steer` method, however. Place the class names and method definitions at the appropriate places in this class diagram.

fly

steer

land

Instance variables belong to the object, not the class!

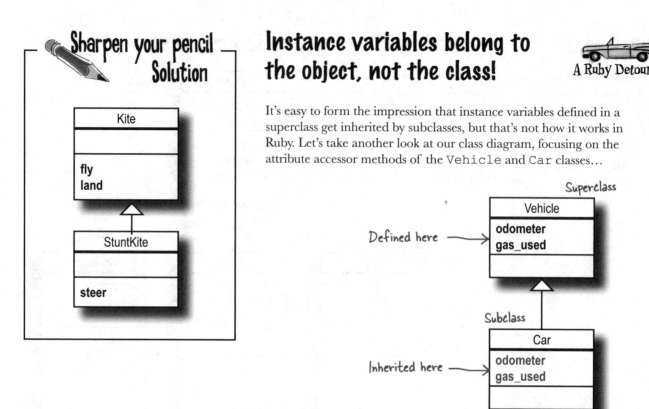

It's easy to form the impression that instance variables defined in a superclass get inherited by subclasses, but that's not how it works in Ruby. Let's take another look at our class diagram, focusing on the attribute accessor methods of the Vehicle and Car classes…

You might assume that Car would inherit @odometer and @gas_used instance variables from Vehicle. Well, let's test that… All Ruby objects have a method called instance_variables that we can call to see what instance variables are defined for that object. Let's try creating a new Car object and see what instance variables it has.

```
car = Car.new
puts car.instance_variables
```

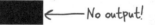 ←— No output!

There's no output because car doesn't *have any* instance variables right now! The object won't get any instance variables until we call some instance methods on it, at which point the *method* will create the variables on the object. Let's call the odometer and gas_used attribute writer methods, then check the list of instance variables again.

```
car.odometer = 22914
car.gas_used = 728
puts car.instance_variables
```

 ←—THERE are the instance variables!

So the Car class didn't inherit the @odometer and @gas_used instance *variables*…it inherited the odometer= and gas_used= instance *methods*, and the *methods* created the instance variables!

In many other object-oriented languages, instance variables are declared on the *class*, so Ruby *differs* in this respect. It's a subtle distinction, but one worth knowing about…

Instance variables belong to the object, not the class! (continued)

A Ruby Detour

So why's it important to know that instance variables belong to the object and not the class? As long as you follow the convention and ensure your instance variable names match your accessor method names, you won't have to worry about it. But if you deviate from that convention, look out! You may find that a subclass can interfere with its superclass's functionality by *overwriting* its instance variables.

Say we had a superclass that breaks from convention and uses the @storage instance variable to hold the value for its name= and name accessor methods. Then suppose that a subclass uses the same variable name, @storage, to hold the value for its salary= and salary accessor methods.

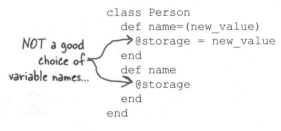

NOT a good choice of variable names...

```
class Person
  def name=(new_value)
    @storage = new_value
  end
  def name
    @storage
  end
end
```

...but we'll use the same name here. (Hey, why not?)

```
class Employee < Person
  def salary=(new_value)
    @storage = new_value
  end
  def salary
    @storage
  end
end
```

When we try to actually use the Employee subclass, we'll find that any time we assign to the salary attribute, we overwrite the name attribute, because both are using the *same* instance variable.

```
employee = Employee.new
employee.name = "John Smith"
employee.salary = 80000
puts employee.name
```

What an unusual name!

80000

Make sure you always use sensible variable names that match your attribute accessor names. That simple practice should be enough to keep you out of trouble!

End of Ruby Detour

Overriding methods

Marcy, the team's experienced object-oriented developer, has rewritten our `Car`, `Truck`, and `Motorcycle` classes as subclasses of `Vehicle`. They don't need any methods or attributes of their own—they inherit everything from the superclass! But Mike points out an issue with this design...

> Pretty slick, Marcy. But you forgot one little detail: the `Motorcycle` class needs a specialized `steer` method!

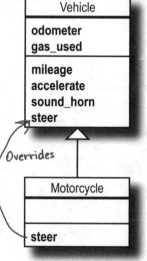

```
motorcycle = Motorcycle.new
motorcycle.steer
```

`Turn front 2 wheels.`

One wheel too many for a motorcycle!

> Not a problem—I can just **override** that method for `Motorcycle`!

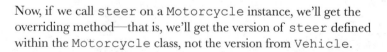

If the superclass's behavior isn't what you need in the subclass, inheritance gives you another mechanism to help: method *overriding*. When you **override** one or more methods in a subclass, you replace the inherited methods from the superclass with methods specific to the subclass.

```
class Motorcycle < Vehicle
  def steer
    puts "Turn front wheel."
  end
end
```

Now, if we call `steer` on a `Motorcycle` instance, we'll get the overriding method—that is, we'll get the version of `steer` defined within the `Motorcycle` class, not the version from `Vehicle`.

```
motorcycle.steer
```

`Turn front wheel.`

Vehicle

odometer
gas_used

mileage
accelerate
sound_horn
steer

Overrides

Motorcycle

steer

Overriding methods (continued)

If we call any other methods on a `Motorcycle` instance, though, we'll get the inherited method.

```
motorcycle.accelerate
```

How does this work?

If Ruby sees that the requested method is defined on a subclass, it will call that method and stop there.

But if the method's not found, Ruby will look for it on the superclass, then the superclass's superclass, and so on, up the chain.

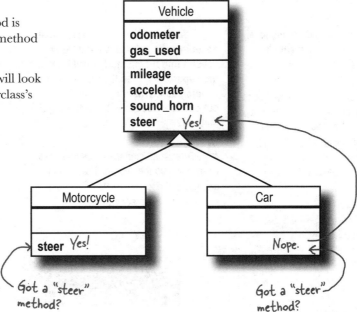

Everything seems to be working again! When changes are needed, they can be made in the `Vehicle` class, and they'll propagate to the subclasses automatically, meaning everyone gets the benefit of updates sooner. If a subclass needs specialized behavior, it can simply override the method it inherited from the superclass.

Nice work cleaning up Got-A-Motor's classes! Next, we'll take another look at the Fuzzy Friends code. They still have a lot of redundant methods in their application's classes. We'll see if inheritance and method overriding can help them out.

there are no Dumb Questions

Q: Can you have more than one level of inheritance? That is, can a subclass have its own subclasses?

A: Yes! If you need to override methods on some of your subclass's instances, but not others, you might consider making a subclass of the subclass.

```
class Car < Vehicle
end

class DragRacer < Car
  def accelerate
    puts "Inject nitrous!"
  end
end
```

Don't overdo it, though! This kind of design can rapidly become very complex. Ruby doesn't place a limit on the number of levels of inheritance, but most Ruby developers don't go more than one or two levels deep.

Q: You said that if a method is called on an instance of a class and Ruby doesn't find the method, it will look on the superclass, then the superclass's superclass... What happens if it runs out of superclasses without finding the method?

A: After searching the last superclass, Ruby gives up the search. That's when you get one of those `undefined method` errors we've been seeing.

```
Car.new.fly
```

```
undefined method
`fly' for
#<Car:0x007ffec48c>
```

Q: When designing an inheritance hierarchy, which should I design first, the subclass or the superclass?

A: Either! You might not even realize you need to use inheritance until after you've started coding your application.

When you discover that two related classes need similar or identical methods, though, just make those classes into subclasses of a new superclass. Then move those shared methods into the superclass. There: you've designed the subclasses first.

Likewise, when you discover that only some instances of a class are using a method, create a new subclass of the existing class and move the method there. You've just designed the superclass first!

Code Magnets

A Ruby program is all scrambled up on the fridge. Can you reconstruct the code snippets to make a working superclass and subclass, so the sample code below can execute and produce the given output?

`class` `Camera` `DigitalCamera` `<` `Camera`

`class` `def` `def` `def` `load`

`end` `end` `end` `end` `load`

`end` `take_picture`

`puts "Triggering shutter."`

`puts "Inserting memory card."`

`puts "Winding film."`

Sample code:

```
camera = Camera.new
camera.load
camera.take_picture

camera2 = DigitalCamera.new
camera2.load
camera2.take_picture
```

Output:

```
File  Edit  Window  Help
Winding film.
Triggering shutter.
Inserting memory card.
Triggering shutter.
```

WHAT'S MY PURPOSE?

Match each of the concepts on the left to a definition on the right.

Subclass

Overriding

Inheritance

Superclass

. Replaces a method inherited from a superclass with new functionality.

Allows a single method or attribute to be shared by multiple classes.

A class that holds the code for methods that are shared by one or more other classes.

A class that inherits one or more methods or attributes from a superclass.

Code Magnets Solution

A Ruby program is all scrambled up on the fridge. Can you reconstruct the code snippets to make a working superclass and subclass, so the sample code below can execute and produce the given output?

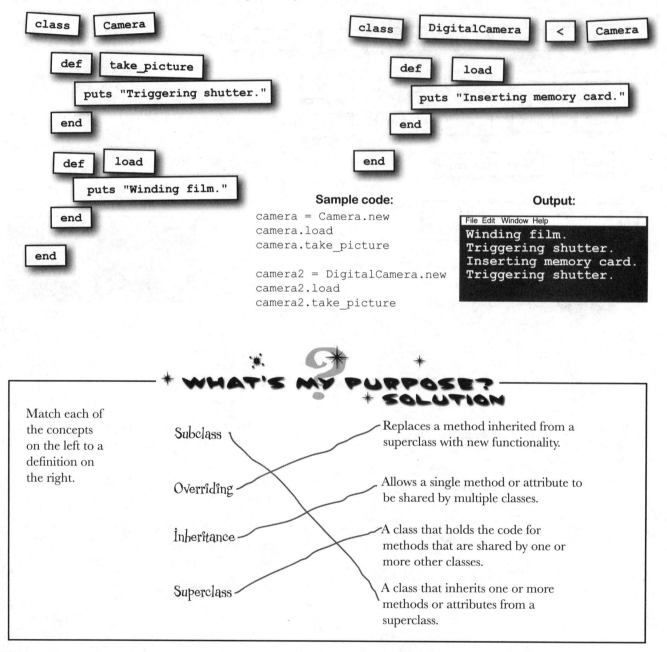

```
class Camera
    def take_picture
        puts "Triggering shutter."
    end
    def load
        puts "Winding film."
    end
end
```

```
class DigitalCamera < Camera
    def load
        puts "Inserting memory card."
    end
end
```

Sample code:

```
camera = Camera.new
camera.load
camera.take_picture

camera2 = DigitalCamera.new
camera2.load
camera2.take_picture
```

Output:

```
File Edit Window Help
Winding film.
Triggering shutter.
Inserting memory card.
Triggering shutter.
```

WHAT'S MY PURPOSE? SOLUTION

Match each of the concepts on the left to a definition on the right.

Subclass — A class that inherits one or more methods or attributes from a superclass.

Overriding — Replaces a method inherited from a superclass with new functionality.

Inheritance — A class that holds the code for methods that are shared by one or more other classes.

Superclass — Allows a single method or attribute to be shared by multiple classes.

Bringing our animal classes up to date with inheritance

Remember the Fuzzy Friends virtual storybook application from last chapter? We did a lot of excellent work on the Dog class. We added name and age attribute accessor methods (with validation), and updated the talk, move, and report_age methods to use the @name and @age instance variables.

Here's a recap of the code we have so far:

Creates methods to get current values of @name and @age ———→

```ruby
class Dog
  attr_reader :name, :age

  def name=(value)
    if value == ""
      raise "Name can't be blank!"
    end
    @name = value
  end

  def age=(value)
    if value < 0
      raise "An age of #{value} isn't valid!"
    end
    @age = value
  end

  def talk
    puts "#{@name} says Bark!"
  end

  def move(destination)
    puts "#{@name} runs to the #{destination}."
  end

  def report_age
    puts "#{@name} is #{@age} years old."
  end

end
```

We create our own attribute writer methods, so we can check that the new values are valid.

Other instance methods for our Dog objects

The Bird and Cat classes have been completely left behind, however, even though they need almost identical functionality.

Let's use this new concept of inheritance to create a design that will bring all our classes up to date at once (and keep them updated in the future).

Designing the animal class hierarchy

We've added lots of new functionality to our Dog class, and now
we want it in the Cat and Bird classes as well...

We want all the classes to have name and
age attributes, as well as talk, move, and
report_age methods. Let's move all of these
attributes and methods up to a new class, which
we'll call Animal.

Then, we'll declare that Dog, Bird, and Cat
are *subclasses* of Animal. All three subclasses
will inherit all the attributes and instance
methods from their superclass. We'll instantly
be caught up!

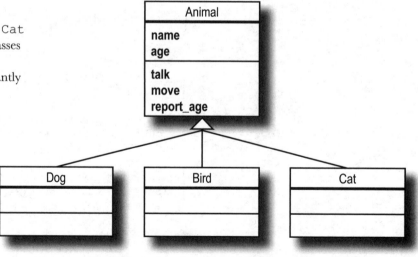

Code for the Animal class and its subclasses

Here's code for the `Animal` superclass, with all the old methods from `Dog` moved into it...

```ruby
class Animal

  attr_reader :name, :age

  def name=(value)
    if value == ""
      raise "Name can't be blank!"
    end
    @name = value
  end

  def age=(value)
    if value < 0
      raise "An age of #{value} isn't valid!"
    end
    @age = value
  end

  def talk
    puts "#{@name} says Bark!"
  end

  def move(destination)
    puts "#{@name} runs to the #{destination}."
  end

  def report_age
    puts "#{@name} is #{@age} years old."
  end

end
```

The exact same code that was in the Dog class!

And here are the other classes, rewritten as subclasses of `Animal`.

```ruby
class Dog < Animal
end

class Bird < Animal
end

class Cat < Animal
end
```

We don't have to write any methods here; these classes will inherit all the methods from the Animal class above!

Overriding a method in the Animal subclasses

With our `Dog`, `Bird`, and `Cat` classes rewritten as subclasses of `Animal`, they don't need any methods or attributes of their own—they inherit everything from the superclass!

```
whiskers = Cat.new
whiskers.name = "Whiskers"
fido = Dog.new
fido.name = "Fido"
polly = Bird.new
polly.name = "Polly"

polly.age = 2
polly.report_age
fido.move("yard")
whiskers.talk
```

```
Polly is 2 years old.
Fido runs to the yard.
Whiskers says Bark!
```

Wait...Whiskers is a Cat...

Looks good, except for one problem…our `Cat` instance is barking.

The subclasses inherited this method from `Animal`:

```
def talk
  puts "#{@name} says Bark!"
end
```

That's appropriate behavior for a `Dog`, but not so much for a `Cat` or a `Bird`.

```
whiskers = Cat.new
whiskers.name = "Whiskers"
polly = Bird.new
polly.name = "Polly"

whiskers.talk
polly.talk
```

```
Whiskers says Bark!
Polly says Bark!
```

This code will override the `talk` method that was inherited from `Animal`:

```
class Cat < Animal
  def talk          ———— Overrides the inherited method
    puts "#{@name} says Meow!"
  end
end
```

```
class Bird < Animal
  def talk          ———— Overrides the inherited method
    puts "#{@name} says Chirp! Chirp!"
  end
end
```

Now, when you call `talk` on `Cat` or `Bird` instances, you'll get the overridden methods.

```
whiskers.talk
polly.talk
```

```
Whiskers says Meow!
Polly says Chirp! Chirp!
```

We need to get at the overridden method!

Next up, Fuzzy Friends wants to add armadillos to their interactive storybook. (That's right, they want the little anteater-like critters that can roll into an armored ball. We're not sure why.) We can simply add `Armadillo` as a subclass of `Animal`.

There's a catch, though: before the armadillos can run anywhere, they have to unroll. The `move` method will have to be overridden to reflect this fact.

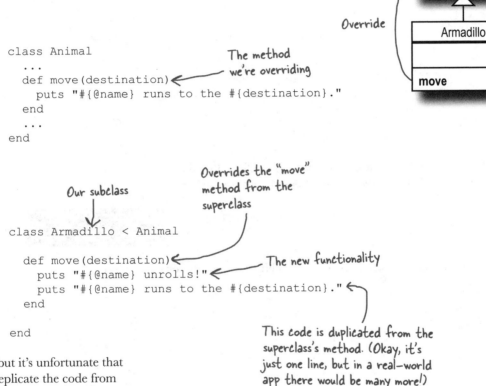

```ruby
class Animal
  ...
  def move(destination)          ← The method
    puts "#{@name} runs to the #{destination}."    we're overriding
  end
  ...
end
```

Our subclass

Overrides the "move" method from the superclass

```ruby
class Armadillo < Animal

  def move(destination)          ← 
    puts "#{@name} unrolls!"          ← The new functionality
    puts "#{@name} runs to the #{destination}."  ←
  end

end
```

This code is duplicated from the superclass's method. (Okay, it's just one line, but in a real–world app there would be many more!)

This works, but it's unfortunate that we have to replicate the code from the `move` method of the `Animal` class.

What if we could override the `move` method with new code, *and* still harness the code from the superclass? Ruby has a mechanism to do just that...

The "super" keyword

When you use the super keyword
within a method, it makes a call to
a method of the same name on the
superclass.

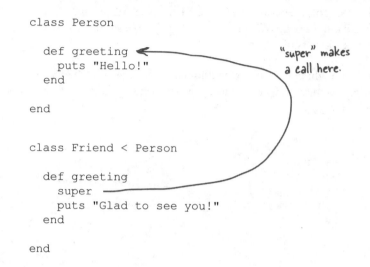

```
class Person

  def greeting
    puts "Hello!"
  end

end


class Friend < Person

  def greeting
    super
    puts "Glad to see you!"
  end

end
```

"super" makes
a call here.

If we make a call to the *overriding* method on the *subclass*, we'll see that the
super keyword makes a call to the *overridden* method on the *superclass*:

```
Friend.new.greeting
```

```
Hello!
Glad to see you!
```

The super keyword works like an ordinary method call in almost every respect.

For example, the superclass method's
return value becomes the value of
the super expression:

```
class Person

  def greeting
    "Hello!"
  end

end

class Friend < Person

  def greeting
    basic_greeting = super
    "#{basic_greeting} Glad to see you!"
  end

end

puts Friend.new.greeting
```

The method return value

Assigns "Hello!" to
basic_greeting

```
Hello! Glad to see you!
```

The "super" keyword (continued)

Another way in which using the super keyword is like a regular method call: you can pass it arguments, and those arguments will be passed to the superclass's method.

```ruby
class Person

  def greet_by_name(name)
    "Hello, #{name}!"
  end

end

class Friend < Person

  def greet_by_name(name)
    basic_greeting = super(name)
    "#{basic_greeting} Glad to see you!"
  end

end

puts Friend.new.greet_by_name("Meghan")
```

Includes the argument in the method call.

```
Hello, Meghan! Glad to see you!
```

But here's a way that super *differs* from a regular method call: if you leave the arguments *off*, the superclass method will automatically be called with the same arguments that were passed to the subclass method.

```ruby
class Friend < Person

  def greet_by_name(name)
    basic_greeting = super
    "#{basic_greeting} Glad to see you!"
  end

end

puts Friend.new.greet_by_name("Bert")
```

Friend's greet_by_name method has to be called with a "name" argument...

...so the "name" argument will be forwarded on to Person's greet_by_name method as well.

```
Hello, Bert! Glad to see you!
```

Watch it!

The calls super and super() are not the same.

By itself, super calls the overridden method with the same arguments the overriding method received. But super() calls the overridden method with __no__ arguments, even if the overriding method __did__ receive arguments.

A super-powered subclass

Now let's use our new understanding of `super` to eliminate a little duplicated code from the `move` method in our `Armadillo` class.

Here's the method we're inheriting from the Animal superclass:

```ruby
class Animal
  ...
  def move(destination)
    puts "#{@name} runs to the #{destination}."
  end
  ...
end
```

Here's that duplicated line.

And here's the overridden version in the Armadillo subclass:

```ruby
class Armadillo < Animal

  def move(destination)
    puts "#{@name} unrolls!"
    puts "#{@name} runs to the #{destination}."
  end

end
```

We can replace the duplicated code in the subclass's `move` method with a call to `super`, and rely on the superclass's `move` method to provide that functionality.

Here, we explicitly pass on the `destination` parameter for `Animal`'s move method to use:

```ruby
class Armadillo < Animal

  def move(destination)
    puts "#{@name} unrolls!"
    super(destination)
  end

end
```

Explicitly specify the argument...

~~~~~~~~ OR... ~~~~~~~~

But we could instead leave off the arguments to `super`, and allow the `destination` parameter to be forwarded to the superclass's move method automatically:

```ruby
class Armadillo < Animal

  def move(destination)
    puts "#{@name} unrolls!"
    super
  end

end
```

Autoforward the same argument(s) "move" was called with.

Either way, the code still works great!

```ruby
dillon = Armadillo.new
dillon.name = "Dillon"
dillon.move("burrow")
```

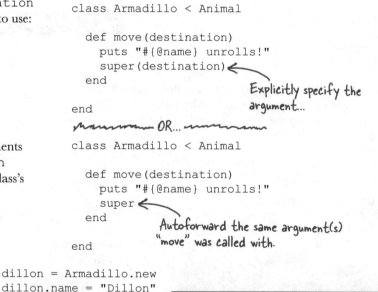

```
Dillon unrolls!
Dillon runs to the burrow.
```

Your mastery of class inheritance has wrung the repetition out of your code like water from a sponge. And your coworkers will thank you—less code means fewer bugs! Great job!

Exercise

Below you'll find code for three Ruby classes. The code snippets on the right use those classes, either directly or through inheritance. Fill in the blanks below each snippet with what you think its output will be. Don't forget to take method overriding and the `super` keyword into account! (We've filled in the first one for you.)

```ruby
class Robot

  attr_accessor :name

  def activate
    puts "#{@name} is powering up"
  end

  def move(destination)
    puts "#{@name} walks to #{destination}"
  end

end

class TankBot < Robot

  attr_accessor :weapon

  def attack
    puts "#{@name} fires #{@weapon}"
  end

  def move(destination)
    puts "#{@name} rolls to #{destination}"
  end

end

class SolarBot < Robot

  def activate
    puts "#{@name} deploys solar panel"
    super
  end

end
```

Your answers:

```ruby
tank = TankBot.new
tank.name = "Hugo"
tank.weapon = "laser"
tank.activate
tank.move("test dummy")
tank.attack
```

Hugo is powering up
....
....

```ruby
sunny = SolarBot.new
sunny.name = "Sunny"
sunny.activate
sunny.move("tanning bed")
```

....
....
....

Below you'll find code for three Ruby classes. The code snippets on the right use those classes, either directly or through inheritance. Fill in the blanks below each snippet with what you think its output will be. Don't forget to take method overriding and the `super` keyword into account!

```ruby
class Robot

  attr_accessor :name

  def activate
    puts "#{@name} is powering up"
  end

  def move(destination)
    puts "#{@name} walks to #{destination}"
  end

end

class TankBot < Robot

  attr_accessor :weapon

  def attack
    puts "#{@name} fires #{@weapon}"
  end

  def move(destination)
    puts "#{@name} rolls to #{destination}"
  end

end

class SolarBot < Robot

  def activate
    puts "#{@name} deploys solar panel"
    super
  end

end
```

```ruby
tank = TankBot.new
tank.name = "Hugo"
tank.weapon = "laser"
tank.activate
tank.move("test dummy")
tank.attack
```

Hugo is powering up..................

Hugo rolls to test dummy............

Hugo fires laser.........................

```ruby
sunny = SolarBot.new
sunny.name = "Sunny"
sunny.activate
sunny.move("tanning bed")
```

Sunny deploys solar panel............

Sunny is powering up...................

Sunny walks to tanning bed.........

Difficulties displaying Dogs

Let's make one more improvement to our `Dog` class, before we declare it finished. Right now, if we pass a `Dog` instance to the `print` or `puts` methods, the output isn't too useful:

```
lucy = Dog.new
lucy.name = "Lucy"
lucy.age = 4

rex = Dog.new
rex.name = "Rex"
rex.age = 2

puts lucy, rex
```

The output we get:

```
#<Dog:0x007fb2b50c4468>
#<Dog:0x007fb2b3902000>
```

We can tell that they're `Dog` objects, but beyond that it's very hard to tell one `Dog` from another. It would be far nicer if we got output like this:

```
Lucy the dog, age 4
Rex the dog, age 2
```

The output we WISH we had...

When you pass an object to the `puts` method, Ruby calls the `to_s` instance method on it to convert it to a string for printing. We can call `to_s` explicitly, and get the same result:

```
puts lucy.to_s, rex.to_s
```

```
#<Dog:0x007fb2b50c4468>
#<Dog:0x007fb2b3902000>
```

Now, here's a question: Where did that `to_s` instance method come from?

Indeed, where did *most* of these instance methods on `Dog` objects come from? If you call the method named `methods` on a `Dog` instance, only the first few instance methods will look familiar...

```
puts rex.methods
```

These are inherited from Animal...

```
name
age
name=
age=
talk
move
report_age
```

Instance methods named `clone`, `hash`, `inspect`... We didn't define them ourselves; they're not on the `Dog` class. They weren't inherited from the `Animal` superclass, either.

But—and here's the part you may find surprising— they *were* inherited from *somewhere*.

...but where did these come from?

```
eql?
hash
class
clone
to_s
inspect
methods
object_id
...
```

There are more than we have room to print!

The Object class

Where could our `Dog` instances have inherited all these instance methods from? We don't define them in the `Animal` superclass. And we didn't specify a superclass for `Animal`...

```
class Dog < Animal
end

class Animal
   ...
end
```

 The superclass for Dog is Animal.

No superclass specified!

Ruby classes have a `superclass` method that you can call to get their superclass. The result of using it on `Dog` isn't surprising:

```
puts Dog.superclass
```

`Animal`

But what happens if we call `superclass` on `Animal`?

```
puts Animal.superclass
```

`Object`

Whoa! Where did *that* come from?

When you define a new class, Ruby implicitly sets a class called `Object` as its superclass (unless you specify a superclass yourself).

So writing this:
```
class Animal
   ...
end
```

...is equivalent to writing this:
```
class Animal < Object
   ...
end
```

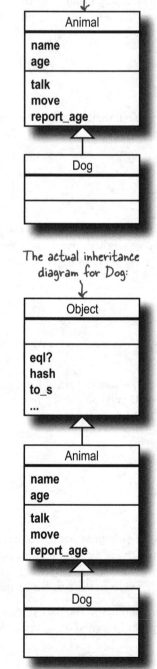

The inheritance diagram for Dog (that we've seen so far):

Animal
name **age**
talk **move** **report_age**

Dog

The actual inheritance diagram for Dog:

Object
eql? **hash** **to_s** ...

Animal
name **age**
talk **move** **report_age**

Dog

Why everything inherits from the Object class

If you don't explicitly specify a superclass for a class you define, Ruby implicitly sets a class named `Object` as the superclass.

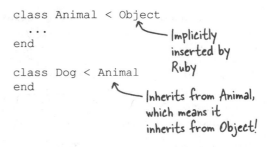

```
class Animal < Object
    ...
end

class Dog < Animal
end
```

Implicitly inserted by Ruby

Inherits from Animal, which means it inherits from Object!

Even if you *do* specify a superclass for your class, that superclass probably inherits from `Object`. That means almost every Ruby object, directly or indirectly, has `Object` as a superclass!

Ruby does this because the `Object` class defines dozens of useful methods that almost all Ruby objects need. This includes a lot of the methods that we've been calling on objects so far:

- The `to_s` method converts an object to a string for printing.

- The `inspect` method converts an object to a debug string.

- The `class` method tells you which class an object is an instance of.

- The `methods` method tells you what instance methods an object has.

- The `instance_variables` method gives you a list of an object's instance variables.

And there are many others. The methods inherited from the `Object` class are fundamental to the way Ruby works with objects.

We hope you've found this little tangent informative, but it doesn't help us with our original problem: our `Dog` objects are still printing in a gibberish format.

Or *does* it?

Ruby objects inherit dozens of essential methods from the Object class.

Overriding the inherited method

We specified that the superclass of the Dog class is the Animal class. And we learned that because we *didn't* specify a superclass for Animal, Ruby automatically set the Object class as its superclass.

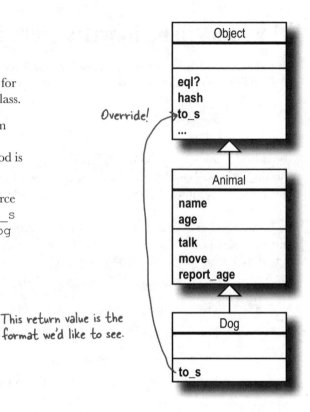

That means that Animal instances inherit a to_s method from Object. Dog instances, in turn, inherit to_s from Animal. When we pass a Dog object to puts or print, its to_s method is called, to convert it to a string.

Do you see where we're headed? If the to_s method is the source of the gibberish strings being printed for Dog instances, and to_s is an *inherited* method, all we have to do is override to_s *on the* Dog *class*!

```ruby
class Dog < Animal

  def to_s
    "#{@name} the dog, age #{age}"
  end

end
```

This return value is the format we'd like to see.

Are you ready? Let's try it.

```ruby
lucy = Dog.new
lucy.name = "Lucy"
lucy.age = 4

rex = Dog.new
rex.name = "Rex"
rex.age = 2

puts lucy.to_s, rex.to_s
```

```
Lucy the dog, age 4
Rex the dog, age 2
```

It works! No more #<Dog:0x007fb2b50c4468>. This is actually readable!

One more tweak: the to_s method is already called when printing objects, so we can leave that off:

```ruby
puts lucy, rex
```

```
Lucy the dog, age 4
Rex the dog, age 2
```

This new output format will make debugging the virtual storybook much easier. And you've gained a key insight into how Ruby objects work: inheritance plays a vital role!

Q: I tried this code in irb instead of using the **ruby** command. After I override **to_s**, if I type **lucy = Dog.new** into irb, I still see something like **#<Dog:0x007fb2b50c4468>**. Why don't I see the dog's name and age?

A: The values that irb shows you are the result of calling inspect on an object, not to_s. You won't see the results of to_s until you set the name and age, and pass the object to puts.

Your Ruby Toolbox

That's it for Chapter 3! You've added inheritance to your toolbox.

Statements

Con Methods
the
is m   Me Classes
Loo   opt
encl   It's   A   Inheritance
a co   end   ob   Inheritance lets a subclass inherit
       An   methods from a superclass.
       Me   kn
       call   do   A subclass can define its own
       ret   methods in addition to the
       sta   methods it inherits.

                     A subclass can override inherited
                     methods, replacing them with its
                     own version.

Up Next...

What would happen if you created a new Dog instance, but called move on it *before* you set its name attribute? (Try it if you want; the result won't look very good.) In the next chapter, we'll look at the initialize method, which can help prevent that sort of mishap.

BULLET POINTS

- Any ordinary Ruby class can be used as a superclass.

- To define a subclass, simply specify a superclass in the class definition.

- Instance variables are *not* inherited from a superclass, but the methods that create and access instance variables *are* inherited.

- The `super` keyword can be used within a subclass method to call the overridden method of the same name on the superclass.

- If you don't specify arguments to the `super` keyword, it takes all arguments that the subclass method was called with, and passes them on to the superclass method.

- The expression value of the `super` keyword is the return value of the superclass method it calls.

- When you define a class, Ruby implicitly sets the `Object` class as the superclass, unless you specify one.

- Almost every Ruby object has instance methods from the `Object` class, inherited either directly or through another superclass.

- The `to_s`, `methods`, `instance_variables`, and `class` methods are all inherited from the `Object` class.

4 initializing instances

Off to a Great Start

That guy Jenkins sent out a new car with a missing timing belt last week. Whole thing fell apart! Not me, though. I make sure all the parts are there!

Right now, your class is a time bomb. Every instance you create starts out as a clean slate. If you call certain instance methods before adding data, an error will be raised that will bring your whole program to a screeching halt.

In this chapter, we're going to show you a couple of ways to create objects that are safe to use right away. We'll start with the `initialize` method, which lets you pass in a bunch of arguments to set up an object's data *at the time you create it*. Then we'll show you how to write **class methods**, which you can use to create and set up an object even **more** easily.

Payroll at Chargemore

You've been tasked with creating a payroll system for Chargemore, a new chain of department stores. They need a system that will print pay stubs for their employees.

Chargemore employees are paid for two-week pay periods. Some employees are paid a two-week portion of their annual salary, and some are paid for the number of hours they work within the two-week period. For starters, though, we're just going to focus on the salaried employees.

A pay stub needs to include the following information:

* The employee name

* The amount of pay an employee received during a two-week pay period

So…here's what the system will need to *know* for each employee:

* Employee name

* Employee salary

And here's what it will need to *do*:

* Calculate and print pay for a two-week period

Pay up!

This sounds like the ideal place to create an `Employee` class! Let's try it, using the same techniques that we covered back in Chapter 2.

We'll set up attribute reader methods for `@name` and `@salary` instance variables, then add writer methods (with validation). Then we'll add a `print_pay_stub` instance method that prints the employee's name and their pay for the period.

Employee
name **salary**
print_pay_stub

@name = "Kara Byrd"
@salary = 45000

@name = "Ben Weber"
@salary = 50000

@name = "Amy Blake"
@salary = 50000

An Employee class

Here's some code to implement our Employee class…

We need to create attribute writer methods manually, so we can validate the data. We can create reader methods automatically, though.

```ruby
class Employee

  attr_reader :name, :salary

  def name=(name)
    if name == ""
      raise "Name can't be blank!"
    end
    @name = name
  end

  def salary=(salary)
    if salary < 0
      raise "A salary of #{salary} isn't valid!"
    end
    @salary = salary
  end

  def print_pay_stub
    puts "Name: #{@name}"
    pay_for_period = (@salary / 365) * 14
    puts "Pay This Period: $#{pay_for_period}"
  end

end
```

Report an error if the name is blank.

Store the name in an instance variable.

Report an error if the salary is negative.

Store the salary in an instance variable.

Print the employee name.

Calculate a 14-day portion of the employee's salary.

Print the amount paid.

(Yes, we realize that this doesn't account for leap years and holidays and a host of other things that real payroll apps must consider. But we wanted a print_pay_stub method that fits on one page.)

Creating new Employee instances

Now that we've defined an `Employee` class, we can create new instances and assign to their `name` and `salary` attributes.

```ruby
amy = Employee.new
amy.name = "Amy Blake"
amy.salary = 50000
```

Thanks to validation code in our `name=` method, we have protection against the accidental assignment of blank names.

```ruby
kara = Employee.new
kara.name = ""
```

Error ⟶
```
in `name=': Name can't be
blank! (RuntimeError)
```

Our `salary=` method has validation to ensure that negative numbers aren't assigned as a salary.

```ruby
ben = Employee.new
ben.salary = -246
```

Error ⟶
```
in `salary=': A salary
of -246 isn't valid!
(RuntimeError)
```

And when an `Employee` instance is properly set up, we can use the stored name and salary to print a summary of the employee's pay period.

```ruby
amy.print_pay_stub
```

```
Name: Amy Blake
Pay This Period: $1904
```
← Close, but where are the cents?

Hmmm… It's typical to display two decimal places when showing currency, though. And did that calculation really come out to an even dollar amount?

Before we go on to perfect our `Employee` class, it looks like we have a bug to fix. And that will require us to go on a couple of brief detours. (But you'll learn some number formatting skills that you'll need later—promise!)

1. Our employee pay is getting its decimal places chopped off. To fix this, we'll need to look at the difference between Ruby's `Float` and `Fixnum` numeric classes.

2. We don't want to display too *many* decimal places, either, so we'll need to look at the `format` method to format our numbers properly.

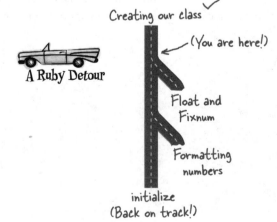

A Ruby Detour

Creating our class ✓

← (You are here!)

Float and Fixnum

Formatting numbers

initialize
(Back on track!)

A Ruby Detour

A division problem

We're working to make the perfect `Employee` class to help us
calculate payroll for the Chargemore department store. But there's a
little detail we have to take care of first…

```
Name: Amy Blake
Pay This Period: $1904
```

Whoa, hold up. This
is close, but where
are the cents? In
fact, this is off by
several dollars!

That's true. Doing the math on paper (or launching a calculator app,
if that's your thing) can confirm that Amy should be earning $1917.81,
rounded to the nearest cent. So where did that other $13.81 go?

To find out, let's launch irb and do the math ourselves, step by step.

First, let's calculate a day's pay.

```
>> 50000 / 365
=> 136
```

← Annual salary, divided by
number of days in a year

That's nearly a dollar a day missing, compared to doing the math by hand:

$$50{,}000 \div 365 = 136.9863\ldots$$

This error is then compounded when we calculate *fourteen* days' pay:

```
>> 136 * 14
=> 1904
```

Compare that to the answer we'd get if we multiplied the *full* daily pay:

$$136.9863 \times 14 = 1917.8082\ldots$$

So we're nearly $14 off. Multiply *that* by many paychecks and many
employees, and you've got yourself an angry workforce. We're going to
have to fix this, and soon…

Division with Ruby's Fixnum class

A Ruby Detour

The result of our Ruby expression to calculate two weeks of an employee's pay doesn't match up with doing the math by hand…

```
>> 50000 / 365 * 14
=> 1904
```

$50{,}000 \div 365 \times 14 = 1917.8082\ldots$

The problem here is that when dividing instances of the `Fixnum` class (a Ruby class that represents integers), Ruby rounds fractional numbers *down* to the nearest whole number.

```
>> 1 / 2
=> 0
```
← The result is rounded down!

It rounds the number because `Fixnum` instances aren't *meant* to store numbers with decimal places. They're intended for use in contexts where only whole numbers make sense, like counting employees in a department or the number of items in a shopping cart. When you create a `Fixnum`, you're telling Ruby: "I expect to only be working with whole numbers here. If anyone does math with you that results in a fraction, I want you to throw those pesky decimal places away."

How can we know whether we're working with `Fixnum` instances? We can call the `class` instance method on them. (Remember we talked about the `Object` class back in Chapter 3? The `class` method is one of the instance methods inherited from `Object`.)

```
>> salary = 50000
=> 50000
>> salary.class
=> Fixnum
```

Or, if you'd rather save yourself the trouble, just remember that any number in your code that *doesn't* have a decimal point in it will be treated as a `Fixnum` by Ruby.

Any number in your code that *does* have a decimal point in it gets treated as a `Float` (the Ruby class that represents floating-point decimal numbers):

```
>> salary = 50000.0
=> 50000.0
>> salary.class
=> Float
```

**If it's got a decimal point, it's a `Float`.
If it doesn't, it's a `Fixnum`.**

273	273.4
Fixnum	**Float**

A Ruby Detour

Division with Ruby's Float class

We loaded up irb and saw that if we divide one `Fixnum` (integer) instance by another `Fixnum`, Ruby rounds the result *down*.

Should be 136.9863... ⟶

```
>> 50000 / 365
=> 136
```

The solution, then, is to use `Float` instances in the operation, which we can get by including a decimal point in our numbers. If you do, Ruby will give you a `Float` instance back:

```
>> 50000.0 / 365.0
=> 136.986301369863
>> (50000.0 / 365.0).class
=> Float
```

It doesn't even matter whether both the dividend and divisor are `Float` instances; Ruby will give you a `Float` back as long as *either* operand is a `Float`.

```
>> 50000.0 / 365
=> 136.986301369863
```

It holds true for addition, subtraction, and multiplication as well: Ruby will give you a `Float` if *either* operand is a `Float`:

```
>> 50000 + 1.5
=> 50001.5
>> 50000 - 1.5
=> 49998.5
>> 50000 * 1.5
=> 75000.0
```

When the first operand is a...	And the second operand is a...	The result is a...
Fixnum	Fixnum	Fixnum
Fixnum	Float	Float
Float	Fixnum	Float
Float	Float	Float

And of course, with addition, subtraction, and multiplication, it doesn't matter whether both operands are `Fixnum` instances, because there's no fractional number to lose in the result. The only operation where it really matters is division. So, remember this rule:

When doing division, make sure at least one operand is a `Float`.

Let's see if we can use this hard-won knowledge to fix our `Employee` class.

Fixing the salary rounding error in Employee

A Ruby Detour

As long as one of the operands is a `Float`, Ruby won't truncate the decimals from our division operation.

```
>> 50000 / 365.0
=> 136.986301369863
```

With this rule in mind, we can revise our `Employee` class to stop truncating the decimals from employees' pay:

```
class Employee
  ...          We're omitting the attribute
               reader/writer code for brevity.

  def print_pay_stub
    puts "Name: #{@name}"
    pay_for_period = (@salary / 365.0) * 14
    puts "Pay This Period: $#{pay_for_period}"
  end

end
```

Now, whether or not @salary is a Float, we'll get a Float result.

Print the amount paid.

```
employee = Employee.new
employee.name = "Jane Doe"
employee.salary = 50000          Using a Fixnum here is just fine!
employee.print_pay_stub
```

Now we have a new problem, though: look what happens to the output!

```
Name: Jane Doe
Pay This Period: $1917.8082191780823
```

We're showing a little *too much* precision! Currency is generally expected to be shown with just two decimal places, after all. So, before we can go back to building the perfect `Employee` class, we need to go on one more detour…

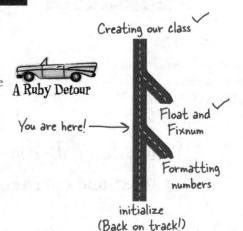

Creating our class ✓

Float and Fixnum ✓

Formatting numbers

You are here! →

initialize
(Back on track!)

A Ruby Detour

Formatting numbers for printing

Our `print_pay_stub` method is displaying too many decimal places. We need to figure out how to round the displayed pay to the nearest penny (two decimal places).

```
Name: Jane Doe
Pay This Period: $1917.8082191780823
```

To deal with these sorts of formatting issues, Ruby provides the `format` method.

Here's a sample of what this method can do. It may look a little confusing, but we'll explain it all on the next few pages!

Rounds the number to two decimal places and prints it

```
result = format("Rounded to two decimal places: %0.2f", 3.14159265)
puts result
```

```
Rounded to two decimal places: 3.14
```

So it looks like `format` *can* help us limit our displayed employee pay to the correct number of places. The question is, *how*? To be able to use this method effectively, we'll need to learn about two features of `format`:

1. Format sequences (the little `%0.2f` above is a format sequence)

2. Format sequence widths (that's the `0.2` in the middle of the format sequence)

Relax

> **We'll explain exactly what those arguments to `format` mean on the next few pages.**
>
> We know, those method calls look a little confusing. We have a ton of examples that should clear that confusion up. We're going to focus on formatting decimal numbers, because it's likely that will be the main thing you use `format` for in your Ruby career.

A Ruby Detour

Format sequences

The first argument to `format` is a string that will be used to format the output. Most of it is formatted exactly as it appears in the string. Any percent signs (%), however, will be treated as the start of a **format sequence**, a section of the string that will be substituted with a value in a particular format. The remaining arguments are used as values for those format sequences.

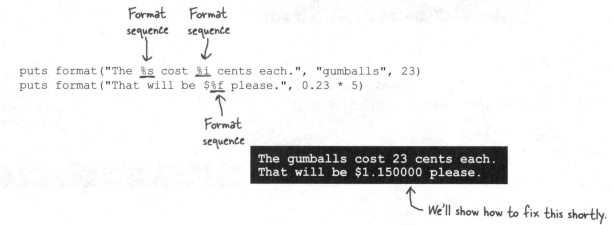

Format sequence

Format sequence

```
puts format("The %s cost %i cents each.", "gumballs", 23)
puts format("That will be $%f please.", 0.23 * 5)
```

Format sequence

```
The gumballs cost 23 cents each.
That will be $1.150000 please.
```

We'll show how to fix this shortly.

Format sequence types

The letter following the percent sign indicates the type of value that's expected. The most common types are:

%s   string

%i   integer

%f   floating-point decimal

```
puts format("A string: %s", "hello")
puts format("An integer: %i", 15)
puts format("A float: %f", 3.1415)
```

```
A string: hello
An integer: 15
A float: 3.141500
```

So %f is for floating-point decimal numbers… We can use that sequence type to format the currency in our pay stubs.

By itself, though, the %f sequence type won't help us. The results still show too many decimal places.

```
puts format("$%f", 1917.8082191780823)
```

```
$1917.808219
```

Up next, we'll look at a fix for that situation: the format sequence *width*.

A Ruby Detour

Format sequence width

Here's the useful part of format sequences: they let you specify the *width* of the resulting field.

Let's say we want to format some data in a plain-text table. We need to ensure the formatted value fills a minimum number of spaces, so that the columns align properly.

You can specify the minimum width after the percent sign in a format sequence. If the argument for that format sequence is shorter than the minimum width, it will be padded with spaces until the minimum width is reached.

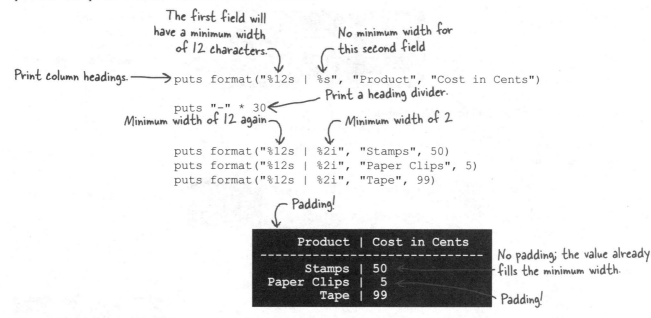

The first field will have a minimum width of 12 characters.

No minimum width for this second field

Print column headings. →
```ruby
puts format("%12s | %s", "Product", "Cost in Cents")
```

Print a heading divider.
```ruby
puts "-" * 30
```

Minimum width of 12 again

Minimum width of 2
```ruby
puts format("%12s | %2i", "Stamps", 50)
puts format("%12s | %2i", "Paper Clips", 5)
puts format("%12s | %2i", "Tape", 99)
```

Padding!

```
    Product | Cost in Cents
------------------------------
     Stamps | 50
Paper Clips | 5
       Tape | 99
```

No padding; the value already fills the minimum width.

Padding!

And now we come to the part that's important for today's task: you can use format sequence widths to specify the precision (the number of displayed digits) for floating-point numbers. Here's the format:

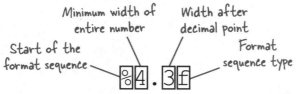

Minimum width of entire number

Width after decimal point

Start of the format sequence

Format sequence type

`%4.3f`

The minimum width of the entire number includes decimal places. If it's included, shorter numbers will be padded with spaces at the start until this width is reached. If it's omitted, no spaces will ever be added.

The width after the decimal point is the maximum number of digits to show. If a more precise number is given, it will be rounded (up or down) to fit in the given number of decimal places.

Format sequence width with floating-point numbers

A Ruby Detour

So when we're working with floating-point numbers, format sequence widths let us specify the number of digits displayed before *and* after the decimal point. Could this be the key to fixing our pay stubs?

Here's a quick demonstration of various width values in action:

```ruby
def test_format(format_string)
  print "Testing '#{format_string}': "
  puts format(format_string, 12.3456)
end
```

```
test_format "%7.3f"      Testing '%7.3f':    12.346    ← Rounded to three places
test_format "%7.2f"      Testing '%7.2f':    12.35     ← Rounded to two places
test_format "%7.1f"      Testing '%7.1f':    12.3      ← Rounded to one place
test_format "%.1f"       Testing '%.1f': 12.3          ← Rounded to one place, no padding
test_format "%.2f"       Testing '%.2f': 12.35         ← Rounded to two places, no padding
```

That last format, `"%.2f"`, will let us take floating-point numbers of any precision and round them to two decimal places. (It also won't do any unnecessary padding.) This format is ideal for showing currency, and it's just what we need for our `print_pay_stub` method!

```ruby
puts format("$%.2f", 2514.2727367874069)     $2514.27   ← All rounded to two places!
puts format("$%.2f", 1150.6849315068494)     $1150.68
puts format("$%.2f", 3068.4931506849316)     $3068.49
```

Previously, our calculated pay for our Employee class's `print_pay_stub` method was displayed with excess decimal places:

```ruby
salary = 50000
puts "$#{(salary / 365.0) * 14}"     $1917.8082191780823
```

But now we finally have a format sequence that will round a floating-point number to two decimal places:

```ruby
puts format("$%.2f", (salary / 365.0) * 14 )     $1917.81
```

Let's try using `format` in the `print_pay_stub` method.

```ruby
class Employee
  ...
  def print_pay_stub
    puts "Name: #{@name}"
    pay_for_period = (@salary / 365.0) * 14
    formatted_pay = format("%.2f", pay_for_period)    ← Get a string with the pay amount
    puts "Pay This Period: $#{formatted_pay}"            rounded to two decimal places.
  end                                                  Print the formatted
end                                                    amount string.
```

Using "format" to fix our pay stubs

A Ruby Detour

We can test our revised `print_pay_stub` using the same values as before:

```ruby
amy = Employee.new
amy.name = "Amy Blake"
amy.salary = 50000
amy.print_pay_stub
```

```
Name: Amy Blake
Pay This Period: $1917.81
```

Excellent! No more extra decimal places! (And more importantly, no more missing money!)

We had to make a couple of detours, but we've finally got our Employee class printing pay stubs as it should! Next, we'll get back to the business of perfecting our class...

End of Ruby Detour

Creating our class ✓

Float and Fixnum ✓

Formatting numbers ✓

You are here! ⟶

initialize
(Back on track!)

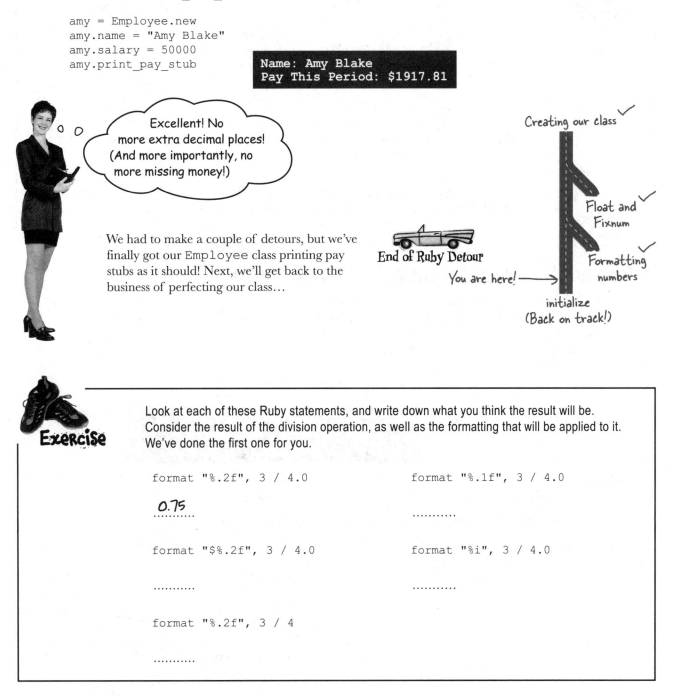

Exercise

Look at each of these Ruby statements, and write down what you think the result will be. Consider the result of the division operation, as well as the formatting that will be applied to it. We've done the first one for you.

```ruby
format "%.2f", 3 / 4.0
```
0.75

```ruby
format "$%.2f", 3 / 4.0
```
....

```ruby
format "%.2f", 3 / 4
```
....

```ruby
format "%.1f", 3 / 4.0
```
....

```ruby
format "%i", 3 / 4.0
```
....

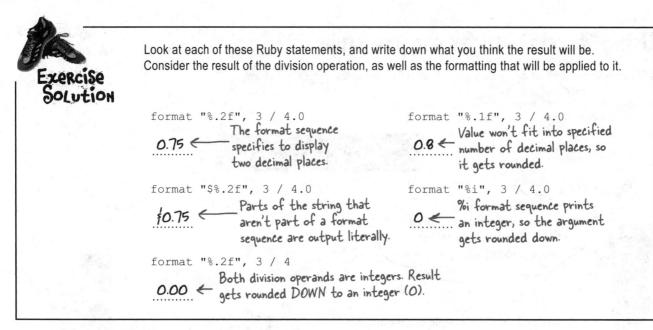

Look at each of these Ruby statements, and write down what you think the result will be. Consider the result of the division operation, as well as the formatting that will be applied to it.

```
format "%.2f", 3 / 4.0
```
_0.75_ ← The format sequence specifies to display two decimal places.

```
format "%.1f", 3 / 4.0
```
_0.8_ ← Value won't fit into specified number of decimal places, so it gets rounded.

```
format "$%.2f", 3 / 4.0
```
_$0.75_ ← Parts of the string that aren't part of a format sequence are output literally.

```
format "%i", 3 / 4.0
```
_0_ ← %i format sequence prints an integer, so the argument gets rounded down.

```
format "%.2f", 3 / 4
```
_0.00_ ← Both division operands are integers. Result gets rounded DOWN to an integer (0).

When we forget to set an object's attributes...

Now that you have the employee pay printing in the correct format, you're puttering along, happily using your new `Employee` class to process payroll. That is, until you create a new `Employee` instance and forget to set the `name` and `salary` attributes before calling `print_pay_stub`:

```
employee = Employee.new
employee.print_pay_stub
```

~ Not an error, but it's blank!

```
Name:
in `print_pay_stub': undefined method
`/' for nil:NilClass
```
← Error!

What happened? It's only natural that the name is empty; we forgot to set it. But what's this "undefined method for nil" error? What the heck is this `nil` thing?

This sort of error is pretty common in Ruby, so let's take a few pages to understand it.

Let's alter the `print_pay_stub` method to print the values of `@name` and `@salary`, so we can figure out what's going on.

```
class Employee

  ...

  def print_pay_stub           ← Print the values.
    puts @name, @salary
  end                ← We'll restore the rest of
                       the code later.
end
```

"nil" stands for nothing

Now let's create a new `Employee` instance and call the revised method:

This should print @name and @salary. →

```
employee = Employee.new
employee.print_pay_stub
```

 ←— Two empty lines!

Well, *that* wasn't very helpful. Maybe we're missing something, though.

Back in Chapter 1, we learned that the `inspect` and `p` methods can reveal information that doesn't show up in ordinary output. Let's try again, using `p`:

```
class Employee
  ...
  def print_pay_stub
    p @name, @salary
  end
end
```
←— Print the values in debug format.

We create another new instance, make another call to the instance method, and…

```
employee = Employee.new
employee.print_pay_stub
```

```
nil
nil
```
←—A-HA!

Ruby has a special value, `nil`, that represents *nothing*. That is, it represents the *absence* of a value.

Just because `nil` *represents* nothing doesn't mean it's *actually* nothing, though. Like everything else in Ruby, it's an object, and it has its own class: `puts nil.class`   `NilClass`

But if there's actually something there, how come we didn't see anything in the output?

It's because the `to_s` instance method from `NilClass` always returns an empty string.   `puts nil.to_s`   ←— Empty string!

The `puts` and `print` methods automatically call `to_s` on an object to convert it to a string for printing. That's why we got two blank lines when we tried to use `puts` to print the values of `@name` and `@salary`; both were set to `nil`, so we wound up printing two empty strings.

Unlike `to_s`, the `inspect` instance method from `NilClass` always returns the string `"nil"`.   `puts nil.inspect`   `nil`

You may recall that the `p` method calls `inspect` on each object before printing it. That's why the `nil` values in `@name` and `@salary` appeared in the output once we called `p` on them.

"/" is a method

So, when you first create an instance of the Employee class, its @name and @salary instance variables have a value of nil. The @salary variable, in particular, causes problems if you call the print_pay_stub method without setting it first:

Error ⟶ `in 'print_pay_stub': undefined method '/' for nil:NilClass`

↖ "nil" value!

It's obvious from the error that the problem is related to the nil value. But it says undefined method '/'... Is division really a method?

In Ruby, the answer is yes; most mathematical operators are implemented as methods. When Ruby sees something like this in your code:

```
6 + 2
```

...it converts it to a call to a method named + on the Fixnum object 6, with the object on the right of the + (that is, 2) as an argument:

A method call! ⤵ ⤵ The other operand is passed as an argument.

```
6.+(2)
```

Both forms are perfectly valid Ruby, and you can try running them yourself:

```
puts 6 + 2
puts 6.+(2)
```
```
8
8
```

The same is true for most of the other mathematical operators.

```
puts 7 - 3
puts 7.-(3)
puts 3.0 * 2
puts 3.0.*(2)
puts 8.0 / 4.0
puts 8.0./(4.0)
```
```
4
4
6.0
6.0
2.0
2.0
```

Even comparison operators are implemented as methods.

```
puts 9 < 7
puts 9.<(7)
puts 9 > 7
puts 9.>(7)
```
```
false
false
true
true
```

But while the Fixnum and Float classes define these operator methods, NilClass does *not*.

```
puts nil./(365.0)
```

Error ⟶ `undefined method '/' for nil:NilClass`

In fact, nil doesn't define *most* of the instance methods you see on other Ruby objects.

And why should it? If you're doing mathematical operations with nil, it's almost certainly because you forgot to assign a value to one of the operands. You *want* an error to be raised, to bring your attention to the problem.

It was a mistake when we forgot to set a salary for an Employee, for example. And now that we understand the source of this error, it's time to prevent it from happening again.

The "initialize" method

We tried to call `print_pay_stub` on an instance of our
Employee class, but we got `nil` when we tried to access the `@name`
and `@salary` instance variables.

```
employee = Employee.new
employee.print_pay_stub
```

Chaos ensued.

Not an error, but it's blank!

```
Name:
in `print_pay_stub': undefined method
`/' for nil:NilClass
```

← *Error!*

Here's the method where the `nil` values caused so much trouble:

Results in call to to_s on @name.
Since it's nil, prints an empty string.

```
def print_pay_stub
  puts "Name: #{@name}"
  pay_for_period = (@salary / 365.0) * 14
  formatted_pay = format("$%.2f", pay_for_period)
  puts "Pay This Period: #{formatted_pay}"
end
```

Results in call to "/"
(actually an instance method)
on @salary. Since it's nil,
raises an error.

Here's the key problem: at the time we create an Employee instance, it's
in an invalid state; it's not safe to call `print_pay_stub` until you set its
`@name` and `@salary` instance variables.

If we could set `@name` and `@salary` *at the same time* as we create an
Employee instance, it would reduce the potential for errors.

Ruby provides a mechanism to help with this situation: the `initialize`
method. The `initialize` method is your chance to step in and make
the object safe to use, before anyone else attempts to call methods on it.

```
class MyClass
  def initialize
    puts "Setting up new instance!"
  end
end
```

When you call `MyClass.new`, Ruby allocates some memory to hold
a new MyClass object, then calls the `initialize` instance method
on that new object.

```
MyClass.new
```
```
Setting up new instance!
```

> **Ruby calls the**
> **initialize method**
> **on new objects after**
> **they're created.**

Employee safety with "initialize"

Let's add an `initialize` method that will set up `@name` and `@salary` for new Employee instances before any other instance methods are called.

```ruby
class Employee

  attr_reader :name, :salary

  def name=(name)
    if name == ""
      raise "Name can't be blank!"
    end
    @name = name
  end

  def salary=(salary)
    if salary < 0
      raise "A salary of #{salary} isn't valid!"
    end
    @salary = salary
  end

  def initialize
    @name = "Anonymous"
    @salary = 0.0
  end

  def print_pay_stub
    puts "Name: #{@name}"
    pay_for_period = (@salary / 365.0) * 14
    formatted_pay = format("$%.2f", pay_for_period)
    puts "Pay This Period: #{formatted_pay}"
  end

end
```

Our new method → `def initialize` ... `end`

Set the @name instance variable.

Set the @salary instance variable.

Now that we've set up an `initialize` method, `@name` and `@salary` will already be set for any new Employee instance. It'll be safe to call `print_pay_stub` on them immediately!

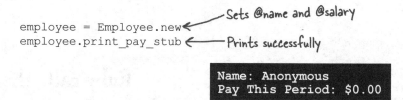

```ruby
employee = Employee.new
employee.print_pay_stub
```

Sets @name and @salary

Prints successfully

```
Name: Anonymous
Pay This Period: $0.00
```

Arguments to "initialize"

Our `initialize` method now sets a default `@name` of `"Anonymous"` and a default `@salary` of `0.0`. It would be better if we could supply a value other than these defaults.

It's for situations like this that any arguments to the new method are passed on to `initialize`.

```
class MyClass
  def initialize(my_param)
    puts "Got a parameter from 'new': #{my_param}"
  end
end
                                    ⌐ Forwarded to "initialize"!
MyClass.new("hello")
```

```
Got a parameter from 'new': hello
```

We can use this feature to let the caller of `Employee.new` specify what the initial name and salary should be. All we have to do is add `name` and `salary` parameters to `initialize`, and use them to set the `@name` and `@salary` instance variables.

```
class Employee

  ...

  def initialize(name, salary)
    @name = name          ⟵  Use the "name" parameter to set the "@name" instance variable.
    @salary = salary ⟵
  end                      Use the "salary" parameter to set the "@salary" instance variable.

  ...

end
```

And just like that, we can set `@name` and `@salary` via arguments to `Employee.new`!

```
employee = Employee.new("Amy Blake", 50000)
employee.print_pay_stub
                            Forwarded to "initialize"!
```

```
Name: Amy Blake
Pay This Period: $1917.81
```

Of course, once you set it up this way, you'll need to be careful. If you don't pass any arguments to new, there will be no arguments to forward on to `initialize`. At that point, you'll get the same result that happens any time you call a Ruby method with the wrong number of arguments: an error.

```
employee = Employee.new          Error ⟶
```

```
in `initialize': wrong number
of arguments (0 for 2)
```

We'll look at a solution for this in a moment.

Using optional parameters with "initialize"

We started with an `initialize` method that set default values for our instance variables, but didn't let you specify your own...

```
class Employee
  ...
  def initialize
    @name = "Anonymous"      ←——— Set the @name instance variable.
    @salary = 0.0 ←
  end                        Set the @salary instance variable.
  ...
end
```

Then we added parameters to `initialize`, which meant that you *had* to specify your own name and salary values, and couldn't rely on the defaults...

```
class Employee
  ...
  def initialize(name, salary)
    @name = name ←——— Use the "name" parameter to set the "@name" instance variable.
    @salary = salary ←
  end            Use the "salary" parameter to set the "@salary" instance variable.
  ...
end
```

Can we have the best of both worlds?

Yes! Since `initialize` is an ordinary method, it can utilize all the features of ordinary methods. And that includes optional parameters. (Remember those from Chapter 2?)

We can specify default values when declaring the parameters. When we omit an argument, we'll get the default value. Then, we just assign those parameters to the instance variables normally.

```
class Employee
  ...
  def initialize(name = "Anonymous", salary = 0.0) ←——— Specify default parameter values.
    @name = name
    @salary = salary
  end
  ...
end
```

With this change in place, we can omit one or both arguments and get the appropriate defaults!

```
Employee.new("Jane Doe", 50000).print_pay_stub
Employee.new("Jane Doe").print_pay_stub
Employee.new.print_pay_stub
```

```
Name: Jane Doe
Pay This Period: $1917.81
Name: Jane Doe
Pay This Period: $0.00
Name: Anonymous
Pay This Period: $0.00
```

Pool Puzzle

Your **job** is to take code snippets from the pool and place them into the blank lines in the code. **Don't** use the same snippet more than once, and you won't need to use all the snippets. Your **goal** is to make code that will run and produce the output shown.

```
class Car

  def _____ (_____)
    _____ = engine
  end

  def rev_engine
    @engine.make_sound
  end

end

class Engine

  def initialize(_____ = _____)
    @sound = sound
  end

  def make_sound
    puts @sound
  end

end

engine = Engine.___
car = Car.new(_____)
car.rev_engine
```

Output:

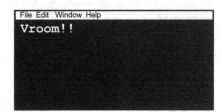

```
File Edit Window Help
Vroom!!
```

Note: each thing from the pool can only be used once!

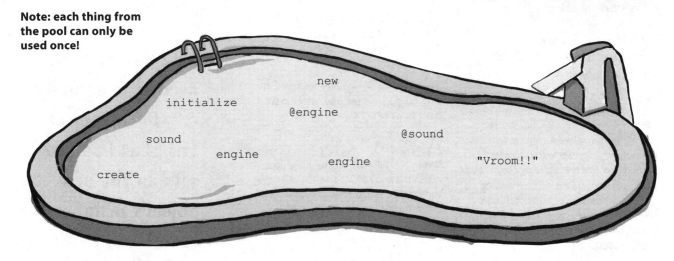

```
new
initialize        @engine
sound                  @sound
       engine      engine    "Vroom!!"
create
```

Pool Puzzle Solution

```
class Car

    def initialize (engine)
        @engine = engine
    end

    def rev_engine
        @engine.make_sound
    end

end

engine = Engine.new
car = Car.new(engine)
car.rev_engine
```

```
class Engine

    def initialize(sound = "Vroom!!")
        @sound = sound
    end

    def make_sound
        puts @sound
    end

end
```

Output:

```
File Edit Window Help
Vroom!!
```

there are no Dumb Questions

Q: What's the difference between `initialize` methods in Ruby and constructors from other object-oriented languages?

A: They both serve the same basic purpose: to let the class prepare new instances for use. Whereas constructors are a special structure in most other languages, though, Ruby's `initialize` is just an ordinary instance method.

Q: Why do I have to call `MyClass.new`? Can't I just call `initialize` directly?

A: The `new` method is needed to actually *create* the object; `initialize` just sets up the new object's instance variables. Without `new`, there would be no object to initialize! For this reason, Ruby doesn't allow you to call the `initialize` method directly from outside an instance. (So we oversimplified a little bit; `initialize` *does* differ from an ordinary instance method in one respect.)

Q: Does `MyClass.new` always call `initialize` on the new object?

A: Yes, always.

Q: Then how have we been calling `new` on the classes we've made so far? They didn't have `initialize` methods!

A: Actually, they *did* have one... All Ruby classes inherit an `initialize` method from the `Object` superclass.

Q: But if `Employee` inherited an `initialize` method, why did we have to write our own?

A: The `initialize` from `Object` takes no arguments, and basically does nothing. It won't set up any instance variables for you; we had to override it with our own version in order to do that.

Q: Can I return a value from an `initialize` method?

A: You can, but Ruby will ignore it. The `initialize` method is intended solely for setting up new instances of your class, so if you need a return value, you should do that elsewhere in your code.

The new method is needed to actually create the object; initialize just sets up the new object's instance variables.

"initialize" does an end-run around our validation

> This new `initialize` method is great. It lets us make sure that an employee's name and salary are always set to **something**. But remember the validation in our accessor methods? The `initialize` method skips it entirely, and we're seeing bad data!

@name = "Steve Wilson (HR Manager)"
@salary = 80000

You remember our `name=` attribute writer method, which prevents the assignment of an empty string as an Employee name:

```
ben = Employee.new
ben.name = ""
```

Error ⟶ ` in `name=': Name can't be blank! (RuntimeError) `

There's also our `salary=` attribute writer method, which ensures that negative numbers aren't assigned as a salary:

```
kara = Employee.new
kara.salary = -246
```

Error ⟶ ` in `salary=': A salary of -246 isn't valid! (RuntimeError) `

We have bad news for you: since your `initialize` method assigns directly to the `@name` and `@salary` instance variables, bad data has a new way to sneak in!

```
employee = Employee.new("", -246)
employee.print_pay_stub
```

Blank name in your output!

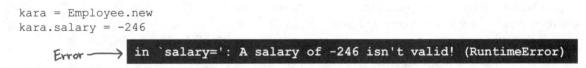
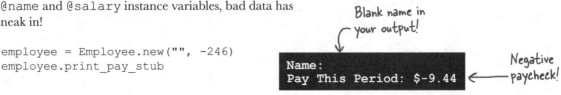

```
Name:
Pay This Period: $-9.44
```

Negative paycheck!

"initialize" and validation

We *could* get our `initialize` method to validate its parameters by adding the same validation code to the `initialize` method...

```ruby
class Employee
  ...
  def name=(name)
    if name == ""
      raise "Name can't be blank!"
    end
    @name = name
  end

  def salary=(salary)
    if salary < 0
      raise "A salary of #{salary} isn't valid!"
    end
    @salary = salary
  end

  def initialize(name = "Anonymous", salary = 0.0)
    if name == ""
      raise "Name can't be blank!"
    end
    @name = name
    if salary < 0
      raise "A salary of #{salary} isn't valid!"
    end
    @salary = salary
  end
  ...
end
```

Duplicated code!

Duplicated code!

But duplicating code like that is a problem. What if we changed the `initialize` validation code later, but forgot to update the `name=` method? There would be different rules for setting the name, depending on how you set it!

Rubyists try to follow the *DRY principle*, where DRY stands for Don't Repeat Yourself. It means that you should avoid duplicating code wherever possible, as it's likely to result in bugs.

What if we called the `name=` and `salary=` methods from *within* the `initialize` method? That would let us set the `@name` and `@salary` instance variables. It would also let us run the validation code, *without* duplicating it!

Call other methods on the same instance with "self"

We need to call the `name=` and `salary=` attribute writer methods from within the `initialize` method *of the same object*. That will let us run the writer methods' validation code before we set the `@name` and `@salary` instance variables.

Unfortunately, code like this *won't* work…

```
class Employee
  ...
  def initialize(name = "Anonymous", salary = 0.0)
    name = name
    salary = salary
  end
  ...
end

amy = Employee.new("Amy Blake", 50000)
amy.print_pay_stub
```

`name = name` ← Doesn't work—Ruby thinks you're assigning to a variable!

`@name` and `@salary` are nil again!

```
Name:
in `print_pay_stub': undefined method
`/' for nil:NilClass (NoMethodError)
```

The code in the `initialize` method treats `name=` and `salary=` *not* as calls to the attribute writer methods, but as resetting the `name` and `salary` local variables to the same values they already contain! (If that sounds like a useless and nonsensical thing to do, that's because it is.)

What we *need* to do is make it clear to Ruby that we intend to call the `name=` and `salary=` instance methods. And to call an instance method, we usually use the dot operator.

But we're inside the `initialize` instance method…what would we put to the left of the dot operator?

We can't use the `amy` variable; it would be silly to refer to one instance of the class within the class itself. Besides, `amy` is out of scope within the `initialize` method.

```
class Employee
  ...
  def initialize(name = "Anonymous", salary = 0.0)
    amy.name = name
    amy.salary = salary
  end
  ...
end

amy = Employee.new("Amy Blake", 50000)
```

Not in scope here! → `amy.name = name`

Error → `in `initialize': undefined local variable or method `amy'`

Call other methods on the same instance with "self" (continued)

We need something to put to the left of the dot operator, so that we can call our Employee class's name= and salary= attribute accessor methods within our initialize method. The problem is, what do we put there? How do you refer to the current instance from *inside* an instance method?

```
class Employee
  ...
  def initialize(name = "Anonymous", salary = 0.0)
    amy.name = name
    amy.salary = salary
  end
  ...
end

amy = Employee.new("Amy Blake", 50000)
```

Not in scope here! ⟶ (pointing to `amy.name = name`)

Ruby has an answer: the self keyword. Within instance methods, self always refers to the current object.

We can demonstrate this with a simple class:

```
class MyClass
  def first_method
    puts "Current instance within first_method: #{self}"
  end
end
```

If we create an instance and call first_method on it, we'll see that inside the instance method, self refers to the object the method is being called on.

```
my_object = MyClass.new
puts "my_object refers to this object: #{my_object}"
my_object.first_method
```

```
my_object refers to this object: #<MyClass:0x007f91fb0ae508>
Current instance within first_method: #<MyClass:0x007f91fb0ae508>
```

← Same object!

The string representations of my_object and self include a unique identifier for the object. (We'll learn more about this in Chapter 8.) The identifiers are the same, so it's the same object!

> **Within instance methods, the keyword self refers to the current object.**

Call other methods on the same instance with "self" (continued)

We can also use `self` with the dot operator to call a second instance method from inside the first one.

```ruby
class MyClass
  def first_method
    puts "Current instance within first_method: #{self}"
    self.second_method       Calls here!
  end

  def second_method
    puts "Current instance within second_method: #{self}"
  end
end

my_object = MyClass.new
my_object.first_method
```

```
Current instance within first_method: #<MyClass:0x007ffd4b077510>      Same
Current instance within second_method: #<MyClass:0x007ffd4b077510>      object!
```

Now that we have `self` to use the dot operator on, we can make it clear to Ruby that we want to call the `name=` and `salary=` instance methods, not to set the `name` and `salary` variables...

```ruby
class Employee
  ...
  def initialize(name = "Anonymous", salary = 0.0)
    self.name = name        DEFINITELY a call to the "name=" method
    self.salary = salary
  end
  ...
end
```

DEFINITELY a call to
the "salary=" method

Let's try calling our new constructor and see if it worked!

```ruby
amy = Employee.new("Amy Blake", 50000)
amy.print_pay_stub
```

```
Name: Amy Blake
Pay This Period: $1917.81
```

Call other methods on the same instance with "self" (continued)

Success! Thanks to `self` and the dot operator, it's now clear to Ruby (and everyone else) that we're making calls to the attribute writer methods, not assigning to variables.

And since we're going through the accessor methods, that means the validation works, without any duplicated code!

```
employee = Employee.new("", 50000)
```

Error ⟶ `in ``name=``: Name can't be blank!`

```
employee = Employee.new("Jane Doe", -99999)
```

Error ⟶ `in ``salary=``: A salary of -99999 isn't valid!`

No more blank names and negative salaries for our new employees? And it won't delay the payroll project? Nice job!

When "self" is optional

Right now, our `print_pay_stub` method accesses the `@name` and `@salary` instance variables directly:

```
class Employee

  def print_pay_stub
    puts "Name: #{@name}"
    pay_for_period = (@salary / 365.0) * 14
    formatted_pay = format("$%.2f", pay_for_period)
    puts "Pay This Period: #{formatted_pay}"
  end

end
```

But we defined `name` and `salary` attribute reader methods in our `Employee` class; we could use those instead of accessing the instance variables directly. (That way, if you ever change the `name` method to display last name first, or change the `salary` method to calculate salary according to an algorithm, the `print_pay_stub` code won't need to be updated.)

We *can* use the `self` keyword and the dot operator when calling `name` and `salary`, and it will work just fine:

```
class Employee

  attr_reader :name, :salary

  ...

  def print_pay_stub
    puts "Name: #{self.name}"
    pay_for_period = (self.salary / 365.0) * 14
    formatted_pay = format("$%.2f", pay_for_period)
    puts "Pay This Period: #{formatted_pay}"
  end

end

Employee.new("Amy Blake", 50000).print_pay_stub
```

```
Name: Amy Blake
Pay This Period: $1917.81
```

When "self" is optional (continued)

But Ruby has a rule that can save us a little typing when calling from one instance method to another... If you don't specify a receiver using the dot operator, the receiver defaults to the current object, `self`.

```ruby
class Employee          "self" omitted; still works!
  ...
  def print_pay_stub          "self" omitted; still works!
    puts "Name: #{name}"
    pay_for_period = (salary / 365.0) * 14
    formatted_pay = format("$%.2f", pay_for_period)
    puts "Pay This Period: #{formatted_pay}"
  end
  ...
end

Employee.new("Amy Blake", 50000).print_pay_stub
```

Still works!

```
Name: Amy Blake
Pay This Period: $1917.81
```

As we saw in the previous section, you *have* to include the `self` keyword when calling attribute writer methods, or Ruby will mistake the = for a variable assignment. But for any other kind of instance method call, you can leave `self` off, if you want.

If you don't specify a receiver using the dot operator, the receiver defaults to the current object, `self`.

Implementing hourly employees through inheritance

The `Employee` class you've created for Chargemore is working great! It prints accurate pay stubs that are formatted properly, and thanks to the `initialize` method you wrote, it's really easy to create new `Employee` instances.

But, at this point, it only handles salaried employees. It's time to look at adding support for employees that are paid by the hour.

The requirements for hourly employees are basically the same as for salaried ones; we need to be able to print pay stubs that include their name and the amount paid. The only difference is the way that we calculate their pay. For hourly employees, we multiply their hourly wage by the number of hours they work per week, then double that amount to get two weeks' worth.

Since salaried and hourly employees are so similar, it makes sense to put the shared functionality in a superclass. Then, we'll make two subclasses that hold the different pay calculation logic.

(salary / 365.0) * 14
Salaried employee pay calculation formula

hourly_wage * hours_per_week * 2
Hourly employee pay calculation formula

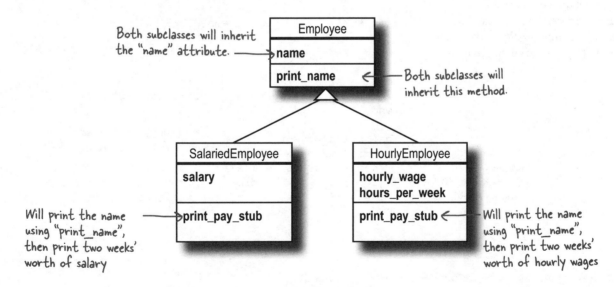

you are here ▶ **137**

Implementing hourly employees through inheritance (continued)

Let's start by ensuring the common logic between
`SalariedEmployee` and `HourlyEmployee` stays in the
`Employee` superclass.

Since pay stubs for both salaried and
hourly employees need to include
their names, we'll leave the `name`
attribute in the superclass, for the
subclasses to share. We'll move
the code that prints the name into
the `print_name` method in the
superclass.

```ruby
class Employee

  attr_reader :name

  def name=(name)
    # Code to validate and set @name
  end

  def print_name
    puts "Name: #{name}"
  end

end
```

← We'll be omitting all attribute accessor code for brevity.

⌐ Remember, this is the same as a call to self.name.

We'll move the logic to calculate
pay for salaried employees to the
`SalariedEmployee` class, but
we'll call the inherited `print_name`
method to print the employee name.

```ruby
class SalariedEmployee < Employee

  attr_reader :salary

  def salary=(salary)
    # Code to validate and set @salary
  end

  def print_pay_stub
    print_name
    pay_for_period = (salary / 365.0) * 14
    formatted_pay = format("$%.2f", pay_for_period)
    puts "Pay This Period: #{formatted_pay}"
  end

end
```

Calls print_name method inherited from superclass

This code is the same as we had in the old Employee print_pay_stub method.

With those changes in place, we can create a new `SalariedEmployee`
instance, set its name and salary, and print a pay stub as before:

```ruby
salaried_employee = SalariedEmployee.new
salaried_employee.name = "Jane Doe"
salaried_employee.salary = 50000
salaried_employee.print_pay_stub
```

```
Name: Jane Doe
Pay This Period: $1917.81
```

Implementing hourly employees through inheritance (continued)

Now we'll build a new `HourlyEmployee` class. It's just like `SalariedEmployee`, except that it holds an hourly wage and number of hours worked per week, and uses those to calculate pay for a two-week period. As with `SalariedEmployee`, storing and printing the employee name is left up to the `Employee` superclass.

```ruby
class HourlyEmployee < Employee

  attr_reader :hourly_wage, :hours_per_week

  def hourly_wage=(hourly_wage)
    # Code to validate and set @hourly_wage
  end

  def hours_per_week=(hours_per_week)
    # Code to validate and set @hours_per_week
  end

  def print_pay_stub
    print_name
    pay_for_period = hourly_wage * hours_per_week * 2
    formatted_pay = format("$%.2f", pay_for_period)
    puts "Pay This Period: #{formatted_pay}"
  end

end
```

And now we can create an `HourlyEmployee` instance. Instead of setting a salary, we set an hourly wage and number of hours per week. Those values are then used to calculate the pay stub amount.

```ruby
hourly_employee = HourlyEmployee.new
hourly_employee.name = "John Smith"
hourly_employee.hourly_wage = 14.97
hourly_employee.hours_per_week = 30
hourly_employee.print_pay_stub
```

```
Name: John Smith
Pay This Period: $898.20
```

That wasn't bad at all! Through the use of inheritance, we've implemented pay stubs for hourly employees, kept pay stubs for salaried employees, and minimized code duplication between the two.

We've lost something in the shuffle, though—our `initialize` method. We used to be able to set up an `Employee` object's data at the time we created it, and these new classes won't let us do that. We'll have to add `initialize` methods back in.

Restoring "initialize" methods

To make `SalariedEmployee` and `HourlyEmployee` objects that are safe to work with as soon as they're created, we'll need to add `initialize` methods to those two classes.

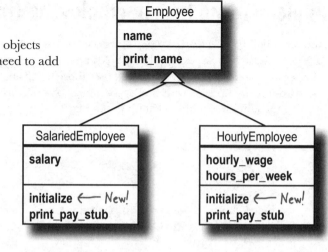

As we did with the `Employee` class before, our `initialize` methods will need to accept a parameter for each object attribute we want to set. The `initialize` method for `SalariedEmployee` will look just like it did for the old `Employee` class (since the attributes are the same), but `initialize` for `HourlyEmployee` will accept a different set of parameters (and set different attributes).

```
class SalariedEmployee < Employee
  ...
  def initialize(name = "Anonymous", salary = 0.0)
    self.name = name
    self.salary = salary
  end
  ...
end
```

This is just like the initialize method for the old Employee class.

```
class HourlyEmployee < Employee
  ...
  def initialize(name = "Anonymous", hourly_wage = 0.0, hours_per_week = 0.0)
    self.name = name
    self.hourly_wage = hourly_wage
    self.hours_per_week = hours_per_week
  end
  ...
end
```

This method needs to accept three parameters, and set three attributes.

Again, we make parameters optional by providing defaults.

With our `initialize` methods added, we can once again pass arguments to the `new` method for each class. Our objects will be ready to use as soon as they're created.

```
salaried_employee = SalariedEmployee.new("Jane Doe", 50000)
salaried_employee.print_pay_stub

hourly_employee = HourlyEmployee.new("John Smith", 14.97, 30)
hourly_employee.print_pay_stub
```

```
Name: Jane Doe
Pay This Period: $1917.81
Name: John Smith
Pay This Period: $898.20
```

Inheritance and "initialize"

There's one small weakness in our new `initialize` methods, though: the code to set the employee name is duplicated between our two subclasses.

```ruby
class SalariedEmployee < Employee
  ...
  def initialize(name = "Anonymous", salary = 0.0)
    self.name = name
    self.salary = salary
  end
  ...
end

class HourlyEmployee < Employee
  ...
  def initialize(name = "Anonymous", hourly_wage = 0.0, hours_per_week = 0.0)
    self.name = name          ←——— Duplicated in SalariedEmployee!*
    self.hourly_wage = hourly_wage
    self.hours_per_week = hours_per_week
  end
  ...
end
```

In all other aspects of our subclasses, we delegate handling of the `name` attribute to the `Employee` superclass. We define the reader and writer methods there. We even print the name via the `print_name` method, which the subclasses call from their respective `print_pay_stub` methods.

```ruby
class Employee

  attr_reader :name

  def name=(name)
    # Code to validate and set @name
  end

  def print_name
    puts "Name: #{name}"
  end

end
```

Superclass holds the "name" attribute.

Superclass holds shared code to print the name.

But we don't do this for `initialize`. Could we?

Yes! We've said it before, and we'll say it again: `initialize` is just an *ordinary instance method*. That means that it gets inherited like any other, that it can be overridden like any other, and that overriding methods can call it via `super` like any other. We'll demonstrate on the next page.

*Okay, we realize it's just one line of duplicated code. But the technique we're about to show you will also help with much larger amounts of duplication.

"super" and "initialize"

To eliminate the repeated `name` setup code in our `Employee` subclasses, we can move the name handling to an `initialize` method in the superclass, then have the subclass `initialize` methods call it with `super`. `SalariedEmployee` will keep the logic to set up a salary, `HourlyEmployee` will keep the logic to set up an hourly wage and hours per week, and the two classes can delegate the shared logic for `name` to their shared superclass.

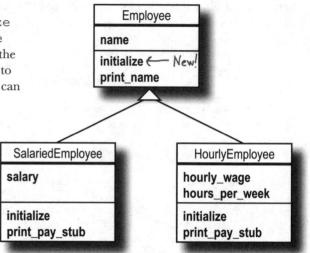

First, let's try moving the name handling from the `initialize` method in `SalariedEmployee` to the `Employee` class.

```ruby
class Employee
  ...
  def initialize(name = "Anonymous")       ←——— New "initialize" method that
    self.name = name                             handles only the name!
  end
  ...
end

class SalariedEmployee < Employee
  ...
  def initialize(name = "Anonymous", salary = 0.0)
    super ←————————————— Attempt to call "initialize" in
    self.salary = salary    Employee to set up the name.
  end
  ...
end
```

Trying to use this revised `initialize` method reveals a problem, though...

```ruby
salaried_employee = SalariedEmployee.new("Jane Doe", 50000)
salaried_employee.print_pay_stub
```

Error ——→ `in 'initialize': wrong number of arguments (2 for 0..1)`

"super" and "initialize" (continued)

Oops! We forgot a key detail about super that we learned earlier—if you don't specify a set of arguments, it calls the superclass method with the same set of arguments that the subclass method received. (This is true when you're using super in other instance methods, and it's true when you're using super within initialize.) The initialize method in SalariedEmployee received *two* parameters, and super passed them *both* on to the initialize method in Employee. (Even though it only accepts *one* argument.)

The fix, then, is to specify which parameter we want to pass on: the name parameter.

```
class SalariedEmployee < Employee
  ...
  def initialize(name = "Anonymous", salary = 0.0)
    super(name)←──────── Call "initialize" in Employee,
    self.salary = salary          passing only the name.
  end
  ...
end
```

Let's try to initialize a new SalariedEmployee again...

```
salaried_employee = SalariedEmployee.new("Jane Doe", 50000)
salaried_employee.print_pay_stub
```

```
Name: Jane Doe
Pay This Period: $1917.81
```

It worked! Let's make the same changes to the HourlyEmployee class...

```
class HourlyEmployee < Employee
  ...
  def initialize(name = "Anonymous", hourly_wage = 0.0, hours_per_week = 0.0)
    super(name)←──────────────── Call "initialize" in Employee,
    self.hourly_wage = hourly_wage     passing only the name.
    self.hours_per_week = hours_per_week
  end
  ...
end
```

```
hourly_employee = HourlyEmployee.new("John Smith", 14.97, 30)
hourly_employee.print_pay_stub
```

```
Name: John Smith
Pay This Period: $898.20
```

Previously, we used super within our print_pay_stub methods in SalariedEmployee and HourlyEmployee to delegate printing of the employee name to the Employee superclass. Now we've just done the same thing with the initialize method, allowing the superclass to handle setting of the name attribute.

Why does it work? Because initialize is an instance method just like any other. Any feature of Ruby that you can use with an ordinary instance method, you can use with initialize.

there are no
Dumb Questions

Q: If I override `initialize` in a subclass, does the superclass's `initialize` method run when the overriding `initialize` method runs?

A: Not unless you explicitly call it with the `super` keyword, no. Remember, in Ruby, `initialize` is just an ordinary method, like any other. If you call the `move` method on a `Dog` instance, does `move` from the `Animal` class get run as well? No, not unless you use `super`. It's no different with the `initialize` method.

Ruby is *not* the same as many other object-oriented languages, which automatically call the superclass's constructor before calling the subclass constructor.

Q: If I use **super** to call the superclass's `initialize` method explicitly, does it have to be the first thing I do in the subclass's `initialize` method?

A: If your subclass depends on instance variables that are set up by the superclass's `initialize` method, then you may want to invoke `super` before doing anything else. But Ruby doesn't require it. As with other methods, you can invoke `super` anywhere you want within `initialize`.

Q: You *say* the superclass's `initialize` method doesn't get run unless you call **super**... If that's true, then how does `@last_name` get set in this sample?

```ruby
class Parent
  attr_accessor :last_name
  def initialize(last_name)
    @last_name = last_name
  end
end

class Child < Parent
end

child = Child.new("Smith")
puts child.last_name
```

A: Because `initialize` is *inherited* from the `Parent` class. With Ruby instance methods, you only need to call `super` to invoke the parent class's method *if* you want it to run, *and* you've overridden it in the subclass. If you haven't overridden it, then the inherited method is run directly. This works the same for `initialize` as it does for any other method.

Code Magnets

A Ruby program is all scrambled up on the fridge. Can you reconstruct the code snippets to make a working superclass and subclass, so the sample code below can execute and produce the given output?

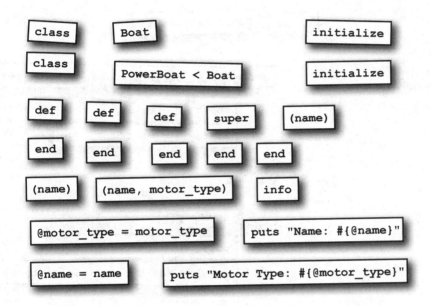

`class`	`Boat`	`initialize`
`class`	`PowerBoat < Boat`	`initialize`

`def`   `def`   `def`   `super`   `(name)`

`end`   `end`   `end`   `end`   `end`

`(name)`   `(name, motor_type)`   `info`

`@motor_type = motor_type`   `puts "Name: #{@name}"`

`@name = name`   `puts "Motor Type: #{@motor_type}"`

Sample code:

```ruby
boat = PowerBoat.new("Guppy", "outboard")
boat.info
```

Output:

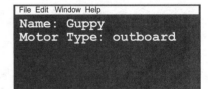

```
File Edit Window Help
Name: Guppy
Motor Type: outboard
```

Code Magnets Solution

A Ruby program is all scrambled up on the fridge. Can you reconstruct the code snippets to make a working superclass and subclass, so the sample code below can execute and produce the given output?

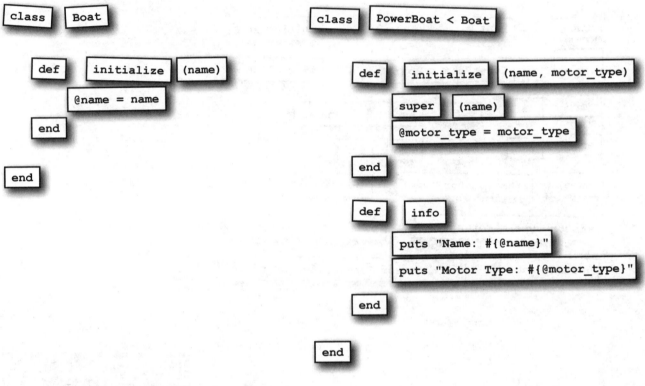

```ruby
class Boat

  def initialize(name)
    @name = name
  end

end


class PowerBoat < Boat

  def initialize(name, motor_type)
    super(name)
    @motor_type = motor_type
  end

  def info
    puts "Name: #{@name}"
    puts "Motor Type: #{@motor_type}"
  end

end
```

Sample code:

```ruby
boat = PowerBoat.new("Guppy", "outboard")
boat.info
```

Output:

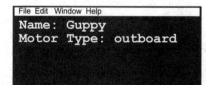

```
File Edit  Window Help
Name: Guppy
Motor Type: outboard
```

Same class, same attribute values

With your `HourlyEmployee` class complete, Chargemore is ready
to begin a hiring blitz to staff their new stores. Here's the set of
employees they need to create for their first store downtown:

> Ruby lets us use as many space characters as we want, so we've aligned this code for easier reading.

```
ivan    = HourlyEmployee.new("Ivan Stokes",      12.75, 25)
harold  = HourlyEmployee.new("Harold Nguyen",    12.75, 25)
tamara  = HourlyEmployee.new("Tamara Wells",     12.75, 25)
susie   = HourlyEmployee.new("Susie Powell",     12.75, 25)

edwin   = HourlyEmployee.new("Edwin Burgess",    10.50, 20)
ethel   = HourlyEmployee.new("Ethel Harris",     10.50, 20)

angela  = HourlyEmployee.new("Angela Matthews",  19.25, 30)
stewart = HourlyEmployee.new("Stewart Sanchez",  19.25, 30)
```

hourly_wage ⟶   hours_per_week

If you look at the above code, you'll probably notice there are large
groups of objects where similar arguments are passed to the `new`
method. There's a good reason for this: the first group are cashiers for
the new store, the second group are janitors, and the third group are
security guards.

Chargemore starts all new cashiers off at the same base pay and
number of hours per week. Janitors get a different rate and number of
hours than cashiers, but it's the same for all janitors. And the same is
true for security guards. (Individuals may get raises later, depending on
performance, but they all start out the same.)

The upshot is that there's a lot of repetition of arguments in those
calls to `new`, and a lot of chances to make a typo. And this is just the
first wave of hiring, for the first Chargemore store, so things can only
get worse. Seems like we can make this easier.

```
down_arrows
short_downward_arrow
downward_arrow
horizontal_arrow
upward_arrow
up_arrows
```

An inefficient factory method

When you need to make many instances of a class that have similar data, you can often save some repetition by making a *factory method* to create objects prepopulated with the needed attribute values. (Factory methods are a programming pattern that can be used in any object-oriented language, not just Ruby.)

But if we use only the tools we have now, any factory method we make will be inefficient at best.

To demonstrate what we mean, let's try making a method to set up new `HourlyEmployee` objects with the default pay and hours per week for cashiers.

```ruby
class HourlyEmployee
  ...
  def turn_into_cashier
    self.hourly_wage = 12.75        Set hourly wage.
    self.hours_per_week = 25        Set hours per week.
  end
  ...
end

ivan = HourlyEmployee.new("Ivan Stokes")
ivan.turn_into_cashier
ivan.print_pay_stub
```

```
Name: Ivan Stokes
Pay This Period: $637.50
```

This works, yes. So what's so inefficient about it? Let's look at our `initialize` method (which of course has to run when we create a new `HourlyEmployee`) again...

```ruby
class HourlyEmployee
  ...
  def initialize(name = "Anonymous", hourly_wage = 0, hours_per_week = 0)
    super(name)
    self.hourly_wage = hourly_wage        Set hourly wage.
    self.hours_per_week = hours_per_week  Set hours per week.
  end
  ...
end
```

We're setting the `hourly_wage` and `hours_per_week` attributes within `initialize`, then immediately turning around and setting them *again* within `turn_into_cashier`!

This is inefficient for Ruby, but there's potential for it to be inefficient for us, too. What if we didn't have default parameters for `hourly_wage` and `hours_per_week` on `initialize`? Then, *we'd* have to specify the arguments we're throwing away!

```ruby
ivan = HourlyEmployee.new("Ivan Stokes", 0, 0)    We won't use either
ivan.turn_into_cashier                            of these values!
```

That's the problem with writing factory methods as instance methods: we're trying to *make* a new instance of the class, but there has to already *be* an instance to run the methods on! There must be a better way...

Fortunately, there is! Up next, we're going to learn about *class methods*.

Class methods

You don't *have* an instance of a class, but you *need* one. And you need a method to set it up for you. Where do you put that method?

You could stick it off by itself in some little Ruby source file, but it would be better to keep it together with the class that it makes instances of. You can't make it an instance method on that class, though. If you *had* an instance of the class, you wouldn't need to *make* one, now would you?

It's for situations like this that Ruby supports **class methods**: methods that you can invoke directly on a class, without the need for any instance of that class. You don't *have* to use a class method as a factory method, but it's *perfect* for the job.

A class method definition is very similar to any other method definition in Ruby. The difference: you specify that you're defining it *on the class itself*.

Specifies that the method is being defined on the <u>class</u>

Method name

```
class MyClass

    def MyClass.my_class_method(p1, p2)    ⟵ Parameters
      puts "Hello from MyClass!"
      puts "My parameters: #{p1}, #{p2}"
    end    ⟵ End of definition

end
```

Method body

Within a class definition (but outside any instance method definitions), Ruby sets `self` to refer to the class that's being defined. So many Rubyists prefer to replace the class name with `self`:

Also refers to MyClass!

```
class MyClass

    def self.my_class_method(p1, p2)
      puts "Hello from MyClass!"
      puts "My parameters: #{p1}, #{p2}"
    end

end
```

In most ways, class method definitions behave just like you're used to:

- You can put as many Ruby statements as you like in the method body.

- You can return a value with the `return` keyword. If you don't, the value of the last expression in the method body is used as the return value.

- You can optionally define one or more parameters that the method accepts, and you can make the parameters optional by defining defaults.

Class methods (continued)

We've defined a new class, `MyClass`, with a single class method:

```
class MyClass

  def self.my_class_method(p1, p2)
    puts "Hello from MyClass!"
    puts "My parameters: #{p1}, #{p2}"
  end

end
```

Once a class method is defined, you can call it directly on the class:

```
MyClass.my_class_method(1, 2)
```

```
Hello from MyClass!
My parameters: 1, 2
```

Perhaps that syntax for calling a class method looks familiar to you...

```
MyClass.new
```

That's right, `new` is a class method! If you think about it, that makes sense; `new` can't be an *instance* method, because you're calling it to *get* an instance in the first place! Instead, you have to ask the *class* for a new instance of itself.

Now that we know how to create class methods, let's see if we can write some factory methods that will create new `HourlyEmployee` objects with the pay rate and hours per week already populated for us. We need methods to set up predefined pay and hours for three positions: cashier, janitor, and security guard.

```
class HourlyEmployee < Employee
  ...
  def self.security_guard(name)
    HourlyEmployee.new(name, 19.25, 30)
  end

  def self.cashier(name)
    HourlyEmployee.new(name, 12.75, 25)
  end

  def self.janitor(name)
    HourlyEmployee.new(name, 10.50, 20)
  end
  ...
end
```

Accept the employee name as a parameter.

Use predefined hourly_wage and hours_per_week for each employee type.

Use the given name to construct an employee.

Same for the cashiers

Same for the janitors

We won't know the name of the employee in advance, so we accept that as a parameter to each of the class methods. We *do* know the values for `hourly_wage` and `hours_per_week` for each employee position, though. We pass those three arguments to the `new` method for the class, and get a new `HourlyEmployee` object back. That new object is then returned from the class method.

Class methods (continued)

Now we can call the factory methods directly on the class, providing only the employee name.

```
angela = HourlyEmployee.security_guard("Angela Matthews")
edwin = HourlyEmployee.janitor("Edwin Burgess")
ivan = HourlyEmployee.cashier("Ivan Stokes")
```

The `HourlyEmployee` instances returned are fully configured with the name we provided, and the appropriate `hourly_wage` and `hours_per_week` for the position. We can begin printing pay stubs for them right away!

```
angela.print_pay_stub
edwin.print_pay_stub
ivan.print_pay_stub
```

```
Name: Angela Matthews
Pay This Period: $1155.00
Name: Edwin Burgess
Pay This Period: $420.00
Name: Ivan Stokes
Pay This Period: $637.50
```

In this chapter, you've learned that there are some pitfalls to creating new objects. But you've also learned techniques to ensure *your* objects are safe to use as soon as you make them. With well-designed `initialize` methods and factory methods, creating and configuring new objects is a snap!

With well-designed `initialize` methods and factory methods, creating and configuring new objects is a snap!

Our complete source code

```
class Employee

  attr_reader :name

  def name=(name)
    if name == ""
      raise "Name can't be blank!"
    end
    @name = name
  end

  def initialize(name = "Anonymous")
    self.name = name
  end

  def print_name
    puts "Name: #{name}"
  end

end

class SalariedEmployee < Employee

  attr_reader :salary

  def salary=(salary)
    if salary < 0
      raise "A salary of #{salary} isn't valid!"
    end
    @salary = salary
  end

  def initialize(name = "Anonymous", salary = 0.0)
    super(name)
    self.salary = salary
  end

  def print_pay_stub
    print_name
    pay_for_period = (salary / 365.0) * 14
    formatted_pay = format("$%.2f", pay_for_period)
    puts "Pay This Period: #{formatted_pay}"
  end

end
```

The "name" attribute is inherited by both SalariedEmployee and HourlyEmployee.

employees.rb

The "initialize" methods of both SalariedEmployee and HourlyEmployee will call this method via "super".

The "print_pay_stub" methods of both SalariedEmployee and HourlyEmployee will call this method.

This attribute is specific to salaried employees.

Called when we call "SalariedEmployee.new"

Call the superclass's "initialize" method, passing only the name.

Set the salary ourselves, since it's specific to this class.

Have the superclass print the name.

Calculate two weeks' pay.

Format the pay with two decimal places.

Continued on next page!

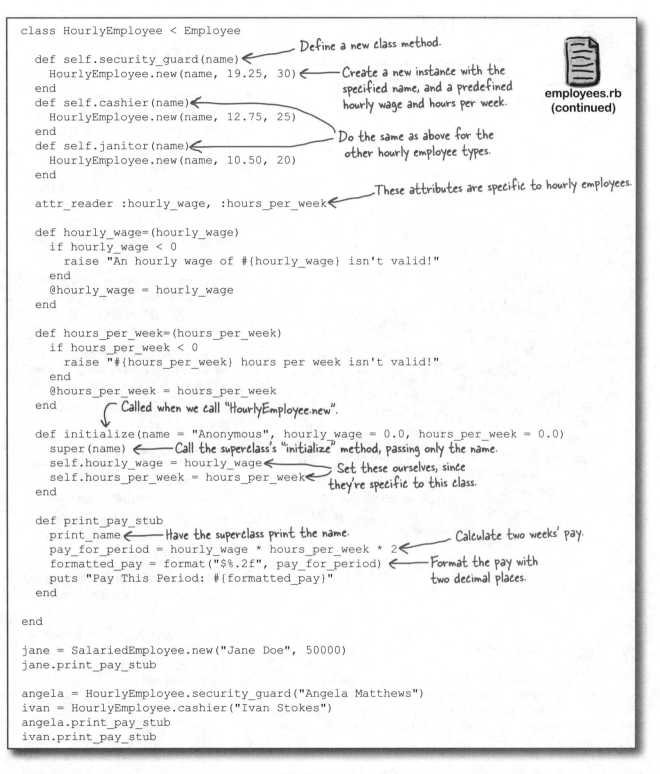

```
class HourlyEmployee < Employee

  def self.security_guard(name)          Define a new class method.
    HourlyEmployee.new(name, 19.25, 30)   Create a new instance with the
  end                                     specified name, and a predefined
  def self.cashier(name)                  hourly wage and hours per week.
    HourlyEmployee.new(name, 12.75, 25)
  end                                     Do the same as above for the
  def self.janitor(name)                  other hourly employee types.
    HourlyEmployee.new(name, 10.50, 20)
  end
                                          These attributes are specific to hourly employees.
  attr_reader :hourly_wage, :hours_per_week

  def hourly_wage=(hourly_wage)
    if hourly_wage < 0
      raise "An hourly wage of #{hourly_wage} isn't valid!"
    end
    @hourly_wage = hourly_wage
  end

  def hours_per_week=(hours_per_week)
    if hours_per_week < 0
      raise "#{hours_per_week} hours per week isn't valid!"
    end
    @hours_per_week = hours_per_week
  end                    Called when we call "HourlyEmployee.new".

  def initialize(name = "Anonymous", hourly_wage = 0.0, hours_per_week = 0.0)
    super(name)             Call the superclass's "initialize" method, passing only the name.
    self.hourly_wage = hourly_wage      Set these ourselves, since
    self.hours_per_week = hours_per_week  they're specific to this class.
  end

  def print_pay_stub
    print_name          Have the superclass print the name.
    pay_for_period = hourly_wage * hours_per_week * 2    Calculate two weeks' pay.
    formatted_pay = format("$%.2f", pay_for_period)     Format the pay with
    puts "Pay This Period: #{formatted_pay}"            two decimal places.
  end

end

jane = SalariedEmployee.new("Jane Doe", 50000)
jane.print_pay_stub

angela = HourlyEmployee.security_guard("Angela Matthews")
ivan = HourlyEmployee.cashier("Ivan Stokes")
angela.print_pay_stub
ivan.print_pay_stub
```

employees.rb (continued)

Your Ruby Toolbox

That's it for Chapter 4! You've added the `initialize` method and class methods to your toolbox.

Statements

Methods

Classes

Inheritance

Creating objects

Ruby calls the "initialize" method on new instances of a class. You can use "initialize" to set up a new object's instance variables.

Class methods can be invoked directly on a class, rather than an instance of that class. They're great as factory methods.

BULLET POINTS

- Number literals *with* a decimal point will be treated as `Float` instances. *Without* a decimal point, they'll be treated as `Fixnum` instances.

- If either operand in a mathematical operation is a `Float`, the result will be a `Float`.

- The `format` method uses format sequences to insert formatted values into a string.

- The format sequence type indicates the type of value that will be inserted. There are types for floating-point numbers, integers, strings, and more.

- The format sequence width determines the number of characters that a formatted value will take up within the string.

- The value `nil` represents *nothing*—the *absence* of a value.

- Operators such as +, −, *, and / are implemented as methods in Ruby. When an operator is encountered in your code, it's converted into a method call.

- Within instance methods, the `self` keyword refers to the instance that the method is being called on.

- If you don't specify a receiver when calling an instance method, the receiver defaults to `self`.

- Within a class body, you can use either `def ClassName.method_name` or `def self.method_name` to define a class method.

Up Next...

So far, we've been working with objects one at a time. But it's much more common to work with *groups* of objects. In the next chapter, we'll show you how to create a group, with *arrays*. We'll also show you how to process each of the items in those arrays, using *blocks*.

5 arrays and blocks

Better Than Loops

"index = 0". "while index < guests.length". Why do I have to mess with this "index" stuff? Can't I just check in each guest?

A whole lot of programming deals with lists of things. Lists of addresses. Lists of phone numbers. Lists of products. Matz, the creator of Ruby, knew this. So he worked *really hard* to make sure that working with lists in Ruby is *really easy*. First, he ensured that **arrays**, which keep track of lists in Ruby, have lots of *powerful methods* to do almost anything you might need with a list. Second, he realized that writing code to *loop over a list* to do something with each item, although tedious, is something developers were doing *a lot*. So he added **blocks** to the language, and removed the need for all that looping code. What is a block, exactly? Read on to find out…

Arrays

Your new client is working on an invoicing program for an online store. They need three different methods, each of which works with the prices on an order. The first method needs to add all the prices together to calculate a total. The second will process a refund to the customer's account. And the third will take 1/3 off each price and display the discount.

Each order will have a list of item prices.

| $ 2.99 |
| $ 25.00 |
| $ 9.99 |

| $ 7.99 |
| $ 25.00 |
| $ 2.99 |
| $ 9.99 |

| $ 3.99 |
| $ 31.00 |
| $ 8.99 |

Hmm, so you have a list of prices (a *collection* of them, if you will), and you don't know in advance how many there will be... That means you can't use variables to store them—there's no way to know how many variables to create. You're going to need to store the prices in an *array*.

An **array** is used to hold a collection of objects. The collection can be any size you need. An array can hold objects of any type (even other arrays). You can even mix multiple types together in the same array.

We can create an array object and initialize it with data by using an array *literal*: square brackets ([]) surrounding a comma-separated list of values..

An array holds a collection of objects.

Start of the array ⟶ ['a', 'b', 'c'] ⟵ End of the array

Objects the array contains go here.

Objects are separated by commas.

Let's create an array to hold the prices from our first order now.

```
prices = [2.99, 25.00, 9.99]
```

You don't have to know an array's entire contents at the time you create it, though. You can also manipulate arrays *after* creating them...

Accessing arrays

So now we've got a place to store all our item prices. To retrieve the prices we stored in the array, we first have to specify which one we want.

Items in an array are numbered from left to right, starting with 0. This is called the array **index**.

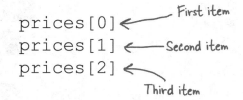

```
[2.99, 25.00, 9.99]
```

Index: 0   1   2   etc...

To retrieve an item, you specify the integer index of the item you want within square brackets:

```
prices[0]
prices[1]
prices[2]
```

First item

Second item

Third item

So we can print out elements from our array like this.

```
puts prices[0]
puts prices[2]
puts prices[1]
```

```
3.99
25.0
8.99
```

You can assign to a given array index with =, much like assigning to a variable.

(The "p" and "inspect" methods are useful for arrays, too!) ⟶

```
prices[0] = 0.99
prices[1] = 1.99
prices[2] = 2.99
p prices
```

```
[0.99, 1.99, 2.99]
```

If you assign to an index that's beyond the end of an array, the array will grow as necessary.

```
prices[3] = 3.99
p prices
```

Here's the new element.

```
[0.99, 1.99, 2.99, 3.99]
```

If you assign to an element that's *way* beyond the end of an array, it will still grow to accommodate your assignment. There just won't be anything at the intervening indexes.

"nil" means "there's nothing here"!

Here's the element we assigned to.

```
prices[6] = 6.99
p prices
```

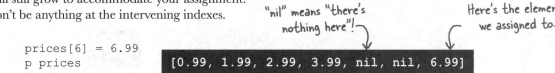

```
[0.99, 1.99, 2.99, 3.99, nil, nil, 6.99]
```

Here, Ruby has placed nil (which, you may recall, represents the absence of a value) at the array indexes you haven't assigned to yet.

You'll also get nil back if you access an element that's beyond the end of an array.

```
p prices[7]
```

The array only extends through index 6!

```
nil
```

Arrays are objects, too!

Like everything else in Ruby, arrays are objects:

```ruby
prices = [7.99, 25.00, 3.99, 9.99]
puts prices.class
```

`Array`

That means they have lots of useful methods attached directly to the array object. Here are some highlights...

Instead of using array indexes like `prices[0]`, there are easy-to-read methods you can use:

```ruby
puts prices.first
```
`7.99`

```ruby
puts prices.last
```
`9.99`

There are methods to find out an array's size:

```ruby
puts prices.length
```
`4`

There are methods to let you search for values within the array:

```ruby
puts prices.include?(25.00)
```
`true`

```ruby
puts prices.find_index(9.99)
```
`3`

There are methods that will let you insert or remove elements, causing the array to grow or shrink:

```ruby
prices.push(0.99)
p prices
```
`[7.99, 25.0, 3.99, 9.99, 0.99]`

```ruby
prices.pop
p prices
```
`[7.99, 25.0, 3.99, 9.99]`

```ruby
prices.shift
p prices
```
`[25.0, 3.99, 9.99]`

The << operator (which, like most operators, is actually a method behind the scenes) also adds elements:

```ruby
prices << 5.99
prices << 8.99
p prices
```
`[25.0, 3.99, 9.99, 5.99, 8.99]`

Arrays have methods that can convert them to strings:

```ruby
puts ["d", "o", "g"].join
puts ["d", "o", "g"].join("-")
```
`dog`
`d-o-g`

And strings have methods that can convert them to arrays:

```ruby
p "d-o-g".chars
```
`["d", "-", "o", "-", "g"]`

```ruby
p "d-o-g".split("-")
```
`["d", "o", "g"]`

Exercise

Open a new terminal window, type **irb**, and hit the Enter/Return key. For each of the Ruby expressions below, write your guess for what the result will be on the line below it. Then try typing the expression into irb and hit Enter. See if your guess matches what irb returns!

```
mix = ["one", 2, "three", Time.new]
```

....

```
mix.length
```

....

```
mix[0]
```

....

```
mix[1]
```

....

```
mix[0].capitalize
```

....

```
mix[1].capitalize
```

....

```
letters = ["b", "c", "b", "a"]
```

....

```
letters.shift
```

....

```
letters
```

....

```
letters.join("/")
```

....

```
letters.pop
```

....

```
letters
```

....

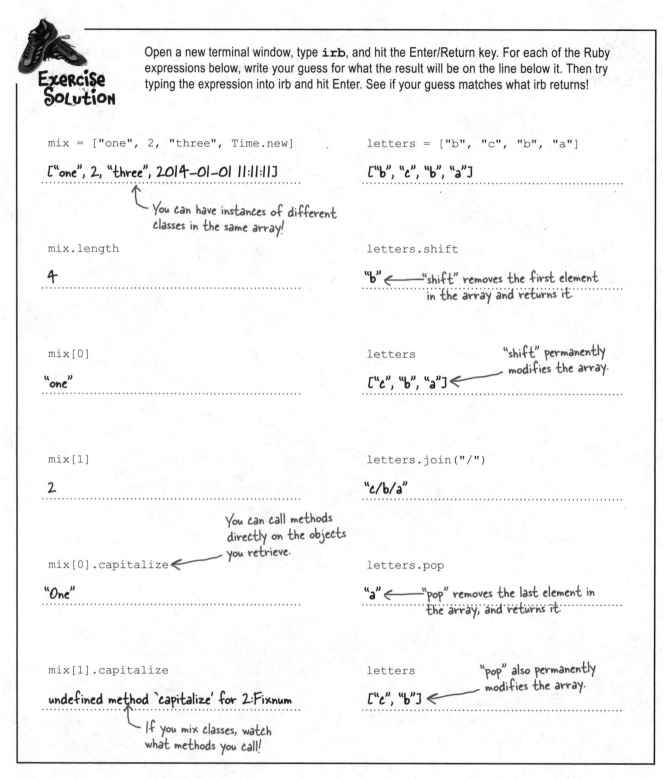

Open a new terminal window, type **irb**, and hit the Enter/Return key. For each of the Ruby expressions below, write your guess for what the result will be on the line below it. Then try typing the expression into irb and hit Enter. See if your guess matches what irb returns!

Exercise Solution

`mix = ["one", 2, "three", Time.new]`

["one", 2, "three", 2014-01-01 11:11:11]

↑ You can have instances of different classes in the same array!

`letters = ["b", "c", "b", "a"]`

["b", "c", "b", "a"]

`mix.length`

4

`letters.shift`

"b" ← "shift" removes the first element in the array and returns it.

`mix[0]`

"one"

`letters`

["c", "b", "a"] ← "shift" permanently modifies the array.

`mix[1]`

2

`letters.join("/")`

"c/b/a"

You can call methods directly on the objects you retrieve.

`mix[0].capitalize` ←

"One"

`letters.pop`

"a" ← "pop" removes the last element in the array, and returns it.

`mix[1].capitalize`

undefined method `capitalize' for 2:Fixnum

↑ If you mix classes, watch what methods you call!

`letters`

["c", "b"] ← "pop" also permanently modifies the array.

Looping over the items in an array

Right now, we can only access the particular array indexes that we specify in our code. Just to print all the prices in an array, we have to write this:

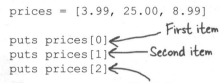

```
prices = [3.99, 25.00, 8.99]

puts prices[0]    ← First item
puts prices[1]    ← Second item
puts prices[2]    ←
                    Third item
```

That won't work when the arrays get very large, or when we don't know their size beforehand.

But we can use a `while` loop to process *all* of an array's elements, one at a time.

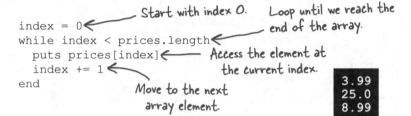

```
index = 0                          ← Start with index 0.    Loop until we reach the
while index < prices.length        ←                         end of the array.
  puts prices[index]               ← Access the element at
  index += 1                       ←    the current index.
end                                                            3.99
        Move to the next                                       25.0
        array element.                                         8.99
```

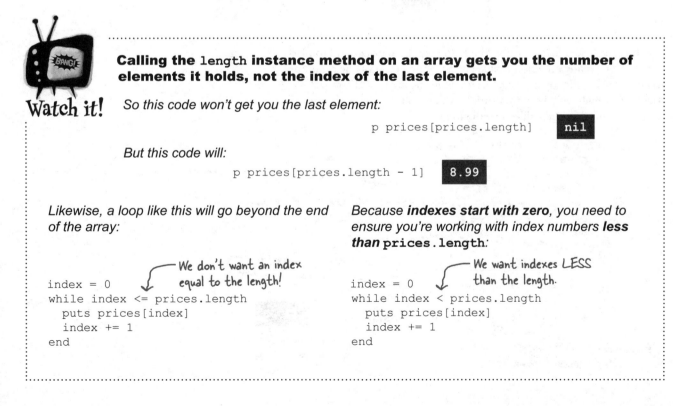

Calling the `length` instance method on an array gets you the number of elements it holds, not the index of the last element.

Watch it!

So this code won't get you the last element:

```
p prices[prices.length]
```
`nil`

But this code will:

```
p prices[prices.length - 1]
```
`8.99`

Likewise, a loop like this will go beyond the end of the array:

```
index = 0                          ← We don't want an index
while index <= prices.length         equal to the length!
  puts prices[index]
  index += 1
end
```

Because **indexes start with zero**, you need to ensure you're working with index numbers **less than `prices.length`**:

```
index = 0                          ← We want indexes LESS
while index < prices.length          than the length.
  puts prices[index]
  index += 1
end
```

The repeating loop

Now that we understand how to store the prices from an order in an array, and how to use a `while` loop to process each of those prices, it's time to work on the three methods your client needs:

☐ Given an array of prices, add them all together and return the total.

☐ Given an array of prices, subtract each price from the customer's account balance.

☐ Given an array of prices, reduce each item's price by 1/3, and print the savings.

The first requested feature is the ability to take these prices and total them. We'll create a method that keeps a running total of the amounts in an array. It will loop over each element in the array and add it to a total (which we'll keep in a variable). After all the elements are processed, the method will return the total.

```ruby
def total(prices)        The total starts at 0.
  amount = 0             Start at the first array index.
  index = 0
  while index < prices.length        While we're still within the array...
    amount += prices[index]          Add the current price
    index += 1                       to the total.
  end
  amount               Move to the next price.
end          Return the total.              Create an array holding
                                             prices from our order.
prices = [3.99, 25.00, 8.99]

puts format("%.2f", total(prices))          37.98

Ensure the correct number          Pass our array of prices
of decimal places is shown.        to the method and
                                   format the result.
```

The repeating loop (continued)

We need a second method that can process a refund for orders. It needs to loop through each item in an array, and subtract the amount from the customer's account balance.

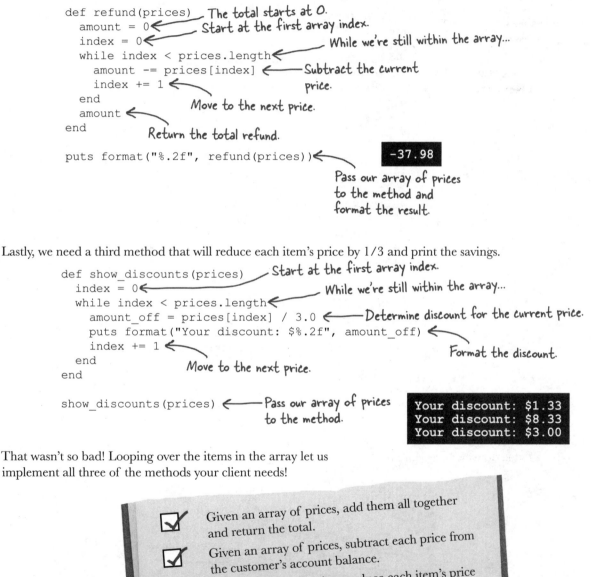

```
def refund(prices)          The total starts at 0.
   amount = 0          Start at the first array index.
   index = 0
                                While we're still within the array...
   while index < prices.length
     amount -= prices[index]      Subtract the current
     index += 1                   price.
   end                  Move to the next price.
   amount
end              Return the total refund.

puts format("%.2f", refund(prices))
```

    -37.98

Pass our array of prices
to the method and
format the result.

Lastly, we need a third method that will reduce each item's price by 1/3 and print the savings.

```
def show_discounts(prices)      Start at the first array index.
   index = 0
                                While we're still within the array...
   while index < prices.length
     amount_off = prices[index] / 3.0      Determine discount for the current price.
     puts format("Your discount: $%.2f", amount_off)
     index += 1                  Format the discount.
   end
end       Move to the next price.

show_discounts(prices)      Pass our array of prices
                            to the method.
```

    Your discount: $1.33
    Your discount: $8.33
    Your discount: $3.00

That wasn't so bad! Looping over the items in the array let us implement all three of the methods your client needs!

- ☑ Given an array of prices, add them all together and return the total.
- ☑ Given an array of prices, subtract each price from the customer's account balance.
- ☑ Given an array of prices, reduce each item's price by 1/3, and print the savings.

The repeating loop (continued)

If we look at the three methods together, though, you'll notice there's a
lot of duplicated code. And it all seems to be related to looping through
the array of prices. We've highlighted the duplicated lines below.

Highlighted lines are duplicated
among the three methods.

This line in the middle
differs, though...

```ruby
def total(prices)
    amount = 0
    index = 0
    while index < prices.length
        amount += prices[index]
        index += 1
    end
    amount
end
```

```ruby
def refund(prices)
    amount = 0
    index = 0
    while index < prices.length
        amount -= prices[index]
        index += 1
    end
    amount
end
```

Differs...

```ruby
def show_discounts(prices)
    index = 0
    while index < prices.length
        amount_off = prices[index] / 3.0
        puts format("Your discount: $%.2f", amount_off)
        index += 1
    end
end
```

Differs...

This is definitely a violation of the DRY (Don't Repeat Yourself) principle.
We need to go back to the drawing board and refactor these methods.

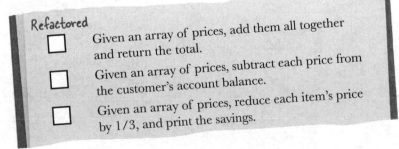

Refactored

- [ ] Given an array of prices, add them all together and return the total.
- [ ] Given an array of prices, subtract each price from the customer's account balance.
- [ ] Given an array of prices, reduce each item's price by 1/3, and print the savings.

Eliminating repetition...the WRONG way...

Our `total`, `refund`, and `show_discounts` methods have a fair amount of repeated code related to looping over array elements. It would be nice if we could extract the repeated code out into another method, and have `total`, `refund`, and `show_discounts` call it.

But a method that combines *all* the logic in `total`, `refund`, and `show_variables` would be *really* cluttered... Sure, the code for the loop *itself* is repeated, but the code in the *middle* of the loop is all different. Also, the `total` and `refund` methods need a variable to track the total amount, but `show_discounts` doesn't.

Let's demonstrate exactly *how* awful such a method would look. (We want you to fully appreciate it when we show you a better solution.) We'll try writing a method with an extra parameter, `operation`. We'll use the value in `operation` to switch which variables we use, and what code gets run in the middle of the loop.

```
def do_something_with_every_item(array, operation)

    if operation == "total" or operation == "refund"
        amount = 0
    end
    index = 0
    while index < array.length

        if operation == "total"
           amount += array[index]
        elsif operation == "refund"
           amount -= array[index]
        elsif operation == "show discounts"
           amount_off = array[index] / 3.0
           puts format("Your discount: $%.2f", amount_off)
        end

        index += 1
    end

    if operation == "total" or operation == "refund"
        return amount
    end

end
```

"operation" should be set to "total", "refund", or "show discounts". Don't make a typo!

We won't need this variable for the "show discounts" operation.

Here's the start of the loop—no more duplication!

Use the correct logic for the current operation.

We don't return the value of this variable for "show discounts".

We warned you it would be bad. We've got `if` statements all over the place, each checking the value of the `operation` parameter. We've got an `amount` variable that we use in some cases, but not others. And we return a value in some cases, but not others. The code is ugly, and it's way too easy to make a mistake when calling it.

But if you *don't* write your code this way, how will you set up the variables you need prior to running the loop? And how will you execute the code you need in the *middle* of the loop?

Chunks of code?

The problem is that the repeated code at the top and bottom of each method *surrounds* the code that needs to change.

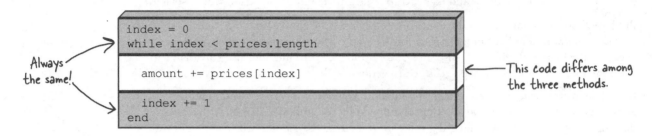

Always the same!

```
index = 0
while index < prices.length

    amount += prices[index]

    index += 1
end
```

This code differs among the three methods.

It would sure be nice if we could take those other chunks of code that *vary*...

```
amount -= prices[index]
```

```
amount_off = prices[index] / 3.0
puts format("Your discount: $%.2f", amount_off)
```

...and *swap* them into the middle of the array loop code. That way we could keep just *one copy* of the code that's always the same.

Keep this.

Instead of this...

...use this!

```
index = 0
while index < prices.length
```

```
amount_off = prices[index] / 3.0
puts format("Your discount: $%.2f", amount_off)
```

```
    index += 1
end
```

Keep this.

```
amount += prices[index]
```

Blocks

What if we could pass a chunk of **code** into a method, like it was an argument? We could put the looping code at the top and bottom of the method, and then in the middle, we could run the code that was passed in!

It turns out we can do just that, using Ruby's <u>blocks</u>.

A **block** is a chunk of code that you associate with a method call. While the method runs, it can *invoke* (execute) the block one or more times. *Methods and blocks work in tandem to process your data.*

Blocks are mind-bending stuff. But stick with it!

We won't mince words. Blocks are going to be the hardest part of this book. Even if you've programmed in other languages, you've probably never seen anything like blocks. But *stick with it*, because the payoff is *big*.

Imagine if, for all the methods you have to write for the rest of your career, someone else *wrote half of the code for you*. For free. *They'd* write all the tedious stuff at the beginning and end, and just leave a little blank space in the middle for you to insert *your* code, the clever code, the code that runs your business.

If we told you that blocks can give you that, you'd be willing to do whatever it takes to learn them, right?

Well, here's what you'll have to do: be patient, and persistent. We're here to help. We'll look at each concept repeatedly, from different angles. We'll provide exercises for practice. Make sure to *do them*, because they'll help you understand and remember how blocks work.

A few hours of hard work now are going to pay dividends for the rest of your Ruby career, we promise. Let's get to it!

When calling a method, you can provide a block. The method can then invoke the code in that block.

Defining a method that takes blocks

Blocks and methods work in tandem. In fact, you can't *have* a block without also having a method to accept it. So, to start, let's define a method that works with blocks.

(On this page, we're going to show you how to use an ampersand, `&`, to accept a block, and the `call` method to call that block. This isn't the quickest way to work with blocks, but it *does* make it more obvious what's going on. We'll show you `yield`, which is more commonly used, in a few pages!)

Since we're just starting off, we'll keep it simple. The method will print a message, invoke the block it received, and print another message.

This method takes a
block as a parameter!

```ruby
def my_method(&my_block)
    puts "We're in the method, about to invoke your block!"
    my_block.call    ←——The "call" method calls the block.
    puts "We're back in the method!"
end
```

If you place an ampersand before the last parameter in a method definition, Ruby will expect a block to be attached to any call to that method. It will take the block, convert it to an object, and store it in that parameter.

```ruby
def my_method(&my_block)
    ...
end
```

When you call this method with a
block, it will be stored in "my_block".

Remember, a block is just a chunk of code that you pass into a method. To execute that code, stored blocks have a `call` instance method that you can call on them. The `call` method invokes the block's code.

```ruby
def my_method(&my_block)
    ...
    my_block.call    ←——Run the block's code.
    ...
end
```

No ampersand; that's
only used when you're
defining the parameter.

Okay, we know, you still haven't *seen* an actual block, and you're going crazy wondering what they look like. Now that the setup's out of the way, we can show you...

Your first block

Are you ready? Here it comes: your first glimpse of a Ruby block.

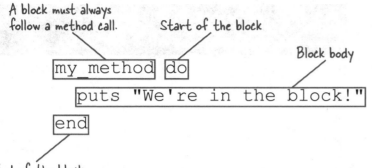

A block must always follow a method call.

Start of the block

Block body

```
my_method do
        puts "We're in the block!"
end
```

End of the block

There it is! Like we said, a block is just a *chunk of code* that you pass to a method. We invoke `my_method`, which we just defined, and then place a block immediately following it. The method will receive the block in its `my_block` parameter.

- The start of the block is marked with the keyword `do`, and the end is marked by the keyword `end`.

- The block *body* consists of one or more lines of Ruby code between `do` and `end`. You can place any code you like here.

- When the block is called from the method, the code in the block body will be executed.

- After the block runs, control returns to the method that invoked it.

there are no
Dumb Questions

Q: Can I use a block by itself?

A: No, that will give you a syntax error. Blocks are meant to be used together with methods.

```
do
    puts "Woooo!"
end
```

```
syntax error,
unexpected
keyword_do_block
```

This shouldn't ever get in your way; if you're writing a block that isn't associated with a method call, then whatever you're trying to express can probably be done with standalone Ruby statements.

So we can call `my_method` and pass it the above block:

```
def my_method(&my_block)
  puts "We're in the method, about to invoke your block!"
  my_block.call
  puts "We're back in the method!"
end

my_method do
  puts "We're in the block!"
end
```

The call to my_method

The block. It will be stored in the "my_block" parameter.

…and here's the output we'd see:

```
We're in the method, about to invoke your block!
We're in the block!
We're back in the method!
```

Flow of control between a method and block

We declared a method named `my_method`, called it with a block, and got
this output:

```
my_method do
    puts "We're in the block!"
end
```

```
We're in the method, about to invoke your block!
We're in the block!
We're back in the method!
```

Let's break down what happened in the method and block, step by step.

1 The first `puts` statement in `my_method`'s body runs.

The method:

```
def my_method(&my_block)
  puts "We're in the method, about to invoke your block!"
  my_block.call
  puts "We're back in the method!"
end
```

The block:

```
do
    puts "We're in the block!"
end
```

```
We're in the method, about to invoke your block!
```

2 The `my_block.call` expression runs, and control is passed to the block.
The `puts` expression in the block's body runs.

```
def my_method(&my_block)
  puts "We're in the method, about to invoke your block!"      do
  my_block.call                                                    puts "We're in the block!"
  puts "We're back in the method!"                             end
end
```

```
We're in the block!
```

3 When the statements within the block body have all run, control returns to
the method. The second call to `puts` within `my_method`'s body runs, and
then the method returns.

```
def my_method(&my_block)
  puts "We're in the method, about to invoke your block!"      do
  my_block.call                                                    puts "We're in the block!"
  puts "We're back in the method!"                             end
end
```

```
We're back in the method!
```

Calling the same method with different blocks

You can pass *many different blocks* to a *single method*.

We can pass different blocks to the method we just defined, and do different things:

```
my_method do
  puts "It's a block party!"
end
```
```
We're in the method, about to invoke your block!
It's a block party!
We're back in the method!
```

```
my_method do
  puts "Wooooo!"
end
```
```
We're in the method, about to invoke your block!
Wooooo!
We're back in the method!
```

The code in the method is always the *same*, but you can *change* the code you provide in the block.

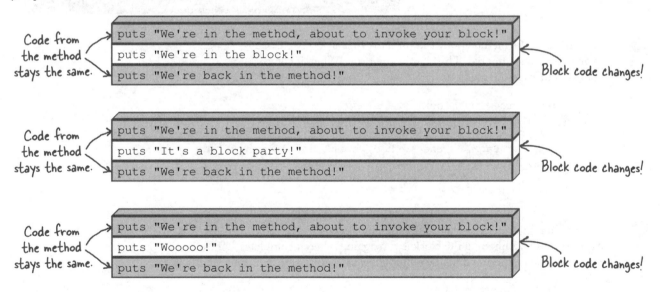

Code from the method stays the same.
```
puts "We're in the method, about to invoke your block!"
puts "We're in the block!"
puts "We're back in the method!"
```
Block code changes!

Code from the method stays the same.
```
puts "We're in the method, about to invoke your block!"
puts "It's a block party!"
puts "We're back in the method!"
```
Block code changes!

Code from the method stays the same.
```
puts "We're in the method, about to invoke your block!"
puts "Wooooo!"
puts "We're back in the method!"
```
Block code changes!

Calling a block multiple times

A method can invoke a block as many times as it wants.

This method is just like our previous one, except that it has *two*
`my_block.call` expressions:

Declaring another ———→
method that
takes a block.

```
def twice(&my_block)
  puts "In the method, about to call the block!"
  my_block.call  ←——— Call the block.
  puts "Back in the method, about to call the block again!"
  my_block.call  ←——— Call the block AGAIN.
  puts "Back in the method, about to return!"
end

twice do
  puts "Woooo!"
end
```

Calling the method ———→
and passing it a block.

The method name is appropriate: as you can see from the output, the method does indeed call our block twice!

```
In the method, about to call the block!
Woooo!
Back in the method, about to call the block again!
Woooo!
Back in the method, about to return!
```

1 Statements in the method body run until the first `my_block.call`
expression is encountered. The block is then run. When it completes,
control returns to the method.

```
def twice(&my_block)
  puts "In the method, about to call the block!"
  my_block.call                                              do
  puts "Back in the method, about to call the block again!"    puts "Woooo!"
  my_block.call                                              end
  puts "Back in the method, about to return!"
end
```

2 The method body resumes running. When the second `my_block.call`
expression is encountered, the block is run again. When it completes, control
returns to the method so that any remaining statements there can run.

```
def twice(&my_block)
  puts "In the method, about to call the block!"
  my_block.call
  puts "Back in the method, about to call the block again!"    do
  my_block.call                                                  puts "Woooo!"
  puts "Back in the method, about to return!"                  end
end
```

Block parameters

We learned back in Chapter 2 that when defining a Ruby method, you can specify that it will accept one or more parameters:

```ruby
def print_parameters(p1, p2)
  puts p1, p2
end
```

You're probably also aware that you can pass arguments when calling the method that will determine the value of those parameters.

```ruby
print_parameters("one", "two")
```

In a similar vein, a method can pass one or more arguments to a block. Block parameters are similar to method parameters; they're values that are passed in when the block is run, and that can be accessed within the block body.

there are no
Dumb Questions

Q: Can I define a block once, and use it across many methods?

A: You can do something like this using Ruby *procs* (which are beyond the scope of this book). But it's not something you'll want to do in practice. A block is intimately tied to a particular method call, so much that a particular block will usually only work with a single method.

Q: Can a method take more than one block at the same time?

A: No. A single block is by far the most common use case, to the point that it's not worth the syntactic mess it would create for Ruby to support multiple blocks. If you ever want to do this, you could also use Ruby procs (but again, that's beyond the scope of this book).

Arguments to `call` get forwarded on to the block:

You can have a block accept one or more parameters from the method by defining them between vertical bar (|) characters at the start of the block:

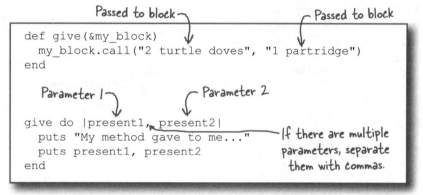

So, when we call our method and provide a block, the arguments to `call` are passed into the block as parameters, which then get printed. When the block completes, control returns to the method, as normal.

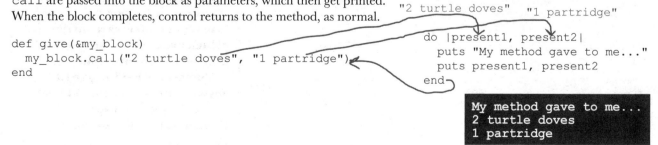

```ruby
def give(&my_block)
  my_block.call("2 turtle doves", "1 partridge")
end
```

Using the "yield" keyword

So far, we've been treating blocks like an argument to our methods. We've been declaring an extra method parameter that takes a block as an object, then using the `call` method on that object.

```
def twice(&my_block)
  my_block.call
  my_block.call
end
```

We mentioned that this wasn't the easiest way to accept blocks, though. Now, let's learn the less obvious but more concise way: the `yield` keyword.

The `yield` keyword will find and invoke the block a method was called with—there's no need to declare a parameter to accept the block.

This method is functionally equivalent to the one above:

```
def twice
  yield
  yield
end
```

Just like with `call`, we can also give one or more arguments to `yield`, which will be passed to the block as parameters. Again, these methods are functionally equivalent:

```
def give(&my_block)
  my_block.call("2 turtle doves", "1 partridge")
end

def give
  yield "2 turtle doves", "1 partridge"
end
```

Conventional Wisdom

Declaring a &block parameter is useful in a few rare instances (which are beyond the scope of this book). But now that you understand what the yield keyword does, you should just use that in most cases. It's cleaner and easier to read.

Block formats

So far, we've been using the `do...end` block format for blocks. Ruby has a second block format, though: "curly brace" style. You'll see both formats being used "in the wild," so you should learn to recognize both.

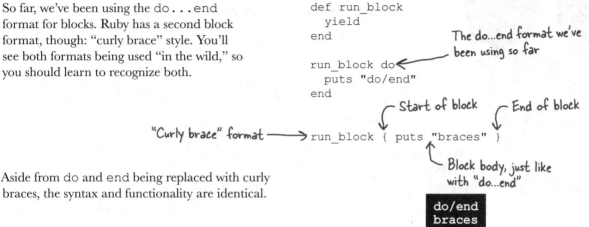

```
def run_block
  yield
end

run_block do
  puts "do/end"
end
```

The do...end format we've been using so far

"Curly brace" format ⟶ `run_block { puts "braces" }`

Start of block · End of block

Block body, just like with "do...end"

do/end braces

Aside from `do` and `end` being replaced with curly braces, the syntax and functionality are identical.

And just as `do...end` blocks can accept parameters, so can curly-brace blocks:

```
def take_this
  yield "present"
end

take_this do |thing|
  puts "do/end block got #{thing}"
end

take_this { |thing| puts "braces block got #{thing}" }
```

```
do/end block got present
braces block got present
```

By the way, you've probably noticed that all our `do...end` blocks span multiple lines, but our curly-brace blocks all appear on a single line. This follows another convention that much of the Ruby community has adopted. It's valid *syntax* to do it the other way:

Breaks convention!

```
take_this { |thing|
  puts "braces: got #{thing}"
}
take_this do |thing| puts "do/end: got #{thing}" end
```

Breaks convention (and is really ugly)!

```
braces: got present
do/end: got present
```

But not only is that out of line with the convention, it's really ugly.

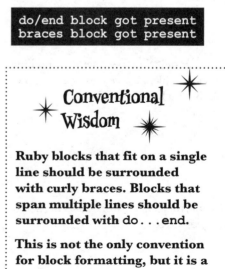

Conventional Wisdom

Ruby blocks that fit on a single line should be surrounded with curly braces. Blocks that span multiple lines should be surrounded with `do...end`.

This is not the only convention for block formatting, but it is a common one.

Fireside Chats

Tonight's talk: **A method and a block talk about how they became associated with each other.**

Method:

Thanks for coming, Block! I called you here tonight so we could educate people on how blocks and methods work together. I've had people ask me exactly what you contribute to the relationship, and I think we can clear those questions up for everyone.

Block:

Sure, Method! I'm here to help whenever you call.

So most parts of a method's job are pretty clearly defined. My task, for example, is to loop through each item in an array.

Right. Not a very glamorous job, but an important one.

Sure! It's a task *lots* of developers need done; there's a lot of demand for my services. But then I encounter a problem: *what do I do* with each of those array elements? Every developer needs something different! And that's where blocks come in...

Precisely. Every developer can write their *own* block that describes exactly what they need done with each element in the array.

I know another method that does nothing but open and close a file. He's *very* good at that part of the task. But he has *no clue* what to do with the *contents* of the file...

...and so he calls on a block, right? And the block prints the file contents, or updates them, or whatever else the developer needs done. It's a great working relationship!

I handle the general work that's needed on a *wide variety* of tasks...

And I handle the logic that's specific to an *individual* task.

Exercise

Here are three Ruby method definitions, each of which takes a block:

```ruby
def call_block(&block)
  puts 1
  block.call
  puts 3
end
```

```ruby
def call_twice
  puts 1
  yield
  yield
  puts 3
end
```

```ruby
def pass_parameters_to_block
  puts 1
  yield 9, 3
  puts 3
end
```

And here are several calls to the above methods. Match each method call to the output it produces.

(We've done the first one for you.)

B ......
```ruby
call_block do
  puts 2
end
```

......
```ruby
call_block { puts "two" }
```

......
```ruby
call_twice { puts 2 }
```

......
```ruby
call_twice do
  puts "two"
end
```

......
```ruby
pass_parameters_to_block do |param1, param2|
  puts param1 + param2
end
```

......
```ruby
pass_parameters_to_block do |param1, param2|
  puts param1 / param2
end
```

A
```
1
2
2
3
```

B
```
1
2
3
```

C
```
1
3
3
```

D
```
1
12
3
```

E
```
1
two
3
```

F
```
1
two
two
3
```

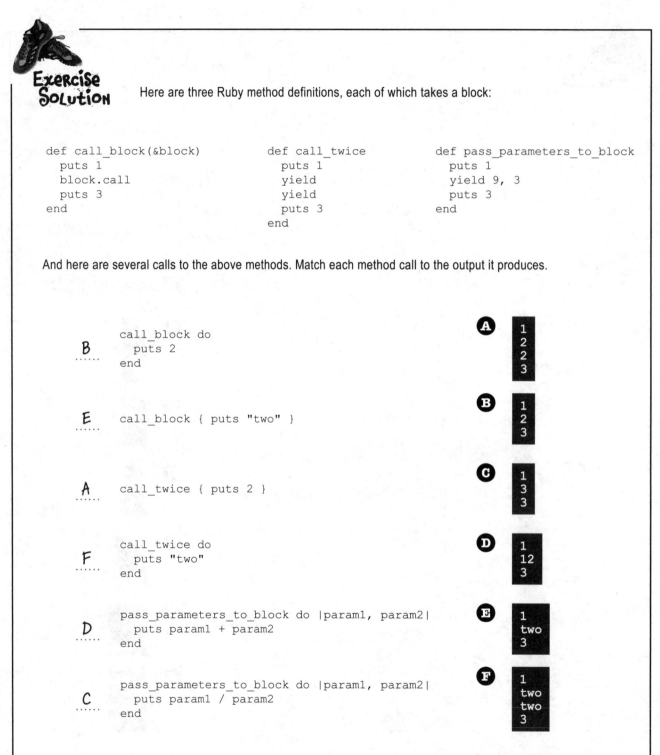

Here are three Ruby method definitions, each of which takes a block:

```ruby
def call_block(&block)      def call_twice        def pass_parameters_to_block
  puts 1                      puts 1                puts 1
  block.call                  yield                 yield 9, 3
  puts 3                      yield                 puts 3
end                          puts 3               end
                           end
```

And here are several calls to the above methods. Match each method call to the output it produces.

B
```ruby
call_block do
  puts 2
end
```

A
```
1
2
2
3
```

E
```ruby
call_block { puts "two" }
```

B
```
1
2
3
```

A
```ruby
call_twice { puts 2 }
```

C
```
1
3
3
```

F
```ruby
call_twice do
  puts "two"
end
```

D
```
1
12
3
```

D
```ruby
pass_parameters_to_block do |param1, param2|
  puts param1 + param2
end
```

E
```
1
two
3
```

C
```ruby
pass_parameters_to_block do |param1, param2|
  puts param1 / param2
end
```

F
```
1
two
two
3
```

The "each" method

We had a lot to learn in order to get here: how to write a block, how a method calls a block, how a method can pass parameters to a block. And now, it's finally time to take a good, long look at the method that will let us get rid of that repeated loop code in our `total`, `refund`, and `show_discounts` methods. It's an instance method that appears on every `Array` object, and it's called `each`.

You've seen that a method can yield to a block more than once, with different values each time:

```
def my_method
  yield 1
  yield 2
  yield 3
end

my_method { |param| puts param }
```

The `each` method uses this feature of Ruby to loop through each of the items in an array, yielding them to a block, one at a time.

```
["a", "b", "c"].each { |param| puts param }
```

```
a
b
c
```

If we were to write our own method that works like `each`, it would look very similar to the code we've been writing all along:

```
class Array

  def each
    index = 0
    while index < self.length
      yield self[index]
      index += 1
    end
  end

end
```

This is just like the loops in our "total", "refund", and "show_discounts" methods!

Remember, "self" refers to the current object—in this case, the current array.

The key difference: we yield the current element to a block!

Then move to the next element, just like before.

We loop through each element in the array, just like in our `total`, `refund`, and `show_discounts` methods. The key difference is that instead of putting code to process the current array element in the *middle of the loop*, we use the `yield` keyword to *pass the element to a block*.

The "each" method, step-by-step

We're using the `each` method and a block to
process each of the items in an array:

```
["a", "b", "c"].each { |param| puts param }
```

a
b
c

Let's go step-by-step through each of the calls to the block and see what it's doing.

1 For the first pass through the `while` loop, `index` is set to 0, so the
first element of the array gets yielded to the block as a parameter. In
the block body, the parameter gets printed. Then control returns to
the method, `index` gets incremented, and the `while` loop continues.

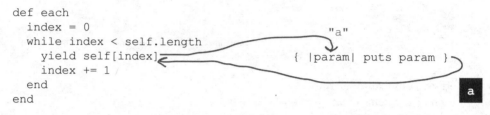

2 Now, on the second pass through the `while` loop, `index` is set to
1, so the *second* element in the array will be yielded to the block as a
parameter. As before, the block body prints the parameter, control
then returns to the method, and the loop continues.

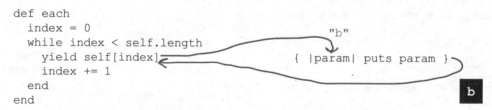

3 After the third array element gets yielded to the block for printing and
control returns to the method, the `while` loop ends, because we've
reached the end of the array. No more loop iterations means no more
calls to the block; we're done!

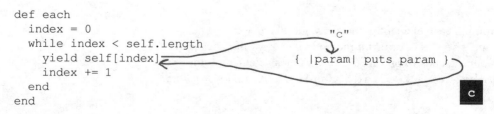

That's it! We've found a method that can handle the repeated looping code, and yet allows
us to run our own code in the middle of the loop (using a block). Let's put it to use!

DRYing up our code with "each" and blocks

Our invoicing system requires us to implement these three methods. All three of them have nearly identical code for looping through the contents of an array.

It's been difficult to get rid of that duplication, though, because all three methods have *different* code in the *middle* of that loop.

Highlighted lines are duplicated among the three methods. ───→

This line in the middle ───→ differs, though...

```
def total(prices)
  amount = 0
  index = 0
  while index < prices.length
    amount += prices[index]
    index += 1
  end
  amount
end

def refund(prices)
  amount = 0
  index = 0
  while index < prices.length
    amount -= prices[index]
    index += 1
  end
  amount
end

def show_discounts(prices)
  index = 0
  while index < prices.length
    amount_off = prices[index] / 3.0
    puts format("Your discount: $%.2f", amount_off)
    index += 1
  end
end
```

Differs... ───→

Differs... {

But now we've finally mastered the `each` method, which loops over the elements in an array and passes them to a block for processing.

```
["a", "b", "c"].each { |param| puts param }
```

a
b
c

Let's see if we can use `each` to refactor our three methods and eliminate the duplication.

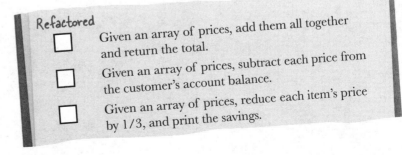

Refactored

☐ Given an array of prices, add them all together and return the total.

☐ Given an array of prices, subtract each price from the customer's account balance.

☐ Given an array of prices, reduce each item's price by 1/3, and print the savings.

DRYing up our code with "each" and blocks (continued)

First up for refactoring is the `total` method. Just like the others, it contains code for looping over prices stored in an array. In the middle of that looping code, `total` adds the current price to a total amount.

The `each` method looks like it will be perfect for getting rid of the repeated looping code! We can just take the code in the middle that adds to the total, and place it in a block that's passed to `each`.

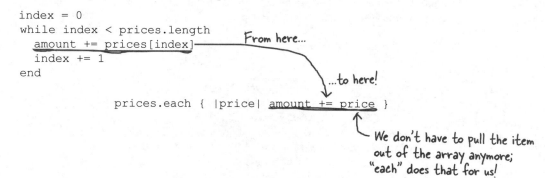

```
index = 0
while index < prices.length
  amount += prices[index]        From here...
  index += 1
end
                                                  ...to here!

            prices.each { |price| amount += price }

                                    We don't have to pull the item
                                    out of the array anymore;
                                    "each" does that for us!
```

Let's redefine our `total` method to utilize `each`, then try it out.

```
def total(prices)        Start the total at 0.
  amount = 0
  prices.each do |price|      Process each price.
    amount += price        Add the current price
  end                        to the total.
  amount
end        Return the final total.

prices = [3.99, 25.00, 8.99]

puts format("%.2f", total(prices))     37.98
```

Perfect! There's our total amount. The `each` method worked!

DRYing up our code with "each" and blocks (continued)

For each element in the array, each passes it as a parameter to the block. The code in the block adds the current array element to the amount variable, and then control returns back to each.

```ruby
prices = [3.99, 25.00, 8.99]
puts format("%.2f", total(prices))
```

```
37.98
```

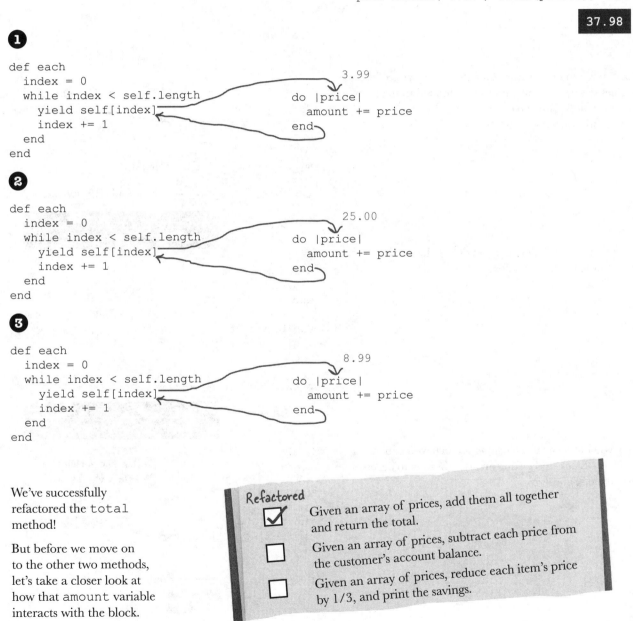

❶

```ruby
def each
  index = 0
  while index < self.length          3.99
    yield self[index]          do |price|
    index += 1                   amount += price
  end                          end
end
```

❷

```ruby
def each
  index = 0
  while index < self.length          25.00
    yield self[index]          do |price|
    index += 1                   amount += price
  end                          end
end
```

❸

```ruby
def each
  index = 0
  while index < self.length          8.99
    yield self[index]          do |price|
    index += 1                   amount += price
  end                          end
end
```

We've successfully refactored the total method!

But before we move on to the other two methods, let's take a closer look at how that amount variable interacts with the block.

Refactored

☑ Given an array of prices, add them all together and return the total.

☐ Given an array of prices, subtract each price from the customer's account balance.

☐ Given an array of prices, reduce each item's price by 1/3, and print the savings.

Blocks and variable scope

We should point something out about our new `total` method. Did you notice that we use the `amount` variable both *inside* and *outside* the block?

```ruby
def total(prices)
  amount = 0
  prices.each do |price|
    amount += price
  end
  amount
end
```

As you may remember from Chapter 2, the *scope* of local variables defined within a method is limited to the body of that method. You can't access variables that are local to the method from *outside* the method.

The same is true of blocks, *if* you define the variable for the first time *inside* the block.

But, if you define a variable *before* a block, you can access it *inside* the block body. You can *also* continue to access it *after* the block ends!

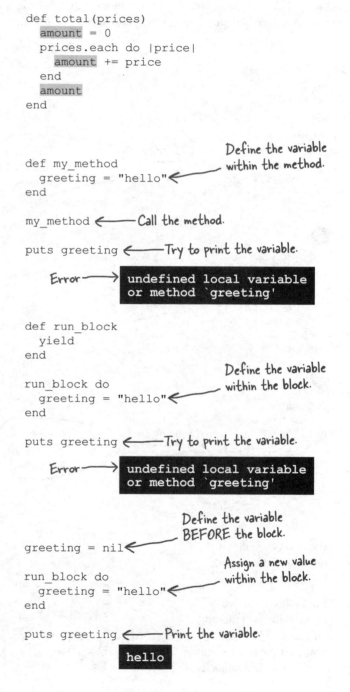

```ruby
def my_method
  greeting = "hello"
end
```
Define the variable within the method.

```ruby
my_method
```
Call the method.

```ruby
puts greeting
```
Try to print the variable.

Error → `undefined local variable or method 'greeting'`

```ruby
def run_block
  yield
end
```

```ruby
run_block do
  greeting = "hello"
end
```
Define the variable within the block.

```ruby
puts greeting
```
Try to print the variable.

Error → `undefined local variable or method 'greeting'`

```ruby
greeting = nil
```
Define the variable BEFORE the block.

```ruby
run_block do
  greeting = "hello"
end
```
Assign a new value within the block.

```ruby
puts greeting
```
Print the variable.

`hello`

Blocks and variable scope (continued)

Since Ruby blocks can access variables declared outside the block body, our `total` method is able to use `each` with a block to update the amount variable.

We can call `total` like this:

```
total([3.99, 25.00, 8.99])
```

```ruby
def total(prices)
  amount = 0
  prices.each do |price|
    amount += price
  end
  amount
end
```

The `amount` variable is set to 0, and then `each` is called on the array. Each of the values in the array is passed to the block. Each time the block is called, `amount` is updated:

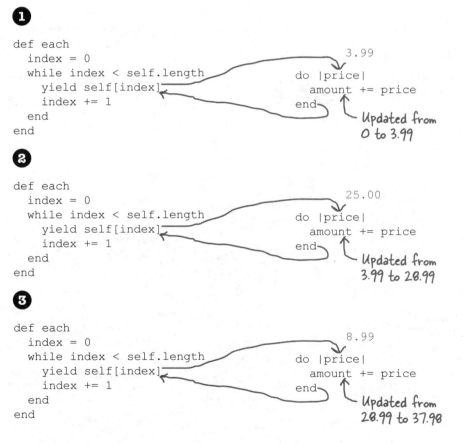

1

```ruby
def each
  index = 0
  while index < self.length
    yield self[index]
    index += 1
  end
end
```
3.99
```
do |price|
  amount += price
end
```
Updated from 0 to 3.99

2

```ruby
def each
  index = 0
  while index < self.length
    yield self[index]
    index += 1
  end
end
```
25.00
```
do |price|
  amount += price
end
```
Updated from 3.99 to 28.99

3

```ruby
def each
  index = 0
  while index < self.length
    yield self[index]
    index += 1
  end
end
```
8.99
```
do |price|
  amount += price
end
```
Updated from 28.99 to 37.98

When the `each` method completes, `amount` is still set to that final value, 37.98. It's that value that gets returned from the method.

there are no
Dumb Questions

Q: Why can blocks access variables that were declared outside their bodies, when methods can't? Isn't that unsafe?

A: A method can be accessed from other places in your program, far from where it was declared (maybe even in a different source file). A block, by contrast, is normally accessible only during the method call it's associated with. A block, and the variables it has access to, is kept in the *same place* in your code. That means you can easily see all the variables a block is interacting with, meaning that accessing them is less prone to nasty surprises.

Using "each" with the "refund" method

We've revised the `total` method to get rid of the repeated loop code. We need to do the same with the `refund` and `show_discounts` methods, and then we'll be done!

The process of updating the `refund` method is very similar to the process we used for `total`. We simply take the specialized code from the middle of the generic loop code, and move it to a block that's passed to `each`.

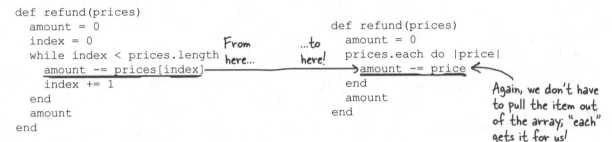

```
def refund(prices)
  amount = 0
  index = 0                    From      ...to    def refund(prices)
  while index < prices.length  here...   here!      amount = 0
    amount -= prices[index]                          prices.each do |price|
    index += 1                                         amount -= price
  end                                                end
  amount                                             amount
end                                                end
```

Again, we don't have to pull the item out of the array; "each" gets it for us!

Much cleaner, and calls to the method still work just the same as before!

```
prices = [3.99, 25.00, 8.99]
puts format("%.2f", refund(prices))
```

 `-37.98`

Within the call to `each` and the block, the flow of control looks very similar to what we saw in the `total` method:

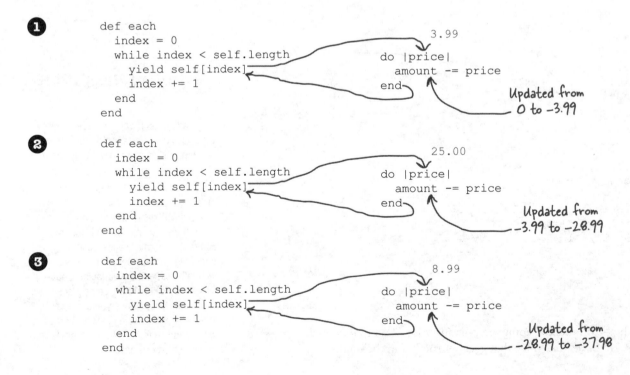

```
1   def each                                3.99
      index = 0
      while index < self.length     do |price|
        yield self[index]             amount -= price
        index += 1                  end
      end
    end                                           Updated from
                                                  0 to -3.99


2   def each                                25.00
      index = 0
      while index < self.length     do |price|
        yield self[index]             amount -= price
        index += 1                  end
      end
    end                                           Updated from
                                                  -3.99 to -28.99


3   def each                                8.99
      index = 0
      while index < self.length     do |price|
        yield self[index]             amount -= price
        index += 1                  end
      end
    end                                           Updated from
                                                  -28.99 to -37.98
```

Using "each" with our last method

One more method, and we're done! Again, with `show_discounts`, it's a matter of taking the code out of the middle of the loop and moving it into a block that's passed to `each`.

```ruby
def show_discounts(prices)
  index = 0
  while index < prices.length
    amount_off = prices[index] / 3.0
    puts format("Your discount: $%.2f", amount_off)
    index += 1
  end
end
```

From here...

To here!

```ruby
def show_discounts(prices)
  prices.each do |price|
    amount_off = price / 3.0
    puts format("Your discount: $%.2f", amount_off)
  end
end
```

Again, as far as users of your method are concerned, no one will notice you've changed a thing!

```ruby
prices = [3.99, 25.00, 8.99]
show_discounts(prices)
```

```
Your discount: $1.33
Your discount: $8.33
Your discount: $3.00
```

Here's what the calls to the block look like:

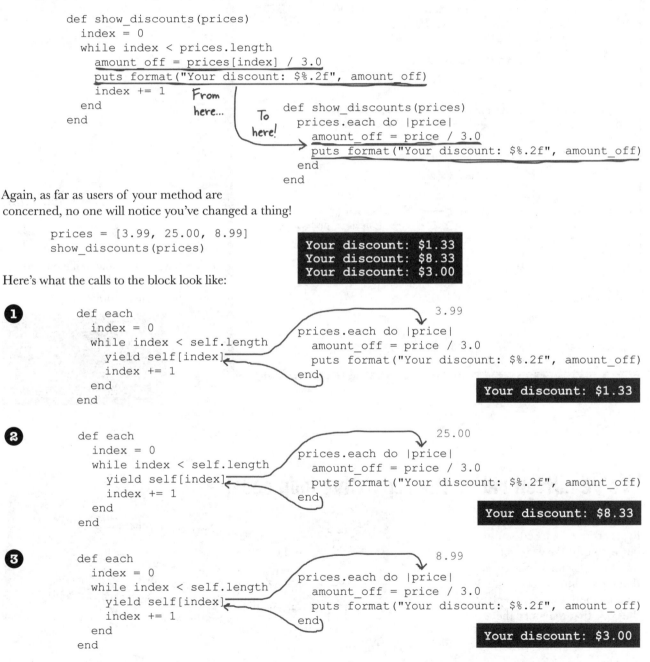

1
```ruby
def each
  index = 0
  while index < self.length
    yield self[index]
    index += 1
  end
end
```

3.99
```ruby
prices.each do |price|
  amount_off = price / 3.0
  puts format("Your discount: $%.2f", amount_off)
end
```
```
Your discount: $1.33
```

2
```ruby
def each
  index = 0
  while index < self.length
    yield self[index]
    index += 1
  end
end
```

25.00
```ruby
prices.each do |price|
  amount_off = price / 3.0
  puts format("Your discount: $%.2f", amount_off)
end
```
```
Your discount: $8.33
```

3
```ruby
def each
  index = 0
  while index < self.length
    yield self[index]
    index += 1
  end
end
```

8.99
```ruby
prices.each do |price|
  amount_off = price / 3.0
  puts format("Your discount: $%.2f", amount_off)
end
```
```
Your discount: $3.00
```

Our complete invoicing methods

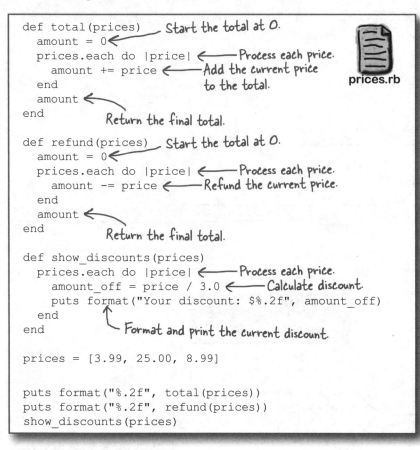

```ruby
def total(prices)
  amount = 0
  prices.each do |price|
    amount += price
  end
  amount
end

def refund(prices)
  amount = 0
  prices.each do |price|
    amount -= price
  end
  amount
end

def show_discounts(prices)
  prices.each do |price|
    amount_off = price / 3.0
    puts format("Your discount: $%.2f", amount_off)
  end
end

prices = [3.99, 25.00, 8.99]


puts format("%.2f", total(prices))
puts format("%.2f", refund(prices))
show_discounts(prices)
```

Start the total at 0.
Process each price.
Add the current price to the total.
Return the final total.

Start the total at 0.
Process each price.
Refund the current price.
Return the final total.

Process each price.
Calculate discount.
Format and print the current discount.

prices.rb

Do this!

Save this code in a file named *prices.rb*. Then try running it from the terminal!

```
$ ruby prices.rb
37.98
-37.98
Your discount: $1.33
Your discount: $8.33
Your discount: $3.00
```

We've gotten rid of the repetitive loop code!

We've done it! We've refactored the repetitive loop code out of our methods! We were able to move the portion of the code that *differed* into blocks, and rely on a method, each, to replace the code that remained the *same!*

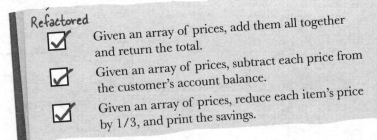

Refactored

☑ Given an array of prices, add them all together and return the total.

☑ Given an array of prices, subtract each price from the customer's account balance.

☑ Given an array of prices, reduce each item's price by 1/3, and print the savings.

Pool Puzzle

Your **job** is to take code snippets from the pool and place them into the blank lines in the code. **Don't** use the same snippet more than once, and you won't need to use all the snippets. Your **goal** is to make code that will run and produce the output shown.

```
def pig_latin(words)

  original_length = 0
  _____ = 0

  words.____ do _____
    puts "Original word: #{word}"
    _____ += word.length
    letters = word.chars
    first_letter = letters.shift
    new_word = "#{letters.join}#{first_letter}ay"
    puts "Pig Latin word: #{_____}"
    _____ += new_word.length
  end

  puts "Total original length: #{_____}"
  puts "Total Pig Latin length: #{new_length}"

end

my_words = ["blocks", "totally", "rock"]
pig_latin(_____)
```

Output:

```
File Edit Window Help
Original word: blocks
Pig Latin word: locksbay
Original word: totally
Pig Latin word: otallytay
Original word: rock
Pig Latin word: ockray
Original total length: 17
Total Pig Latin length: 23
```

Note: each thing from the pool can only be used once!

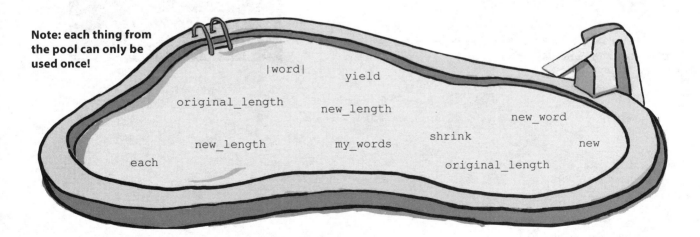

|word| yield

original_length   new_length

new_word

new_length   my_words   shrink   new

each   original_length

Pool Puzzle Solution

```
def pig_latin(words)

  original length = 0
  new_length = 0

  words.each do |word|
    puts "Original word: #{word}"
    original_length += word.length
    letters = word.chars
    first_letter = letters.shift
    new_word = "#{letters.join}#{first_letter}ay"
    puts "Pig Latin word: #{new_word}"
    new_length += new_word.length
  end

  puts "Total original length: #{original_length}"
  puts "Total Pig Latin length: #{new_length}"

end

my_words = ["blocks", "totally", "rock"]
pig_latin(my_words)
```

Output:

```
File Edit Window Help
Original word: blocks
Pig Latin word: locksbay
Original word: totally
Pig Latin word: otallytay
Original word: rock
Pig Latin word: ockray
Original total length: 17
Total Pig Latin length: 23
```

Utilities and appliances, blocks and methods

Imagine two electric appliances: a mixer and a drill. They have very different jobs: one is used for baking, the other for carpentry. And yet they have a very similar need: electricity.

Now, imagine a world where, any time you wanted to use an electric mixer or drill, you had to wire your appliance into the power grid yourself. Sounds tedious (and fairly dangerous), right?

That's why, when your house was built, an electrician came and installed *power outlets* in every room. The outlets provide the same utility (electricity) through the same interface (an electric plug) to very different appliances.

The electrician doesn't know the details of how your mixer or drill works, and he doesn't care. He just uses his skills and training to get the current safely from the electric grid to the outlet.

Likewise, the designers of your appliances don't have to know how to wire a home for electricity. They only need to know how to take power from an outlet and use it to make their devices operate.

You can think of the author of a method that takes a block as being kind of like an electrician. They don't know how the block works, and they don't care. They just use their knowledge of a problem (say, looping through an array's elements) to get the necessary data to the block.

```ruby
def wire
  yield "current"
end
```

You can think of calling a method with a block as being kind of like plugging an appliance into an outlet. Like the outlet supplying power, the block parameters offer a safe, consistent interface for the method to supply data to your block. Your block doesn't have to worry about how the data got there, it just has to process the parameters it's been handed.

Like a power outlet

```ruby
wire { |power| puts "Using #{power} to turn drill bit" }
wire { |power| puts "Using #{power} to spin mixer" }
```

```
Using current to turn drill bit
Using current to spin mixer
```

Not every appliance uses electricity, of course; some require other utilities. There are stoves and furnaces that require gas. There are automatic sprinklers and spray nozzles that use water.

Just as there are many kinds of utilities to supply many kinds of appliances, there are many methods in Ruby that supply data to blocks. The each method was just the beginning. We'll be looking at some of the others over the next chapter.

Your Ruby Toolbox

That's it for Chapter 5! You've added arrays and blocks to your toolbox.

Statements

Methods

Classes

Inheritance

Creating objects

Arrays

An array holds a collection of objects.

Arrays can be any size and can grow or shrink as needed.

Arrays are ordinary Ruby objects and have many useful instance methods.

Blocks

A block is a chunk of code that you associate with a method call.

When a method runs, it can invoke the block it was called with one or more times.

Each time a block finishes running, it returns control to the method that invoked it.

BULLET POINTS

- The index is a number that can be used to retrieve a particular item from an array. An array's index starts with 0.

- You can also use the index to assign a new value to a particular array location.

- The `length` method can be used to get the number of items in an array.

- Ruby blocks are only allowed following a method call.

- There are two ways to write a block: with `do...end` or with curly braces (`{}`).

- You can specify that the last method parameter should be a block by preceding the parameter name with an ampersand (`&`).

- It's more common to use the `yield` keyword, though. You don't have to specify a method parameter to take the block—`yield` will find and invoke it for you.

- A block can receive one or more parameters from the method. Block parameters are similar to method parameters.

- A block can get or update the value of local variables that appear in the same scope as the block.

- Arrays have an `each` method, which invokes a block once for each item in an array.

Up Next...

You haven't seen everything that blocks can do yet! A block can also *return* a value to the method, and methods can use those return methods in a thousand interesting ways. We'll show you all the details in the next chapter!

6 block return values

How Should I Handle This?

Let me go over the list with you... Should I keep the steak? OK, I'll keep it. The chicken? Keep, OK. The liver? Get rid of it? Consider it done!

You've seen only a fraction of the power of blocks. Up until now, the *methods* have just been handing data off to a *block*, and expecting the block to handle everything. But a *block* can also return data to the *method*. This feature lets the method get *directions* from the block, allowing it to do more of the work.

In this chapter, we'll show you some methods that will let you take a *big*, *complicated* collection, and use **block return values** to cut it down to size.

A big collection of words to search through

Word got out on the great work you did on the invoicing program, and your next client has already come in—a movie studio. They release a lot of films each year, and the task of making commercials for all of them is enormous. They want you to write a program that will go through the text of movie reviews, find adjectives that describe a given movie, and generate a collage of those adjectives:

The critics agree, *Hindenburg* is:

"Romantic"

"Thrilling"

"Explosive"

They've given you a sample text file to work off of, and they want you to see if you can make a collage for their new release, *Truncated*.

Looking at the file, though, you can see your work is cut out for you:

Lines are wrapped so they fit here...

Line 1   Normally producers and directors would stop this kind of garbage from getting published. Truncated is amazing in that it got past those hurdles.

Line 2   --Joseph Goldstein, "Truncated: Awful," New York Minute   ←   *These reviewer bylines need to be ignored.*

Line 3   Guppies is destined to be the family film favorite of the   ←   *There are reviews for other movies mixed in here.* summer.

Line 4   --Bill Mosher, "Go see Guppies," Topeka Obscurant

Line 5   Truncated is funny: it can't be categorized as comedy, romance, or horror, because none of those genres would want to be associated with it.   *The adjectives are capitalized in the collage, but not in the text.*

Line 6   --Liz Smith, "Truncated Disappoints," Chicago Some-Times

Line 7   I'm pretty sure this was shot on a mobile phone. Truncated is astounding in its disregard for filmmaking aesthetics.

Line 8   --Bill Mosher, "Don't See Truncated," Topeka Obscurant

reviews.txt

It's true, this job is a bit complex. But don't worry: arrays and blocks can help!

A big collection of words to search through (continued)

Let's break our tasks down into a checklist:

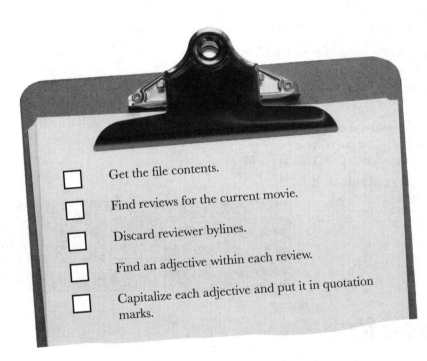

☐ Get the file contents.

☐ Find reviews for the current movie.

☐ Discard reviewer bylines.

☐ Find an adjective within each review.

☐ Capitalize each adjective and put it in quotation marks.

Five tasks to accomplish. Sounds simple enough. Let's get to it!

Opening the file

Our first task is to open the text file with the review contents. This is easier than it sounds—Ruby has a built-in class named `File` that represents files on disk. To open a file named *reviews.txt* in the current directory (folder) so you can read data from it, call the `open` method on the `File` class:

```ruby
review_file = File.open("reviews.txt")
```

The `open` method returns a new `File` object. (It actually calls `File.new` for you, and returns the result of that.)

```ruby
puts review_file.class
```

```
File
```

There are many different methods that you can call on this `File` instance, but the most useful one for our current purpose is the `readlines` method, which returns all the lines in the file as an array.

```ruby
lines = review_file.readlines
puts "Line 4: #{lines[3]}"
puts "Line 1: #{lines[0]}"
```

(Wrapped to fit this page.)

```
Line 4:      --Bill Mosher, "Go see Guppies",
Topeka Obscurant
Line 1: Normally producers and directors would
stop this kind of garbage from getting published.
Truncated is amazing in that it got past those
hurdles.
```

Safely closing the file

We've opened the file and read its contents. Your next step should be to *close the file*. Closing the file tells the operating system, "I'm done with this file; others can use it now."

```ruby
review_file.close
```

Why are we so emphatic about doing this? Because *bad things happen* when you forget to close files.

You can get errors if your operating system detects that you have too many files open at once. If you try to read all the contents of the same file multiple times without closing it, it will appear to be empty on subsequent attempts (because you've already read to the end of the file, and there's nothing after that). If you're writing to a file, no other program can see the changes you made until you *close the file*. It is *very important* not to forget.

Are we making you nervous? Don't be. As usual, Ruby has a developer-friendly solution to this problem.

Safely closing the file, with a block

Ruby offers a way to open a file, do whatever you need with it, and *automatically* close it again when you're done with it. The secret is to call `File.open`...with *a block*!

We just change our code from this:

File object is returned and needs to be stored in a variable.

```
review_file = File.open("reviews.txt")
lines = review_file.readlines
review_file.close
```

We need to call "close" when done.

...to this!

```
File.open("reviews.txt") do |review_file|
  lines = review_file.readlines
end
```

File object is passed as a parameter to the block.

When the block finishes, the file is automatically closed for you!

Why does `File.open` use a block for this purpose? Well, the first and last steps in the process are pretty well defined...

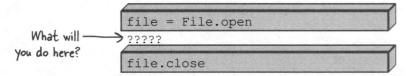

What will you do here? →

...but the creators of `File.open` have *no idea* what you intend to do with that file while it's open. Will you read it one line at a time? All at once? That's why they let *you* decide what to do, by passing in a block.

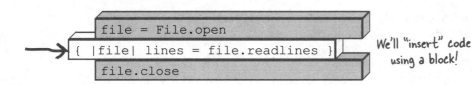

We'll "insert" code using a block!

Don't forget about variable scope!

When we're *not* using a block, we can access the array of lines from the `File` object just fine.

```
review_file = File.open("reviews.txt")
lines = review_file.readlines
review_file.close

puts lines.length
```
`8`

Switching to the block form of `File.open` has introduced a problem, however. We store the array returned by `readlines` in a variable *within* the block, but we can't access it *after* the block.

```
File.open("reviews.txt") do |review_file|
  lines = review_file.readlines
end

puts lines.length
```
`undefined local variable`
`or method `lines'`

The problem is that we're *creating* the `lines` variable *within* the block. As we learned back in Chapter 5, any variable created within a block has a scope that's limited to the body of that block. Those variables can't be "seen" from outside the block.

But, as we also learned in Chapter 5, local variables declared *before* a block *can* be seen *within* the block body (and are still visible after the block, of course). So the simplest solution is to create the `lines` variable *before* declaring the block.

```
lines = []

File.open("reviews.txt") do |review_file|
  lines = review_file.readlines   ⟵——Still in scope!
end

puts lines.length
```
`8`
⤒— Still in scope!

Okay, we've safely closed the file, and we've got our review contents. What do we do with them? We'll be tackling that problem next.

Q: How can `File.open` work both with a block *and* without one?

A: Within a Ruby method, you can call the `block_given?` method to check whether the method caller used a block, and change the method behavior accordingly.

If we were coding our own (simplified) version of `File.open`, it might look like this:

```
def File.open(name, mode)
  file = File.new(name, mode)
  if block_given?
    yield(file)
  else
    return file
  end
end
```

If a block is given, the file is passed to it for use within the block. If it's not, the file is returned.

Three Ruby scripts are below. Fill in the blank in each script so that it will run successfully and produce the specified output.

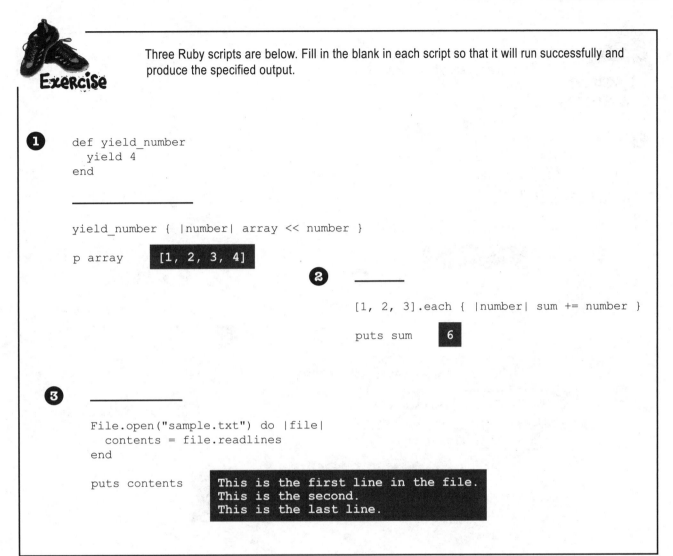

①
```
def yield_number
  yield 4
end
```

_____

```
yield_number { |number| array << number }

p array        [1, 2, 3, 4]
```

② _____

```
[1, 2, 3].each { |number| sum += number }

puts sum        6
```

③ _____

```
File.open("sample.txt") do |file|
  contents = file.readlines
end

puts contents   This is the first line in the file.
                This is the second.
                This is the last line.
```

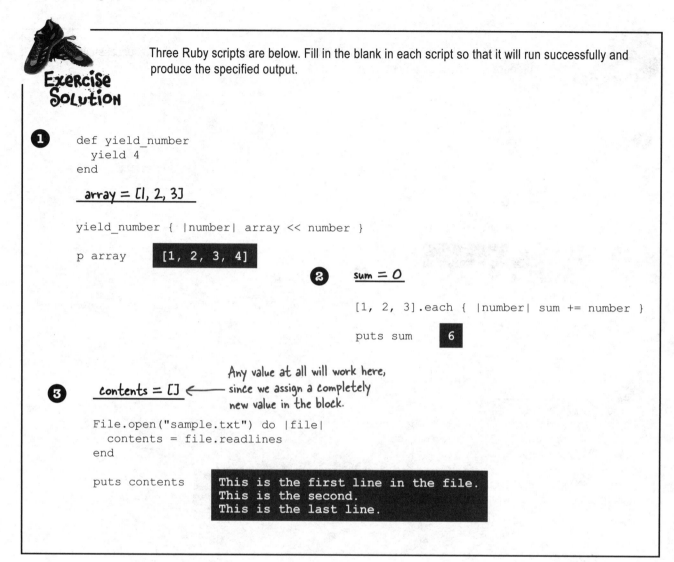

Three Ruby scripts are below. Fill in the blank in each script so that it will run successfully and produce the specified output.

1
```
def yield_number
  yield 4
end
```

array = [1, 2, 3]

```
yield_number { |number| array << number }

p array          [1, 2, 3, 4]
```

2 _sum = 0_

```
[1, 2, 3].each { |number| sum += number }

puts sum          6
```

Any value at all will work here,
3   _contents = []_ ← since we assign a completely
                         new value in the block.

```
File.open("sample.txt") do |file|
  contents = file.readlines
end

puts contents     This is the first line in the file.
                  This is the second.
                  This is the last line.
```

Finding array elements we want, with a block

We've opened the file and used the `readlines` method to get an array with every line from the file in its own element. The first feature from our checklist is complete!

Let's see what remains:

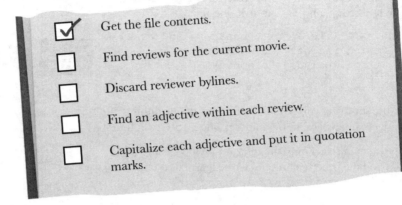

☑ Get the file contents.

☐ Find reviews for the current movie.

☐ Discard reviewer bylines.

☐ Find an adjective within each review.

☐ Capitalize each adjective and put it in quotation marks.

It seems we can't expect the text file to contain only reviews for the movie we want. Reviews for other movies are mixed in there, too:

Line 1
```
Normally producers and directors would stop this kind of
garbage from getting published. Truncated is amazing in that
it got past those hurdles.
```
Line 2
```
      --Joseph Goldstein, "Truncated: Awful," New York Minute
```
Line 3
```
Guppies is destined to be the family film favorite of the
summer.
```
⟵ A review for a completely different movie!

Line 4
```
      --Bill Mosher, "Go see Guppies," Topeka Obscurant
```
Line 5
```
Truncated is funny: it can't be categorized as comedy,
romance, or horror, because none of those genres would want
to be associated with it.
```
Line 6
```
      --Liz Smith, "Truncated Disappoints," Chicago Some-Times
```
...

reviews.txt

Fortunately, it also looks like every review mentions the name of the movie at least once. We can use that fact to find only the reviews for our target movie.

```
Normally producers and directors would stop this kind of
garbage from getting published. Truncated is amazing in that it
got past those hurdles.
```
↑ We can look for this within the string.

The verbose way to find array elements, using "each"

You can call the `include?` method on any instance of the `String` class to determine if it includes a substring (which you pass as an argument). Remember, by convention, methods that end in `?` return a Boolean value. The `include?` method will return `true` if the string contains the specified substring, and `false` if it doesn't.

```
my_string = "I like apples, bananas, and oranges"
puts my_string.include?("bananas")
puts my_string.include?("elephants")
```

```
true
false
```

It doesn't matter if the substring you're looking for is at the beginning of the string, at the end, or somewhere in the middle; `include?` will find it.

So here's one way you could select only the relevant reviews, using the `include?` method and the other techniques we've learned so far...

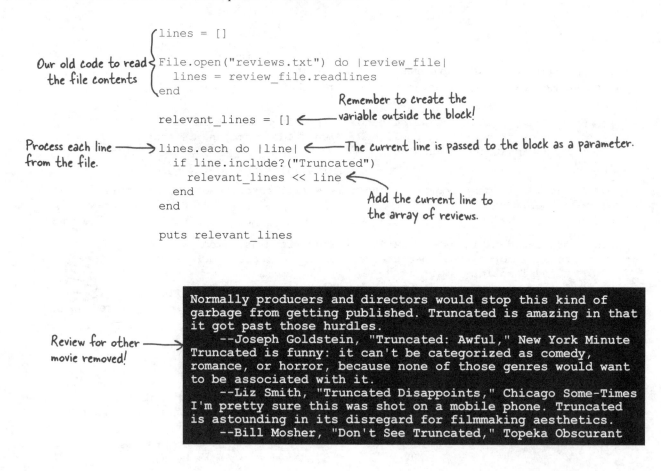

Our old code to read the file contents

```
lines = []

File.open("reviews.txt") do |review_file|
    lines = review_file.readlines
end
```

```
relevant_lines = []
```
← Remember to create the variable outside the block!

Process each line from the file.
```
lines.each do |line|
```
← The current line is passed to the block as a parameter.
```
    if line.include?("Truncated")
        relevant_lines << line
```
← Add the current line to the array of reviews.
```
    end
end

puts relevant_lines
```

Review for other movie removed! →

```
Normally producers and directors would stop this kind of
garbage from getting published. Truncated is amazing in that
it got past those hurdles.
    --Joseph Goldstein, "Truncated: Awful," New York Minute
Truncated is funny: it can't be categorized as comedy,
romance, or horror, because none of those genres would want
to be associated with it.
    --Liz Smith, "Truncated Disappoints," Chicago Some-Times
I'm pretty sure this was shot on a mobile phone. Truncated
is astounding in its disregard for filmmaking aesthetics.
    --Bill Mosher, "Don't See Truncated," Topeka Obscurant
```

Introducing a faster method...

But actually, Ruby offers a much quicker way to do this. The `find_all` method uses a block to run a test against each element in an array. It returns a new array that contains only the elements for which the test returned a true value.

We can use the `find_all` method to achieve the same result, by calling `include?` in its block:

```
lines = []

File.open("reviews.txt") do |review_file|
  lines = review_file.readlines
end

relevant_lines = lines.find_all { |line| line.include?("Truncated") }
```

This shortened code works just as well: only lines that include the substring `"Truncated"` are copied to the new array!

```
puts relevant_lines
```

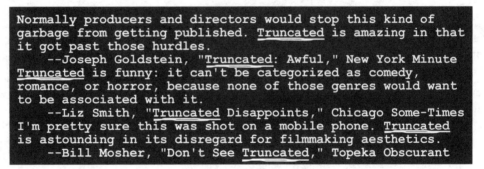

```
Normally producers and directors would stop this kind of
garbage from getting published. Truncated is amazing in that
it got past those hurdles.
    --Joseph Goldstein, "Truncated: Awful," New York Minute
Truncated is funny: it can't be categorized as comedy,
romance, or horror, because none of those genres would want
to be associated with it.
    --Liz Smith, "Truncated Disappoints," Chicago Some-Times
I'm pretty sure this was shot on a mobile phone. Truncated
is astounding in its disregard for filmmaking aesthetics.
    --Bill Mosher, "Don't See Truncated," Topeka Obscurant
```

Replacing six lines of code with a single line…not bad, huh?

Uh, oh. Did we just blow your mind again?

Relax

We'll explain everything that one line of code is doing behind the scenes.

Over the next few pages, we'll walk you through everything you need in order to fully understand how `find_all` works. There are many other Ruby methods that work in a similar way, so trust us, the effort will be worth it!

Blocks have a return value

We just saw the `find_all` method. You pass it a block with selection logic, and `find_all` finds only the elements in an array that match the block's criteria.

```
lines.find_all { |line| line.include?("Truncated") }
```

By "elements that match the block's criteria," we mean elements for which the block *returns* a true value. The `find_all` method uses the *return value of the block* to determine which elements to keep, and which to discard.

As we've progressed, you've probably noticed a few similarities between blocks and methods...

Methods:

- Accept parameters

- Have a body that holds Ruby expressions

- Return a value

Blocks:

- Accept parameters

- Have a body that holds Ruby expressions

- Return a value ← *Wait, what? Do they?*

That's right, just like methods, Ruby blocks return the value of the last expression they contain! It's returned to the method as the result of the `yield` keyword.

We can create a simple method that shows this in action, and then call it with different blocks to see their return values:

```
def print_block_result
  block_result = yield
  puts block_result
end
```
Assigns the result of the block to a variable

```
print_block_result { 1 + 1 }
```
Code is evaluated; block returns 2.

```
print_block_result do
  "I'm not the last expression, so I'm not the return value."
  "I'm the result!"
end
```
Only the last expression's value is returned.

```
print_block_result { "I hated Truncated".include?("Truncated") }
```
Code is evaluated; block returns true.

The value of the last expression in a block gets returned to the method.

```
2
I'm the result!
true
```

Blocks have a return value (continued)

The method isn't limited to *printing* the block return value, of course. It can also do math with it:

```ruby
def triple_block_result
  puts 3 * yield
end

triple_block_result { 2 }
triple_block_result { 5 }
```

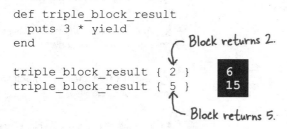

```
6
15
```

Block returns 2.

Block returns 5.

Or use it in a string:

```ruby
def greet
  puts "Hello, #{yield}!"
end

greet { "Liz" }
```

```
Hello, Liz!
```

Block returns this string.

Or use it in a conditional:

```ruby
def alert_if_true
  if yield
    puts "Block returned true!"
  else
    puts "Block returned false."
  end
end

alert_if_true { 2 + 2 == 5 }
alert_if_true { 2 > 1 }
```

Block returns false.

```
Block returned false.
Block returned true!
```

Block returns true.

Up next, we'll take a detailed look at how `find_all` uses the block's return value to give you just the array elements you want.

Watch it!

We say that blocks have a "return value," but that doesn't mean you should use the return keyword.

Using the `return` *keyword within a block isn't a syntax error, but we don't recommend it. Within a block body, the* `return` *keyword returns <u>from the method where the block is being defined</u>, not the block itself. It's very unlikely that this is what you want to do.*

```
def print_block_value
  puts yield
end

def other_method
  print_block_value { return 1 + 1 }
end

other_method
```

The above code <u>won't print anything</u>, because `other_method` *exits <u>as the block is being defined</u>.*

If you change the block to simply use its last expression as a return value, then everything works as expected:

```
def other_method
  print_block_value { 1 + 1 }
end

other_method
```

---

there are no Dumb Questions

Q: Do *all* blocks return a value?

A: Yes! They return the result of the last expression in the block body.

Q: If that's true, then why didn't we learn about this sooner?

A: We haven't needed to. A block may `return` a value, but the associated method doesn't have to *use* it. The `each` method, for example, ignores the values returned from its block.

Q: Can I pass parameters to a block *and* use its return value?

A: Yes! You can pass parameters, use the return value, do both, or do neither; it's up to you.

```
def one_two
  result = yield(1, 2)
  puts result
end

one_two do |param1, param2|
  param1 + param2
end
```

Code Magnets

A Ruby program is all scrambled up on the fridge. Can you reconstruct the code snippets so that they produce the given output?

```
puts "Preheat oven to 375 degrees"
```

```
puts "Place #{ingredients} in dish"
```

```
puts "Bake for 20 minutes"
```

```
"rice, broccoli, and chicken"
```

```
"noodles, celery, and tuna"
```

```
def        end        =
```

```
do        end        yield
```

```
do        end        ingredients
```

```
make_casserole
```

```
make_casserole
```

```
make_casserole
```

Output:

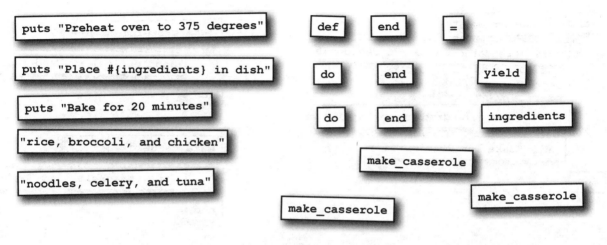

```
File Edit Window Help
Preheat oven to 375 degrees
Place noodles, celery, and tuna in dish
Bake for 20 minutes
Preheat oven to 375 degrees
Place rice, broccoli, and chicken in dish
Bake for 20 minutes
```

Code Magnets Solution

A Ruby program is all scrambled up on the fridge. Can you reconstruct the code snippets so that they produce the given output?

```
def    make_casserole
         puts "Preheat oven to 375 degrees"
         ingredients  =  yield
         puts "Place #{ingredients} in dish"
         puts "Bake for 20 minutes"
end
```

```
make_casserole    do
         "noodles, celery, and tuna"
end
```

```
make_casserole    do
         "rice, broccoli, and chicken"
end
```

Output:

```
File Edit Window Help
Preheat oven to 375 degrees
Place noodles, celery, and tuna in dish
Bake for 20 minutes
Preheat oven to 375 degrees
Place rice, broccoli, and chicken in dish
Bake for 20 minutes
```

How the method uses a block return value

We're close to deciphering how this snippet of code works:

```
lines.find_all { |line| line.include?("Truncated") }
```

The last step is understanding the `find_all` method. It passes each element in an array to a block, and builds a new array including only the elements for which the block returns a true value.

```
p [1, 2, 3, 4, 5].find_all { |number| number.even? }
p [1, 2, 3, 4, 5].find_all { |number| number.odd? }
```

```
[2, 4]
[1, 3, 5]
```

You can think of the values the block returns as a set of *instructions* for the method. The `find_all` method's job is to keep some array elements and discard others. But it relies on the block's return value to tell it which elements to keep.

All that matters in this selection process is the block's return value. The block body doesn't even have to use the parameter with the current array element (although in most practical programs, it will). If the block returns `true` for everything, *all* the array elements will be included...

```
p ['a', 'b', 'c'].find_all { |item| true }
```

```
["a", "b", "c"]
```

...but if it returns `false` for everything, *none* of them will be.

```
p ['a', 'b', 'c'].find_all { |item| false }
```

```
[]
```

Think of block return values as <u>instructions</u> from the block to the method.

If we were to write our own version of `find_all`, it might look like this:

```
def find_all
  matching_items = []
  self.each do |item|
    if yield(item)
      matching_items << item
    end
  end
  matching_items
end
```

Create a new array to hold the elements for which the block returns true.

Process each element.

Pass the element to the block. If the result is true...

...add it to the array of matching elements.

If this code looks familiar, it should. It's a more generalized version of our earlier code to find lines that were relevant to our target movie!

The old code:

```
relevant_lines = []
lines.each do |line|
  if line.include?("Truncated")
    relevant_lines << line
  end
end
puts relevant_lines
```

Putting it all together

Now that we know how the `find_all` method works, we're really close to understanding this code.

```
lines = []

File.open("reviews.txt") do |review_file|
  lines = review_file.readlines
end

relevant_lines = lines.find_all { |line| line.include?("Truncated") }
```

We've almost got this!

Here's what we've learned (not necessarily in order):

- The last expression in a block becomes its return value.

  Result will be used as block return value.

  ```
  lines.find_all { |line| line.include?("Truncated") }
  ```

- The `include?` method returns `true` if the string contains the specified substring, and `false` if it doesn't.

  ```
  lines.find_all { |line| line.include?("Truncated") }
  ```

  Returns true if line contains "Truncated"

- The `find_all` method passes each element in an array to a block, and builds a new array including only the elements for which the block returns a true value.

  ```
  lines.find_all { |line| line.include?("Truncated") }
  ```

  Result will be an array with all the elements of "lines" that contain string "Truncated."

Let's look inside the `find_all` method and the block as they process the first few lines of the file, to see what they're doing…

A closer look at the block return values

1 The `find_all` method passes the first line from the file to the block, which receives it in the `line` parameter. The block tests whether `line` includes the string `"Truncated"`. It does, so the return value of the block is `true`. Back in the method, the line gets added to the array of matching items.

"find_all" passes the full text lines; we've just shortened them to fit this page!

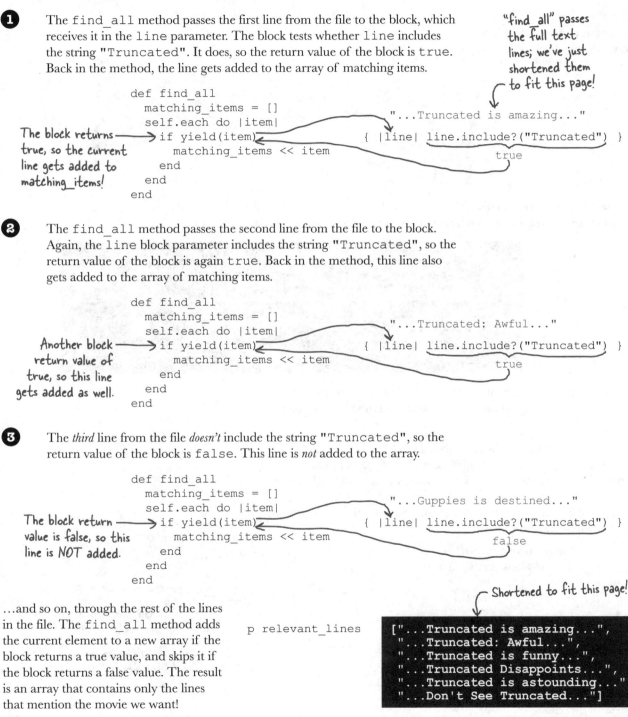

The block returns true, so the current line gets added to matching_items!

```
def find_all
  matching_items = []
  self.each do |item|
    if yield(item)
      matching_items << item
    end
  end
end
```

`"...Truncated is amazing..."`

`{ |line| line.include?("Truncated") }`

`true`

2 The `find_all` method passes the second line from the file to the block. Again, the `line` block parameter includes the string `"Truncated"`, so the return value of the block is again `true`. Back in the method, this line also gets added to the array of matching items.

Another block return value of true, so this line gets added as well.

```
def find_all
  matching_items = []
  self.each do |item|
    if yield(item)
      matching_items << item
    end
  end
end
```

`"...Truncated: Awful..."`

`{ |line| line.include?("Truncated") }`

`true`

3 The *third* line from the file *doesn't* include the string `"Truncated"`, so the return value of the block is `false`. This line is *not* added to the array.

The block return value is false, so this line is NOT added.

```
def find_all
  matching_items = []
  self.each do |item|
    if yield(item)
      matching_items << item
    end
  end
end
```

`"...Guppies is destined..."`

`{ |line| line.include?("Truncated") }`

`false`

...and so on, through the rest of the lines in the file. The `find_all` method adds the current element to a new array if the block returns a true value, and skips it if the block returns a false value. The result is an array that contains only the lines that mention the movie we want!

`p relevant_lines`

Shortened to fit this page!

```
["...Truncated is amazing...",
 "...Truncated: Awful...",
 "...Truncated is funny...",
 "...Truncated Disappoints...",
 "...Truncated is astounding...",
 "...Don't See Truncated..."]
```

Eliminating elements we don't want, with a block

Using the `find_all` method, we've successfully found all the reviews for our target movie and placed them in the `relevant_lines` array. We can check another requirement off our list!

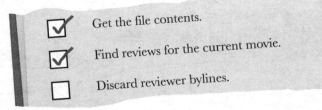

☑ Get the file contents.

☑ Find reviews for the current movie.

☐ Discard reviewer bylines.

Our next requirement is to discard the reviewer bylines, because we're only interested in retrieving adjectives from the main text of each review.

We want to get rid of these:

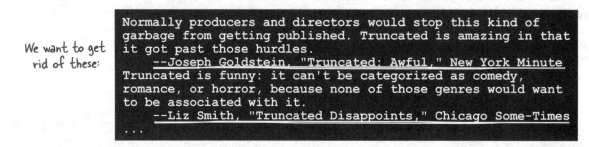

```
Normally producers and directors would stop this kind of
garbage from getting published. Truncated is amazing in that
it got past those hurdles.
    --Joseph Goldstein, "Truncated: Awful," New York Minute
Truncated is funny: it can't be categorized as comedy,
romance, or horror, because none of those genres would want
to be associated with it.
    --Liz Smith, "Truncated Disappoints," Chicago Some-Times
...
```

Fortunately, they're clearly marked. Each one starts with the characters `--`, so it should be easy to use the `include?` method to determine if a string contains a byline.

Before, we used the `find_all` method to *keep* lines that included a particular string. The `reject` method is basically the opposite of `find_all`—it passes elements from an array to a block, and *rejects* an element if the block returns a true value. If `find_all` relies on the block to tell it which items to *keep*, `reject` relies on the block to tell it which items to *discard*.

If we were to implement our own version of `reject`, it would look very similar to `find_all`:

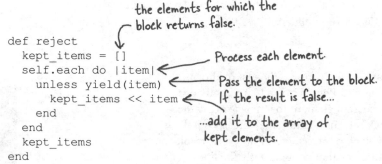

Create a new array to hold the elements for which the block returns false.

```
def reject
  kept_items = []
  self.each do |item|
    unless yield(item)
      kept_items << item
    end
  end
  kept_items
end
```

Process each element.

Pass the element to the block.

If the result is false...

...add it to the array of kept elements.

The return values for "reject"

So `reject` works just like `find_all`, except that instead of *keeping* elements that the block returns a true value for, it *rejects* them. If we use `reject`, it should be easy to get rid of the bylines!

```
reviews = relevant_lines.reject { |line| line.include?("--") }
```

1 The `reject` method passes the first line from the file to the block. The `line` block parameter does *not* include the string `"--"`, so the return value of the block is `false`. Back in the method, this line gets added to the array of items we're keeping.

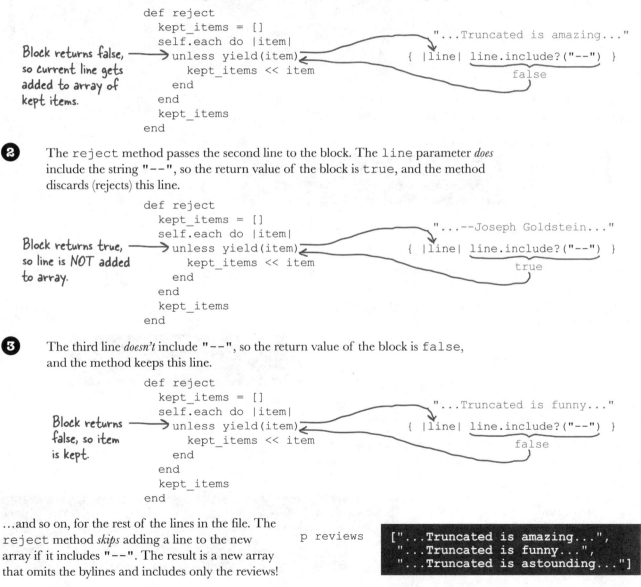

```
def reject
  kept_items = []
  self.each do |item|
    unless yield(item)
      kept_items << item
    end
  end
  kept_items
end
```

Block returns false, so current line gets added to array of kept items.

`"...Truncated is amazing..."`
`{ |line| line.include?("--") }`
`false`

2 The `reject` method passes the second line to the block. The `line` parameter *does* include the string `"--"`, so the return value of the block is `true`, and the method discards (rejects) this line.

```
def reject
  kept_items = []
  self.each do |item|
    unless yield(item)
      kept_items << item
    end
  end
  kept_items
end
```

Block returns true, so line is NOT added to array.

`"...--Joseph Goldstein..."`
`{ |line| line.include?("--") }`
`true`

3 The third line *doesn't* include `"--"`, so the return value of the block is `false`, and the method keeps this line.

```
def reject
  kept_items = []
  self.each do |item|
    unless yield(item)
      kept_items << item
    end
  end
  kept_items
end
```

Block returns false, so item is kept.

`"...Truncated is funny..."`
`{ |line| line.include?("--") }`
`false`

...and so on, for the rest of the lines in the file. The `reject` method *skips* adding a line to the new array if it includes `"--"`. The result is a new array that omits the bylines and includes only the reviews!

`p reviews`

```
["...Truncated is amazing...",
 "...Truncated is funny...",
 "...Truncated is astounding..."]
```

Breaking a string into an array of words

We've discarded the reviewer bylines, leaving us with an array containing only the text of each review. That's another requirement down! Two to go...

☑ Get the file contents.

☑ Find reviews for the current movie.

☑ Discard reviewer bylines.

☐ Find an adjective within each review.

☐ Capitalize each adjective and put it in quotation marks.

For our next requirement, we're going to need a couple of new methods. They don't take blocks at all, but they *are* super-useful.

We need to find an adjective in each review:

```
p reviews
```
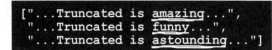

["...Truncated is <u>amazing</u>...",
"...Truncated is <u>funny</u>...",
"...Truncated is <u>astounding</u>..."]

We need to select just the adjectives...

If you look above, you'll notice a pattern... The adjective we want always seems to follow the word *is*.

So we need to get one word that follows another word... What we have right now are *strings*. How can we convert those to *words*?

Strings have a `split` instance method that you can call to split them into an array of substrings.

```
p "1-800-555-0199".split("-")
p "his/her".split("/")
p "apple, avocado, anvil".split(", ")
```
```
["1", "800", "555", "0199"]
["his", "her"]
["apple", "avocado", "anvil"]
```

The argument to `split` is the *separator*: one or more characters that separate the string into sections.

What separates words in the English language? A space! If we pass `" "` (a space character) to `split`, we'll get an array back. Let's try it with our first review.

```
string = reviews.first
words = string.split(" ")
p words
```
```
["Normally", "producers", "and", "directors",
"would", "stop", "this", "kind", "of", "garbage",
"from", "getting", "published.", "Truncated", "is",
"amazing", "in", "that", "it", "got", "past",
"those", "hurdles."]
```

There you have it—an array of words!

Finding the index of an array element

The `split` method converted our review string into an array of words.
Now, we need to find the word *is* within that array. Again, Ruby has a
method ready to go for us. If you pass an argument to the `find_index`
method, it will find us the first index where that element occurs in the array.

```
p ["1", "800", "555", "0199"].find_index("800")
p ["his", "her"].find_index("his")
p ["apple", "avocado", "anvil"].find_index("anvil")
```

```
1
0
2
```

Using `find_index`, let's write a method that will split a string into
an array of words, find the index of the word *is*, and return the word
that comes *after* that.

```
def find_adjective(string)
  words = string.split(" ")          Split the sentences
                                     into words.
  index = words.find_index("is")     Find the array index of "is".
  words[index + 1]
end                       Find the word AFTER
                          "is" and return it.
```

We can easily test our method on one of our reviews...

```
adjective = find_adjective(reviews.first)        amazing
```

There's our adjective! That only takes care of one review, though.
Next, we need to process *all* the reviews and create an array of the
adjectives we find. With the `each` method, that's easy enough to do.

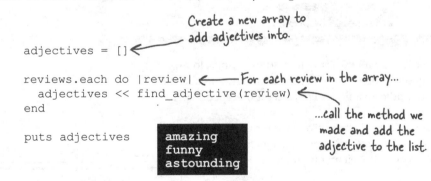

```
                          Create a new array to
                          add adjectives into.
adjectives = []

reviews.each do |review|     For each review in the array...
  adjectives << find_adjective(review)
end                                    ...call the method we
                                       made and add the
puts adjectives    amazing            adjective to the list.
                   funny
                   astounding
```

Now we have an array of adjectives, one for each review!

Would you believe there's an even *easier* way to create an array of
adjectives based on the array of reviews, though?

Making one array that's based on another, the hard way

We had no problem looping through our array of reviews to build up an array of adjectives using `each` and our new `find_adjective` method.

But creating a new array based on the contents of another array is a really common operation, one that requires similar code each time. Some examples:

```
numbers = [2, 3, 4]

squares = []          ◄——Make an array        Loop
                          to hold results.   through
numbers.each do |number|◄                    source
  squares << number ** 2                      array.
end
                      ◄— Perform an operation and
p squares                copy result to results array.
```
```
[4, 9, 16]
```

```
numbers = [2, 3, 4]

cubes = []          ◄——Make an array
                        to hold results.   Loop
numbers.each do |number|◄                  through
  cubes << number ** 3                      source
end                                         array.
                      ◄— Perform an operation and
p cubes                  copy result to results array.
```
```
[8, 27, 64]
```

```
phone_numbers = ["1-800-555-0199", "1-402-555-0123"]

area_codes = []          ◄——Make an array      Loop through
                             to hold results.  source array.
phone_numbers.each do |phone_number|◄
  area_codes << phone_number.split("-")[1]
end
                      ◄— Perform an operation and
p area_codes             copy result to results array.
```
```
["800", "402"]
```

In each of these examples, we have to set up a new array to hold the results, loop through the original array and apply some logic to each of its members, and add the result to the new array. (Just like in our adjective finder code.) It's a bit repetitive…

Wouldn't it be great if there were some sort of magic processor for arrays? You drop in your array, it runs some (interchangeable) logic on its elements, and out pops a new array with the elements you need!

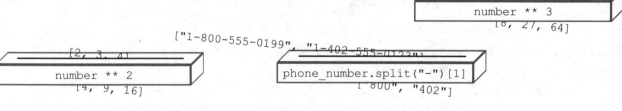

Making one array based on another, using "map"

Ruby has just the magic array processor we're looking for: the `map` method. The `map` method takes each element of an array, passes it to a block, and builds a new array out of the values the block returns.

No need to create the result arrays beforehand—"map" creates them for us!

Make a new array with the squares of each number.

Make a new array with the cubes of each number.

```ruby
squares = [2, 3, 4].map { |number| number ** 2 }
cubes = [2, 3, 4].map { |number| number ** 3 }
area_codes = ['1-800-555-0199', '1-402-555-0123'].map do |phone|
  phone.split("-")[1]
end
p squares, cubes, area_codes
```

Make a new array with just area codes.

```
[4, 9, 16]
[8, 27, 64]
["800", "402"]
```

The `map` method is similar to `find_all` and `reject`, in that it processes each element in an array. But `find_all` and `reject` use the block's return value to decide whether to copy *the original element* from the old array to the new one. The `map` method adds the block's *return value itself* to the new array.

If we were to code our own version of `map`, it might look like this:

Make a new array to hold the block return values.

Loop through each element.

```ruby
def map
  results = []
  self.each do |item|
    results << yield(item)
  end
  results
end
```

Pass the element to the block, and add the return value to the new array.

Return the array of block return values.

The `map` method can shorten our code to gather adjectives down to a single line!

An array with all the return values from find_adjective

```ruby
adjectives = reviews.map { |review| find_adjective(review) }
```

Call our method. Its return value will be the return value of the block.

The return value of `map` is an array with all the values the block returned:

```ruby
p adjectives
```
```
["amazing", "funny", "astounding"]
```

Making one array based on another, using "map" (continued)

Let's look at how the map method and our block process the array of reviews, step by step...

```
["...Truncated is amazing...",
 "...Truncated is funny...",
 "...Truncated is astounding..."]
```

find_adjective(review)

```
["amazing",
 "funny",
 "astounding"]
```

```
adjectives = reviews.map { |review| find_adjective(review) }
```

1 The map method passes our first review to the block. The block, in turn, passes the review to find_adjective, which returns "amazing". The return value of find_adjective also becomes the return value of the block. Back in the map method, "amazing" is added to the results array.

```
def map
  results = []                "...Truncated is amazing..."
  self.each do |item|
    results << yield(item)                 { |review| find_adjective(review) }
  end                                                    "amazing"
  results
end
```

2 The second review is passed to the block, and find_adjective returns "funny". Back in the method, the new adjective is added to the results array.

```
def map
  results = []                "...Truncated is funny..."
  self.each do |item|
    results << yield(item)                 { |review| find_adjective(review) }
  end                                                    "funny"
  results
end
```

3 For the third review, find_adjective returns "astounding", which gets added to the array with the others.

```
def map
  results = []                "...Truncated is astounding..."
  self.each do |item|
    results << yield(item)                 { |review| find_adjective(review) }
  end                                                    "astounding"
  results
end
```

Another requirement finished! We have just one more, and this one will be easy!

☑ Find an adjective within each review.

☐ Capitalize each adjective and put it in quotation marks.

Some additional logic in the "map" block body

We're already using `map` to find the adjectives for each review:

```ruby
adjectives = reviews.map { |review| find_adjective(review) }
```

Lastly, we need to capitalize the adjective and enclose it in quotation marks. We can do this in the block, right after the call to our `find_adjective` method.

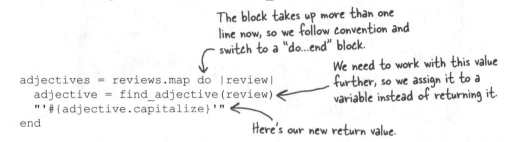

The block takes up more than one line now, so we follow convention and switch to a "do...end" block.

We need to work with this value further, so we assign it to a variable instead of returning it.

```ruby
adjectives = reviews.map do |review|
  adjective = find_adjective(review)
  "'#{adjective.capitalize}'"
end
```

Here's our new return value.

Here are the new return values that this updated code produces:

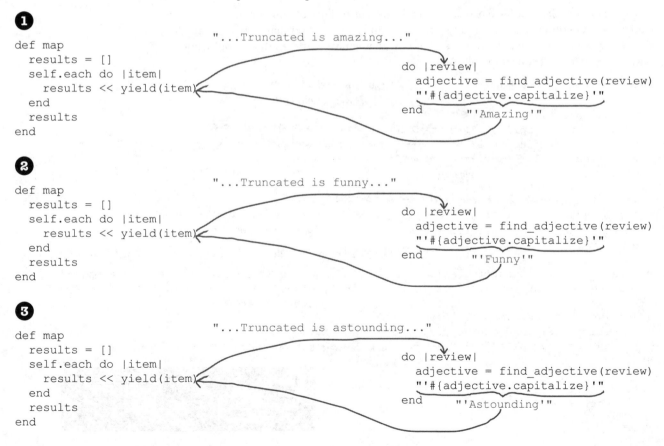

1

```ruby
def map
  results = []
  self.each do |item|
    results << yield(item)
  end
  results
end
```

`"...Truncated is amazing..."`

```ruby
do |review|
  adjective = find_adjective(review)
  "'#{adjective.capitalize}'"
end
```
`"'Amazing'"`

2

```ruby
def map
  results = []
  self.each do |item|
    results << yield(item)
  end
  results
end
```

`"...Truncated is funny..."`

```ruby
do |review|
  adjective = find_adjective(review)
  "'#{adjective.capitalize}'"
end
```
`"'Funny'"`

3

```ruby
def map
  results = []
  self.each do |item|
    results << yield(item)
  end
  results
end
```

`"...Truncated is astounding..."`

```ruby
do |review|
  adjective = find_adjective(review)
  "'#{adjective.capitalize}'"
end
```
`"'Astounding'"`

The finished product

That's our last requirement. Congratulations, we're done!

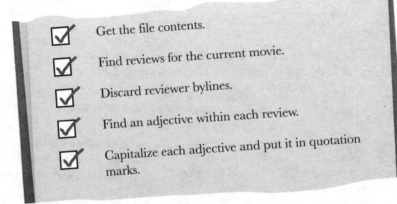

- ☑ Get the file contents.
- ☑ Find reviews for the current movie.
- ☑ Discard reviewer bylines.
- ☑ Find an adjective within each review.
- ☑ Capitalize each adjective and put it in quotation marks.

You've successfully learned to use block return values to find elements you want within an array, to reject elements you don't want, and even to use an algorithm to create an entirely new array!

Processing a complex text file like this would take dozens of lines of code in other languages, with lots of repetition. The `find_all`, `reject`, and `map` methods handled all of that for you! They can be difficult to learn to use, but now that you've mastered them, you've got powerful new tools at your disposal!

Here's our complete code listing:

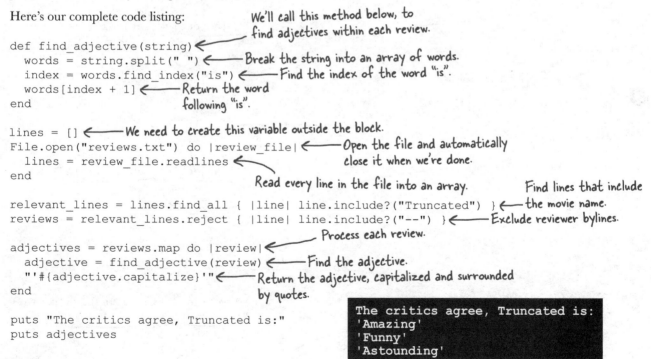

```ruby
def find_adjective(string)          # We'll call this method below, to
  words = string.split(" ")         #   find adjectives within each review.
  index = words.find_index("is")    # Break the string into an array of words.
  words[index + 1]                  # Find the index of the word "is".
end                                 # Return the word following "is".

lines = []                          # We need to create this variable outside the block.
File.open("reviews.txt") do |review_file|   # Open the file and automatically
  lines = review_file.readlines     #   close it when we're done.
end                                 # Read every line in the file into an array.

relevant_lines = lines.find_all { |line| line.include?("Truncated") }   # Find lines that include the movie name.
reviews = relevant_lines.reject { |line| line.include?("--") }          # Exclude reviewer bylines.

adjectives = reviews.map do |review|        # Process each review.
  adjective = find_adjective(review)        # Find the adjective.
  "'#{adjective.capitalize}'"               # Return the adjective, capitalized and surrounded by quotes.
end

puts "The critics agree, Truncated is:"
puts adjectives
```

```
The critics agree, Truncated is:
'Amazing'
'Funny'
'Astounding'
```

Exercise

Open a new terminal window, type **irb**, and hit the Enter/Return key. For each of the Ruby expressions below, write your guess for what the result will be on the line next to it. Then try typing the expression into irb and hit Enter. See if your guess matches what irb returns!

```
[1, 2, 3, 4].find_all { |number| number.odd? }
```
....

```
[1, 2, 3, 4].find_all { |number| true }
```
....

```
[1, 2, 3, 4].find_all { |number| false }
```
....

```
[1, 2, 3, 4].find { |number| number.even? }
```
....

```
[1, 2, 3, 4].reject { |number| number.odd? }
```
....

```
[1, 2, 3, 4].all? { |number| number.odd? }
```
....

```
[1, 2, 3, 4].any? { |number| number.odd? }
```
....

```
[1, 2, 3, 4].none? { |number| number > 4 }
```
....

```
[1, 2, 3, 4].count { |number| number.odd? }
```
....

```
[1, 2, 3, 4].partition { |number| number.odd? }
```
....

```
['$', '$$', '$$$'].map { |string| string.length }
```
....

```
['$', '$$', '$$$'].max_by { |string| string.length }
```
....

```
['$', '$$', '$$$'].min_by { |string| string.length }
```
....

Exercise Solution

Open a new terminal window, type `irb`, and hit the Enter/Return key. For each of the Ruby expressions below, write your guess for what the result will be on the line next to it. Then try typing the expression into irb and hit Enter. See if your guess matches what irb returns!

`[1, 2, 3, 4].find_all { |number| number.odd? }`

[1, 3] ← An array of all values for which the block returns true

`[1, 2, 3, 4].find_all { |number| true }`

[1, 2, 3, 4] ← If it always returns true, all values get included.

`[1, 2, 3, 4].find_all { |number| false }`

[] ← If it NEVER returns true, NO values are included.

`[1, 2, 3, 4].find { |number| number.even? }`

2 ← "find" returns the FIRST value for which the block returns true.

`[1, 2, 3, 4].reject { |number| number.odd? }`

[2, 4] ← An array of all values for which the block returns false

`[1, 2, 3, 4].all? { |number| number.odd? }`

false ← "all?" returns true if the block returned true for ALL elements.

`[1, 2, 3, 4].any? { |number| number.odd? }`

true ← "any?" returns true if the block returned true for ANY elements.

`[1, 2, 3, 4].none? { |number| number > 4 }`

true ← "none?" returns true if the block returned FALSE for all elements.

`[1, 2, 3, 4].count { |number| number.odd? }`

2 ← The number of elements for which the block returned true

`[1, 2, 3, 4].partition { |number| number.odd? }`

[[1, 3], [2, 4]] ←

Two arrays, the first with all the elements where the block returned TRUE, the second with all the elements where it returned FALSE

`['$', '$$', '$$$'].map { |string| string.length }`

[1, 2, 3] ← An array with all the values the block returns

`['$', '$$', '$$$'].max_by { |string| string.length }`

"$$$" ← The element for which the block returned the LARGEST value

`['$', '$$', '$$$'].min_by { |string| string.length }`

"$" ← The element for which the block returned the SMALLEST value

Your Ruby Toolbox

That's it for Chapter 6! You've added block return values to your toolbox.

Arrays

An Blocks

Block Return Values

The value of the last expression in a block's body is returned to the method, as the value of the yield keyword.

Methods can use the block return value to find elements in a collection, decide how to sort elements, and more.

Up Next...

Arrays have their limitations. If you need to find a particular value within an array, you have to start at the beginning and search through the items one by one. In the next chapter, we'll show you another kind of collection that will help you find things much more quickly: *hashes*.

7 hashes

Labeling Data

Wilson, Wilson... Not here, either. If only this data had labels on it... I could find things more quickly!

Throwing things in piles is fine, until you need to find something again. You've already seen how to create a collection of objects using an *array*. You've seen how to process *each item* in an array, and how to *find items* you want. In both cases, you start at the beginning of the array, and *look through Every. Single. Object.* You've also seen methods that take big collections of parameters. You've seen the problems this causes: method calls require a big, *confusing collection of arguments* that you have to remember the exact order for.

What if there were a kind of collection where *all the data had labels* on it? You could *quickly find the elements* you needed! In this chapter, we'll learn about Ruby **hashes**, which do just that.

Counting votes

A seat on the Sleepy Creek County School Board is up for grabs this year, and polls have been showing that the election is really close. Now that it's election night, the candidates are excitedly watching the votes roll in.

I'm confident that the voters will choose the candidate who will put our children first!

It's time to bring financial responsibility and accountability back to our school system!

```
{"name" => "Amber Graham",
 "occupation" => "Manager"}
```

```
{"name" => "Brian Martin",
 "occupation" => "Accountant"}
```

The electronic voting machines in use this year record the votes to text files, one vote per line. (Budgets are tight, so the city council chose the cheap voting machine vendor.)

Here's a file with all the votes for District A:

Each line represents one vote.

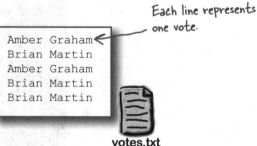

```
Amber Graham
Brian Martin
Amber Graham
Brian Martin
Brian Martin
```

votes.txt

We need to process each line of the file and tally the total number of times each name occurs. The name with the most votes will be our winner!

The development team's first order of business is to read the contents of the *votes.txt* file. That part is easy; it's just like the code we used to read the movie reviews file back in Chapter 6.

Create a variable that will still be accessible after the block.

```
lines = []
File.open("votes.txt") do |file|
  lines = file.readlines
end
```

Open the file and pass it to the block.

Store all the file lines in an array.

Now we need to get the name from each line of the file, and increment a tally of the number of times that name has occurred.

An array of arrays...is not ideal

But how do we keep track of all those names *and* associate a vote total with each of them? We'll show you two ways. The first approach uses arrays, which we already know about from Chapter 5. The second way uses a new data structure, *hashes*.

If all we had to work with were arrays, we might build an *array of arrays* to hold everything. That's right: Ruby arrays can hold any object, including *other arrays*. So we could create an array with the candidate's name and the number of votes we've counted for it:

```
["Brian Martin", 1]
```

We could put this array *inside* another array that holds all the *other* candidate names and *their* totals:

Outer array ──────▶ [
An inner array ─────▶ ["Amber Graham", 1],
                     ["Brian Martin", 1] ◀──── Insert the new array here...
                  ]

For each name we encountered in the text file...   "Mikey Moose"

...we'd need to loop through the *outer* array and check whether the first element of the *inner* array matches it.

"Mikey Moose"? Nope...   [
"Mikey Moose"? Nope...   ["Amber Graham", 1],
                                 ["Brian Martin", 1],
                                 ...
                              ]

If none matched, we'd add a new inner array with the new name.

```
[
  ["Amber Graham", 1],
  ["Brian Martin", 1],
  ["Mikey Moose", 1]  ◀──── Insert the new array here...
]
```

But if we encountered a name in the text file that *did* already exist in the array of arrays...   "Brian Martin"

...then we'd update the existing total for that name.

"Brian Martin"? Nope.   [
"Brian Martin"? Yes!   ["Amber Graham", 1],
                                 ["Brian Martin", 2], ◀──── Update this vote count.
                                 ["Mikey Moose", 1]
                              ]

You *could* do all that. But it would require extra code, and all that looping would take a long time when processing large lists. As usual, Ruby has a better way.

Hashes

The problem with storing the vote tally for each candidate in an array is the inefficiency of looking it up again later. For each name we want to find, we have to search through *all* the others.

```
                                          [
"Mikey Moose"? Nope...      ["Amber Graham", 4],
"Mikey Moose"? Nope...      ["Brian Martin", 5],
        "Mikey Moose"?      ["Mikey Moose", 2]
                                          ]
```

Putting data in an array is like stacking it in a big pile; you can get particular items back out, but you'll have to search through *everything* to find them.

Ruby has another way of storing collections of data: *hashes*. A **hash** is a collection where each value is accessed via a *key*. Keys are an easy way to get data back out of your hash. It's like having neatly labeled file folders instead of a messy pile.

Start at the top; search the whole pile.

Array

AMBER GRAHAM

Keys let you quickly find data again!

Hash

Just as with arrays, you can create a new hash and add some data to it at the same time using a hash literal. The syntax looks like this:

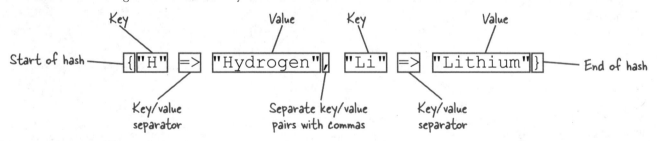

```
Start of hash — {"H" => "Hydrogen", "Li" => "Lithium"} — End of hash
```

Key / Value / Key / Value
Key/value separator / Separate key/value pairs with commas / Key/value separator

Those => symbols show which key points to which value. They look a bit like a rocket, so they are sometimes called "hash rockets."

We can assign a new hash to a variable:

```
elements = {"H" => "Hydrogen", "Li" => "Lithium"}
```

Then we can access values from that hash using the keys we set up for them. Whereas hash literals use *curly braces*, you use *square brackets* to access individual values. It looks just like the syntax to access values from an array, except you place the hash key within the brackets instead of a numeric index.

Use a hash key here, and you'll get the corresponding value.

```
puts elements["Li"]
puts elements["H"]
```

```
Lithium
Hydrogen
```

Hashes (continued)

We can also add new keys and values to an existing hash. Again, the syntax looks a lot like the syntax to assign to an array element:

Hash key we're assigning a value for ⟶

New value ⟵

```
elements["Ne"] = "Neon"
puts elements["Ne"]
```
`Neon`

Whereas an array can only use *integers* as indexes, a hash can use *any object* as a key. That includes numbers, strings, and symbols.

```
mush = {1 => "one", "two" => 2, :three => 3.0}

p mush[:three]
p mush[1]
p mush["two"]
```
`3.0`
`"one"`
`2`

An array can only use integers as indexes, but a hash can use _any object_ as a key.

Although arrays and hashes have major differences, there are enough similarities that it's worth taking a moment to compare them…

Arrays:

- Arrays grow and shrink as needed.

- Arrays can hold any object, even hashes or other arrays.

- Arrays can hold instances of more than one class at the same time.

- Literals are surrounded by *square brackets*.

- You access elements by specifying their index within *square brackets*.

- Only integers can be used as indexes.

- The index of an element is determined by its position within the array.

```
[2.99, 25.00, 9.99]
```
  ↑   ↑   ↑
  0   1   2

Hashes:

- Hashes grow and shrink as needed.

- Hashes can hold any object, even arrays or other hashes.

- Hashes can hold instances of more than one class at the same time.

- Literals are surrounded by *curly braces*.

- You access values by specifying their key within *square brackets*.

- Any object can be used as a key.

- Keys are not calculated; each key must be specified whenever a value is added.

```
{"M" => "Monday", "T" => "Tuesday"}
```
  ↑   ↑   ↑   ↑
 Key   Value   Key   Value

Exercise

Fill in the blanks in the code below so that it will produce the output shown.

```
my_hash = {"one" => _____, :three => "four", _ => "six"}
puts my_hash[5]
puts my_hash["one"]
puts my_hash[_____]
my_hash[_____] = 8
puts my_hash["seven"]
```

Output:

```
six
two
four
8
```

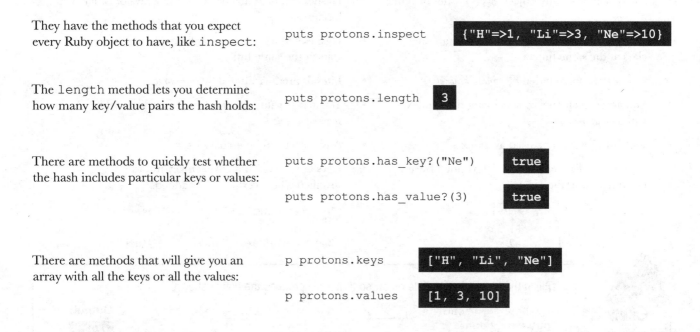

Fill in the blanks in the code below so that it will produce the output shown.

```
my_hash = {"one" => "two", :three => "four", 5 => "six"}
puts my_hash[5]
puts my_hash["one"]
puts my_hash[:three]
my_hash["seven"] = 8
puts my_hash["seven"]
```

Exercise Solution

Output:

```
six
two
four
8
```

Hashes are objects

We've been hearing over and over that everything in Ruby is an object. We saw that arrays are objects, and it probably won't surprise you to learn that hashes are objects, too.

```
protons = {"H" => 1, "Li" => 3, "Ne" => 10}
puts protons.class
```

`Hash`

And, like most Ruby objects, hashes have lots of useful instance methods. Here's a sampling…

They have the methods that you expect every Ruby object to have, like `inspect`:

```
puts protons.inspect
```

`{"H"=>1, "Li"=>3, "Ne"=>10}`

The `length` method lets you determine how many key/value pairs the hash holds:

```
puts protons.length
```

`3`

There are methods to quickly test whether the hash includes particular keys or values:

```
puts protons.has_key?("Ne")
```

`true`

```
puts protons.has_value?(3)
```

`true`

There are methods that will give you an array with all the keys or all the values:

```
p protons.keys
```

`["H", "Li", "Ne"]`

```
p protons.values
```

`[1, 3, 10]`

And, as with arrays, there are methods that will let you use a block to iterate over the hash's contents. The `each` method, for example, takes a block with *two* parameters, one for the key and one for the value. (More about `each` in a few pages.)

```
protons.each do |element, count|
  puts "#{element}: #{count}"
end
```

```
H: 1
Li: 3
Ne: 10
```

Exercise

Open a new terminal or command prompt, type **irb**, and hit the Enter/Return key. For each of the Ruby expressions below, write your guess for what the result will be on the line next to it. Then try typing the expression into irb and hit Enter. See if your guess matches what irb returns!

```
protons = { "He" => 2 }
```
....

```
protons["He"]
```
....

```
protons["C"] = 6
```
....

```
protons["C"]
```
....

```
protons.has_key?("C")
```
....

```
protons.has_value?(119)
```
....

```
protons.keys
```
....

```
protons.values
```
....

```
protons.merge({ "C" => 0, "Uh" => 147.2 })
```
....

there are no Dumb Questions

Q: Why is it called a "hash"?

A: Frankly, it's not the best possible name. Other languages refer to this kind of structure as "maps," "dictionaries," or "associative arrays" (because keys are associated with values). In Ruby, it's called a "hash" because an algorithm called a *hash table* is used to quickly look up keys within the hash. The details of that algorithm are beyond the scope of this book, but you can visit your favorite search engine to learn more.

Exercise Solution

Open a new terminal or command prompt, type **irb**, and hit the Enter/Return key. For each of the Ruby expressions below, write your guess for what the result will be on the line next to it. Then try typing the expression into irb and hit Enter. See if your guess matches what irb returns!

```
protons = { "He" => 2 }
```
{"He"=>2}

Result of an assignment statement, as always, is the value that was assigned.

```
protons["He"]
```
2

Provide the key, get the corresponding value.

```
protons["C"] = 6
```
6

The value that was assigned

```
protons["C"]
```
6

Retrieving the value we just assigned from the hash

```
protons.has_key?("C")
```
true

Returns true because the hash includes the given key

```
protons.has_value?(119)
```
false

Returns false because no key in the hash has the given value

```
protons.keys
```
["He", "C"]

An array containing every key in the hash

```
protons.values
```
[2, 6]

An array containing every value in the hash

If a key in the new hash already exists in the old hash, the old value is overridden.

If a key didn't already exist, it just gets added.

```
protons.merge({ "C" => 0, "Uh" => 147.2 })
```
{"He"=>2, "C"=>0, "Uh"=>147.2}

Hashes return "nil" by default

Let's take a look at the array of lines we read from the sample file of votes. We need to tally the number of times each name occurs within this array.

votes.txt

```
Amber Graham
Brian Martin
Amber Graham
Brian Martin
Brian Martin
```

```
p lines
```

```
["Amber Graham\n", "Brian Martin\n", "Amber Graham\n",
  "Brian Martin\n", "Brian Martin\n"]
```

↑ These newline characters were read from the file.

In the place of the array of arrays we discussed earlier, let's use a hash to store the vote counts. When we encounter a name within the `lines` array, if that name doesn't exist, we'll add it to the hash.

If we read this line... ⟶ `"Amber Graham"`

```
{
    "Amber Graham" => 1,    ←——...we'll add this key and
}                                value to the hash.
```

Each new name we encounter will get its own key and value added to the hash.

If we read this line... ⟶ `"Brian Martin"`

```
{
    "Amber Graham" => 1,
    "Brian Martin" => 1,    ←——...we'll add this key and
}                                value to the hash.
```

If we encounter a name that we've already added, we'll update its count instead.

If we read the same ⟶ `"Amber Graham"`
name again...

```
{
    "Amber Graham" => 2,    ←——...we'll update the
    "Brian Martin" => 1,         corresponding value.
}
```

...and so on, until we've counted all the votes.

That's the plan, anyway. But our first version of the code to do this fails with an error...

⌐ Set up an empty hash.

```
votes = {}

lines.each do |line|
   name = line.chomp
   votes[name] += 1
end

p votes
```

Remove the newline character.

Increment the total for the current name.

⌐ Error

```
undefined
method `+' for
nil:NilClass
```

So what happened? As we saw in Chapter 5, if you try to access an *array element* that hasn't been assigned to yet, you'll get `nil` back. If you try to access a *hash key* that has never been assigned to, the default value is *also* `nil`.

```
array = []
p array[999]      ←—— Doesn't exist
hash = {}
p hash["I don't exist"]  ←—— Doesn't exist
```

```
nil
nil
```

When we try to access the votes for a candidate name that has never been assigned to, we get `nil` back. And trying to add to `nil` produces an error.

Hashes return "nil" by default (continued)

The first time we encounter a candidate's name, instead of getting a vote tally back from the hash, we get `nil`. This results in an error when we try to add to it.

```
lines.each do |line|
  name = line.chomp
  votes[name] += 1
end
```

```
undefined method `+'
for nil:NilClass
```

To fix this, we can test whether the value for the current hash key is `nil`. If it's not, then we can safely increment whatever number is there. But if it *is* `nil`, then we'll need to set up an initial value (a tally of 1) for that key.

```
lines = []
File.open("votes.txt") do |file|
  lines = file.readlines
end

votes = {}

lines.each do |line|
  name = line.chomp
  if votes[name] != nil      ←——— If we've seen this name before...
    votes[name] += 1      ←———...increment its total.
  else      ←——— If this is our first sight of this name...
    votes[name] = 1      ←———...add it to the hash with a value of 1.
  end
end
```

And in the output, we see the populated hash. Our code is working!

```
p votes
```

```
{"Amber Graham"=>2, "Brian Martin"=>3}
```

nil (and only nil) is "falsy"

There's a small improvement to be made, though; that conditional is a little ugly.

```
if votes[name] != nil
```

We can clean that up by taking advantage of the fact that *any* Ruby expression can be used in a conditional statement. Most of them will be treated as if they were a true value. (Rubyists often say these values are "truthy.")

```
if "any string"  ←——Truthy
  puts "I'll be printed!"
end
```

```
if 42  ←——Truthy
  puts "I'll be printed!"
end
```

```
if ["any array"]  ←——Truthy
  puts "I'll be printed!"
end
```

In fact, aside from the `false` Boolean value, there is only *one* value that Ruby treats as if it were false: `nil`. (Rubyists often say that `nil` is "falsy.")

```
if false  ←——Actually false
  puts "I won't be printed!"
end
```

```
if nil  ←——Falsy
  puts "I won't, either!"
end
```

nil (and only nil) is "falsy" (continued)

Ruby treats `nil` like it's false to make it easier to test whether values have been assigned or not. For example, if you access a hash value within an `if` statement, the code within will be run if the value exists. If the value doesn't exist, the code won't be run.

Value is nil, ———→ which is falsy.

Value is 1, ———→ which is truthy.

```ruby
votes = {}
if votes["Kremit the Toad"]
    puts "I won't be printed!"
end
votes ["Kremit the Toad"] = 1
if votes["Kremit the Toad"]
    puts "I'll be printed!"
end
```

We can make our conditional read a little better by changing it from
`if votes[name] != nil` to just
`if votes[name]`.

Our code still works the same as before; it's just a bit cleaner looking. This may be a small victory now, but the average program has to test for the existence of objects a *lot*. Over time, this technique will save you many keystrokes!

```ruby
lines.each do |line|
  name = line.chomp
  if votes[name]  ←——— We don't need that ugly
    votes[name] += 1       "if votes[name] != nil"
  else                     anymore!
    votes[name] = 1
  end
end

p votes
```

```
{"Amber Graham"=>2, "Brian Martin"=>3}
```

Watch it!

We mean it when we say that <u>only</u> nil is falsy.

Most values that are treated as falsy in some other languages—such as empty strings, empty arrays, and the number 0—are <u>truthy</u> in Ruby.

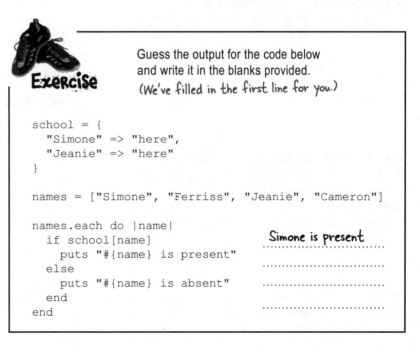

Exercise

Guess the output for the code below and write it in the blanks provided.
(We've filled in the first line for you.)

```ruby
school = {
  "Simone" => "here",
  "Jeanie" => "here"
}

names = ["Simone", "Ferriss", "Jeanie", "Cameron"]

names.each do |name|
  if school[name]
    puts "#{name} is present"
  else
    puts "#{name} is absent"
  end
end
```

Simone is present
....
....
....
....

Exercise Solution

Guess the output for the code below and write it in the blanks provided.

```
school = {
  "Simone" => "here",
  "Jeanie" => "here"
}

names = ["Simone", "Ferriss", "Jeanie", "Cameron"]

names.each do |name|
  if school[name]
    puts "#{name} is present"
  else
    puts "#{name} is absent"
  end
end
```

Simone is present
Ferriss is absent
Jeanie is present
Cameron is absent

Returning something other than "nil" by default

A disproportionate amount of our code for tallying the votes lies in the `if`/`else` statement that checks whether a key exists within the hash…

```
votes = {}

lines.each do |line|
  name = line.chomp
  if votes[name]          ← If votes[name] is not nil…
    votes[name] += 1      ← …increment the existing total.
  else                    ← If votes[name] IS nil…
    votes[name] = 1       ← …add the name to the
  end                        hash with a value of 1.
end
```

And we *need* that `if` statement. Normally, when you try to access a hash key that hasn't had a value assigned yet, you get `nil` back. The first time we tried to add to the tally for a key that didn't yet exist, we'd get an error (because you can't add to `nil`).

```
lines.each do |line|
  name = line.chomp
  votes[name] += 1
end
```

On the first name, gets "nil" and tries to add 1 to it…

Error →
```
undefined method `+'
for nil:NilClass
```

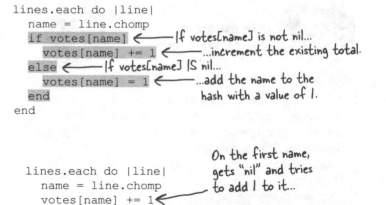

But what if we got a value *other* than `nil` for the unassigned keys? A value that we *can* increment? Let's find out how to make that happen…

Returning something other than "nil" by default (continued)

Instead of using a hash literal ({ }), you can also call `Hash.new` to create new hashes. Without any arguments, `Hash.new` works just like { }, giving you a hash that returns `nil` for unassigned keys.

Create a new hash.

```
votes = Hash.new
votes["Amber Graham"] = 1
p votes["Amber Graham"]
p votes["Brian Martin"]
```

When we access a value that's been assigned to, we get that value back.

When we access a value that HASN'T been assigned to, we get "nil".

```
1
nil
```

But when you call `Hash.new` and pass an object as an argument, that argument becomes that hash's default object. Any time you access a key in that hash that hasn't been assigned to yet, instead of `nil`, you'll get the default object you specified.

Create a new hash with a default object of "0".

```
votes = Hash.new(0)
votes["Amber Graham"] = 1
p votes["Amber Graham"]
p votes["Brian Martin"]
```

When we access a value that's been assigned to, we get that value back.

When we access a value that HASN'T been assigned to, we get the default object.

```
1
0
```

Let's use a hash default object to shorten up our vote counting code...

If we create our hash with `Hash.new(0)`, it will return the default object (0) when we try to access the vote tally for any key that hasn't been assigned to yet. That 0 value gets incremented to 1, then 2, and so on as the same name is encountered again and again.

Watch it!

Using anything other than a number as a hash default object may cause bugs!

We'll cover ways to safely use other objects in Chapter 8. Until then, don't use anything other than a number as a default!

```
lines = []
File.open("votes.txt") do |file|
  lines = file.readlines
end

votes = Hash.new(0)

lines.each do |line|
  name = line.chomp
  votes[name] += 1
end

p votes
```

Create a new hash with a default object of "0".

Increment whatever value is returned: "0" if the key has never been updated, or the current tally otherwise.

We can get rid of the `if` statement entirely!

And as you can see from the output, the code still works.

```
{"Amber Graham"=>2, "Brian Martin"=>3}
```

Normalizing hash keys

Okay, so you've got counts for each candidate. But that won't help if the counts are <u>wrong</u>. We just got the final votes in, and look what happened!

```
Amber Graham
Brian Martin
Amber Graham
Brian Martin
Brian Martin
amber graham
brian martin
amber graham
amber graham
```
votes.txt

```
{"name" => "Kevin Wagner",
 "occupation" => "Election Volunteer"}
```

Here's what we get if we run this new file through our existing code:

```
{"Amber Graham"=>2, "Brian Martin"=>3, "amber graham"=>3, "brian martin"=>1}
```

These two shouldn't be separate items!

Well, this won't do... It looks like the last few votes were added with the candidates' names in lowercase, and they were treated as *entirely separate* candidates!

This highlights a problem when you're working with hashes: if you want to access or modify a value, whatever you provide as a key needs to match the existing key *exactly*. Otherwise, it will be treated as an entirely new key.

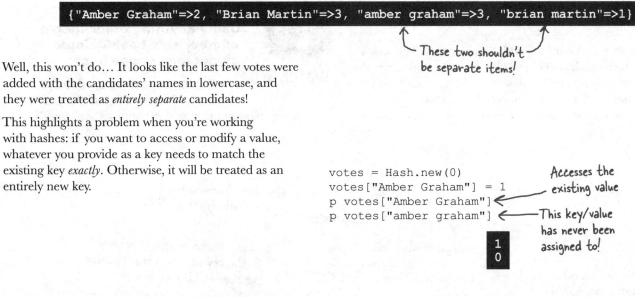

```
votes = Hash.new(0)
votes["Amber Graham"] = 1
p votes["Amber Graham"]
p votes["amber graham"]
```

Accesses the existing value

This key/value has never been assigned to!

```
1
0
```

So how will we ensure that the new lowercase entries in our text file get matched with the capitalized entries? We need to *normalize* the input: we need one standard way of representing candidates' names, and we need to use *that* for our hash keys.

Normalizing hash keys (continued)

Fortunately, in this case, normalizing the candidate names
is really easy. We'll add one line of code to ensure the case
on each name matches prior to storing it in the hash.

```ruby
lines = []
File.open("votes.txt") do |file|
  lines = file.readlines
end

votes = Hash.new(0)

lines.each do |line|
  name = line.chomp
  name.upcase!        ←——— Change the name to ALL CAPS
  votes[name] += 1           before using it as a hash key.
end

p votes
```

And in the output we see the updated contents
of our hash: votes from the lowercase entries
have been added to the totals for the capitalized
entries. Our counts are fixed!

```
{"AMBER GRAHAM"=>5, "BRIAN MARTIN"=>4}
```

We have our winner!

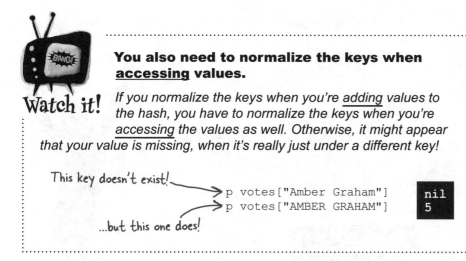

**You also need to normalize the keys when
<u>accessing</u> values.**

*If you normalize the keys when you're <u>adding</u> values to
the hash, you have to normalize the keys when you're
<u>accessing</u> the values as well. Otherwise, it might appear
that your value is missing, when it's really just under a different key!*

This key doesn't exist!

```ruby
p votes["Amber Graham"]
p votes["AMBER GRAHAM"]
```

```
nil
5
```

...but this one does!

Watch it!

Hashes and "each"

We've processed the lines in the sample file and built a hash with the total number of votes:

```
p votes
```
```
{"AMBER GRAHAM"=>5, "BRIAN MARTIN"=>4}
```

It would be far better, though, if we could print one line for each candidate name, together with its vote count.

As we saw back in Chapter 5, arrays have an `each` method that takes a block with a single parameter. The `each` method passes each element of the array to the block for processing, one at a time. Hashes also have an `each` method, which works in about the same way. The only difference is that on hashes, `each` expects a block with *two* parameters: one for the key, and one for the corresponding value.

```
hash = { "one" => 1, "two" => 2 }
hash.each do |key, value|
  puts "#{key}: #{value}"
end
```
```
one: 1
two: 2
```

there are no Dumb Questions

Q: What happens if I call **each** on a hash, but pass it a block with *one* parameter?

A: The `each` method for hashes allows that; it will pass the block a two-element array with the key and value from each key/value pair in the hash. It's much more common to use blocks with two parameters, though.

We can use `each` to print the name of each candidate in the `votes` hash, along with the corresponding vote count:

```
lines = []
File.open("votes.txt") do |file|
  lines = file.readlines
end

votes = Hash.new(0)

lines.each do |line|
  name = line.chomp
  name.upcase!
  votes[name] += 1          Key      Value
end                         goes     goes
                            here.    here.

Process each ──→  votes.each do |name, count|
key/value pair.     puts "#{name}: #{count}"
                  end
```
```
AMBER GRAHAM: 5
BRIAN MARTIN: 4
```

There are our totals, neatly formatted!

Now you've seen one of the classic uses of hashes—a program where we need to look up values for a given key repeatedly. Up next, we'll look at another common way to use hashes: as method arguments.

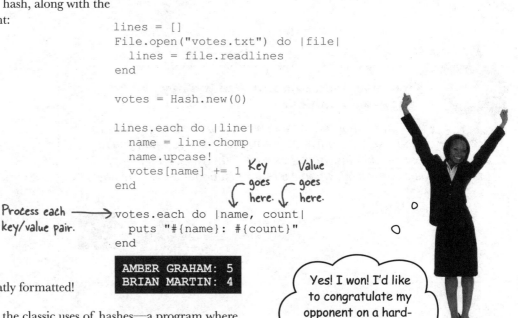

Yes! I won! I'd like to congratulate my opponent on a hard-fought campaign...

Fireside Chats

Tonight's talk: **An array and a hash work out their differences.**

Hash:

Nice to see you again, Array.

There's no need to be like that.

Well, I do have a certain glamor about me… But even I know there are still times when developers *should* use an array instead of a hash.

It's true; it's a lot of work keeping all of my elements where I can retrieve them quickly! It pays off if someone wants to retrieve a particular item from the middle of the collection, though. If they give me the correct key, I always know right where to find a value.

Yes, but the developer has to know the exact index where the data is stored, right? All those numbers are a pain to keep track of! But it's either that, or wait for the array to search through all its elements, one by one…

Agreed. Developers should know about both arrays *and* hashes, and pick the right one for their current task.

Array:

I didn't really want to be here, but whatever, Hash.

Isn't there? I was doing a perfectly fine job storing everyone's collections, and then you come along, and developers everywhere are like, "Ooh! Why use an array when I can use a hash? Hashes are so cool!"

Darn right! Arrays are way more efficient than hashes! If you're happy retrieving elements in the same order you added them (say, with each), then you want an array, because you won't have to wait while a hash organizes your data for you.

Hey, we arrays can get data back too, you know.

But the point is, we *can* do it. And if you're just building a simple queue, we're still the better choice.

Fair enough.

A mess of method arguments

Suppose we're making an app to track basic information regarding candidates so voters can learn about them. We've created a `Candidate` class to keep all of a candidate's info in one place. For convenience, we've set up an `initialize` method so that we can set all of an instance's attributes directly from a call to `Candidate.new`.

```ruby
class Candidate
  attr_accessor :name, :age, :occupation, :hobby, :birthplace
  def initialize(name, age, occupation, hobby, birthplace)
    self.name = name
    self.age = age
    self.occupation = occupation
    self.hobby = hobby
    self.birthplace = birthplace
  end
end
```

Set up attribute accessors.

Set up Candidate.new to take arguments.

Use the parameters to set the object attributes.

Let's add some code following the class definition to create a `Candidate` instance and print out its data.

```ruby
def print_summary(candidate)
  puts "Candidate: #{candidate.name}"
  puts "Age: #{candidate.age}"
  puts "Occupation: #{candidate.occupation}"
  puts "Hobby: #{candidate.hobby}"
  puts "Birthplace: #{candidate.birthplace}"
end

candidate = Candidate.new("Carl Barnes", 49, "Attorney", nil, "Miami")
print_summary(candidate)
```

We have to provide an argument even if we're not using it.

```
Candidate: Carl Barnes
Age: 49
Occupation: Attorney
Hobby:
Birthplace: Miami
```

Our very first attempt at calling `Candidate.new` shows that its usage could be a lot smoother. We have to provide all the arguments whether we're going to use them or not.

We could just make the `hobby` parameter optional, *if* it didn't have the `birthplace` parameter following it…

```ruby
class Candidate
  attr_accessor :name, :age, :occupation, :hobby, :birthplace
  def initialize(name, age, occupation, hobby = nil, birthplace)
    ...
  end
end
```

Provide a default value to make the parameter optional…

Since `birthplace` is present, though, we get an error if we try to omit hobby…

```ruby
Candidate.new("Carl Barnes", 49, "Attorney", , "Miami")
```

Error →

```
syntax error, unexpected ',', expecting ')'
```

A mess of method arguments (continued)

We encounter another problem if we forget the order that method arguments should appear in...

```
candidate = Candidate.new("Amy Nguyen", 37, "Lacrosse", "Engineer", "Seattle")
print_summary(candidate)
```

Wait, what order do these go in?

It's becoming clear that there are some issues with using a long list of parameters for a method. The order is confusing, and it's hard to leave unwanted arguments off.

Whoops! We got these two backward!

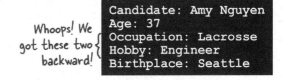

```
Candidate: Amy Nguyen
Age: 37
Occupation: Lacrosse
Hobby: Engineer
Birthplace: Seattle
```

Using hashes as method parameters

Historically, Rubyists have dealt with these issues by using hashes as method parameters. Here's a simple `area` method that, instead of separate `length` and `width` parameters, accepts a single hash. (We realize this is a bit messy. Over the next few pages, we'll show you some shortcuts to make hash parameters much more readable!)

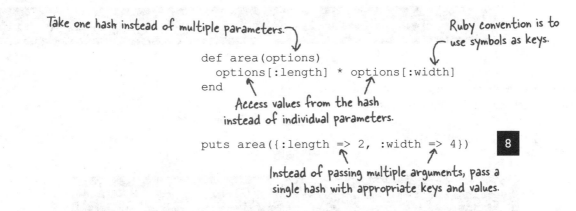

Take one hash instead of multiple parameters.

Ruby convention is to use symbols as keys.

```
def area(options)
  options[:length] * options[:width]
end
```

Access values from the hash instead of individual parameters.

```
puts area({:length => 2, :width => 4})
```

8

Instead of passing multiple arguments, pass a single hash with appropriate keys and values.

The convention in Ruby is to use symbols instead of strings for hash parameter keys, because looking up symbol keys is more efficient than looking up strings.

Using hash parameters offers several benefits over regular method parameters...

With regular parameters:

- Arguments must appear in exactly the right order.

- Arguments can be hard to tell apart.

- Required parameters have to appear before optional parameters.

With hash parameters:

- Keys can appear in any order.

- Keys act as "labels" for each value.

- You can skip providing a value for any key you want.

Hash parameters in our Candidate class

Here's a revision of our `Candidate` class's `initialize` method
using a hash parameter.

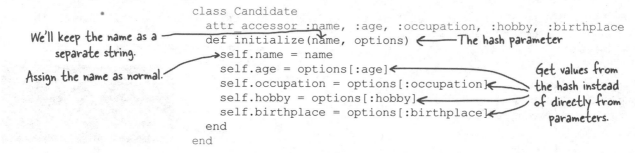

We'll keep the name as a separate string.

Assign the name as normal.

The hash parameter

Get values from the hash instead of directly from parameters.

```
class Candidate
  attr_accessor :name, :age, :occupation, :hobby, :birthplace
  def initialize(name, options)
    self.name = name
    self.age = options[:age]
    self.occupation = options[:occupation]
    self.hobby = options[:hobby]
    self.birthplace = options[:birthplace]
  end
end
```

We can now call `Candidate.new` by passing the name as a string,
followed by a hash with the values for all the other `Candidate` attributes:

Now it's clear which attribute is which!

```
candidate = Candidate.new("Amy Nguyen",
  {:age => 37, :occupation => "Engineer", :hobby => "Lacrosse", :birthplace => "Seattle"})

p candidate
```

```
#<Candidate:0x007fbd7a02e858 @name="Amy Nguyen", @age=37,
  @occupation="Engineer", @hobby="Lacrosse", @birthplace="Seattle">
```

No more switched attributes!

We can leave one or more of the hash keys off, if we want. The
attribute will just get assigned the hash default object, `nil`.

We can leave the hobby off.

```
candidate = Candidate.new("Carl Barnes",
  {:age => 49, :occupation => "Attorney", :birthplace => "Miami"})

p candidate
```

```
#<Candidate:0x007f8aaa042a68 @name="Carl Barnes", @age=49,
  @occupation="Attorney", @hobby=nil, @birthplace="Miami">
```

Omitted attributes default to nil.

We can put the hash keys in any order we want:

```
candidate = Candidate.new("Amy Nguyen",
  {:birthplace => "Seattle", :hobby => "Lacrosse", :occupation => "Engineer", :age => 37})

p candidate
```

```
#<Candidate:0x007f81a890e8c8 @name="Amy Nguyen", @age=37,
  @occupation="Engineer", @hobby="Lacrosse", @birthplace="Seattle">
```

Leave off the braces!

We'll admit that the method calls we've been showing so far are a little uglier than method calls with regular arguments, what with all those curly braces:.

```ruby
candidate = Candidate.new("Carl Barnes",
  {:age => 49, :occupation => "Attorney"})
```

...which is why Ruby lets you leave the curly braces off, as long as the hash argument is the final argument:

```ruby
candidate = Candidate.new("Carl Barnes",
  :age => 49, :occupation => "Attorney")    No braces!
p candidate
```

```
#<Candidate:0x007fb412802c30
 @name="Carl Barnes", @age=49,
 @occupation="Attorney",
 @hobby=nil, @birthplace=nil>
```

For this reason, you'll find that most methods that define a hash parameter define it as the last parameter.

Leave out the arrows!

Ruby offers one more shortcut we can make use of. If a hash uses symbols as keys, hash literals let you leave the colon (:) off the symbol and replace the hash rocket (=>) with a colon.

```ruby
candidate = Candidate.new("Amy Nguyen", age: 37,
  occupation: "Engineer", hobby: "Lacrosse")
p candidate
```

The same symbols, but more readable!

```
#<Candidate:0x007f9dc412aa98
 @name="Amy Nguyen", @age=37,
 @occupation="Engineer",
 @hobby="Lacrosse",
 @birthplace=nil>
```

Those hash arguments started out pretty ugly, we admit. But now that we know all the tricks to make them more readable, they're looking rather nice, don't you think? Almost like regular method arguments, but with handy labels next to them!

```ruby
Candidate.new("Carl Barnes", age: 49, occupation: "Attorney")
Candidate.new("Amy Nguyen", age: 37, occupation: "Engineer")
```

Conventional Wisdom

When you're defining a method that takes a hash parameter, ensure the hash parameter comes <u>last</u>, so that callers to your method can leave the curly braces off their hash. When calling a method with a hash argument, you should leave the curly braces off if possible—it's easier to read. And lastly, you should use symbols as keys whenever you're working with a hash parameter; it's more efficient.

Making the entire hash optional

There's one last improvement we can make to our `Candidate` class's `initialize` method. Currently we can include all of our hash keys:

```
Candidate.new("Amy Nguyen", age: 37, occupation: "Engineer",
  hobby: "Lacrosse", birthplace: "Seattle")
```

Or we can leave *most* of them off:

```
Candidate.new("Amy Nguyen", age: 37)
```

But if we try to leave them *all* off, we get an error:

```
p Candidate.new("Amy Nguyen")
```

Error ⟶
```
in `initialize': wrong number
of arguments (1 for 2)
```

If we leave all the keys off, then as far as Ruby is concerned, we didn't pass a hash argument at all.

We can avoid this inconsistency by setting an empty hash as a default for the `options` argument:

```
class Candidate
  attr_accessor :name, :age, :occupation, :hobby, :birthplace
  def initialize(name, options = {})        ⟵— If no hash is passed, use an empty one.
    self.name = name
    self.age = options[:age]
    self.occupation = options[:occupation]
    self.hobby = options[:hobby]
    self.birthplace = options[:birthplace]
  end
end
```

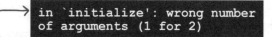

Now, if no hash argument is passed, the empty hash will be used by default. All the `Candidate` attributes will be set to the `nil` default value from the empty hash.

```
p Candidate.new("Carl Barnes")
```

```
#<Candidate:0x007fbe0981ec18 @name="Carl Barnes", @age=nil,
  @occupation=nil, @hobby=nil, @birthplace=nil>
```

If we specify at least one key/value pair, though, the hash argument will be treated as before:

```
p Candidate.new("Carl Barnes", occupation: "Attorney")
```

```
#<Candidate:0x007fbe0981e970 @name="Carl Barnes", @age=nil,
  @occupation="Attorney", @hobby=nil, @birthplace=nil>
```

Code Magnets

A Ruby program is all scrambled up on the fridge. Can you reconstruct the code snippets to make a working Ruby program that will produce the given output?

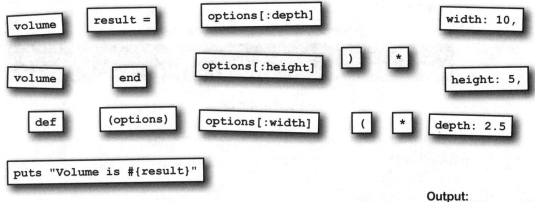

```
volume        result =        options[:depth]                    width: 10,

volume        end             options[:height]      )      *     height: 5,

     def      (options)       options[:width]      (      *      depth: 2.5

puts "Volume is #{result}"
```

Output:

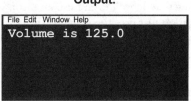

File Edit Window Help
Volume is 125.0

Code Magnets Solution

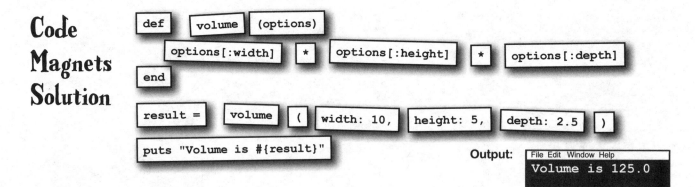

```
def    volume    (options)
    options[:width]  *  options[:height]  *  options[:depth]
end

result =   volume   (  width: 10,   height: 5,   depth: 2.5   )
puts "Volume is #{result}"
```

Output:

```
File Edit Window Help
Volume is 125.0
```

Typos in hash arguments are dangerous

There's a downside to hash arguments that we haven't discussed yet, and it's just waiting to cause trouble for us… For example, you might expect this code to set the `occupation` attribute of the new `Candidate` instance, and you might be surprised when it doesn't:

```
p Candidate.new("Amy Nguyen", occupaiton: "Engineer")
```

```
#<Candidate:0x007f862a022cb0 @name="Amy Nguyen", @age=nil,
 @occupation=nil, @hobby=nil, @birthplace=nil>
```

Why is this still nil?

Why didn't it work? Because we misspelled the symbol name in the hash key!

```
p Candidate.new("Amy Nguyen", occupaiton: "Engineer")
```

Whoops!

The code doesn't even raise an error. Our `initialize` method just uses the value of the correctly spelled `options[:occupation]` key, which is of course `nil`, because it's never been assigned to.

> Silent failures now mean hard-to-diagnose bugs later. This doesn't make me want to use hash arguments…

Don't worry. In version 2.0, Ruby added <u>keyword arguments</u>, which can prevent this sort of issue.

Keyword arguments

Rather than require a single hash parameter in method definitions, we can specify the individual hash keys we want callers to provide, using this syntax:

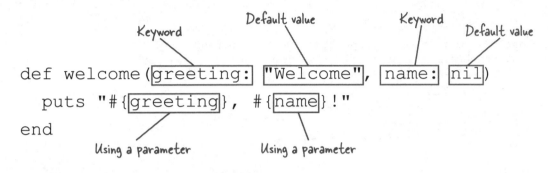

When we define the method this way, we don't have to worry about providing keys to a hash in the method body. Ruby stores each value in a separate parameter, which can be accessed directly by name, just like a regular method parameter.

With the method defined, we can call it by providing keys and values, just like we have been:

```ruby
welcome(greeting: "Hello", name: "Amy")
```
```
Hello, Amy!
```

In fact, callers are actually just passing a hash, like before:

```ruby
my_arguments = {greeting: "Hello", name: "Amy"}
welcome(my_arguments)
```
```
Hello, Amy!
```

The hash gets some special treatment within the method, though. Any keywords omitted from the call get set to the specified default values:

```ruby
welcome(name: "Amy")
```
```
Welcome, Amy!
```

And if any unknown keywords are provided (or you make a typo in a key), an error will be raised:

```ruby
welcome(greeting: "Hello", nme: "Amy")
```
Error ⟶
```
ArgumentError: unknown
keywords: greting, nme
```

Using keyword arguments with our Candidate class

Currently, our `Candidate` class is using a hash parameter in its `initialize` method. The code is a bit ugly, and it won't warn a caller if they make a typo in a hash key.

```ruby
class Candidate
  attr_accessor :name, :age, :occupation, :hobby, :birthplace
  def initialize(name, options = {})        ⟵— Hash parameter
    self.name = name
    self.age = options[:age]
    self.occupation = options[:occupation]      Accessing values
    self.hobby = options[:hobby]                from the hash
    self.birthplace = options[:birthplace]
  end
end
```

Let's revise our `Candidate` class's `initialize` method to take keyword arguments.

```ruby
class Candidate                                      We replace the hash parameter
  attr_accessor :name, :age, :occupation, :hobby, :birthplace    with keywords and default values.
  def initialize(name, age: nil, occupation: nil, hobby: nil, birthplace: "Sleepy Creek")
    self.name = name
    self.age = age
    self.occupation = occupation        We use parameter names
    self.hobby = hobby                  instead of hash keys.
    self.birthplace = birthplace
  end
end
```

We use `"Sleepy Creek"` as a default value for the `birthplace` keyword, and `nil` as a default for the others. We also replace all those references to the `options` hash in the method body with parameter names. The method is a lot easier to read now!

It can still be called the same way as before…

```ruby
p Candidate.new("Amy Nguyen", age: 37, occupation: "Engineer")
```

```
#<Candidate:0x007fbf5b14e520 @name="Amy Nguyen",
  @age=37, @occupation="Engineer", @hobby=nil, @birthplace="Sleepy Creek">
```

└─ Specified values! ─┘   └─ Defaults! ─┘

…and it will warn callers if they make a typo in a keyword!

```ruby
p Candidate.new("Amy Nguyen", occupaiton: "Engineer")
```

Error ⟶ `ArgumentError: unknown keyword: occupaiton`

Required keyword arguments

Right now, we can still call `Candidate.new` even if we fail to provide the most basic information about a candidate:

```
p Candidate.new("Carl Barnes")
```

All attributes are set to the defaults!

```
#<Candidate:0x007fe743885d38 @name="Carl Barnes",
 @age=nil, @occupation=nil, @hobby=nil, @birthplace="Sleepy Creek">
```

This isn't ideal. We want to require callers to provide at least an age and an occupation for a candidate.

Back when the `initialize` method was using ordinary method parameters, this wasn't a problem; *all* the arguments were required.

```
class Candidate
  attr_accessor :name, :age, :occupation, :hobby, :birthplace
  def initialize(name, age, occupation, hobby, birthplace)
    ...
  end
end
```

The only way to make a method parameter optional is to provide a default value for it.

```
class Candidate
  attr_accessor :name, :age, :occupation, :hobby, :birthplace
  def initialize(name, age = nil, occupation = nil, hobby = nil, birthplace = nil)
    ...
  end
end
```

But wait—we provide default values for all our keywords now.

```
class Candidate
  attr_accessor :name, :age, :occupation, :hobby, :birthplace
  def initialize(name, age: nil, occupation: nil, hobby: nil, birthplace: "Sleepy Creek")
    ...
  end
end
```

If you take away the default value for an ordinary method parameter, that parameter is required; you can't call the method without providing a value. What happens if we take away the default values for our *keyword* arguments?

Required keyword arguments (continued)

Let's try removing the default values for the age and occupation keywords, and see if they'll be required when we call `initialize`.

We can't just remove the colon after the keyword, though. If we did, Ruby wouldn't be able to tell age and occupation apart from ordinary method parameters.

> **Required keyword arguments were only added in Ruby 2.1.**
>
> *If you're running Ruby 2.0, you'll get a syntax error if you try to use required keyword arguments. You'll need to either upgrade to 2.1 (or later) or provide default values.*

Watch it!

```ruby
class Candidate
  attr_accessor :name, :age, :occupation, :hobby, :birthplace
  def initialize(name, age, occupation, hobby: nil, birthplace: "Sleepy Creek")
    ...
  end
end
```

Ordinary parameters, not keywords!

What if we removed the default value but left the colon after the keyword?

```ruby
class Candidate
  attr_accessor :name, :age, :occupation, :hobby, :birthplace
  def initialize(name, age:, occupation:, hobby: nil, birthplace: "Sleepy Creek")
    self.name = name
    self.age = age
    self.occupation = occupation
    self.hobby = hobby
    self.birthplace = birthplace
  end
end
```

Keywords, but with no defaults!

We can still call `Candidate.new`, as long as we provide the required keywords:

```ruby
p Candidate.new("Carl Barnes", age: 49, occupation: "Attorney")
```

```
#<Candidate:0x007fcec281e5a0 @name="Carl Barnes",
@age=49, @occupation="Attorney", @hobby=nil, @birthplace="Sleepy Creek">
```

…and if we leave the required keywords off, Ruby will warn us!

```ruby
p Candidate.new("Carl Barnes")
```

Error →
```
ArgumentError: missing
keywords: age, occupation
```

You used to have to provide a long list of unlabeled arguments to `Candidate.new`, and you had to get the order *exactly* right. Now that you've learned to use hashes as arguments, whether explicitly or behind the scenes with keyword arguments, your code will be a lot cleaner!

Exercise

Here are definitions for two Ruby methods. Match each of the six method calls below to the output it would produce. (We've filled in the first one for you.)

```ruby
def create(options = {})
  puts "Creating #{options[:database]} for owner #{options[:user]}..."
end

def connect(database:, host: "localhost", port: 3306, user: "root")
  puts "Connecting to #{database} on #{host} port #{port} as #{user}..."
end
```

A   `create(database: "catalog", user: "carl")`

B   `create(user: "carl")`

C   `create`

D   `connect(database: "catalog")`

E   `connect(database: "catalog", password: "1234")`

F   `connect(user: "carl")`

...... `Creating  for owner carl...`

...... `unknown keyword: password`

...... `Connecting to catalog on localhost port 3306 as root...`

A ...... `Creating catalog for owner carl...`

...... `Creating  for owner ...`

...... `missing keyword: database`

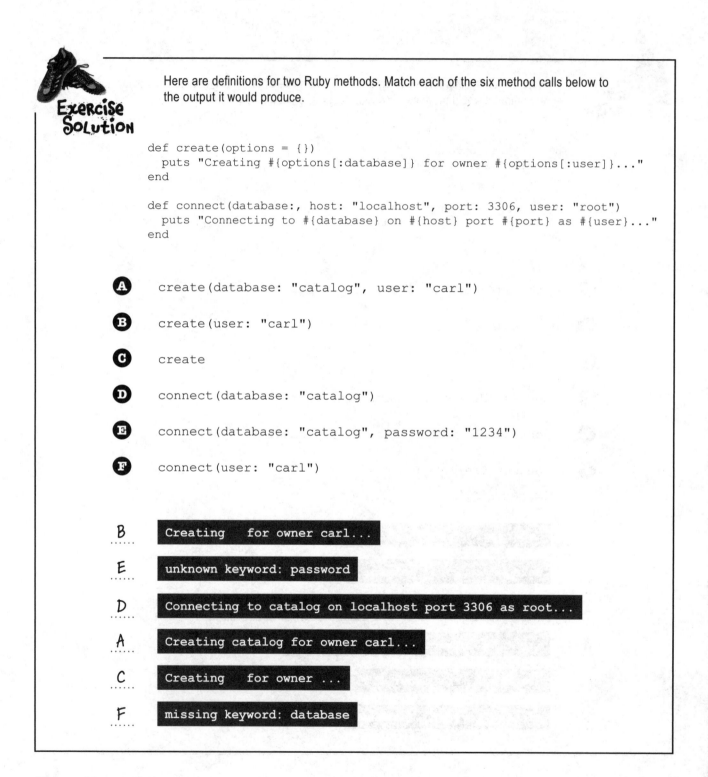

Here are definitions for two Ruby methods. Match each of the six method calls below to the output it would produce.

```ruby
def create(options = {})
  puts "Creating #{options[:database]} for owner #{options[:user]}..."
end

def connect(database:, host: "localhost", port: 3306, user: "root")
  puts "Connecting to #{database} on #{host} port #{port} as #{user}..."
end
```

A `create(database: "catalog", user: "carl")`

B `create(user: "carl")`

C `create`

D `connect(database: "catalog")`

E `connect(database: "catalog", password: "1234")`

F `connect(user: "carl")`

B .... `Creating   for owner carl...`

E .... `unknown keyword: password`

D .... `Connecting to catalog on localhost port 3306 as root...`

A .... `Creating catalog for owner carl...`

C .... `Creating   for owner ...`

F .... `missing keyword: database`

Your Ruby Toolbox

That's it for Chapter 7! You've added hashes to your toolbox.

Here are our notes on arrays from Chapter 5, just for comparison...

Arrays

An array holds a collection of objects.

Arrays can be any size and can grow or shrink as needed.

Arrays are ordinary Ruby objects and have many useful instance methods.

Hashes

A hash holds a collection of objects, each "labeled" with a key.

You can use any object as a hash key. This is different than arrays, which can only use integers as indexes.

Hashes are also Ruby objects and have many useful instance methods.

...and here are our notes for this chapter!

Up Next...

We've shown you how to set up a hash default value. But when used incorrectly, hash default values can cause strange bugs. The problem has to do with *references* to objects, which we'll learn about in the next chapter...

BULLET POINTS

- A hash literal is surrounded by curly braces. It needs to include a key for each value, like this: `{"one" => 1, "two" => 2}`

- When a hash key is accessed that a value has never been assigned to, `nil` is returned by default.

- Any Ruby expression can be used in conditional statements. Aside from the `false` Boolean value, the only other value Ruby will treat as false is `nil`.

- You can use `Hash.new` instead of a hash literal to create a new hash. If you pass an object as an argument to `Hash.new`, that object becomes the hash default object. When any key that hasn't been assigned to is accessed, the default object will be returned as the value (instead of `nil`).

- If the key you access isn't exactly equal to the key in the hash, it will be treated as an entirely different key.

- Hashes have an `each` method that works a lot like the `each` method on arrays. The difference is that the block you provide should (normally) accept two parameters (instead of one): one for each key, and one for the corresponding value.

- If you pass a hash as the last argument to a method, Ruby lets you leave the braces off.

- If a hash uses symbols as keys, you can leave the colon off the symbol, and replace => with a colon, like this: `{name: "Kim", age: 28}`

- When defining a method, you can specify that callers should provide keyword arguments. The keywords and values are actually just a hash behind the scenes, but the values are placed into named parameters within the method.

- You can require keyword arguments, or make them optional by defining a default value.

8 references

Crossed Signals

> Mama, the nice man asked if we were ready for a delivery, and I said okay. Um, what's an orangutan?

Ever sent an email to the wrong contact? You probably had a hard time sorting out the confusion that ensued. Well, *Ruby objects* are *just like those contacts* in your address book, and *calling methods* on them is like *sending messages* to them. If your address book gets *mixed up*, it's possible to send messages to the *wrong object*. This chapter will help you *recognize the signs* that this is happening, and help you *get your programs running smoothly* again.

Some confusing bugs

The word continues to spread—if someone has a Ruby problem, your company can solve it. And so people are showing up at your door with some unusual dilemmas…

I'm making a star cataloging program. But the stars' names are getting overwritten!

This astronomer thinks he has a clever way to save some coding. Instead of typing `my_star = CelestialBody.new` and `my_star.type = 'star'` for every star he wants to create, he wants to just *copy* the original star and set a new name for it.

```ruby
class CelestialBody
  attr_accessor :type, :name
end

altair = CelestialBody.new
altair.name = 'Altair'      To save time, he wants to
altair.type = 'star'        copy the previous star...
polaris = altair
polaris.name = 'Polaris'    ...and just change
vega = polaris                 the name.
vega.name = 'Vega'          Same
                            here
puts altair.name, polaris.name, vega.name
```

But it looks like the names on all three stars are now identical!

But the plan seems to be backfiring. All three of his `CelestialBody` instances are reporting that they have the *same* name!

The heap

The bug in the star catalog program stems from an underlying problem: the developer *thinks* he's working with *multiple* objects, when actually he's operating on the *same* object over and over.

To understand how that can be, we're going to need to learn about where objects really live, and how your programs communicate with them.

Rubyists often talk about "placing objects in variables," "storing objects in arrays," "storing an object in a hash value," and so forth. But that's just a simplification of what actually happens. Because you can't actually put an object *in* a variable, array, or hash.

Instead, all Ruby objects live on the **heap**, an area of your computer's memory allocated for object storage.

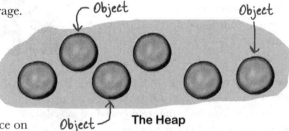

When a new object is created, Ruby allocates space on the heap where it can live.

Generally, you don't need to concern yourself with the heap—Ruby manages it for you. The heap grows in size if more space is needed. Objects that are no longer used get cleared off the heap. It's not something you usually have to worry about.

But we *do* need to be able to *retrieve* items that are stored on the heap. And we do that with *references*. Read on to learn more about them.

References

When you want to send a letter to a particular person, how do you get it to them? Each residence in a city has an *address* that mail can be sent to. You simply write the address on an envelope. A postal worker then uses that address to find the residence and deliver the letter.

When a friend of yours moves into a new residence, they give you their address, which you then write down in an address book or other convenient place. This allows you to communicate with them in the future.

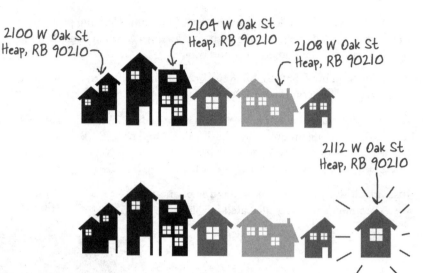

Ruby uses **references** to locate objects on the heap, like you might use an address to locate a house. When a new object is created, it returns a reference to itself. You store that reference in a variable, array, or other convenient place. Similar to a house address, the reference tells Ruby where the object "lives" on the heap.

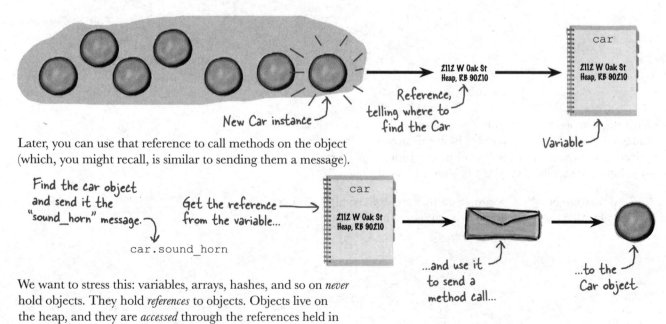

Later, you can use that reference to call methods on the object (which, you might recall, is similar to sending them a message).

We want to stress this: variables, arrays, hashes, and so on *never* hold objects. They hold *references* to objects. Objects live on the heap, and they are *accessed* through the references held in variables.

When references go wrong

Andy met not one, but *two*, gorgeous women last week: Betty and Candace. Better yet, they both live on his street.

Betty Bell
2106 W Oak St
Heap, RB 90210

Candace Camden
2110 W Oak St
Heap, RB 90210

Andy Adams
2100 W Oak St
Heap, RB 90210

Oak Street in reality

Andy intended to write down both their addresses in his address book. Unfortunately for him, he accidentally wrote down the *same* address (Betty's) for *both* women.

Betty Bell
2106 W Oak St
Heap, RB 90210

Candace Camden
2106 W Oak St
Heap, RB 90210

Oak Street according to Andy's address book

Later that week, Betty received *two* letters from Andy:

Dear Betty,

It was great to meet you on Tuesday! I really enjoyed chatting about that thing you like.

Say, I was wondering, would you go to the big dance with me next week? I think we'd have a good time. Let me know!

Yours,

Andy

Dear Candace,

It was great to meet you on Monday! I really enjoyed chatting about that thing you like.

Say, I was wondering, would you go to the movies with me next week? I think we'd have a good time. Let me know!

Yours,

Andy

Now, Betty is angry at Andy, and Candace (who never received a letter) thinks Andy is ignoring her.

What does any of this have to do with fixing our Ruby programs? You're about to find out…

Aliasing

Andy's dilemma can be simulated in Ruby with this simple class, called `LoveInterest`. A `LoveInterest` has an instance method, `request_date`, which will print an affirmative response just once. If the method is called again after that, the `LoveInterest` will report that it's busy.

```
class LoveInterest

  def request_date
    if @busy
      puts "Sorry, I'm busy."
    else
      puts "Sure, let's go!"
      @busy = true
    end
  end

end
```

`@busy` is nil (and treated as false) until it gets set to something else. → `if @busy` ← If this is not the first request...

`puts "Sorry, I'm busy."` ← ...give a negative response.

`puts "Sure, let's go!"` ← Give an affirmative response.

`@busy = true` ← Mark this object as unable to accept any future requests.

Normally, when using this class, we would create two separate objects and store references to them in two separate variables:

```
betty = LoveInterest.new
candace = LoveInterest.new
```

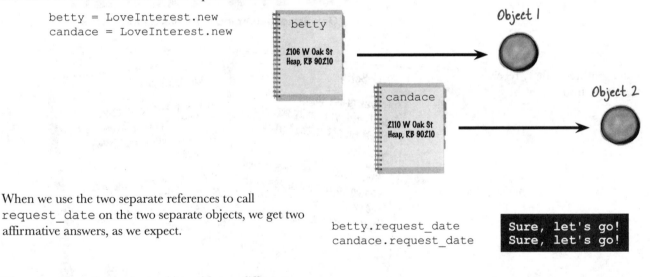

betty
2106 W Oak St
Heap, RB 90210

Object 1

candace
2110 W Oak St
Heap, RB 90210

Object 2

When we use the two separate references to call `request_date` on the two separate objects, we get two affirmative answers, as we expect.

```
betty.request_date
candace.request_date
```

```
Sure, let's go!
Sure, let's go!
```

We can confirm that we're working with two different objects by using the `object_id` instance method, which almost all Ruby objects have. It returns a unique identifier for each object.

```
p betty.object_id
p candace.object_id
```

```
70115845133840
70115845133820
```
} Two different objects

Aliasing (continued)

But if we *copy* the reference instead, we wind up with two references to the *same* object, under two different *names* (the variables `betty` and `candace`).

This sort of thing is known as *aliasing*, because you have multiple *names* for a single thing. This can be dangerous if you're not expecting it!

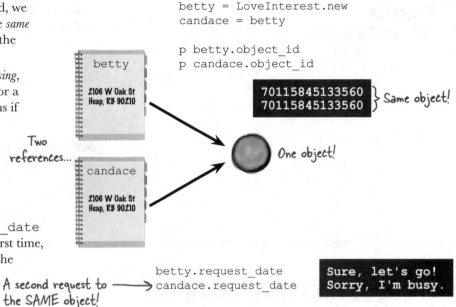

```
betty = LoveInterest.new
candace = betty

p betty.object_id
p candace.object_id
```

70115845133560
70115845133560 } Same object!

Two references...

One object!

In this case, the calls to `request_date` both go to the same object. The first time, it responds that it's available, but the second request is rejected.

A second request to the SAME object! ⟶

```
betty.request_date
candace.request_date
```

Sure, let's go!
Sorry, I'm busy.

This aliasing behavior seems *awfully* familiar... Remember the malfunctioning star catalog program? Let's go back and take another look at that next.

Exercise

Here is a Ruby class:

```ruby
class Counter

  def initialize
    @count = 0
  end

  def increment
    @count += 1
    puts @count
  end

end
```

And here is some code that uses that class:

```ruby
a = Counter.new
b = Counter.new
c = b
d = c

a.increment
b.increment
c.increment
d.increment
```

Guess what the code will output, and write your answer in the blanks.
(We've filled in the first one for you.)

| 1 |
| ..... |
| ..... |
| ..... |
| ..... |

EXERCISE SOLUTION

Here is a Ruby class:

```ruby
class Counter

  def initialize
    @count = 0
  end

  def increment
    @count += 1
    puts @count
  end

end
```

And here is some Ruby code that uses that class:

```ruby
a = Counter.new
b = Counter.new
c = b
d = c

a.increment
b.increment
c.increment
d.increment
```

Guess what the code will output, and write your answer in the blanks.

    1
    .....
    1
    .....
    2
    .....
    3
    .....

Fixing the astronomer's program

Now that we've learned about aliasing, let's take another look at the astronomer's malfunctioning star catalog, and see if we can figure out the problem this time…

```ruby
class CelestialBody
  attr_accessor :type, :name
end

altair = CelestialBody.new
altair.name = 'Altair'      To save time, he wants to
altair.type = 'star'        copy the previous star…
polaris = altair
polaris.name = 'Polaris'    …and just change
vega = polaris              the name.
vega.name = 'Vega'          Same
                            here
puts altair.name, polaris.name, vega.name
```

Vega
Vega
Vega

But it looks like the names on all three stars are now identical!

If we try calling `object_id` on the objects in the three variables, we'll see that all three variables refer to the *same* object. The same object under three different names…sounds like another case of aliasing!

```ruby
puts altair.object_id
puts polaris.object_id
puts vega.object_id
```

70189936850940
70189936850940   Same object!
70189936850940

Fixing the astronomer's program (continued)

By copying the contents of the variables, the astronomer did *not* get three distinct `CelestialBody` instances as he thought. Instead, he's a victim of unintentional aliasing — he got *one* `CelestialBody` with *three* references to it!

Stores a reference to a new CelestialBody

Copies the SAME reference to a new variable!

Copies the same reference to a THIRD variable!

```
altair = CelestialBody.new
altair.name = 'Altair'
altair.type = 'star'
polaris = altair
polaris.name = 'Polaris'
vega = polaris
vega.name = 'Vega'

puts altair.name, polaris.name, vega.name
```

To this poor, bewildered object, the sequence of instructions looked like this:

1. "Set your `name` attribute to `'Altair'`, and your `type` attribute is now `'star'`."

2. "Now set your `name` to `'Polaris'`."

3. "Now your `name` is `'Vega'`."

4. "Give us your `name` attribute 3 times."

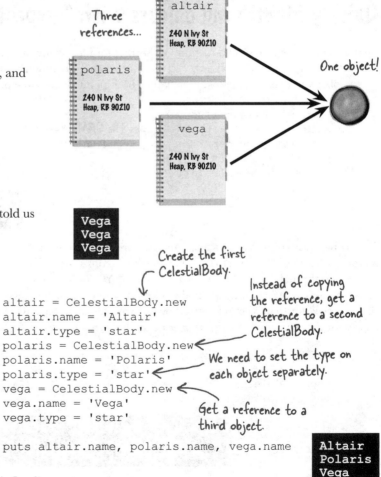

Three references...

One object!

```
Vega
Vega
Vega
```

The `CelestialBody` dutifully complied, and told us three times that its `name` was now Vega.

Fortunately, a fix will be easy. We just need to skip the shortcuts and actually create *three* `CelestialBody` instances.

Create the first CelestialBody.

Instead of copying the reference, get a reference to a second CelestialBody.

We need to set the type on each object separately.

Get a reference to a third object.

```
altair = CelestialBody.new
altair.name = 'Altair'
altair.type = 'star'
polaris = CelestialBody.new
polaris.name = 'Polaris'
polaris.type = 'star'
vega = CelestialBody.new
vega.name = 'Vega'
vega.type = 'star'

puts altair.name, polaris.name, vega.name
```

```
Altair
Polaris
Vega
```

And as we can see from the output, the problem is fixed!

So, all we have to do is avoid copying references from one variable to another, and we'll never have problems with aliasing, right?

It's definitely good policy to avoid copying references from variable to variable. But there are other circumstances where you need to be aware of how aliasing works, as we'll see shortly.

Quickly identifying objects with "inspect"

Before we move on, we should mention a shortcut for identifying objects. We've already shown you how to use the `object_id` instance method. If it outputs the same value for the object in two variables, you know they both point to the same object.

```
altair = CelestialBody.new
altair.name = 'Altair'        Copies the SAME reference
altair.type = 'star'          to a new variable!
polaris = altair
polaris.name = 'Polaris'

puts altair.object_id, polaris.object_id
```
```
70350315190400     } The SAME object!
70350315190400
```

The string returned by the `inspect` instance method also includes a representation of the object ID, in hexadecimal (consisting of the numbers 0 through 9 and the letters *a* through *f*). You don't need to know the details of how hexadecimal works; just know that if you see the *same value* for the object referenced by two variables, you have two aliases for the *same object*. A *different value* means a *different object*.

```
puts altair.inspect, polaris.inspect

vega = CelestialObject.new
puts vega.inspect
```

A hexadecimal representation of the object ID

The SAME object! {
A different object ⟶
```
#<CelestialBody:0x007ff76b17f100 @name="Polaris", @type="star">
#<CelestialBody:0x007ff76b17f100 @name="Polaris", @type="star">
#<CelestialBody:0x007ff76b17edb8>
```

Problems with a hash default object

The astronomer is back, with more problematic code...

> I'm trying to put stars and planets in a hash, but everything's mixed up again!

He needs his hash to be a mix of planets and moons. Since most of his objects will be planets, he set the hash default object to a `CelestialBody` with a `type` attribute of `"planet"`. (We saw hash default objects last chapter; they let you set an object the hash will return any time you access a key that hasn't been assigned to.)

```
class CelestialBody
  attr_accessor :type, :name
end
```

Set up a planet.
```
default_body = CelestialBody.new
default_body.type = 'planet'
bodies = Hash.new(default_body)
```

Make the planet the default value for all unassigned hash keys.

He believes that will let him add planets to the hash simply by assigning names to them. And it seems to work:

```
bodies['Mars'].name = 'Mars'
p bodies['Mars']
```

A CelestialBody with the correct type attribute...

```
#<CelestialBody:0x007fc60d13e6f8 @type="planet", @name="Mars">
```

When the astronomer needs to add a moon to the hash, he can do that, too. He just has to set the `type` attribute in addition to the `name`.

```
bodies['Europa'].name = 'Europa'
bodies['Europa'].type = 'moon'

p bodies['Europa']
```

A CelestialBody with a type of "moon"

```
#<CelestialBody:0x007fc60d13e6f8 @type="moon", @name="Europa">
```

But then, as he continues adding new `CelestialBody` objects to the hash, it starts behaving strangely...

Problems with a hash default object (continued)

The problems with using a `CelestialBody` as a hash default object become apparent as the astronomer tries to add more objects to the hash. When he adds another planet after adding a moon, the planet's `type` attribute is set to `"moon"` as well!

```
bodies['Venus'].name = 'Venus'

p bodies['Venus']
```

This is supposed to be a planet. Why is it set to "moon"?!

```
#<CelestialBody:0x007fc60d13e6f8 @type="moon", @name="Venus">
```

If he goes back and gets the value for the keys he added previously, *those* objects appear to have been modified as well!

```
p bodies['Mars']
p bodies['Europa']
```

Isn't one of these supposed to be a "planet"?

What happened to the names "Mars" and "Europa"?

```
#<CelestialBody:0x007fc60d13e6f8 @type="moon", @name="Venus">
#<CelestialBody:0x007fc60d13e6f8 @type="moon", @name="Venus">
```

> But we're not altering multiple objects... Look at the object IDs. All these different hash keys are giving us references to the **same** object!

Good observation! Remember we said that the `inspect` method string includes a representation of the object ID? And as you know, the `p` method calls `inspect` on each object before printing it. Using the `p` method shows us that all the hash keys refer to the *same* object!

```
p bodies['Venus']
p bodies['Mars']
p bodies['Europa']
```

These are all the SAME object!

```
#<CelestialBody:0x007fc60d13e6f8 @type="moon", @name="Venus">
#<CelestialBody:0x007fc60d13e6f8 @type="moon", @name="Venus">
#<CelestialBody:0x007fc60d13e6f8 @type="moon", @name="Venus">
```

Looks like we've got a problem with aliasing again! On the next few pages, we'll see how to fix it.

We're actually modifying the hash default object!

The central problem with this code is that we're not actually modifying hash values. Instead, we're modifying the *hash default object*.

We can confirm this using the `default` instance method, which is available on all hashes. It lets us look at the default object after we create the hash.

Let's inspect the default object both before and after we attempt to add a planet to the hash.

```
class CelestialBody
  attr_accessor :type, :name
end

default_body = CelestialBody.new
default_body.type = 'planet'
bodies = Hash.new(default_body)

p bodies.default          ←——— Inspect the default object.

bodies['Mars'].name = 'Mars'  ←——— Try to add a value to the hash.

p bodies.default          ←——— Inspect the default object again.
```

The hash default object BEFORE we attempt to add a hash value

The hash default object AFTER we attempt to add a hash value

```
#<CelestialBody:0x007f868a8274c8 @type="planet">
#<CelestialBody:0x007f868a8274c8 @type="planet", @name="Mars">
```

The name got added to the default object instead!

So why is a name being added to the default object? Shouldn't it be getting added to the hash value for `bodies['Mars']`?

If we look at the object IDs for both `bodies['Mars']` and the hash default object, we'll have our answer:

```
p bodies['Mars']
p bodies.default
```

Same object ID!

The SAME object!

```
#<CelestialBody:0x007f868a8274c8 @type="planet", @name="Mars">
#<CelestialBody:0x007f868a8274c8 @type="planet", @name="Mars">
```

When we access `bodies['Mars']`, we're still getting a reference to the hash default object! But why?

A more detailed look at hash default objects

When we introduced the hash default object in the last chapter, we said that you get the default object any time you access a key *that hasn't been assigned to yet.* Let's take a closer look at that last detail.

Create a new hash with a default object.
↓

```
grades = Hash.new('A')
```

Let's suppose we've created a hash that will hold student names as the keys, and their grades as the corresponding values. We want the default to be a grade of `'A'`.

At first, the hash is completely empty. Any student name that we request a grade for will come back with the hash default object, `'A'`.

```
p grades['Regina']
```

`'A'`

grades['Regina']

Got a value for "Regina"?

Hash   **Default Object**

`{ }` ——— `"A"`

Nope.   *Yes!*

When we assign a value to a hash key, we'll get that value back instead of the hash default the next time we try to access it.

```
grades['Regina'] = 'B'
p grades['Regina']
```

`"B"`

grades['Regina']

Got a value for "Regina"?

Hash   **Default Object**

`{"Regina" => "B"}` ——— `"A"`

Yes!

Even when some keys have had values assigned, we'll still get the default object for any key that hasn't been assigned previously.

```
p grades['Carl']
```

`"A"`

grades['Carl']

Got a value for "Carl"?

Hash   **Default Object**

`{"Regina" => "B"}` ——— `"A"`

Nope.   *Yes!*

But *accessing* a hash value is not the same as *assigning* to it. If you access a hash value once and then access it again without making an assignment, you'll still be getting the default object.

```
p grades['Carl']
```

`"A"`

grades['Carl']

Got a value for "Carl"?

Hash   **Default Object**

`{"Regina" => "B"}` ——— `"A"`

Nope.   *Yes!*

Only when a value is *assigned to* the hash (not just *retrieved from* it) will anything other than the default object be returned.

```
grades['Carl'] = 'C'
p grades['Carl']
```

`"C"`

grades['Carl']

Got a value for "Carl"?

Hash   **Default Object**

`{"Regina" => "B", "Carl" => "C"}` ——— `"A"`

Yes!

Back to the hash of planets and moons

And *that* is why, when we try to set the `type` and `name` attributes of objects in the hash of planets and moons, we wind up altering the default object instead. We're not actually assigning any values to the hash. In fact, if we inspect the hash itself, we'll see that it's totally empty!

```ruby
class CelestialBody
  attr_accessor :type, :name
end

default_body = CelestialBody.new
default_body.type = 'planet'
bodies = Hash.new(default_body)

bodies['Mars'].name = 'Mars'
bodies['Europa'].name = 'Europa'
bodies['Europa'].type = 'moon'
bodies['Venus'].name = 'Venus'

p bodies
```

> I thought we **were** assigning values to the hash. Aren't those assignment statements right there?

Isn't this assigning to the hash?

```ruby
bodies['Mars'].name = 'Mars'
bodies['Europa'].name = 'Europa'
bodies['Europa'].type = 'moon'
bodies['Venus'].name = 'Venus'
```

`{}` ← —Empty!

Actually, those are calls to the `name=` and `type=` attribute writer methods on the hash default object. Don't mistake them for assignment to the hash.

When we access a key for which no value has been assigned, we get the default object back.

```ruby
default_body = CelestialBody.new
default_body.type = 'planet'
bodies = Hash.new(default_body)

p bodies['Mars']
```

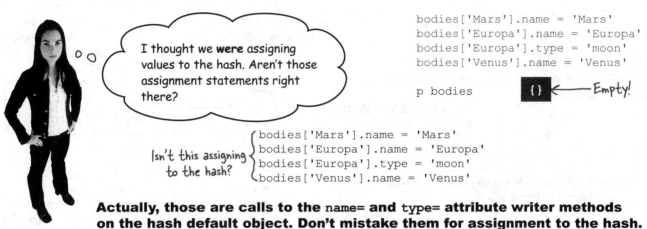

```
#<CelestialBody:
   0x007fe0b98a76f8
   @type="planet">
```

bodies['Mars']

Got a value for "Mars"? → Nope.

Hash   `{}`

Default Object   `#<CelestialBody @type="planet">`   ↑ Yes!

The statement below is *not* an assignment to the hash. It attempts to *access* a value for the key `'Mars'` from the hash (which is still empty). Since there is no value for `'Mars'`, it gets a reference to the default object, *which it then modifies*.

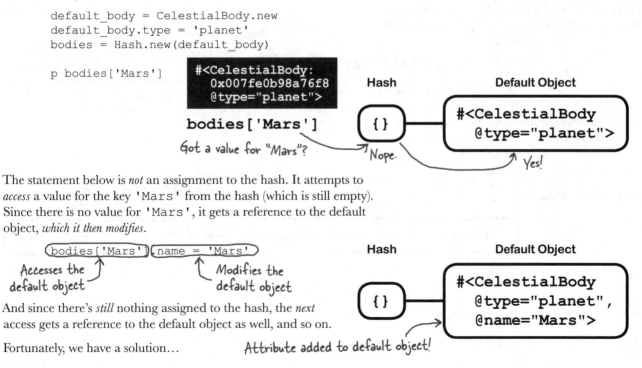

`bodies['Mars']` `name = 'Mars'`

Accesses the default object   *Modifies the default object*

Hash   `{}`

Default Object
```
#<CelestialBody
   @type="planet",
   @name="Mars">
```

And since there's *still* nothing assigned to the hash, the *next* access gets a reference to the default object as well, and so on.

Attribute added to default object!

Fortunately, we have a solution…

Our wish list for hash defaults

We've determined that this code doesn't *assign* a value to the hash, it just *accesses* a value. It gets a reference to the default object, which it then (unintentionally) modifies.

```
default_body = CelestialBody.new
default_body.type = 'planet'
bodies = Hash.new(default_body)
```

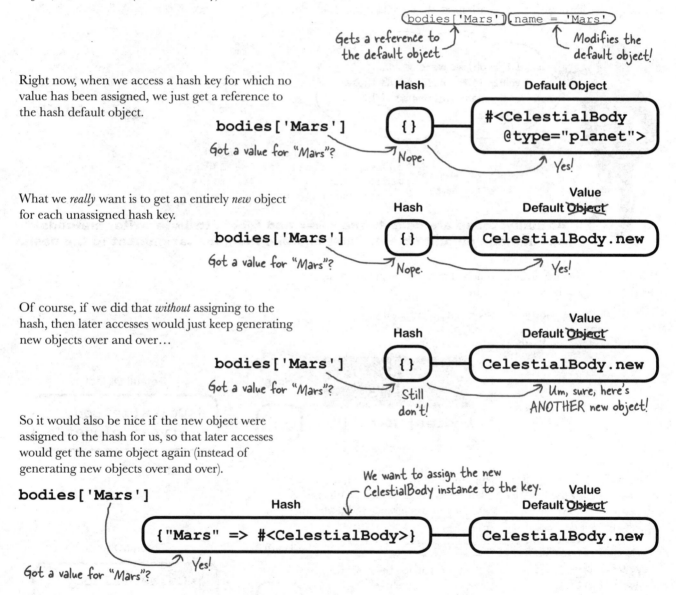

bodies['Mars'] · name = 'Mars'

Gets a reference to the default object

Modifies the default object!

Right now, when we access a hash key for which no value has been assigned, we just get a reference to the hash default object.

bodies['Mars']

Got a value for "Mars"?

Hash
{}
Nope.

Default Object
#<CelestialBody @type="planet">
Yes!

What we *really* want is to get an entirely *new* object for each unassigned hash key.

bodies['Mars']

Got a value for "Mars"?

Hash
{}
Nope.

Value ~~Default Object~~
CelestialBody.new
Yes!

Of course, if we did that *without* assigning to the hash, then later accesses would just keep generating new objects over and over…

bodies['Mars']

Got a value for "Mars"?

Hash
{}
Still don't!

Value ~~Default Object~~
CelestialBody.new
Um, sure, here's ANOTHER new object!

So it would also be nice if the new object were assigned to the hash for us, so that later accesses would get the same object again (instead of generating new objects over and over).

bodies['Mars']

We want to assign the new CelestialBody instance to the key.

Hash
{"Mars" => #<CelestialBody>}

Value ~~Default Object~~
CelestialBody.new

Got a value for "Mars"?
Yes!

Hashes have a feature that can do *all* of this for us!

Hash default blocks

Instead of passing an argument to `Hash.new` to be used as a hash default *object*, you can pass a *block* to `Hash.new` to be used as the hash default *block*. When a key is accessed for which no value has been assigned:

- The block is called.

- The block receives references to the hash and the current key as block parameters. These can be used to assign a value to the hash.

- The block return value is returned as the current value of the hash key.

Those rules are a bit complex, so we'll go over them in more detail in the next few pages. But for now, let's take a look at your first hash default block:

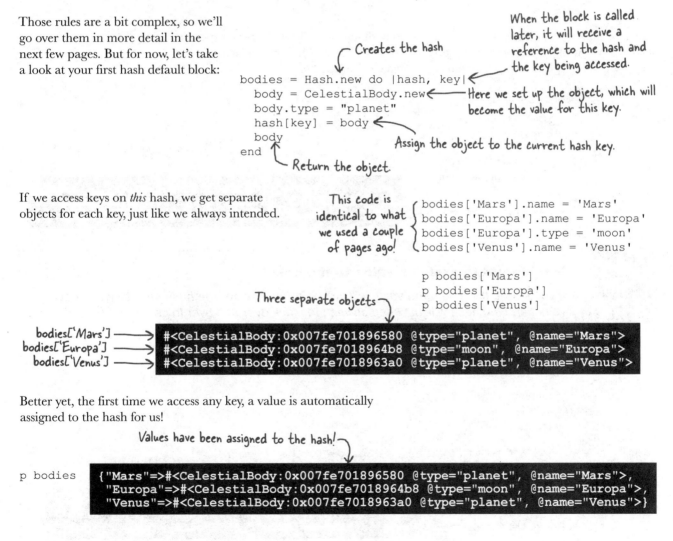

Creates the hash

When the block is called later, it will receive a reference to the hash and the key being accessed.

```ruby
bodies = Hash.new do |hash, key|
  body = CelestialBody.new
  body.type = "planet"
  hash[key] = body
  body
end
```

Here we set up the object, which will become the value for this key.

Assign the object to the current hash key.

Return the object.

If we access keys on *this* hash, we get separate objects for each key, just like we always intended.

This code is identical to what we used a couple of pages ago!

```ruby
bodies['Mars'].name = 'Mars'
bodies['Europa'].name = 'Europa'
bodies['Europa'].type = 'moon'
bodies['Venus'].name = 'Venus'

p bodies['Mars']
p bodies['Europa']
p bodies['Venus']
```

Three separate objects

bodies['Mars'] ⟶
bodies['Europa'] ⟶
bodies['Venus'] ⟶

```
#<CelestialBody:0x007fe701896580 @type="planet", @name="Mars">
#<CelestialBody:0x007fe7018964b8 @type="moon", @name="Europa">
#<CelestialBody:0x007fe7018963a0 @type="planet", @name="Venus">
```

Better yet, the first time we access any key, a value is automatically assigned to the hash for us!

Values have been assigned to the hash!

```
p bodies
```

```
{"Mars"=>#<CelestialBody:0x007fe701896580 @type="planet", @name="Mars">,
 "Europa"=>#<CelestialBody:0x007fe7018964b8 @type="moon", @name="Europa">,
 "Venus"=>#<CelestialBody:0x007fe7018963a0 @type="planet", @name="Venus">}
```

Now that we know it will work, let's take a closer look at the components of that block...

Hash default blocks: Assigning to the hash

In most cases, you'll want to assign the value created by your hash
default block to the hash. A reference to the hash and the current key
are passed to the block, in order to allow you to do so.

When the block is called later, it will receive a reference to the hash and the key being accessed.

```
bodies = Hash.new do |hash, key|
  body = CelestialBody.new
  body.type = "planet"
  hash[key] = body
  body
end
```

Assign the object to the current hash key.

When we assign values to the hash in the block body, things work like we've been expecting
all along. A new object is generated for each new key you access. On subsequent accesses,
we get the same object back again, with any changes we've made intact.

Generates a new object.
Gives us the same object as the line above

```
p bodies['Europa']
p bodies['Europa']
bodies['Europa'].type = 'moon'
p bodies['Europa']
```

Changes we make will be saved.

All the same object

Type attribute is intact.

```
#<CelestialBody:0x007fb6389eed00 @type="planet">
#<CelestialBody:0x007fb6389eed00 @type="planet">
#<CelestialBody:0x007fb6389eed00 @type="moon">
```

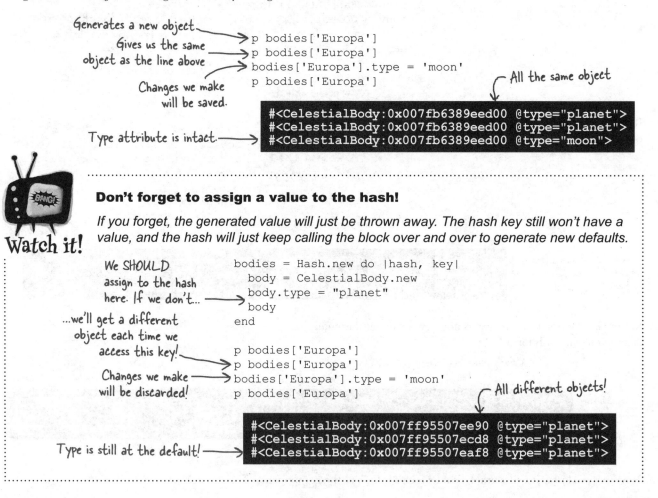

Don't forget to assign a value to the hash!

*If you forget, the generated value will just be thrown away. The hash key still won't have a
value, and the hash will just keep calling the block over and over to generate new defaults.*

We SHOULD assign to the hash here. If we don't...

```
bodies = Hash.new do |hash, key|
  body = CelestialBody.new
  body.type = "planet"
  body
end
```

...we'll get a different object each time we access this key!

Changes we make will be discarded!

```
p bodies['Europa']
p bodies['Europa']
bodies['Europa'].type = 'moon'
p bodies['Europa']
```

All different objects!

Type is still at the default!

```
#<CelestialBody:0x007ff95507ee90 @type="planet">
#<CelestialBody:0x007ff95507ecd8 @type="planet">
#<CelestialBody:0x007ff95507eaf8 @type="planet">
```

Hash default blocks: Block return value

When you access an unassigned hash key for the first time, the hash default block's return value is returned as the value for the key.

```ruby
bodies = Hash.new do |hash, key|
  body = CelestialBody.new
  body.type = "planet"
  hash[key] = body
  body          ←——This return value...
end

p bodies['Mars']   ←————...is what we get here!
```

```
#<CelestialBody:0x007fef7a9132c0 @type="planet">
```

As long as you assign a value to the key within the block body, the hash default block won't be invoked for subsequent accesses of that key; instead, you'll get whatever value was assigned.

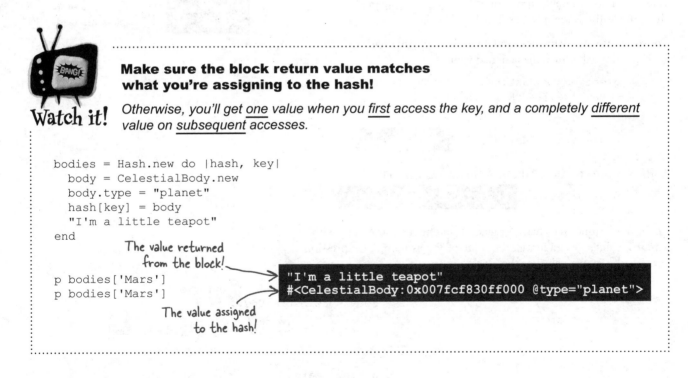

Make sure the block return value matches what you're assigning to the hash!

Otherwise, you'll get <u>one</u> value when you <u>first</u> access the key, and a completely <u>different</u> value on <u>subsequent</u> accesses.

```ruby
bodies = Hash.new do |hash, key|
  body = CelestialBody.new
  body.type = "planet"
  hash[key] = body
  "I'm a little teapot"
end

p bodies['Mars']
p bodies['Mars']
```

The value returned from the block!

```
"I'm a little teapot"
#<CelestialBody:0x007fcf830ff000 @type="planet">
```

The value assigned to the hash!

Generally speaking, you won't need to work very hard to remember this rule. As we'll see on the next page, setting up an appropriate return value for your hash default block happens quite naturally...

Hash default blocks: A shortcut

Thus far, we've been returning a value from the hash default block on a separate line:

```ruby
bodies = Hash.new do |hash, key|
  body = CelestialBody.new
  body.type = "planet"
  hash[key] = body
  body          ⟵——— Separate block return value
end

p bodies['Mars']
```

```
#<CelestialBody:0x007fef7a9132c0 @type="planet">
```

But Ruby offers a shortcut that can reduce the amount of code in your default block a bit...

You've already learned that the value of the last expression in a block is treated as the block's return value... What we *haven't* mentioned is that in Ruby, the value of an assignment expression is the same as the value being assigned.

```ruby
p my_hash = {}
p my_array = []
p my_integer = 20
p my_hash['A'] = ['Apple']
p my_array[0] = 245
```

```
{}
[]
20
["Apple"]
245
```

} Values of expressions are the same as values assigned.

So we can use an assignment statement by itself in a hash default block, and it will return the assigned value.

```ruby
greetings = Hash.new do |hash, key|
  hash[key] = "Hi, #{key}"
end

p greetings["Kayla"]
```

```
"Hi, Kayla"
```

And, of course, it will add the value to the hash as well.

```ruby
p greetings
```

```
{"Kayla"=>"Hi, Kayla"}
```

So, in the astronomer's hash, instead of adding a separate line with a return value, we can just let the value of the assignment expression provide the return value for the block.

```ruby
bodies = Hash.new do |hash, key|
  body = CelestialBody.new
  body.type = "planet"
  hash[key] = body     ⟵——— Let this be the block
end                            return value.

p bodies['Mars']
```

```
#<CelestialBody:0x007fa769a3f2d8 @type="planet">
```

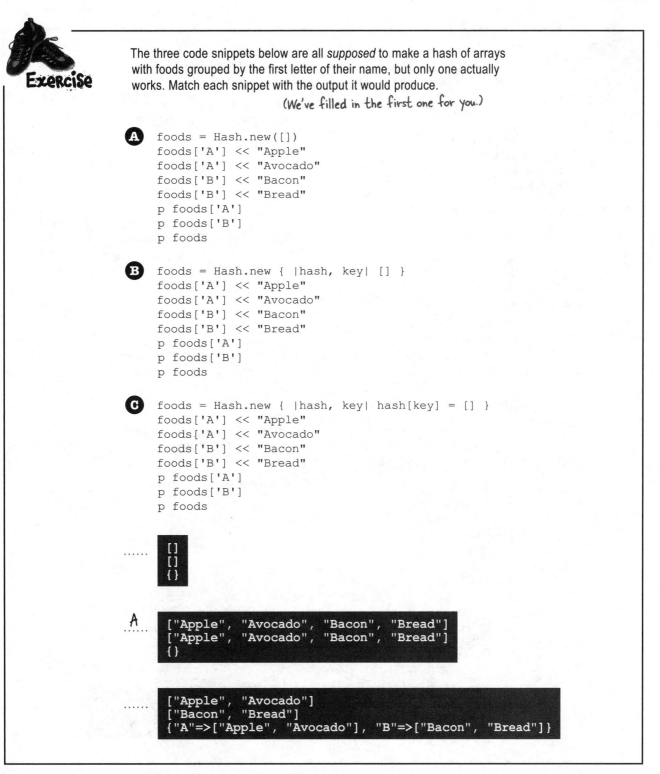

The three code snippets below are all *supposed* to make a hash of arrays with foods grouped by the first letter of their name, but only one actually works. Match each snippet with the output it would produce.

(We've filled in the first one for you.)

A
```ruby
foods = Hash.new([])
foods['A'] << "Apple"
foods['A'] << "Avocado"
foods['B'] << "Bacon"
foods['B'] << "Bread"
p foods['A']
p foods['B']
p foods
```

B
```ruby
foods = Hash.new { |hash, key| [] }
foods['A'] << "Apple"
foods['A'] << "Avocado"
foods['B'] << "Bacon"
foods['B'] << "Bread"
p foods['A']
p foods['B']
p foods
```

C
```ruby
foods = Hash.new { |hash, key| hash[key] = [] }
foods['A'] << "Apple"
foods['A'] << "Avocado"
foods['B'] << "Bacon"
foods['B'] << "Bread"
p foods['A']
p foods['B']
p foods
```

......
```
[]
[]
{}
```

A
......
```
["Apple", "Avocado", "Bacon", "Bread"]
["Apple", "Avocado", "Bacon", "Bread"]
{}
```

......
```
["Apple", "Avocado"]
["Bacon", "Bread"]
{"A"=>["Apple", "Avocado"], "B"=>["Bacon", "Bread"]}
```

**Exercise
Solution**

The three code snippets below are all *supposed* to make a hash of arrays with foods grouped by the first letter of their name, but only one actually works. Match each snippet with the output it would produce.

This ONE array will be used as the default value for all hash keys!

A
```
foods = Hash.new([])
foods['A'] << "Apple"
foods['A'] << "Avocado"
foods['B'] << "Bacon"
foods['B'] << "Bread"
p foods['A']
p foods['B']
p foods
```

All of these will get added to the SAME array!

Returns a new, empty array each time the block is called, but doesn't add it to the hash!

B
```
foods = Hash.new { |hash, key| [] }
foods['A'] << "Apple"
foods['A'] << "Avocado"
foods['B'] << "Bacon"
foods['B'] << "Bread"
p foods['A']
p foods['B']
p foods
```

Each string is added to a new array. The array is then discarded!

Assigns a new array to the hash, under the current key

C
```
foods = Hash.new { |hash, key| hash[key] = [] }
foods['A'] << "Apple"     ← Added to a new array
foods['A'] << "Avocado"   ← Added to same array as "Apple"
foods['B'] << "Bacon"     ← Added to a new array
foods['B'] << "Bread"
p foods['A']
p foods['B']
p foods
```

Added to same array as "Bacon"

B
```
[]
[]
{}
```

A
```
["Apple", "Avocado", "Bacon", "Bread"]
["Apple", "Avocado", "Bacon", "Bread"]
{}
```

C
```
["Apple", "Avocado"]
["Bacon", "Bread"]
{"A"=>["Apple", "Avocado"], "B"=>["Bacon", "Bread"]}
```

The astronomer's hash: Our final code

> The hash is working perfectly. Hash default blocks are just what I needed!

Here's our final code for the hash default block:

```ruby
class CelestialBody
  attr_accessor :type, :name
end

bodies = Hash.new do |hash, key|
  body = CelestialBody.new
  body.type = "planet"
  hash[key] = body
end
```

Receives a reference to the hash and the current key

Creates a new object just for the current key

Assigns to the hash AND returns the new value

These lines all work as expected now!

```ruby
bodies['Mars'].name = 'Mars'
bodies['Europa'].name = 'Europa'
bodies['Europa'].type = 'moon'
bodies['Venus'].name = 'Venus'

p bodies
```

Each hash value is a separate object.

Type defaults to "planet" but can be overridden.

Names are all intact.

(Output aligned for easier reading.)

```
{"Mars"  =>#<CelestialBody:0x007fcde388aaa0 @type="planet", @name="Mars"  >,
 "Europa"=>#<CelestialBody:0x007fcde388a9d8 @type="moon",   @name="Europa">,
 "Venus" =>#<CelestialBody:0x007fcde388a8c0 @type="planet", @name="Venus" >}
```

Here's how the program works now:

- We use a hash default block to create a *unique* object for each hash key. (This is unlike a hash default object, which gives references to *one* object as the default for *all* keys.)

- Within the block, we assign the new object to the current hash key.

- The new object becomes the value of the assignment expression, which also becomes the block's return value. So the first time a given hash key is accessed, a new object is returned as the corresponding value.

Using hash default objects safely

I have one more question. Why would anyone use a hash default object when you can use a hash default block instead?

Hash default objects work very well if you use a number as the default.

I should only use numbers? Then why did Ruby let us use a `CelestialBody` as a default object earlier, without even a warning?

Okay, it's a little more complicated than that. Hash default objects work very well if you don't change the default, and if you assign values back to the hash. It's just that numbers make it easy to follow these rules.

Take this example, which counts the number of times letters occur in an array. (It works just like the vote counting code from last chapter.)

```ruby
letters = ['a', 'c', 'a', 'b', 'c', 'a']

counts = Hash.new(0)

letters.each do |letter|
  counts[letter] += 1
end

p counts
```

If this value is unassigned, gets the hash default but does NOT modify it

Assigns the incremented value back to the hash

`{"a"=>3, "c"=>2, "b"=>1}`

Using a hash default object here works because we follow the above two rules…

Hash default object rule #1: Don't modify the default object

If you're going to use a hash default object, it's important not to modify that object. Otherwise, you'll get unexpected results the next time you access the default. We saw this happen when we used a default object (instead of a default block) for the astronomer's hash, and it caused havoc:

```
default_body = CelestialBody.new
default_body.type = 'planet'
bodies = Hash.new(default_body)
```
← Sets the hash's default object

bodies['Mars']   name = 'Mars'

Gets a reference to → the default object

↑ Modifies the default object!

*Okay, but then why does it work with a **number** as the default object? We modify the default when we add to it, don't we?*

```
letters = ['a', 'c', 'a', 'b', 'c', 'a']

counts = Hash.new(0)

letters.each do |letter|
  counts[letter] += 1
end
```

Isn't this modifying ← the default object?

In Ruby, doing math operations on a numeric object doesn't modify that object; it returns an entirely *new* object. We can see this if we look at object IDs before and after an operation.

```
number = 0
puts number.object_id
number = number + 1
puts number.object_id
```

1
3
} Two different objects! (Object IDs for integers are much lower than for other objects, but that's an implementation detail, so don't worry about it. The key point is, they're different.)

In fact, numeric objects are *immutable*: they don't *have* any methods that modify the object's state. Any operation that might change the number gives you back an entirely new object.

That's what makes numbers safe to use as hash default objects; you can be certain that the default number won't be changed accidentally.

Numbers make good hash default objects because they are <u>immutable</u>.

Hash default object rule #2: Assign values to the hash

If you're going to use a hash default object, it's also important to ensure that you're actually assigning values to the hash. As we saw with the astronomer's hash, sometimes it can look like you're assigning to the hash when you're not…

```
default_body = CelestialBody.new
default_body.type = 'planet'
bodies = Hash.new(default_body)

bodies['Mars'].name = 'Mars'

p bodies
```

A call to an attribute writer method. This does NOT assign to the hash!

`{}` ← *The hash is still empty, actually!*

When we use a *number* as a default object, though, it's much more natural to actually assign values to the hash. (Because numbers are immutable, we *can't* store the incremented values *unless* we assign them to the hash!)

```
hash = Hash.new(0)

hash['a'] += 1
hash['c'] += 1

p hash.default
p hash
```

The hash default object is unchanged.

```
0
{"a"=>1, "c"=>1}
```

We assigned the values to the hash!

The rule of thumb for hash defaults

All of this seems like a lot to remember just to be able to use hash defaults.

That's true. So we have a rule of thumb that will keep you out of trouble...

If your default is a <u>number</u>, you can use a hash default <u>object</u>.
If your default is <u>anything else</u>, you should use a hash default <u>block</u>.

As you gain more experience with references, all of this will become second nature, and you can break this rule of thumb when the time is right. Until then, this should prevent most problems you'll encounter.

Understanding Ruby references and the issue of aliasing won't help you write more powerful Ruby programs. It *will* help you quickly find and fix problems when they arise, however. Hopefully this chapter has helped you form a basic understanding of how references work, and will let you avoid trouble in the first place.

Your Ruby Toolbox

That's it for Chapter 8! You've added references to your toolbox.

Hashes
References

The "heap" is an area of your computer's memory reserved for storing Ruby objects.

Ruby uses references to find objects on the heap.

Variables, arrays, hashes, and other data structures don't contain objects, just references to them.

BULLET POINTS

- If you need to store more objects, Ruby will increase the size of the heap for you. If you're no longer using an object, Ruby will delete it from the heap for you.

- Aliasing is the copying of a reference to an object, and it can cause bugs if you do it unintentionally.

- Most Ruby objects have an `object_id` instance method, which returns a unique identifier for the object. You can use it to determine whether you have multiple references to a single object.

- The string returned by the `inspect` method also includes a representation of the object ID.

- If you set a default object for a hash, all unassigned hash keys will return references to that single default object.

- For this reason, it's best to only use immutable objects (objects that can't be modified), such as numbers, as hash default objects.

- If you need any other kind of object as a hash default, it's better to use a hash default block, so that a unique object is created for each key.

- Hash default blocks receive a reference to the hash and the current key as block parameters. In most cases, you'll want to use these parameters to assign a new object as a value for the given hash key.

- The hash default block's return value is treated as the initial default value for the given key.

- The value of a Ruby assignment expression is the same as the value being assigned. So if an assignment expression is the last expression in a block, the value assigned becomes the block's return value.

Up Next...

In the next chapter, we're going to get back to the topic of organizing your code. You've already learned how to share methods between classes with inheritance. But even in situations where inheritance isn't appropriate, Ruby offers a way to share behavior across classes: *mixins*. We'll learn about those next!

9 mixins

Mix It Up

Eggs for the casserole, eggs for the cake batter... Oh, but Uncle Harold's allergic. Better leave eggs out of the meatloaf.

Inheritance has its limitations. You can only inherit methods from one class. But what if you need to share *several sets of behavior* across several classes? Like methods for starting a battery charge cycle and reporting its charge level—you might need those methods on phones, power drills, and electric cars. Are you going to create a *single* superclass for all of *those*? (It won't end well if you try.) Or methods for starting and stopping a motor. Sure, the drill and the car might need those, but the phone won't!

In this chapter, we'll learn about **modules** and **mixins**, a powerful way to *group methods together* and then share them *only with particular classes that need them*.

The media-sharing app

This week's client project is an app for sharing videos, music, and other media. Music and videos both need some of the same functionality: users need to be able to play songs and videos back, as well as leave comments on them. (To keep this example simple, we'll omit functionality like pausing, rewinding, etc.)

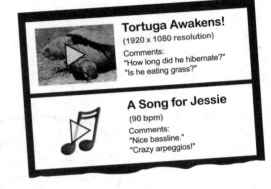

There are some aspects that differ, however. We need the ability to track the number of beats per minute on songs, to separate the fast music from the slow music. Videos don't need a number of beats per minute, but they *do* need to keep track of their resolution (how wide and how tall they are in pixels).

Since we're mixing data and behavior (we need data like resolution, beats per minute, etc., as well as behavior like playback), it makes sense to put everything in `Video` and `Song` classes. Some of that behavior (playback and commenting) is shared, however. The best tool we have so far for sharing behavior between classes is inheritance. So we'll make `Video` and `Song` subclasses of a superclass called `Clip`. `Clip` will have an attribute reader method named `comments`, as well as `play` and `add_comment` instance methods.

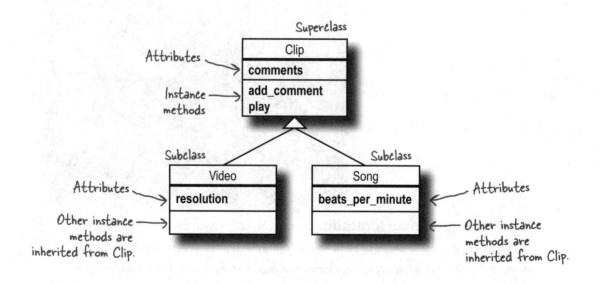

The media-sharing app...using inheritance

Here's some code to define the `Clip`, `Video`, and `Song` classes and test them out. The `resolution` and `beats_per_minute` attributes are very straightforward, so we'll focus on trying the `add_comment` and `comments` methods instead.

```ruby
class Clip

  attr_reader :comments          ← Define a method to return the value of
                                     the "@comments" instance variable.
  def initialize
    @comments = []               ← When a new instance is created, set up
  end                              an empty array to add comments to.

  def add_comment(comment)
    comments << comment          ← Call the "comments" method to get the array
  end                              in "@comments", and append a comment to it.

  def play
    puts "Playing #{object_id}..."  ← Show the ID of the
  end                                 object we're playing.

end
```

Superclass — `class Clip` ... `end`

```ruby
class Video < Clip
  attr_accessor :resolution
end
```

Subclass — `class Video < Clip`

```ruby
class Song < Clip
  attr_accessor :beats_per_minute
end
```

Subclass — `class Song < Clip`

```ruby
video = Video.new                             ← Set up a new Video object.
video.add_comment("Cool slow motion effect!")  ← Add comments to it.
video.add_comment("Weird ending.")
song = Song.new                               ← Set up a new Song object.
song.add_comment("Awesome beat.")             ← Add a comment to it.

p video.comments, song.comments               ← Inspect all comments.
```

```
["Cool slow motion effect!", "Weird ending."]
["Awesome beat."]
```

All this seems to be working pretty well! But then your client throws you a curveball...

One of these classes is not (quite) like the others

Your client wants to add photos to the media-sharing site. Like videos and music, photos should allow users to add comments. *Unlike* videos and music, of course, photos should not have a `play` method; they should have a `show` method instead.

So, if you make a `Photo` class, its instances will need a `comments` attribute accessor method and an `add_comment` method, just like the ones that `Video` and `Song` inherit from the `Clip` superclass.

Using only the things we've learned about Ruby classes so far, we have a couple of possible solutions, but each has its own problems…

Option one: Make Photo a subclass of Clip

We *could* just make `Photo` a subclass of `Clip`, and let it inherit `comments` and `add_comment` just like the other subclasses.

But there's a weakness with this approach: it (wrongly) implies that a `Photo` is a kind of `Clip`. If you make `Photo` a subclass of `Clip`, it will inherit the `comments` and `add_comment` methods, yes. But it will *also* inherit the `play` method.

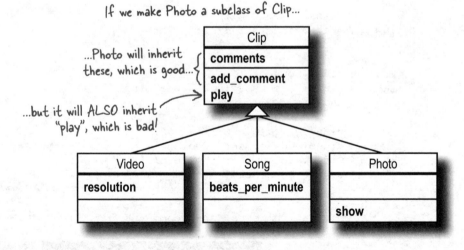

You can't *play* a photo. Even if you overrode the `play` method in the `Photo` subclass so that it didn't raise errors, every developer who looks at your code in the future will scratch their head wondering why `Photo` has a `play` method on it.

So it doesn't seem like a good option to subclass `Clip` just to get the `comments` and `add_comment` methods.

Option two: Copy the methods you want into the Photo class

The second option isn't much better: we could skip setting up a superclass for Photo, and implement the comments and add_comment methods *again* in the Photo class. (In other words, copy and paste the code.)

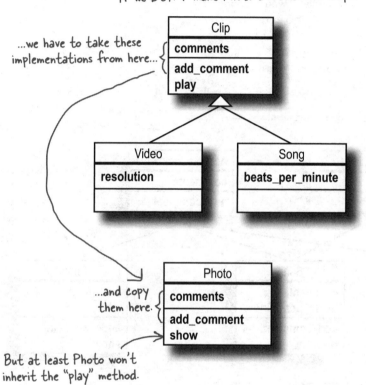

If we DON'T make Photo a subclass of Clip...

...we have to take these implementations from here...

Clip

comments
add_comment **play**

Video

resolution

Song

beats_per_minute

Photo

comments
add_comment **show**

...and copy them here.

But at least Photo won't inherit the "play" method.

We learned the downsides to this approach at the start of Chapter 3, though. If we make a change to comments or add_comment in the Photo class, we have to make sure to change the code in the Clip class as well. Otherwise, the methods will behave differently, which could be a nasty surprise for future developers working with these classes.

So *this* isn't a good option, either.

Not an option: Multiple inheritance

We need a solution that will let us share the implementation of the `comments` and `add_comment` methods between the `Video`, `Song`, and `Photo` classes, *without* `Photo` inheriting the `play` method.

It would sure be nice if we could move the `comments` and `add_comment` methods to a separate `AcceptsComments` superclass, while leaving the `play` method in the `Clip` superclass. That way, `Video` and `Song` could inherit the `play` method from `Clip` *and* inherit the `comments` and `add_comment` methods from `AcceptsComments`. `Photo` would only need `AcceptsComments` as a superclass, so it would inherit `comments` and `add_comment` *without* inheriting `play`.

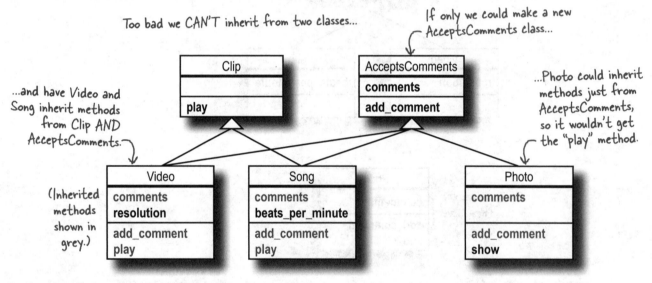

Too bad we CAN'T inherit from two classes...

If only we could make a new AcceptsComments class...

...and have Video and Song inherit methods from Clip AND AcceptsComments.

...Photo could inherit methods just from AcceptsComments, so it wouldn't get the "play" method.

(Inherited methods shown in grey.)

But here's a spoiler: we can't. This concept of inheriting from more than one class is called *multiple inheritance*, and Ruby doesn't allow it. (It's not just Ruby; Java, C#, Objective-C, and many other object-oriented languages intentionally leave out support for multiple inheritance.)

The reason? It's messy. Multiple inheritance gives rise to ambiguities that would require complex rules to resolve. Supporting multiple inheritance would make the Ruby interpreter much larger, and it would make Ruby code much uglier.

So Ruby has another solution...

Using modules as mixins

We need to add a group of methods to multiple classes *without* using inheritance. What can we do?

Ruby offers us **modules** as a way to group related methods. A module starts with the keyword `module` and the module name (which must be capitalized) and ends with the keyword `end`. In between, in the module body, you can declare one or more methods.

Start of module   Module name

```
module  MyModule
        def first_method
          puts "first_method called"
        end
        def second_method
          puts "second_method called"
        end
end
```

Module body

End of module

Looks similar to a class, right? That's because a class is actually a *kind* of module. There's a key difference, though. You can create instances of a class, but you can't create instances of a module:

```
MyModule.new
```
Error ⟶ `undefined method 'new' for MyModule:Module`

Instead, you can declare a class and then "mix in" a module. When you do so, the class gains all the module's methods as instance methods.

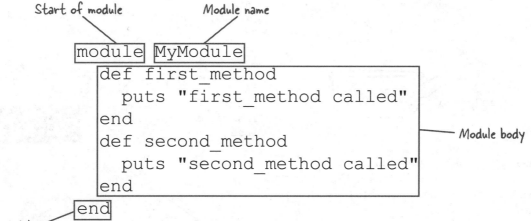

This will become an instance method on any class that mixes this module in.

```
module MyModule
  def first_method
    puts "first_method called"
  end
  def second_method
    puts "second_method called"
  end
end

class MyClass
  include MyModule
end
```

Same here

Mix MyModule into this class.

MyModule
adds:
first_method
second_method
...to any class!

Create an instance of MyClass.

```
my_object = MyClass.new
my_object.first_method
my_object.second_method
```

Call the instance methods mixed in from MyModule.

```
first_method called
second_method called
```

Using modules as mixins (continued)

Modules that are *designed* to be mixed into classes are often referred to as **mixins**. Just as a superclass can have more than one subclass, a mixin can be mixed into any number of classes:

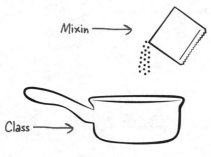

Mixin →

Class →

```ruby
module Friendly
  def my_method
    puts "hello from Friendly"
  end
end

class ClassOne
  include Friendly
end

class ClassTwo
  include Friendly
end

ClassOne.new.my_method
ClassTwo.new.my_method
```

→ Add my_method to ClassOne.

→ Add my_method to ClassTwo.

```
hello from Friendly
hello from Friendly
```

Now, here's the cool part: any number of *modules* can be mixed into a single *class*. The class will gain the functionality of *all* the modules!

```ruby
module Friendly
  def method_one
    puts "hello from Friendly"
  end
end

module Friendlier
  def method_two
    puts "hello from Friendlier!!"
  end
end

class MyClass
  include Friendly
  include Friendlier
end

my_object = MyClass.new
my_object.method_one
my_object.method_two
```

← Add method_one.
← Add method_two.

```
hello from Friendly
hello from Friendlier!!
```

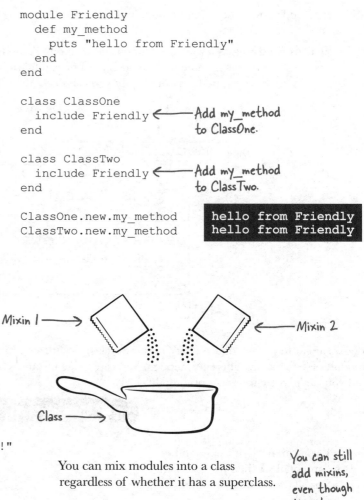

Mixin 1 →

← Mixin 2

Class →

You can mix modules into a class regardless of whether it has a superclass.

You can still add mixins, even though there's a superclass!

```ruby
class MySuperclass
end

class MySubclass < MySuperclass
  include Friendly
  include Friendlier
end

subclass_instance = MySubclass.new
subclass_instance.method_one
subclass_instance.method_two
```

```
hello from Friendly
hello from Friendlier!!
```

Mixins, behind the scenes

When we learned about method overriding back in Chapter 3, we saw that Ruby looks for instance methods on a class first, then looks on the superclass...

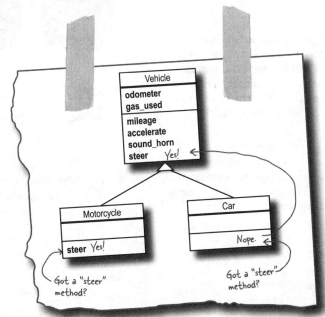

When you mix in a module, it works in a very similar fashion. Ruby adds the module to the list of places it will look for methods, between the class you're mixing it into and its superclass.

```
class MySuperclass
end

module MyModule
  def my_method
    puts "hello from MyModule"
  end
end

class MyClass < MySuperclass
  include MyModule
end

my_object = MyClass.new
my_object.my_method
```

```
hello from MyModule
```

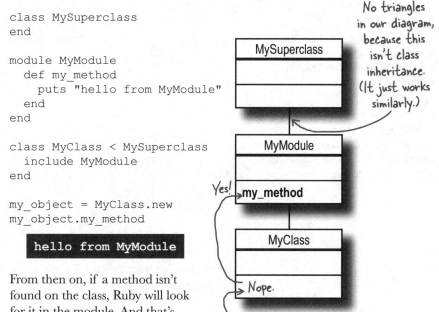

From then on, if a method isn't found on the class, Ruby will look for it in the module. And that's how mixins add methods to a class!

there are no Dumb Questions

Q: You said that modules are added to the list of places Ruby will look for methods, between the class you're mixing it into and its superclass. What happens if you don't define a superclass?

A: Remember, all Ruby classes have `Object` as a superclass. So if you have a class that doesn't explicitly define an superclass, and you mix a module into it:

```
module MyModule
end

class MyClass
  include MyModule
end
```

...then `MyModule` will be added between `MyClass` and `Object` in the `ancestors` list.

Q: What happens if a module is mixed into a superclass? Will subclasses inherit the mixed-in methods?

A: Yes! If Ruby doesn't see a method in the superclass, it will then look for it in the superclass's mixins. So if a method is available to the superclass, it will be available to subclasses, too.

Fireside Chats

Tonight's talk: **A module talks to a class about a delicate subject.**

Module:

Sometimes, I really envy you, Class.

Right, but that's *all* I am—a collection of methods. You can create *instances* of yourself!

And you can inherit methods from a superclass!

But what good is that?

Oh, and so you move the methods that apply only to *some* classes to a module instead?

Well, that *does* sound useful. I guess I don't feel so bad anymore!

Class:

Why's that, Module? We're both just collections of methods.

True, but that's not as much fun as you might think.

I can inherit methods from *one* superclass. Ruby doesn't allow more than that. Which is fine; that sounds like it would get… complicated. But I can mix in as many modules as I want!

Well, with inheritance, you can put related methods for several classes in a single place. But you have to share *all* of those methods with *every* subclass! That might make sense for some methods, but not others.

…and then mix it into those classes; that's right!

It's *really* useful. We make a great team!

Code Magnets

A Ruby program is all scrambled up on the fridge. It includes two modules, a class, and some code to create an instance of the class and call methods on it. Can you reconstruct the snippets to make a working Ruby program that will produce the given output?

| Monkey | Curious | Clumsy | Curious | Clumsy |

| end | | `puts "Looks at #{thing}"` |

| end | end | `puts "Knocks over #{thing}"` |

| end | end | `bubbles =` | `Monkey.new` |

| module | module | class |

| `def investigate(thing)` | `investigate("vase")` |

| `def break(thing)` | `break("vase")` |

| include | include | `bubbles.` | `bubbles.` |

Output:

```
File Edit Window Help
Looks at vase
Knocks over vase
```

Code Magnets Solution

A Ruby program is all scrambled up on the fridge. It includes two modules, a class, and some code to create an instance of the class and call methods on it. Can you reconstruct the snippets to make a working Ruby program that will produce the given output?

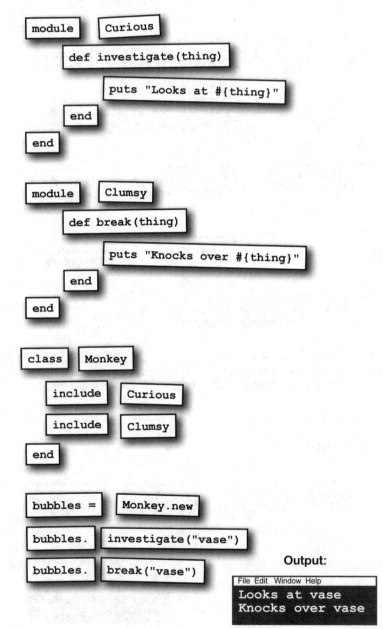

```ruby
module Curious
  def investigate(thing)
    puts "Looks at #{thing}"
  end
end


module Clumsy
  def break(thing)
    puts "Knocks over #{thing}"
  end
end


class Monkey
  include Curious
  include Clumsy
end


bubbles = Monkey.new
bubbles.investigate("vase")
bubbles.break("vase")
```

Output:

```
File Edit Window Help
Looks at vase
Knocks over vase
```

Creating a mixin for comments

We need our `Video`, `Song`, and `Photo` classes to share a single implementation of the `comments` and `add_comment` methods, but we've learned that we *can't* use multiple inheritance.

Too bad we CAN'T inherit from two classes...

If only we could make a new AcceptsComments class...

...and have Video and Song inherit methods from Clip AND AcceptsComments.

...Photo could inherit methods just from AcceptsComments, so it wouldn't get the "play" method.

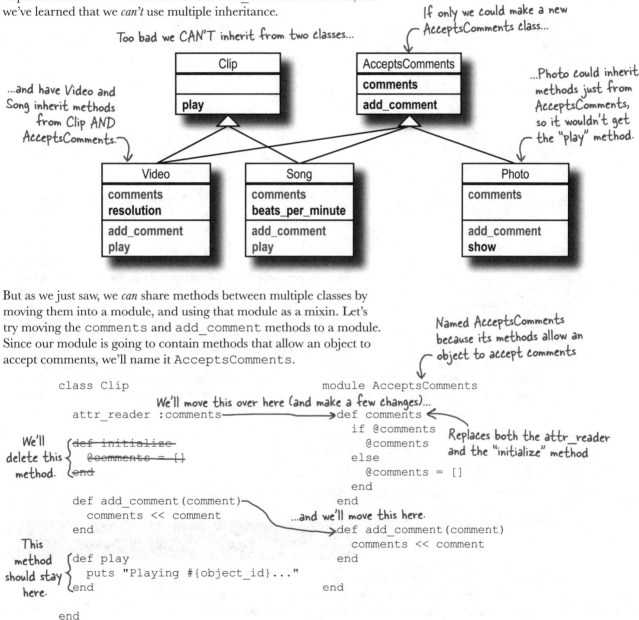

But as we just saw, we *can* share methods between multiple classes by moving them into a module, and using that module as a mixin. Let's try moving the `comments` and `add_comment` methods to a module. Since our module is going to contain methods that allow an object to accept comments, we'll name it `AcceptsComments`.

Named AcceptsComments because its methods allow an object to accept comments

```
class Clip
  attr_reader :comments

  def initialize
    @comments = []
  end

  def add_comment(comment)
    comments << comment
  end

  def play
    puts "Playing #{object_id}..."
  end

end
```

We'll move this over here (and make a few changes)...

We'll delete this method.

This method should stay here.

...and we'll move this here.

```
module AcceptsComments
  def comments
    if @comments
      @comments
    else
      @comments = []
    end
  end

  def add_comment(comment)
    comments << comment
  end

end
```

Replaces both the attr_reader and the "initialize" method

In addition to moving some methods to the module, we've added some logic to `comments` and gotten rid of the `initialize` method. We'll explain why, but first let's try out our changes.

Using our comments mixin

Let's mix the new `AcceptsComments` module into the `Video` and `Song` classes ✱ and see if everything still works the same way...

We'll explain this code, but first we want to try the module out.

```ruby
module AcceptsComments
  def comments
    if @comments
      @comments
    else
      @comments = []
    end
  end
  def add_comment(comment)
    comments << comment
  end
end

class Clip
  def play
    puts "Playing #{object_id}..."
  end
end

class Video < Clip
  include AcceptsComments
  attr_accessor :resolution
end

class Song < Clip
  include AcceptsComments
  attr_accessor :beats_per_minute
end
```

Mix in all methods from the AcceptsComments module.

Mix in all methods from the AcceptsComments module.

✱ We could also have included AcceptsComments in the Clip class and let both Video and Song inherit the methods, but we felt this was a bit clearer.

there are no Dumb Questions

Q: You said that you can't create instances of a module. So how can a module have instance variables?

A: Remember back in Chapter 3, we talked about how instance variables belong to the *object*, not the *class*? It's the same thing with modules. Methods from a module that refer to an instance variable get mixed into a class as instance methods. It's only when those instance methods are called on an object that the instance variables are created—*on that object*. The instance variables don't belong to the module at all; they belong to the instances of the classes that mix the module in.

Same code as before

```ruby
video = Video.new
video.add_comment("Cool slow motion effect!")
video.add_comment("Weird ending.")
song = Song.new
song.add_comment("Awesome beat.")

p video.comments, song.comments
```

Same output

```
["Cool slow motion effect!", "Weird ending."]
["Awesome beat."]
```

The mixin worked! `Video` and `Song` still have their `comments` and `add_comment` methods, except that now they get them from mixing in `AcceptsComments` instead of inheriting them from `Clip`. We can also confirm that `Video` and `Song` successfully inherited a `play` method from `Clip`:

```
video.play        Playing 70322929946360...
song.play         Playing 70322929946280...
```

Using our comments mixin (continued)

Now let's create a `Photo` class and see if we can *also* mix the
`AcceptsComments` module into that...

```ruby
class Photo
  include AcceptsComments          ⟵——— Mix in the "comments" and "add_comment"
  def show                                  methods from the AcceptsComments module.
    puts "Displaying #{object_id}..."
  end
end

photo = Photo.new
photo.add_comment("Beautiful colors.")

p photo.comments
```
```
["Beautiful colors."]
```

The new `Photo` class has a `show` method, as it should, but it does *not* have the unwanted `play`
method. (Only the subclasses of `Clip` have that.) Everything is working as we intended!

```ruby
photo.show
```
```
Displaying 70139324385180...
```

A closer look at the revised "comments" method

Now that we know it works, let's take a closer look at that `comments` method. Our new
version of the method looks for a `@comments` instance variable on the current object. If
`@comments` has never been assigned to, it will have a value of `nil`. In that event, we assign
an empty array to `@comments`, and return that empty array from the `comments` method.

After that, `@comments` is no
longer `nil`. So subsequent
calls to the `comments`
method will return the array
we assigned to `@comments`.

This replaces the
`attr_reader` AND the
"initialize" method.

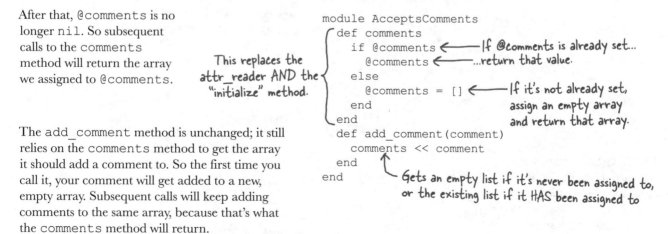

```ruby
module AcceptsComments
  def comments
    if @comments          ⟵——— If @comments is already set...
      @comments           ⟵——— ...return that value.
    else
      @comments = []      ⟵——— If it's not already set,
    end                          assign an empty array
  end                            and return that array.
  def add_comment(comment)
    comments << comment
  end
end
```

Gets an empty list if it's never been assigned to,
or the existing list if it HAS been assigned to

The `add_comment` method is unchanged; it still
relies on the `comments` method to get the array
it should add a comment to. So the first time you
call it, your comment will get added to a new,
empty array. Subsequent calls will keep adding
comments to the same array, because that's what
the `comments` method will return.

Because the `comments` method ensures the `@comments` instance method is initialized for us,
we no longer need the `initialize` method on the `Clip` superclass. So we're free to delete it!

Why you shouldn't add "initialize" to a mixin

The revised `comments` method on our `AcceptsComments` module works every bit as well as the `comments` attribute reader method worked on our old `Clip` superclass. We no longer need the `initialize` method.

```
class Clip                                    module AcceptsComments
                          We'll move this here (and make a few changes)...
   attr_reader :comments ─────────────────────▶def comments   ◀──
                                                  if @comments        Replaces both the attr_reader
  We'll    ┌ def initialize                         @comments         and the "initialize" method
 delete this┤   @comments = []                    else
  method.  └ end                                    @comments = []
             ...                                  end
           end                                  end
                                                ...
                                              end
```

But why did we go to the trouble of updating the `comments` method? Couldn't we just move the `initialize` method from `Clip` to `AcceptsComments`?

```
class Clip         What if we had done this?    module AcceptsComments
   attr_reader :comments ─────────────────────▶attr_reader :comments

   def initialize ────────────────────────────▶def initialize
      @comments = []                              @comments = []
   end                                          end
   ...                                          ...
end                                            end
```

Well, if we *had* done it that way, the `initialize` method would work just fine...at first.

```
module AcceptsComments
   attr_reader :comments          Sets @comments to an empty array
   def initialize            ◀─── when the object is created.
      @comments = []  ◀──
   end
   def add_comment(comment)
      comments << comment
   end                   ▲
end                      └── On the first call, @comments
                              is already set!
class Photo
   include AcceptsComments
   def show
      puts "Displaying #{object_id}..."
   end
end
                              Calls the mixed-in
                              "initialize" method.
photo = Photo.new  ◀──
photo.add_comment("Beautiful colors.")      ┌─────────────────────────┐
p photo.comments                            │ ["Beautiful colors."]   │
                                            └─────────────────────────┘
```

The `initialize` method gets mixed into the `Photo` class, and it gets called when we call `Photo.new`. It sets the `@comments` instance variable to an empty array, before the `comments` reader method is ever called.

Why you shouldn't add "initialize" to a mixin (continued)

Using an `initialize` method in our module works…*until* we add
an `initialize` method to one of the classes we're mixing it into.

Suppose we needed to add an `initialize`
method to our `Photo` class, to set a default format:

```ruby
class Photo
  include AcceptsComments
  def initialize
    @format = 'JPEG'
  end
  ...
end
```

After we add the `initialize` method, if we create a new `Photo`
instance and call `add_comment` on it, we'll get an error!

```ruby
photo = Photo.new
photo.add_comment("Beautiful colors.")
```

Error ⟶ `in ` add_comment': undefined method `<<' for nil:NilClass`

If we add some `puts` statements to the two `initialize` methods to help debug, the issue becomes clear…

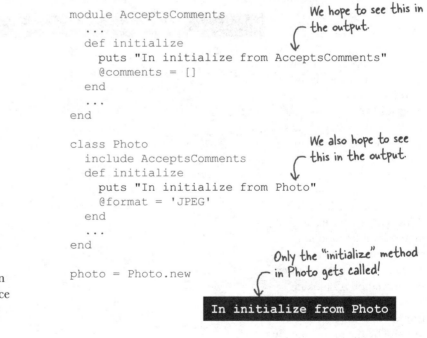

```ruby
module AcceptsComments
  ...
  def initialize
    puts "In initialize from AcceptsComments"
    @comments = []
  end
  ...
end
```

We hope to see this in the output.

```ruby
class Photo
  include AcceptsComments
  def initialize
    puts "In initialize from Photo"
    @format = 'JPEG'
  end
  ...
end

photo = Photo.new
```

We also hope to see this in the output.

The `initialize` method defined
in the `Photo` class gets called, but
the `initialize` method in
`AcceptsComments` doesn't! And so, in
the code above, the `@comments` instance
variable is still set to `nil` when we call
`add_comment`, and we get an error.

Only the "initialize" method in Photo gets called!

`In initialize from Photo`

The problem is that the `initialize` method from the class is
overriding the `initialize` method from the mixin.

Mixins and method overriding

As we saw, when you mix a module into a class, Ruby inserts the module into the chain of places it will look for methods, between the class and its superclass.

```ruby
class MySuperclass
end

module MyModule
  def my_method
    puts "hello from MyModule"
  end
end

class MyClass < MySuperclass
  include MyModule
end
```

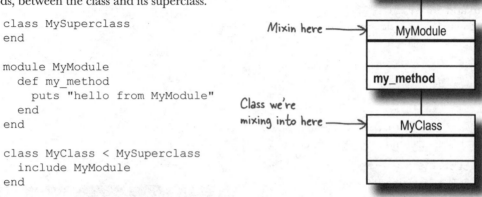

Mixin here →

Class we're mixing into here →

For a given class, you can get a list of all the places that Ruby will look for methods (both mixins and superclasses) by using the `ancestors` class method. It will return an array with all of the class's mixins and superclasses, in the order that they'll be searched.

```ruby
p MyClass.ancestors
```

⌐ Here's the mixin.

```
[MyClass, MyModule, MySuperclass, Object, Kernel, BasicObject]
```

Back in Chapter 3, we saw that when Ruby finds the method it's looking for on a class, it invokes the method *and then stops looking*. That's what allows subclasses to override methods from superclasses.

The same is true for mixins. Ruby searches for instance methods in the modules and classes shown in a class's `ancestors` array, in order. If the method it's looking for is found in a class, it just invokes that method. Any method by the same name in a mixin is ignored; that is, it gets *overridden* by the class's method.

```ruby
module MyModule
  def my_method
    puts "hello from MyModule"
  end
end

class MyClass
  include MyModule
  def my_method
    puts "hello from MyClass"
  end
end

p MyClass.ancestors

MyClass.new.my_method
```

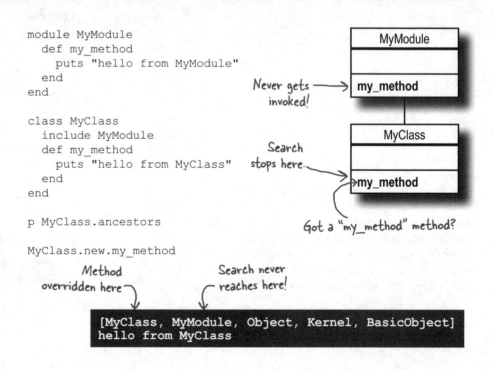

Never gets → invoked!

Search stops here.

Got a "my_method" method?

Method overridden here ⌐

Search never ⌐ reaches here!

```
[MyClass, MyModule, Object, Kernel, BasicObject]
hello from MyClass
```

Exercise

Guess the output for the code below, and write it in the blanks provided.

```ruby
module JetPropelled
  def move(destination)
    puts "Flying to #{destination}."
  end
end

class Robot
  def move(destination)
    puts "Walking to #{destination}."
  end
end

class TankBot < Robot
  include JetPropelled
  def move(destination)
    puts "Rolling to #{destination}."
  end
end

class HoverBot < Robot
  include JetPropelled
end

class FarmerBot < Robot
end

TankBot.new.move("hangar")
HoverBot.new.move("lab")
FarmerBot.new.move("field")
```

....
....
....

Avoid using "initialize" methods in modules

So that's why, if we were to include an `initialize` method in the AcceptsComments mixin, it would cause problems later. If we added an `initialize` method to the Photo class, it would override `initialize` in the mixin, and the `@comments` instance variable wouldn't get initialized.

```ruby
module AcceptsComments
  attr_reader :comments
  def initialize
    @comments = []
  end
  def add_comment(comment)
    comments << comment
  end
end

class Photo
  include AcceptsComments
  def initialize
    @format = 'JPEG'
  end
end

photo = Photo.new
photo.add_comment("Beautiful colors.")
```

The `@comments` instance variable is nil, so this fails!

Overrides "initialize" in the mixin, so it never runs!

Error →
```
in `add_comment': undefined
method `<<' for nil:NilClass
```

Avoid using "initialize" methods in modules (continued)

And that's why, instead of relying on an `initialize` method in `AcceptsComments`, we initialize the `@comments` instance variable within the `comments` method.

This replaces the attr_reader AND the "initialize" method.

```
module AcceptsComments
  def comments
    if @comments            If @comments
      @comments             is already set...
    else                    ...return
      @comments = []        that value.
    end
  end
  ...                  If it's not
end                    already set,
                       assign an
                       empty array
                       and return
                       that array.
```

It doesn't matter that there's an `initialize` method in the `Photo` class, because there's no `initialize` method in `AcceptsComments` for it to override. The `@comments` instance variable gets set to an empty array when `comments` is first called, and everything works great!

```
photo = Photo.new
photo.add_comment("Beautiful colors.")
p photo.comments
```

```
["Beautiful colors."]
```

So here's the lesson: avoid using `initialize` methods in your modules. If you need to set up an instance variable before it's used, do so in an accessor method within the module.

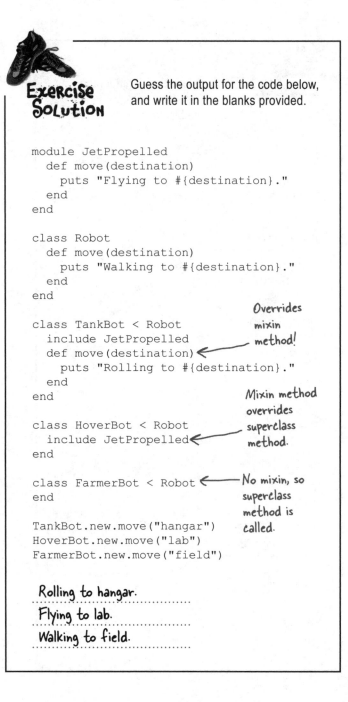

Exercise Solution

Guess the output for the code below, and write it in the blanks provided.

```
module JetPropelled
  def move(destination)
    puts "Flying to #{destination}."
  end
end

class Robot
  def move(destination)
    puts "Walking to #{destination}."
  end
end

class TankBot < Robot
  include JetPropelled           Overrides
  def move(destination)          mixin
    puts "Rolling to #{destination}."  method!
  end
end

class HoverBot < Robot
  include JetPropelled           Mixin method
end                             overrides
                                superclass
                                method.

class FarmerBot < Robot         No mixin, so
end                             superclass
                                method is
TankBot.new.move("hangar")      called.
HoverBot.new.move("lab")
FarmerBot.new.move("field")
```

Rolling to hangar.

Flying to lab.

Walking to field.

Using the Boolean "or" operator for assignment

It's a bit of a pain, though: the `comments` method is several lines long. It would be nice if we could make our attribute accessor methods more concise, especially if we'll be adding more of them.

Well, what if we told you that we could reduce those *five* lines of code in the `comments` method down to just *one*, while keeping the same functionality? Here's one way:

```
module AcceptsComments
  def comments
    if @comments
      @comments
    else
      @comments = []
    end
  end
end
```

Assigns a new value to @comments, but only if @comments is nil

```
module AcceptsComments
  def comments
    @comments = @comments || []
  end
end
```

Assigns a new value to @comments, but only if @comments is nil

Same functionality in a single line!

As we learned back in Chapter 1, the `||` operator (read it aloud as "or") tests whether either of two expressions is `true` (or not `nil`). If the lefthand expression is true, the value of the lefthand expression will be the value of the `||` expression. Otherwise, the value of the righthand expression will be the value of the `||` expression. That's a bit of a mouthful, so it's probably easier to just observe it in action:

p true || false	`true`
p false || true	`true`
p nil || true	`true`
p true || "righthand value"	`true`
p "lefthand value" || "righthand value"	`"lefthand value"`
p nil || []	`[]`
p [] || "righthand value"	`[]`

So if `@comments` is `nil`, the value of the `||` expression in the `comments` method will be an empty array. If `@comments` is *not* `nil`, the value of the `||` expression will be the value in `@comments`.

@comments = nil p @comments || []	`[]`
@comments = ["Beautiful colors."] p @comments || []	`["Beautiful colors."]`

The conditional assignment operator

The value of the `||` expression is what gets assigned back to `@comments`. So `@comments` gets reassigned its current value, *or*, if its current value is `nil`, it gets assigned an empty array.

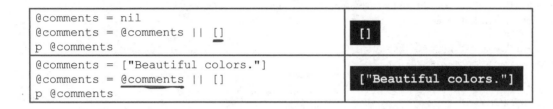

This shortcut is so useful that Ruby offers the `||=` operator, also known as the *conditional assignment operator*, to do the same thing. If a variable's value is `nil` (or false), the conditional assignment operator will assign the variable a new value. But if the variable's value is anything else, `||=` will leave that value intact.

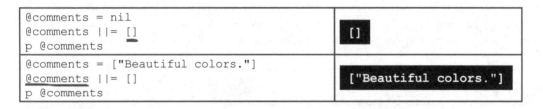

The conditional assignment operator is perfect for use in our `AcceptsComments` mixin's `comments` method...

```ruby
module AcceptsComments
  def comments
    @comments ||= []      ⟵——— If @comments is nil, assign an empty array
  end                            to it. Return the value of @comments.
  def add_comment(comment)
    comments << comment
  end
end

class Photo
  include AcceptsComments
  def initialize
    @format = 'JPEG'
  end
end
```

The `comments` method works the same as before, but now it's one line instead of five!

```ruby
photo = Photo.new
photo.add_comment("Beautiful colors.")
p photo.comments
```

`["Beautiful colors."]`

Exercise

Guess the output for each snippet of code below, and write it in the blanks provided.

(We've filled in the first one for you.)

```
puts true || "my"
```
true

```
puts false || "friendship"
```
....

```
puts nil || "is"
```
....

```
puts "not" || "often"
```
....

```
first = nil
puts first || "easily"
```
....

```
second = "earned."
puts second || "purchased."
```
....

```
third = false
third ||= true
puts third
```
....

```
fourth = "love"
fourth ||= "praise"
puts fourth
```
....

```
fifth = "takes"
fifth ||= "gives"
puts fifth
```
....

```
sixth = nil
sixth ||= "work."
puts sixth
```
....

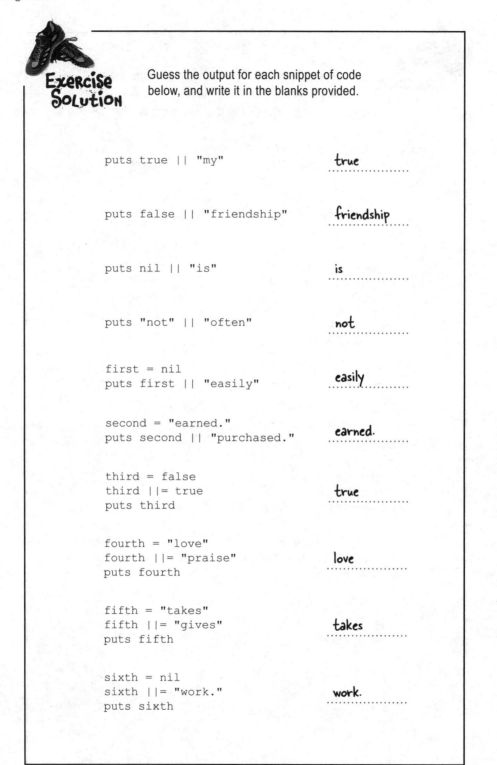

Exercise Solution

Guess the output for each snippet of code below, and write it in the blanks provided.

```
puts true || "my"
```
true

```
puts false || "friendship"
```
friendship

```
puts nil || "is"
```
is

```
puts "not" || "often"
```
not

```
first = nil
puts first || "easily"
```
easily

```
second = "earned."
puts second || "purchased."
```
earned.

```
third = false
third ||= true
puts third
```
true

```
fourth = "love"
fourth ||= "praise"
puts fourth
```
love

```
fifth = "takes"
fifth ||= "gives"
puts fifth
```
takes

```
sixth = nil
sixth ||= "work."
puts sixth
```
work.

Our complete code

Here's our complete updated code for
the media-sharing app. We don't need
that pesky `initialize` method in the
`AcceptsComments` mixin, now that the
`comments` method initializes the `@comments`
array itself. Everything is working great!

Gives either a default value for @comments, or the current value. No need for "initialize"!

```ruby
module AcceptsComments
  def comments
    @comments ||= []
  end
  def add_comment(comment)
    comments << comment
  end
end
```

Add a new comment to the array.

Use the "comments" method to get the value of @comments.

Superclass
```ruby
class Clip
  def play
    puts "Playing #{object_id}..."
  end
end
```
Video and Song will inherit this.

Subclass
```ruby
class Video < Clip
  include AcceptsComments
  attr_accessor :resolution
end
```
Mix in the "comments" and "add_comment" methods.

Subclass
```ruby
class Song < Clip
  include AcceptsComments
  attr_accessor :beats_per_minute
end
```
Mix in the "comments" and "add_comment" methods.

Standalone class
```ruby
class Photo
  include AcceptsComments
  def initialize
    @format = 'JPEG'
  end
end
```
Mix in the "comments" and "add_comment" methods.

No need to worry about this interfering with AcceptsComments!

Create a Video, Song, and Photo, then use methods from the mixin to add and print comments.
```ruby
video = Video.new
video.add_comment("Cool slow motion effect!")
video.add_comment("Weird ending.")
song = Song.new
song.add_comment("Awesome beat.")
photo = Photo.new
photo.add_comment("Beautiful colors.")

p video.comments, song.comments, photo.comments
```

```
["Cool slow motion effect!", "Weird ending."]
["Awesome beat."]
["Beautiful colors."]
```

Your Ruby Toolbox

**That's it for Chapter 9!
You've added modules
and mixins to your toolbox.**

Hashes

Modules

A module is a collection of methods.

The main difference between a
module and a class is that you
can't create instances of a module.

Mixins

When you mix a module into a class,
it's like adding all of the module's
methods to the class as instance
methods.

Although a class can only inherit
from one superclass, you can mix
any number of modules into a class.

BULLET POINTS

- Module names must begin with a capital letter. It's conventional to use camel case for the remaining letters.

- Since mixin modules usually describe one aspect of an object's behavior, it's also conventional to use a description (like `Traceable` or `PasswordProtected`) as the module name.

- Ruby maintains a list of places it will look for methods for instances of any given class. When you mix a module into a class, Ruby adds the module to that list, just after the class.

- You can see the list of places that Ruby will look for methods for a given class by calling the `ancestors` class method.

- If there are instance methods by the same name on both a class and a mixin, the class's instance method will override the mixin's instance method.

- Just like instance methods from a class, mixin methods can create instance variables on the current object.

- The conditional assignment operator, `||=`, assigns a new value to a variable only if it is `nil` (or `false`). It's a good way to set a default value for a variable.

Up Next...

Now you know how to create and use a mixin. But what do you *do* with this
amazing new tool? Well, Ruby has some ideas! It includes some powerful modules
that are ready to mix into your classes. We'll learn about them in the next chapter!

10 comparable and enumerable

Ready-Made Mixes

> **Sometimes** the paint store has just the right color, but I find it pays to be good at mixing...

You've seen that mixins can be useful. But you haven't seen their full power yet. The Ruby core library includes two mixins that will *blow your mind*. The first, `Comparable`, is used for comparing objects. You've used operators like <, >, and == on numbers and strings, but `Comparable` will let you use them on *your* classes.

The second mixin, `Enumerable`, is used for working with collections. Remember those super-useful `find_all`, `reject`, and `map` methods that you used on arrays before? Those came from `Enumerable`. But that's a tiny fraction of what `Enumerable` can do. And again, you can mix it into *your* classes. Read on to see how!

Mixins built into Ruby

Now that you know how modules work, let's take a look at some useful modules that are included with the Ruby language…

Believe it or not, you've been using mixins ever since Chapter 1. You just didn't know it.

Remember comparing numbers using <, >, and == in the guessing game in Chapter 1? You may recall that comparison operators are actually methods in Ruby.

All the numeric classes need comparison operators, so the creators of Ruby *could* have just added them to the `Numeric` class, which is a superclass of `Fixnum`, `Float`, and all the other numeric classes in Ruby.

But the `String` class needs comparison operators, too. And it doesn't seem wise to make `String` a subclass of `Numeric`. For one thing, `String` would inherit a bunch of methods like `abs` (which gives the absolute value of a number) and `modulo` (the remainder of a division operation) that aren't appropriate to a `String` at all.

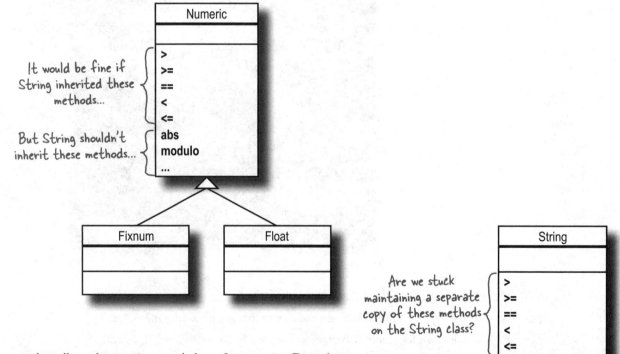

So we can't really make `String` a subclass of `Numeric`. Does that mean Ruby's maintainers have to keep one copy of the comparison methods on the `Numeric` class, and duplicate the methods on the `String` class?

As you learned in the last chapter, the answer is no! They can just mix in a module instead.

A preview of the Comparable mixin

Because so many different kinds of classes need the <, <=, ==, >, and >= methods, it wasn't practical to use inheritance. Instead, Ruby's creators put these five methods (plus a sixth, between?, which we'll talk about later) into a module named Comparable.

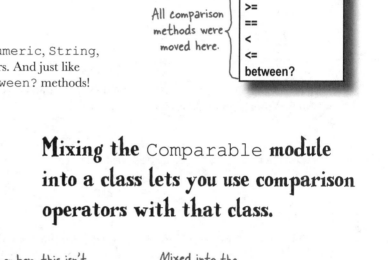

All comparison methods were moved here.

Then, they mixed the Comparable module into Numeric, String, and any other class that needed comparison operators. And just like that, those classes gained <, <=, ==, >, >=, and between? methods!

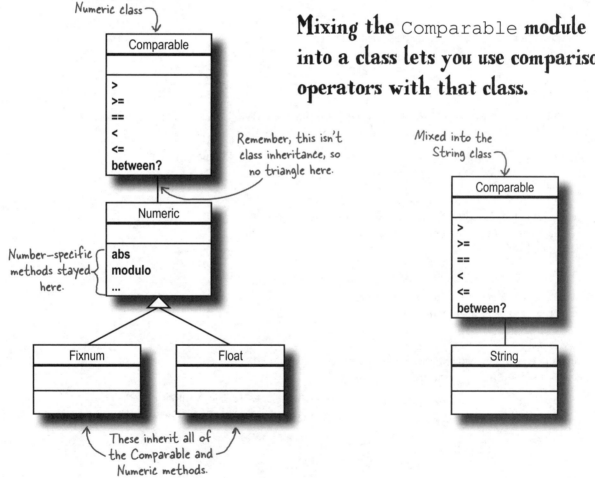

Mixed into the Numeric class

Remember, this isn't class inheritance, so no triangle here.

Number-specific methods stayed here.

Mixing the Comparable **module into a class lets you use comparison operators with that class.**

Mixed into the String class

These inherit all of the Comparable and Numeric methods.

And here's the really great part: *you* can mix Comparable into *your* classes, too! Hmm…but what class shall we use it for?

Choice (of) beef

We'd like to take a moment to talk to you about a topic near and dear to our hearts: steak. In the USA, there are three "grades" of beef, which describe its quality. In order, from best to worst, they are:

- Prime
- Choice
- Select

Beef grades

So a "Prime" steak is going to give you a more delicious dining experience than a "Choice" steak, and "Choice" will be better than "Select."

Suppose we have a simple `Steak` class, with a `grade` attribute that can be set to either `"Prime"`, `"Choice"`, or `"Select"`:

```
class Steak
  attr_accessor :grade
end
```

We want to be able to easily compare `Steak` objects, so that we know which to buy. In other words, we want to be able to write code like this:

```
if first_steak > second_steak        We can't do this (yet)!
  puts "I'll take #{first_steak}"
end
```

As we learned back in Chapter 4, comparison operators like > are actually calls to an instance method on the object being compared. So if you see code like this:

```
4 > 3
```

…it actually gets converted to a call to an instance method named > on the 4 object, with 3 as its argument, like this:

```
4.>(3)
```

So what we need is an instance method on our `Steak` class, named >, that accepts a second `Steak` instance to compare to.

```
first_steak.>(second_steak)        When we can write this, we'll also be able
                                   to write "if first_steak > second_steak"…
```

Implementing a greater-than method on the Steak class

Here's our first attempt at a > method for our `Steak` class. It will compare the current object, `self`, to a second object and return `true` if `self` is "greater," or `false` if the other object is "greater." We'll compare the `grade` attribute of the two objects to determine which is greater.

```ruby
class Steak

  attr_accessor :grade

  def >(other)
    grade_scores = {"Prime" => 3, "Choice" => 2, "Select" => 1}
    grade_scores[grade] > grade_scores[other.grade]
  end

end

first_steak = Steak.new
first_steak.grade = "Prime"
second_steak = Steak.new
second_steak.grade = "Choice"

if first_steak > second_steak
  puts "I'll take #{first_steak.inspect}."
end
```

This is the "other" instance of Steak that we're going to compare this instance to.

This hash lets us convert the "grade" string to a number, for easy comparison.

Returns true if the numeric score of this Steak's grade is greater than the numeric score of the other Steak. Otherwise, returns false.

Use our new method to compare two Steak instances.

```
I'll take #<Steak:0x007fc0bc20eae8 @grade="Prime">.
```

The key to our new > method is the `grade_scores` hash, which lets us look up a grade (`"Prime"`, `"Choice"`, or `"Select"`) and get a numeric score instead. Then, all we have to do is compare the scores!

```ruby
grade_scores = {"Prime" => 3, "Choice" => 2, "Select" => 1}
puts grade_scores["Prime"]
puts grade_scores["Choice"]
puts grade_scores["Prime"] > grade_scores["Select"]
```

```
3
2
true
```

With the > method in place, we're able to use the > operator in our code to compare `Steak` instances. A `Steak` with an assigned grade of `"Prime"` will be "greater" than a `Steak` with a grade of `"Choice"`, and a `Steak` with a grade of `"Choice"` will be greater than a `Steak` with a grade of `"Select"`.

There's just one problem with this code: it creates a new hash object and assigns it to the `grade_scores` variable every time the > method runs. That's pretty inefficient. So, if you'll bear with us, we need to take a quick detour to talk about *constants*...

Constants  A Ruby Detour

The > method on our `Steak` class creates a new hash object and assigns it to the `grade_scores` variable every time it runs. That's pretty inefficient, considering the contents of the hash *never change*.

```ruby
class Steak

  attr_accessor :grade

  def >(other)
    grade_scores = {"Prime" => 3, "Choice" => 2, "Select" => 1}
    grade_scores[grade] > grade_scores[other.grade]
  end

end
```

A new, identical hash gets created every time the > method runs!

For situations like this, Ruby offers the **constant**: a reference to an object that never changes.

If you assign a value to a name that begins with a capital letter, Ruby will treat it as a constant rather than a variable. By convention, constant names should be `ALL_CAPS`. You can assign a value to a constant within a class or module body, and then access that constant from anywhere within that class or module.

```ruby
class MyClass
  MY_CONSTANT = 42
  def my_method
    puts MY_CONSTANT
  end
end

MyClass.new.my_method
```

```
42
```

> ### ✴ Conventional Wisdom ✴
>
> **Use ALL CAPS for constant names. Separate words with underscores.**
>
> ```
> PHI = 1.618
> SPEED_OF_LIGHT = 299792458
> ```

Instead of redefining our hash of numeric equivalents for beef grades every time we call the > method, let's define it as a constant. Then, we can simply access the constant within the > method.

```ruby
class Steak

  GRADE_SCORES = {"Prime" => 3, "Choice" => 2, "Select" => 1}

  attr_accessor :grade

  def >(other)
    GRADE_SCORES[grade] > GRADE_SCORES[other.grade]
  end

end
```

Define the constant within the class body.

We can access the constant within this or any other method within the Steak class.

Our code will work the same using a constant as it did using a variable, but we only have to create the hash once. This should be much more efficient!

End of Ruby Detour

We have a lot more methods to define...

Our revised > method for comparing Steak methods is working great...

```ruby
class Steak

  GRADE_SCORES = {"Prime" => 3, "Choice" => 2, "Select" => 1}

  attr_accessor :grade

  def >(other)
    GRADE_SCORES[grade] > GRADE_SCORES[other.grade]
  end

end

first_steak = Steak.new
first_steak.grade = "Prime"
second_steak = Steak.new
second_steak.grade = "Choice"

if first_steak > second_steak
  puts "I'll take #{first_steak.inspect}."
end
```

```
I'll take #<Steak:0x007fa5b5816ca0 @grade="Prime">.
```

But that's all we have: the > operator. If we try to use <, for example, our code will fail:

```ruby
if first_steak < second_steak
  puts "I'll take #{second_steak}."
end
```

```
undefined method `<' for #<Steak:0x007facdb0f2fa0 @grade="Prime">
```

The same goes for <= and >=. Object has an == method that Steak inherits, so the == operator won't raise an error, but that version of == doesn't work for our needs (it only returns true if you're comparing two references to the *exact same object*).

We'll need to implement methods for all of these methods before we can use them. Doesn't sound like a fun task, does it? Well, there's a better solution. It's time to break out the Comparable module!

The Comparable mixin

Ruby's built-in Comparable module allows you to *compare* instances of your class. Comparable provides methods that allow you to use the <, <=, ==, >, and >= operators (as well as a between? method you can call to determine if one instance of a class is ranked "between" two other instances).

Comparable is mixed into Ruby's string and numeric classes (among others) to implement all of the above operators, and you can use it, too! All you have to do is add a specific method to your class that Comparable relies on, then mix in the module, and you gain all these methods "for free"!

If we were to write our own version of Comparable, it might look like this:

```
module Comparable
  def <(other)
    (self <=> other) == -1
  end
  def >(other)
    (self <=> other) == 1
  end
  def ==(other)
    (self <=> other) == 0
  end
  def <=(other)
    comparison = (self <=> other)
    comparison == -1 || comparison == 0
  end
  def >=(other)
    comparison = (self <=> other)
    comparison == 1 || comparison == 0
  end
  def between?(first, second)
    (self <=> first) >= 0 && (self <=> second) <= 0
  end
end
```

As before, "other" is the other instance we're comparing this instance to.

"self" refers to the current instance, of course.

All the remaining methods use "other" and "self" in the same way.

The spaceship operator

What are those <=> symbols everywhere? They look like a <= or >= operator...sort of.

That's the "spaceship operator."
It's a kind of comparison operator.

Many Rubyists call <=> the "spaceship operator," because it looks like a spaceship.

You can think of <=> as a combination of the <, ==, and > operators. It returns −1 if the expression on the left is *less than* the expression on the right, 0 if the expressions are *equal*, and 1 if the expression on the left is *greater than* the expression on the right.

```
puts 3 <=> 4        -1
puts 3 <=> 3         0
puts 4 <=> 3         1
```

Implementing the spaceship operator on Steak

We mentioned that `Comparable` relies on a specific method being in your class... That's the spaceship operator method.

Just like <, >, ==, and so on, <=> is actually a method behind the scenes. When Ruby encounters something like this in your code:

```
3 <=> 4
```

...it converts it to an instance method call, like this:

```
3.<=>(4)
```

Here's what that means: if we add a <=> instance method to the `Steak` class, then whenever we use the <=> operator to compare some `Steak` instances, our method will be called! Let's try it now.

```ruby
class Steak

  GRADE_SCORES = {"Prime" => 3, "Choice" => 2, "Select" => 1}

  attr_accessor :grade

  def <=>(other)
    if GRADE_SCORES[self.grade] < GRADE_SCORES[other.grade]
      return -1
    elsif GRADE_SCORES[self.grade] == GRADE_SCORES[other.grade]
      return 0
    else
      return 1
    end
  end

end

first_steak = Steak.new
first_steak.grade = "Prime"
second_steak = Steak.new
second_steak.grade = "Choice"

puts first_steak <=> second_steak
puts second_steak <=> first_steak
```

If this steak's grade is lower than the other steak's grade, return -1.

If the grades are equal, return 0.

Otherwise, this steak's grade must be higher than the other steak's grade, so return 1.

```
1
-1
```

If the steak to the left of the <=> operator is "greater" than the steak to the right, we'll get a result of 1. If they're equal, we'll get a result of 0. And if the steak on the left is "lesser" than the steak on the right, we'll get a result of -1.

Of course, code that used <=> everywhere wouldn't be very readable. Now that we can use <=> on `Steak` instances, we're ready to mix the `Comparable` module into the `Steak` class, and get the <, >, <=, >=, ==, and `between?` methods working!

Mixing Comparable into Steak

We've got the spaceship operator working on our `Steak` class:

```
puts first_steak <=> second_steak
puts second_steak <=> first_steak
```

```
1
-1
```

...which is all the `Comparable` mixin needs in order to work with `Steak`. Let's try mixing in `Comparable`. We just have to add one more line of code to do so:

```
class Steak

  include Comparable         ← All Steak instances are now Comparable!

  GRADE_SCORES = {"Prime" => 3, "Choice" => 2, "Select" => 1}

  attr_accessor :grade

  def <=>(other)
    if GRADE_SCORES[self.grade] < GRADE_SCORES[other.grade]
      return -1
    elsif GRADE_SCORES[self.grade] == GRADE_SCORES[other.grade]
      return 0
    else
      return 1
    end
  end

end
```

With `Comparable` mixed in, all the comparison operators (and the `between?` method) should instantly begin working for `Steak` instances:

```
prime = Steak.new
prime.grade = "Prime"
choice = Steak.new
choice.grade = "Choice"
select = Steak.new
select.grade = "Select"

puts "prime > choice: #{prime > choice}"
puts "prime < select: #{prime < select}"
puts "select == select: #{select == select}"
puts "select <= select: #{select <= select}"
puts "select >= choice: #{select >= choice}"
print "choice.between?(select, prime): "
puts choice.between?(select, prime)
```

```
prime > choice: true
prime < select: false
select == select: true
select <= select: true
select >= choice: false
choice.between?(select, prime): true
```

How the Comparable methods work

When a > comparison operator appears in your code, the > method is called on the object to the left of the > operator, with the object to the right of the > as the `other` argument.

```
prime = Steak.new
prime.grade = "Prime"
choice = Steak.new
choice.grade = "Choice"

puts prime > choice
```

This will call the > method on the Steak in the "prime" variable.

This works because `Comparable` has been mixed in to your class, so the > method is now available as an instance method on all `Steak` instances.

```
module Comparable
  ...
  def >(other)
    (self <=> other) == 1
  end
  ...
end
```

This will call the <=> method.

The > method, in turn, calls the <=> instance method (defined directly within the `Steak` class) to determine which `Steak`'s `grade` is "greater." The > method returns `true` or `false` according to the return value of <=>.

```
class Steak

  include Comparable

  GRADE_SCORES = {"Prime" => 3, "Choice" => 2, "Select" => 1}

  attr_accessor :grade
```

This will return –1, 0, or 1 to the > method. →

```
  def <=>(other)
    if GRADE_SCORES[self.grade] < GRADE_SCORES[other.grade]
      return -1
    elsif GRADE_SCORES[self.grade] == GRADE_SCORES[other.grade]
      return 0
    else
      return 1
    end
  end

end
```

And *we* wind up selecting the tastiest steak!

The <, <=, ==, >=, and `between?` methods work similarly, relying on the <=> method to determine whether to return `true` or `false`. Implement the <=> method and mix in `Comparable`, and you get the <, <=, ==, >, >=, and `between?` methods for free! Not bad, eh?

Well, if you like *that*, you're going to *love* the `Enumerable` module...

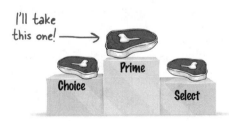

I'll take this one! →

Pool Puzzle

Your **job** is to take code snippets from the pool and place them into the blank lines in the code. **Don't** use the same snippet more than once, and you won't need to use all the snippets. Your **goal** is to make code that will run and produce the output shown.

```
class Apple

    _____ Comparable

    attr_accessor _____

    def _____(weight)
        _____.weight = weight
    end

    def ___(other)
        self.weight <=> _____.weight
    end

end

small_apple = Apple.new(0.17)
medium_apple = Apple.new(0.22)
big_apple = Apple.new(0.25)

puts "small_apple > medium_apple:"
puts small_apple > medium_apple
puts "medium_apple < big_apple:"
puts medium_apple < big_apple
```

Output:

```
File Edit Window Help Pie
small_apple > medium_apple:
false
medium_apple < big_apple:
true
```

Note: each thing from the pool can only be used once!

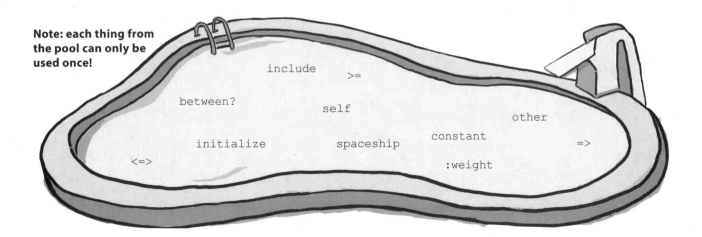

include
>=
between?
self
other
initialize
spaceship
constant
=>
<=>
:weight

Pool Puzzle Solution

```
class Apple

  include  Comparable

  attr_accessor :weight

  def initialize (weight)
    self.weight = weight
  end

  def <=>(other)
    self.weight <=> other.weight
  end

end

small_apple = Apple.new(0.17)
medium_apple = Apple.new(0.22)
big_apple = Apple.new(0.25)

puts "small_apple > medium_apple:"
puts small_apple > medium_apple
puts "medium_apple < big_apple:"
puts medium_apple < big_apple
```

Output:

```
File Edit Window Help
small_apple > medium_apple:
false
medium_apple < big_apple:
true
```

Our next mixin

Remember that awesome `find_all` method from Chapter 6? The one that let us easily select elements from an array based on whatever criteria we wanted?

```
relevant_lines = lines.find_all { |line| line.include?("Truncated") }
```

This shortened code works just as well: only lines that include the substring `"Truncated"` are copied to the new array!

```
puts relevant_lines
```

```
Normally producers and directors would stop this kind of
garbage from getting published. Truncated is amazing in that
it got past those hurdles.
   --Joseph Goldstein, "Truncated: Awful," New York Minute
Truncated is funny: it can't be categorized as comedy,
romance, or horror, because none of those genres would want
to be associated with it.
   --Liz Smith, "Truncated Disappoints," Chicago Some-Times
I'm pretty sure this was shot on a mobile phone. Truncated
is astounding in its disregard for filmmaking aesthetics.
   --Bill Mosher, "Don't See Truncated," Topeka Obscurant
```

Remember the super-useful `reject` and `map` methods from the same chapter? All of those methods come from the same place, and it *isn't* the `Array` class...

The Enumerable module

Just as Ruby's string and numeric classes mix in `Comparable` to implement their comparison methods, many of Ruby's collection classes (like `Array` and `Hash`) mix in the `Enumerable` module to implement their methods that work with collections. This includes the `find_all`, `reject`, and `map` methods we used back in Chapter 6 , as well as 47 others:

Mixing the `Enumerable` **module into a class adds methods for working with collections.**

Instance methods from Enumerable:

all?	find_all	none?
any?	find_index	one?
chunk	first	partition
collect	flat_map	reduce
collect_concat	grep	reject
count	group_by	reverse_each
cycle	include?	select
detect	inject	slice_before
drop	lazy	sort
drop_while	map	sort_by
each_cons	max	take
each_entry	max_by	take_while
each_slice	member?	to_a
each_with_index	min	to_h
each_with_object	min_by	to_set
entries	minmax	zip
find	minmax_by	

And just like `Comparable`, you can mix in `Enumerable` to get all of these methods on your *own* class! You just have to provide a specific method that `Enumerable` needs to call. It's a method you've worked with before on other classes: the `each` method. The methods in `Enumerable` will call on your `each` method to loop through the items in your class, and perform whatever operation you need on them.

Comparable:

- Provides <, >, ==, and three other methods

- Is mixed in by `String`, `Fixnum`, and other numeric classes

- Relies on host class to provide <=> method

Enumerable:

- Provides `find_all`, `reject`, `map` and 47 other methods

- Is mixed in by `Array`, `Hash`, and other collection classes

- Relies on host class to provide `each` method

We don't have nearly enough space in this book to cover *all* the methods in `Enumerable`, but we'll try out a few in the next few pages. And in the upcoming chapter on Ruby documentation, we'll show you where you can read up on the rest of them!

A class to mix Enumerable into

To test out the `Enumerable` module, we're going to need a class to mix it into. And not just any class will do…we need one with an `each` method.

That's why we've created `WordSplitter`, a class that can process each word in a string. Its `each` method splits the string on space characters to get the individual words, then yields each word to a block. The code is short and sweet:

```ruby
class WordSplitter

  attr_accessor :string          # Holds the string we want to split

  def each                        # The Enumerable methods will be calling this.
    string.split(" ").each do |word|   # Split the string into words (split it on space characters) and process each word.
      yield word                  # Yield the current word to the block that was passed to "each".
    end
  end

end
```

We can test that the `each` method works by creating a new `WordSplitter`, assigning it a string, and then calling `each` with a block that prints each word:

```ruby
splitter = WordSplitter.new
splitter.string = "one two three four"   # Here's the string we want to split.

splitter.each do |word|          # The block will receive each word as a parameter.
  puts word                       # Print the current word.
end
```

```
one
two
three
four
```

That one `each` method is cool and all…but we want our 50 `Enumerable` methods! Well, now that we have `each`, getting the additional methods is as easy as mixing `Enumerable` in…

Mixing Enumerable into our class

Without further ado, let's mix Enumerable into our `WordSplitter` class:

```ruby
class WordSplitter

  include Enumerable          ← — Mix in Enumerable.

  attr_accessor :string

  def each
    string.split(" ").each do |word|
      yield word
    end
  end

end
```

We'll create another instance and set its `string` attribute:

```ruby
splitter = WordSplitter.new
splitter.string = "how do you do"
```

Now, let's try calling some of those new methods! The `find_all`, `reject`, and `map` methods work just like we saw back in Chapter 6, except that instead of passing array elements to the block, they pass words! (Because that's what they get from `WordSplitter`'s each method.)

```ruby
p splitter.find_all { |word| word.include?("d") }    ← — Find all items for which the block returns true.
p splitter.reject { |word| word.include?("d") }      ← — Reject items for which the block returns true.
p splitter.map { |word| word.reverse }
```
Returns an array with all of the block's return values

```
["do", "do"]
["how", "you"]
["woh", "od", "uoy", "od"]
```

We get lots of other methods, too:

```ruby
p splitter.any? { |word| word.include?("e") }    ← — The method returns true if the block returns true for any item.
p splitter.count     ← — Count of all items
p splitter.first     ← — First item
p splitter.sort      ←
```
These methods don't require a block.

An array with all the items sorted

```
false
4
"how"
["do", "do", "how", "you"]
```

We get 50 methods in all! That's a lot of power just for adding *one* line to our class!

Inside the Enumerable module

If we were to write our own version of the Enumerable module, every method would include a call to the each method of the host class. Enumerable's methods rely on each in order to get items to process.

Here's what the find_all, reject, and map methods might look like:

```
module Enumerable

  def find_all
    matching_items = []
    self.each do |item|
      if yield(item)
        matching_items << item
      end
    end
    matching_items
  end

  def reject
    kept_items = []
    self.each do |item|
      unless yield(item)
        kept_items << item
      end
    end
    kept_items
  end

  def map
    results = []
    self.each do |item|
      results << yield(item)
    end
    results
  end

  ...
end
```

Create a new array to hold the elements for which the block returns true.

Process each element.

Pass the element to the block. If the result is true...

...add it to the array of matching elements.

Create a new array to hold the elements for which the block returns false.

Process each element.

Pass the element to the block. If the result is false...

...add it to the array of kept elements.

Make a new array to hold the block return values.

Loop through each element.

Pass the element to the block, and add the return value to the new array.

Return the array of block return values.

Many more methods here!

Our custom Enumerable would have other methods besides find_all, reject, and map, though. *Many* others. All of them would be related to working with collections. And all of them would include a call to each.

Just as the methods in Comparable rely on the <=> method to compare two items, the methods in Enumerable rely on the each method to process each item in a collection. Enumerable doesn't have its own each method; instead, it relies on the class you're mixing it into to provide one.

This chapter has given you just a taste of what the Comparable and Enumerable modules can do for you. We encourage you to experiment with other classes. Remember, if you can write a <=> method for it, you can mix Comparable into it. And if you can write an each method for it, you can mix Enumerable into it!

Let's load up our `Enumerable`-enhanced `WordSplitter` class in irb and try it out!

Step One:

Save this class definition to a
file, named *word_splitter.rb*.

```ruby
class WordSplitter

  include Enumerable

  attr_accessor :string

  def each
    string.split(" ").each do |word|
      yield word
    end
  end

end
```

word_splitter.rb

Step Two:

From a system command prompt, navigate into the directory
where you saved your file.

Step Three:

Type the following to launch irb:

```
irb -I .
```
Remember, this part lets you load
files from the current directory.

Step Four:

As before, we need to load the file with our saved Ruby code. Type this line:

```
require "word_splitter"
```

Exercise (Continued)

With our `WordSplitter` class's code loaded, you can create as many instances as you like, set their `string` attributes, and test out all the `Enumerable` methods at your disposal! Try the following for starters:

```
splitter = WordSplitter.new
splitter.string = "salad beefcake corn beef pasta beefy"
```
Find all words that include "beef".
```
splitter.find_all { |word| word.include?("beef") }
```
Reject all words that include "beef".
```
splitter.reject { |word| word.include?("beef") }
```
Get an array with all the words capitalized.
```
splitter.map { |word| word.capitalize }
```
Get the number of words.
```
splitter.count
```
Find the first word that includes "beef".
```
splitter.find { |word| word.include?("beef") }
```
Get the first word.
```
splitter.first
```
Split the words into two arrays: words that include "beef" and words that don't.
```
splitter.group_by { |word| word.include?("beef") }
```
Find the longest word.
```
splitter.max_by { |word| word.length }
```
Get an array with all the words.
```
splitter.to_a
```

Here's a sample session:

```
File Edit Window Help Cow
$ irb -I .
irb(main):001:0> require "word_splitter"
 => true
irb(main):001:0> splitter = WordSplitter.new
 => #<WordSplitter:0x007fbf6c801eb0>
irb(main):001:0> splitter.string = "salad beefcake corn beef pasta beefy"
 => "salad beefcake corn beef pasta beefy"
irb(main):001:0> splitter.find_all { |word| word.include?("beef") }
 => ["beefcake", "beef", "beefy"]
irb(main):001:0> splitter.reject { |word| word.include?("beef") }
 => ["salad", "corn", "pasta"]
irb(main):001:0> splitter.map { |word| word.capitalize }
 => ["Salad", "Beefcake", "Corn", "Beef", "Pasta", "Beefy"]
irb(main):001:0>
```

Your Ruby Toolbox

That's it for Chapter 10! You've **added** Comparable **and** Enumerable **to your toolbox.**

Mixins

When you mix a module into a class, it's like adding all of the module's methods to the class as instance methods.

Although a class can only inherit from one superclass, you can mix any number of modules into a class.

Comparable

The Comparable module provides methods that let you use the <, <=, ==, >=, and > comparison operators on instances of a class.

Comparable can be mixed into any class that has a "<=>" method.

Enumerable

The Enumerable module provides 50 different methods for working with collections.

Enumerable can be mixed into any class that has an "each" method.

Up Next...

In the next chapter, you'll find out where *we* learned about all of these cool classes, modules, and methods: Ruby's documentation. And you'll learn how to use it yourself!

BULLET POINTS

- A constant is a reference to an object that never changes.

- You can define a constant by assigning a value to it, similar to creating a new variable.

- By convention, a constant's name should be ALL_CAPS, with multiple words separated by underscores.

- You add the <, <=, ==, >, >=, and between? methods to the Numeric and String classes by mixing in the Comparable module.

- The so-called spaceship operator, <=>, compares the expressions to its left and right.

- <=> returns −1 if the expression on its left is less than the expression on its right, 0 if the two expressions are equal, and 1 if the expression on its left is greater than the expression on its right.

- Comparable's methods use <=> to determine which of two objects is greater, or if they are equal.

- Many of Ruby's collection classes (like Array and Hash) get their collection-related methods from the Enumerable module.

- Enumerable's methods call the each method on the host class to get the members of a collection.

11 documentation

Read the Manual

There isn't enough room in this book to teach you <u>all</u> of Ruby.

There's an old saying: "Give someone a fish, and you feed them for a day. Teach them how to fish, and you feed them for a lifetime." We've been *giving you fish* so far. We've shown you how to use a few of Ruby's classes and modules. But there are dozens more, some of them applicable to your problems, that we don't have room to cover.

So it's time to *teach you how to fish*. There's excellent **documentation** freely available on all of Ruby's classes, modules, and methods. You just have to know where to find it, and how to interpret it. That's what this chapter will show you.

Learning how to learn more

Your team is really enjoying the transition to Ruby. They're impressed with the `Array` and `Hash` classes, and all the capabilities of the `Comparable` and `Enumerable` modules. But one developer has a concern...

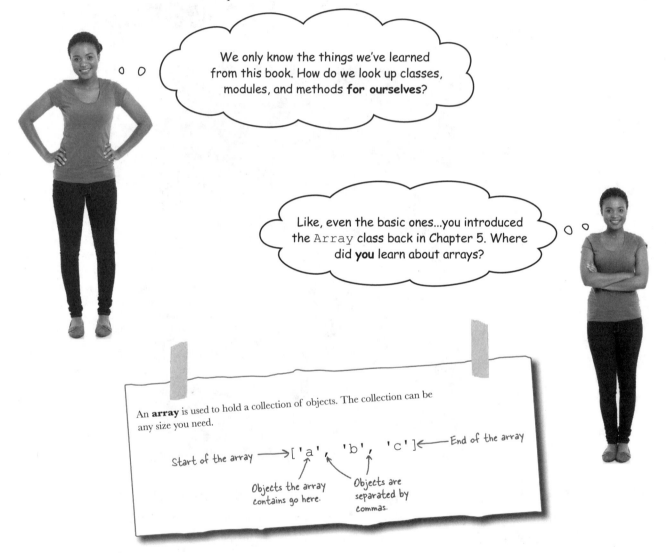

We only know the things we've learned from this book. How do we look up classes, modules, and methods **for ourselves**?

Like, even the basic ones...you introduced the `Array` class back in Chapter 5. Where did **you** learn about arrays?

An **array** is used to hold a collection of objects. The collection can be any size you need.

Start of the array ——→ `['a', 'b', 'c']` ←—— End of the array

Objects the array contains go here.

Objects are separated by commas.

Good question... Now is probably a good time to talk about Ruby's documentation.

Ruby's core classes and modules

As we've said before, Ruby comes with a huge collection of classes and modules to handle a wide variety of common computing tasks. Many of these are automatically loaded every time Ruby runs, without the need to load any external libraries; these are known as Ruby's **core** classes and modules.

> **Ruby's core classes and modules are loaded automatically, every time Ruby starts.**

Here's an *incomplete* list of core classes and modules:

Classes and modules that we've already learned about are underlined.

<u>Array</u>	FalseClass	MatchData	Rational
BasicObject	Fiber	Math	Regexp
Bignum	<u>File</u>	Method	Signal
Binding	FileTest	Module	<u>String</u>
Class	<u>Fixnum</u>	Mutex	Struct
<u>Comparable</u>	<u>Float</u>	<u>NilClass</u>	<u>Symbol</u>
Complex	GC	<u>Numeric</u>	Thread
Dir	<u>Hash</u>	<u>Object</u>	ThreadGroup
Encoding	Integer	ObjectSpace	Time
<u>Enumerable</u>	Interrupt	Proc	TracePoint
Enumerator	IO	Process	TrueClass
Errno	Kernel	Random	UnboundMethod
Exception	Marshal	Range	

Documentation

The only obstacle we face at this point is knowing *what these classes are* and *how to use them*. This chapter will show you how to find out, using Ruby's *documentation*.

We're not talking about looking up blog posts or help forums. A programming language's documentation is in a specific, standardized format. It will list all the available classes and modules, and offer descriptions of each. Then it will list all the methods available for each class/module, and offer descriptions for those as well.

If you've used documentation for other languages, you'll find that Ruby's style isn't too different. But there *are* a few quirks to the notation that you'll need to know about. This chapter will show you what to look out for.

Here's what we'll be covering:

* Documentation for classes and modules

* Documentation for methods

* Adding your own documentation to Ruby source

Let's get started!

Relax

> **You don't need to know about all these classes and modules right now.**
>
> After you've learned to read Ruby documentation, it would be a great idea to look some of them up, just to familiarize yourself with them. But you might not *ever* use some of these classes and modules, so don't worry if you don't get to all of them.

HTML documentation

As you'll see later in the chapter, Ruby developers add documentation directly to their source code, using specially formatted comments. Programs are available to extract that documentation into a variety of formats, the most popular of which is HTML.

Thanks to sites that host this HTML documentation, information about any new class or module is usually just an Internet search away. Just load up your favorite search engine and type **ruby** followed by the name of the class, module, or method you want to know more about. (Including the word *ruby* helps to filter out results for similarly named classes from other programming languages.)

For each class or module, the documentation includes a description, examples of its use, and a list of its class and instance methods.

Popular Ruby documentation sites:

- *http://docs.ruby-lang.org*

- *http://ruby-doc.org*

- *http://www.rubydoc.info*

Documentation for the Hash class

There are a few things you'll need to know in order to navigate the HTML documentation. We'll describe the specifics over the next few pages.

Listing available classes and modules

Ruby documentation sites will generally have an index of the available classes and modules.

For example, if you visit this page in your browser:

http://www.rubydoc.info/stdlib/core

…you'll see a list of classes on the lefthand side. Just click on the one you want.

The class name is a link; click it!

You'll be taken to a page with all the details on your chosen class, including:

- The class name

- The name of the superclass and a link to its documentation

- Links to the documentation of any modules the class mixes in

- A description of the class's purpose, usually including example code showing how to use it

Class documentation page

Class name

Superclass

Mixins included in class

Class description

```
ary = [1, "two", 3.0] #=> [1, "two", 3.0]
```

```
ary = Array.new   #=> []
```

Looking up instance methods

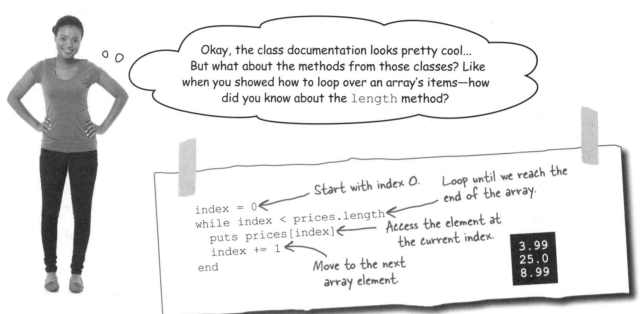

Okay, the class documentation looks pretty cool... But what about the methods from those classes? Like when you showed how to loop over an array's items—how did you know about the `length` method?

Start with index 0.   Loop until we reach the end of the array.

```
index = 0
while index < prices.length
    puts prices[index]
    index += 1
end
```

Access the element at the current index.

Move to the next array element.

```
3.99
25.0
8.99
```

Ruby's class documentation includes info on the class's instance methods.

On every class's documentation page, we'll find an index of all the class's instance methods. (On the rubydoc.info site, you'll see the index if you scroll down the page.)

As with the index of class names, each method name is a link to the method's documentation. So just click the name of the method you want to know more about.

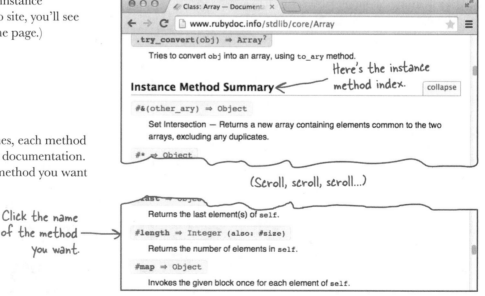

Here's the instance method index.

Click the name of the method you want.

(Scroll, scroll, scroll...)

Instance methods denoted with # in the docs

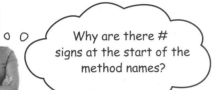

Why are there # signs at the start of the method names?

That's the convention used in Ruby documentation to mark instance methods.

The documentation needs to distinguish instance methods from class methods, since they're called differently. So, by convention, instance methods are labeled with a hash mark (#) at the start of their name.

Indicates instance methods

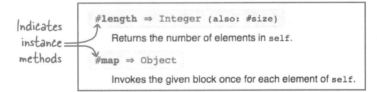

```
#length ⇒ Integer (also: #size)
        Returns the number of elements in self.

#map ⇒ Object
        Invokes the given block once for each element of self.
```

So, if you see `Array#length` mentioned in the docs, you can read it as "the `Array` class's `length` instance method."

Note that # is only used to denote instance methods *in the documentation*. In actual Ruby code, # marks a comment. So don't try typing `[1, 2, 3]#length` in your actual code! If you do, Ruby will view `#length` as a comment, and ignore it.

Watch it!

Don't use # to denote an instance method in actual code!

In Ruby code, # denotes a comment (unless it's within a string). If you try to use # in place of a dot operator, Ruby will think that everything following the # is a comment, and will probably report an error!

Instance method documentation

Once you've found the instance method you want and clicked on its name, you'll be taken to detailed documentation for the method.

Here's documentation for the `length` instance method on `Array` objects:

Call signature ——→

Method return value ⌐

Description ⎰

```
● ● ●        ✎ Class: Array — Documenta  ×

←  →  C   📄 www.rubydoc.info/stdlib/core/Array#length-instance_method  ★  ≡
```

```
#length ⇒ Integer                                          permalink
Also known as: size
```

Returns the number of elements in `self`. May be zero.

```
[ 1, 2, 3, 4, 5 ].length    #=> 5
[].length                   #=> 0
```

Returns:

- (Integer)

[View source]

Generally, the method documentation will include a description of its purpose, and possibly some code samples showing its use.

At the top of the method's documentation, you'll find its *call signature*, which shows how to call the method and what return value to expect.

If the method doesn't take any arguments or a block (like the `length` method above), its call signature will simply consist of the method name and the class of the return value you should expect.

Arguments in call signatures

If a method *does* take arguments, the call signature will list them.

Here's the documentation for the `insert` instance method on the `String` class, which lets you insert one string in the middle of another. The first argument is the integer index of the character it should insert before, and the second argument is the string it should insert.

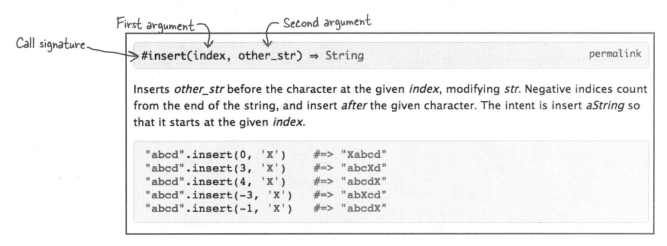

First argument

Second argument

Call signature

```
#insert(index, other_str) ⇒ String                              permalink
```

Inserts *other_str* before the character at the given *index*, modifying *str*. Negative indices count from the end of the string, and insert *after* the given character. The intent is insert *aString* so that it starts at the given *index*.

```
"abcd".insert(0, 'X')      #=> "Xabcd"
"abcd".insert(3, 'X')      #=> "abcXd"
"abcd".insert(4, 'X')      #=> "abcdX"
"abcd".insert(-3, 'X')     #=> "abXcd"
"abcd".insert(-1, 'X')     #=> "abcdX"
```

Sometimes, there will be multiple ways to call the same method. Such methods will have more than one call signature listed at the top of their documentation.

As an example, the `index` instance method for strings is below. Its first argument can be either a string or a regular expression. (We'll talk briefly about what regular expressions are in the appendix; all you need to know now is that they're a different class than strings.) So the documentation includes two call signatures for `index`: one with a string as the first argument, and one with a regular expression.

The square brackets (`[]`) around the second argument to `index` indicate that the argument is optional.

First call signature for this method

Second call signature for this method

```
#index(substring[, offset]) ⇒ Fixnum                            permalink
#index(regexp[, offset]) ⇒ Fixnum
```

Returns the index of the first occurrence of the given *substring* or pattern (*regexp*) in *str*. Returns `nil` if not found. If the second parameter is present, it specifies the position in the string to begin the search.

```
"hello".index('e')          #=> 1
"hello".index('lo')         #=> 3
"hello".index('a')          #=> nil
"hello".index(?e)           #=> 1
"hello".index(/[aeiou]/, -3) #=> 4
```

Blocks in call signatures

If the method takes a block, that will be shown in the call signature as well. If the block is optional, then there will be call signatures both with and without the block.

For example, with the `each` instance method on arrays, the block is optional, so you'll have two sample calls listed (one with the block, and one without).

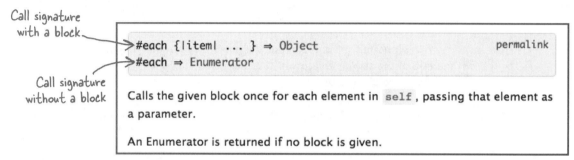

Call signature with a block

Call signature without a block

```
#each {|item| ... } ⇒ Object                          permalink
#each ⇒ Enumerator
```

Calls the given block once for each element in `self`, passing that element as a parameter.

An Enumerator is returned if no block is given.

These two sample calls show different return values as well, because the call *with* a block will return the same array that `each` was called on, whereas the call *without* a block will return an instance of the `Enumerator` class. (Enumerators are beyond the scope of this book, but basically they're a means of looping through a collection without using a block.)

Here's a closer look at the call signature that shows the way we've been calling the `each` method in this book. You can see that it takes a block with a single parameter. It also returns an object—the array that `each` was called on.

Shows that "each" takes a block, which receives one parameter.

When called with a block, "each" returns the array it was called on.

Shows that "each" must be called on an Array instance.

```
#each {|item| ... } ⇒ Object
```

It's worth noting that call signatures are in *pseudocode*: informal code you can't actually run. The code *resembles* Ruby, but it will reference variable names that don't exist, and will generally not be suitable for pasting into a real program. Nonetheless, call signatures are a great way to quickly get an idea of how a method should be used.

Read the docs for the superclass and mixins, too!

I found the documentation for the `Array` class's `length` and `each` instance methods with no problem. But you also showed us the `find_all` method, and I don't see docs for that anywhere!

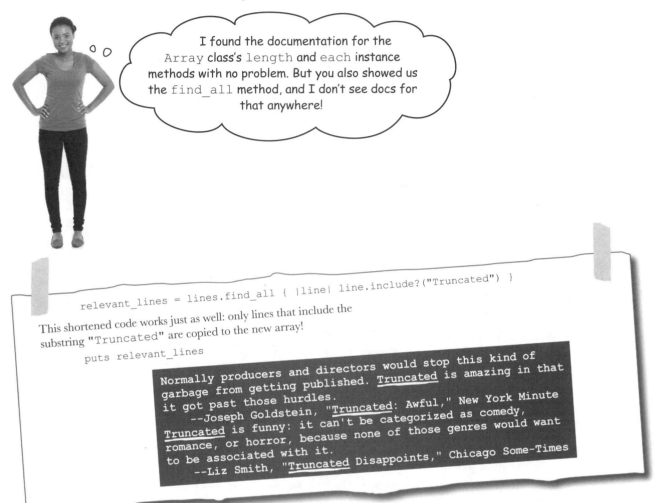

```
relevant_lines = lines.find_all { |line| line.include?("Truncated") }
```

This shortened code works just as well: only lines that include the substring "Truncated" are copied to the new array!

```
puts relevant_lines
```

Normally producers and directors would stop this kind of garbage from getting published. <u>Truncated</u> is amazing in that it got past those hurdles.
   --Joseph Goldstein, "<u>Truncated</u>: Awful," New York Minute
<u>Truncated</u> is funny: it can't be categorized as comedy, romance, or horror, because none of those genres would want to be associated with it.
   --Liz Smith, "<u>Truncated</u> Disappoints," Chicago Some-Times

To find documentation for methods that come from a mixin or superclass, you need to go to the docs for that mixin or superclass.

Remember in Chapter 10 we learned that the `Array` class's `find_all` instance method came from the `Enumerable` mixin? The `Enumerable` module is where you'll find the documentation for `find_all` as well!

The documentation for a class doesn't repeat the methods that it inherits from a superclass or mixes in from a module. (The docs would be huge and repetitive if it did.) So when you're trying to learn about a new class, make sure you read the documentation for its superclass and for any modules it mixes in as well!

Read the docs for the superclass and mixins, too! (continued)

HTML documentation will include convenient links to the docs for the superclass and all mixins. Just click on the class or module name to be taken there.

Class documentation page

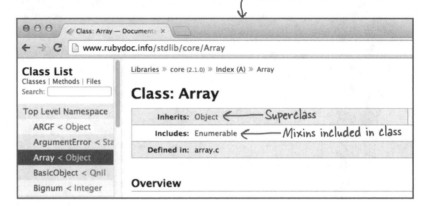

If we click the link for `Enumerable` and scroll to the instance method index for the module, we'll see `find_all` listed there. (Then, as before, we can click the method name to view the full details.)

Module documentation page

We're taken to the docs for the mixin.

there are no
Dumb Questions

Q: The `find_all` method may not be documented on the **Array** class, but **map** and several other **Enumerable** methods are! What gives?

A: You remember that if a method exists on a class, it overrides any methods with the same name on a mixin? Some of Ruby's core classes mix in `Enumerable`, but then override some of its methods for performance reasons. In that event, method documentation will *also* appear on the class. They don't override everything, though, so it's still important to check the module's documentation so you don't miss any!

Pool Puzzle

Your **job** is to take instance method calls from the pool and place them into the blank lines in the code. There's a catch this time, though: these are all methods we **haven't covered** in this book (at least, not extensively). Visit *http://www.rubydoc.info/stdlib/core/Array* (or just do a web search for "ruby array") to learn about the methods in the pool and figure out which ones you should call. Don't forget to look at the documentation for `Array`'s superclass and mixin, too! Your **goal** is to make code that will run and produce the output shown.

```ruby
array = [10, 5, 7, 3, 9]

first = array._____
puts "We pulled #{first} off the start of the array."

last = array._____
puts "We pulled #{last} off the end of the array."

largest = array._____
puts "The largest remaining number is #{largest}."
```

Output:

```
We pulled 10 off the start of the array.
We pulled 9 off the end of the array.
The largest remaining number is 7.
```

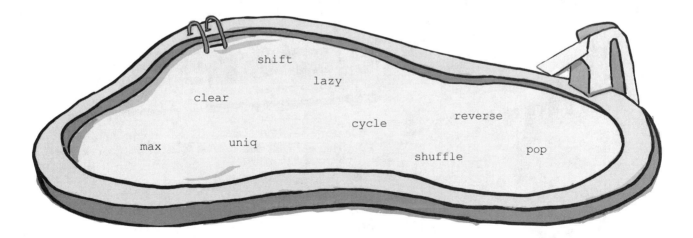

shift
lazy
clear
cycle
reverse
max
uniq
shuffle
pop

Pool Puzzle Solution

```
array = [10, 5, 7, 3, 9]

first = array.shift
puts "We pulled #{first} off the start of the array."

last = array.pop
puts "We pulled #{last} off the end of the array."

largest = array.max
puts "The largest remaining number is #{largest}."
```

Output:

```
We pulled 10 off the start of the array.
We pulled 9 off the end of the array.
The largest remaining number is 7.
```

Looking up class methods

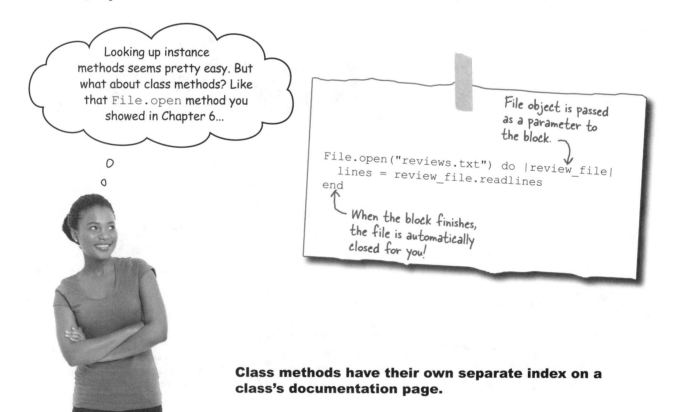

Looking up instance methods seems pretty easy. But what about class methods? Like that `File.open` method you showed in Chapter 6...

File object is passed as a parameter to the block.

```
File.open("reviews.txt") do |review_file|
    lines = review_file.readlines
end
```

When the block finishes, the file is automatically closed for you!

Class methods have their own separate index on a class's documentation page.

Looking up class methods (continued)

Looking up class method documentation is pretty much like looking up instance method documentation, with a couple of exceptions:

*   Class methods are listed under a separate index from instance methods.

*   Class methods are marked with a different symbol at the start of their name than instance methods.

So if we wanted to look up the `File.open` class method, we'd bring up the `File` class's documentation, then scroll down the page until we got to the index of class methods. (It should appear right before the index of instance methods.) Then we'd scroll through that index until we found the `open` method, and click its name to go to its detailed documentation.

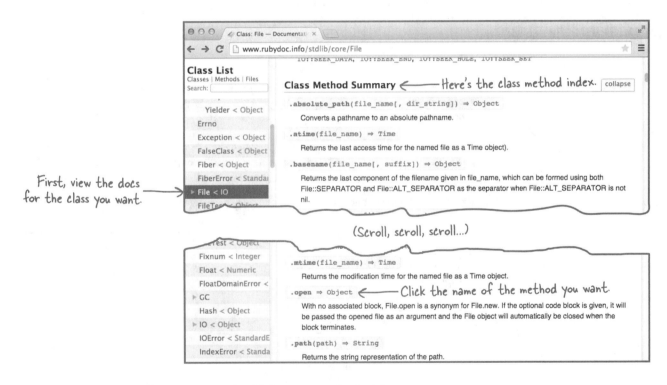

It's important not to confuse class methods with instance methods. After all, you need to call `open` on the `File` class, not an instance of `File`. So while instance methods are marked with `#` at the start of their names, class methods are marked with a dot operator (`.`), as you see above.

(As we'll see later, other HTML documentation marks class methods with `::`, Ruby's scope resolution operator, which is used to access constants or methods inside a class or module. If you see either `.` or `::` at the start of the method name, you know you're looking at a class method.)

Class method documentation

Once you've clicked the link in the class method index to bring up a specific method's documentation, everything looks pretty similar to the docs for instance methods.

At the top, you'll still see pseudocode call signatures for the method. Again, the method name will be marked with . instead of the # you'd see on instance methods. The class name is often omitted in call signatures, but you'll need to include it in your actual code. Below the call signatures, you'll find a description of the method's purpose, and possibly some code samples showing how to use it.

Here are the docs for the `File.open` method. Passing a block to `File.open` is optional, so there are two call signatures shown: one with the block and one without.

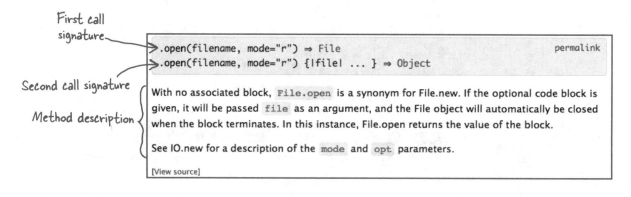

First call signature

Second call signature

Method description

```
.open(filename, mode="r") ⇒ File                                    permalink
.open(filename, mode="r") {|file| ... } ⇒ Object

With no associated block, File.open is a synonym for File.new. If the optional code block is
given, it will be passed file as an argument, and the File object will automatically be closed
when the block terminates. In this instance, File.open returns the value of the block.

See IO.new for a description of the mode and opt parameters.

[View source]
```

Once again, the call signatures also show different return values. If you omit the block, `File.open` will simply return a new `File` object.

Class name omitted ⟶

A new File is returned if you omit the block...

```
.open(filename, mode="r") ⇒ File
```

But if a block is provided, the `File` object is passed to the block, and `File.open` instead returns the block's return value.

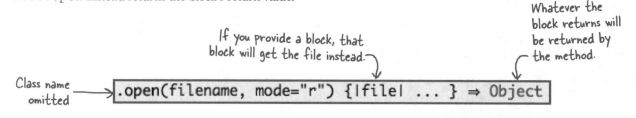

If you provide a block, that block will get the file instead.

Whatever the block returns will be returned by the method.

Class name omitted ⟶

```
.open(filename, mode="r") {|file| ... } ⇒ Object
```

Docs for a class that doesn't exist?!

> I'm stuck. I did a web search and found documentation for this Date class that looks really useful...

Class: Date

Inherits:	Object
Includes:	Comparable

Documentation for the Date class

Oh, yes, the Date class is heavily used in Ruby.

Date has a today class method that creates an object representing the current date...

Documentation for the "today" class method

```
.today([start = Date::ITALY]) ⇒ Object

Date.today #=> #<Date: 2011-06-11 ..>

Creates a date object denoting the present day.
```

...and it also has year, month, and day instance methods that can be used to get the year, month, and day.

Documentation for the "month" instance method

Documentation for the "day" instance method

```
#year ⇒ Integer

Returns the year.
```

Documentation for the "year" instance method

```
#mon ⇒ Fixnum
#month ⇒ Fixnum

Returns the month (1-12).
```

```
#mday ⇒ Fixnum
#day ⇒ Fixnum

Returns the day of the month (1-31).
```

> That's great, but when I try to use the Date class in my code, I get an error! What's going on?

```
today = Date.today
puts "#{today.year}-#{today.month}-#{today.day}"
```

Error → `uninitialized constant Date (NameError)`

That class isn't one of Ruby's core classes, which means it isn't loaded automatically.

The Ruby standard library

At the start of the chapter, we said the "Ruby core" classes and modules are loaded into memory every time a program runs. But it would be terrible if *every* available class and module were loaded; Ruby would take much longer to start up, and would consume more of your computer's memory. So, if a class or module isn't likely to be needed by every program, it isn't loaded automatically.

Instead, programs that need these specialized classes have to load them explicitly. You can load additional Ruby code via the `require` method.

Ruby comes with several directories full of library files containing useful classes and modules—these make up the Ruby **standard library**.

> # The standard library is a collection of classes and modules that are distributed with Ruby, but aren't loaded at startup.

Library directory ——→

abbrev.rb

csv.rb

date.rb

Library files

Standard library classes aren't essential to *every* program, so they aren't loaded automatically. But it's easy to load them yourself. In your code, you can call `require` and pass it a string with the name of the file you want to load. You can leave off the filename extension (the characters following the dot).

```
require 'date'
```
←—— No ".rb" extension needed

Ruby will look through all the library directories it knows of. When the requested file is found, it'll be loaded, and all the classes and modules it contains will become available for use in your program.

Load this one!

Inside the directory...

abbrev.rb   csv.rb   date.rb

We can fix the code simply by passing `'date'` to the `require` method. Doing so will load the `Date` class, which we can then use as much as we please!

```
require 'date'
today = Date.today
puts "#{today.year}-#{today.month}-#{today.day}"
```
←—— Load the Date class.

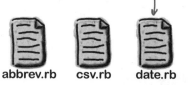

2015-10-17

The Ruby standard library (continued)

There are many more classes and modules in Ruby's standard library. Here's an incomplete list:

File to require	Classes/modules
'abbrev'	Abbrev
'base64'	Base64
'benchmark'	Benchmark
'bigdecimal'	BigDecimal
'cgi'	CGI
'complex'	Complex
'coverage'	Coverage
'csv'	CSV
'curses'	Curses
'date'	Date DateTime
'dbm'	DBM
'delegate'	Delegator
'digest/md5'	Digest::MD5
'digest/sha1'	Digest::SHA1
'drb'	DRb
'erb'	ERB
'fiber'	Fiber
'fiddle'	Fiddle
'fileutils'	FileUtils
'find'	Find
'forwardable'	Forwardable
'getoptlong'	GetoptLong
'gserver'	GServer
'ipaddr'	IPAddr
'irb'	IRB
'json'	JSON

File to require	Classes/modules
'logger'	Logger
'matrix'	Matrix
'minitest'	MiniTest
'monitor'	Monitor
'net/ftp'	Net::FTP
'net/http'	Net::HTTP
'net/imap'	Net::IMAP
'net/pop'	Net::POP3
'net/smtp'	Net::SMTP
'net/telnet'	Net::Telnet
'nkf'	NKF
'observer'	Observable
'open-uri'	OpenURI
'open3'	Open3
'openssl'	OpenSSL
'optparse'	OptionParser
'ostruct'	OpenStruct
'pathname'	Pathname
'pp'	PP
'prettyprint'	PrettyPrint
'prime'	Prime
'pstore'	PStore
'pty'	PTY
'readline'	Readline
'rexml'	REXML
'rinda'	Rinda
'ripper'	Ripper

File to require	Classes/modules
'rss'	RSS
'set'	Set
'shellwords'	Shellwords
'singleton'	Singleton
'socket'	TCPServer TCPSocket UDPSocket
'stringio'	StringIO
'strscan'	StringScanner
'syslog'	Syslog
'tempfile'	Tempfile
'test/unit'	Test::Unit
'thread'	Thread
'thwait'	ThreadsWait
'time'	Time
'timeout'	Timeout
'tk'	Tk
'tracer'	Tracer
'tsort'	TSort
'uri'	URI
'weakref'	WeakRef
'webrick'	WEBrick
'win32ole'	WIN32OLE
'xmlrpc/client'	XMLRPC::Client
'xmlrpc/server'	XMLRPC::Server
'yaml'	YAML
'zlib'	ZLib

Relax ·············· **Again, no need to learn all these right now.**

By all means look up the classes and modules above that interest you, but don't feel you have to learn about *all* of them. We're just showing this list to give you a feel for what's available in the standard library.

Looking up classes and modules in the standard library

There are far more classes in Ruby's standard library than we have
room to document here. But as always, more information is just a web
search away; just search for "ruby standard library."

Suppose we needed more info about the Date class. Here's how we
might go about learning more...

This is one of many pages that will likely appear in your search results:

http://www.rubydoc.info/stdlib

1   If you visit that page, you'll see a list of
packages on the lefthand side. Click on
the package you want info on, and you'll
be taken to a new page.

Click here! ——→

Standard library
index page

csv (2.2.2, 2.1.6, 2.1.0, 2.0.0, 1.9.3)

curses (2.2.2, 2.1.6, 2.1.0, 2.0.0, 1.9.3)

date (2.2.2, 2.1.6, 2.1.0, 2.0.0, 1.9.3)

date2 (1.8.7, 1.8.6)

dbm (2.2.2, 2.1.6, 2.1.0, 2.0.0, 1.9.3)

2   As with Ruby core, you'll see an index of classes
and modules (although this will be much smaller,
since it will only have the contents of the selected
package). Click on the class or module you want.

Package index page

Class List
Classes | Methods | Files
Search:

Top Level Namespace

Click here! ——→ ▸ Date < Object

DateTime < Date

3   You'll be taken to the class's documentation page,
where you can read up on all its available class
and instance methods!

Class documentation page

Libraries » date (2.2.2) » Index (D) » Date

Class: Date

Inherits:	Object
Includes:	Comparable
Defined in:	lib/date.rb

Where Ruby docs come from: rdoc

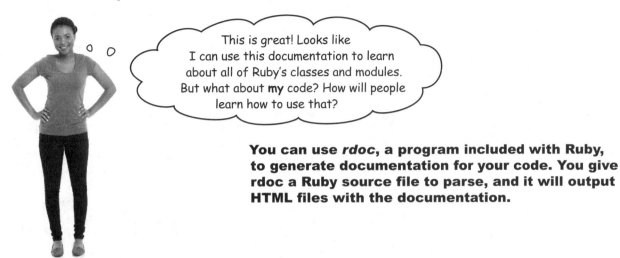

This is great! Looks like I can use this documentation to learn about all of Ruby's classes and modules. But what about **my** code? How will people learn how to use that?

You can use *rdoc*, a program included with Ruby, to generate documentation for your code. You give rdoc a Ruby source file to parse, and it will output HTML files with the documentation.

Below, we've copied the `WordSplitter` class that we created back in Chapter 10. Let's see if we can use rdoc to generate HTML documentation for it.

1 If you haven't already, save this code to a file named *word_splitter.rb*.

```ruby
class WordSplitter

  include Enumerable

  attr_accessor :string

  def each
    string.split(" ").each do |word|
      yield word
    end
  end

end
```

word_splitter.rb

Where Ruby docs come from: rdoc (continued)

2 In your terminal, change to the directory where you saved the file. Then type this command:

```
rdoc word_splitter.rb
```

Change to the directory where you saved word_splitter.rb.

Run "rdoc" with the name of the source file to process.

A subdirectory named doc will be created to hold the HTML documentation.

```
File  Edit  Window  Help
$ cd /code
$ rdoc word_splitter.rb
Parsing sources...
100% [ 1/ 1]  word_splitter.rb

Generating Darkfish format into /code/doc...

  Files:        1

  Classes:      1  (1 undocumented)
  Modules:      0  (0 undocumented)
  Constants:    0  (0 undocumented)
  Attributes:   1  (1 undocumented)
  Methods:      1  (1 undocumented)

  Total:        3  (3 undocumented)
    0.00% documented

  Elapsed: 0.1s
$
```

You'll see output like this as rdoc processes your code. It will create a new subdirectory of the current directory (named *doc* by default) and write HTML files into it.

3 Among the files that rdoc creates in the *doc* subdirectory, you'll find a file named *index.html*. Open this in your web browser (usually by double-clicking it).

Open this in your web browser.

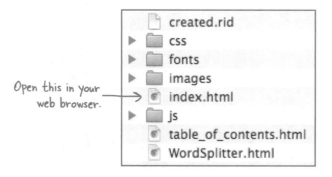

```
    created.rid
▶   css
▶   fonts
▶   images
    index.html
▶   js
    table_of_contents.html
    WordSplitter.html
```

What rdoc can deduce about your classes

When you open the *index.html* file that rdoc generated, the first thing you'll see is an index of classes and modules. Since our source file contained only the `WordSplitter` class, that's the only class listed. Click on its name, and you'll be taken to its documentation page.

Home
Pages Classes Methods

Class and Module Index

Click on the class name.———→ WordSplitter

Validate
Generated by RDoc 4.2.0.
Based on Darkfish by Michael Granger.

When rdoc processed our code, it noted several details about it. The class name is easy to pick out, of course. Less obvious is the fact that we *didn't* declare a superclass, which means that the superclass of `WordSplitter` must be `Object`; rdoc notes this as well. It notes any modules we mix in, and any attributes we declare (including whether the attribute is readable, writable, or both).

When it reaches the instance method definition, rdoc's analysis gets *really* detailed. It notes the method name, of course. But it also notes whether we've defined any parameters for it (we haven't). It even looks inside the method body to find the `yield` statement, from which it deduces that we must be expecting a block. It also notes the name of the variable we're yielding.

```
class WordSplitter          ←——— Class name

    include Enumerable       ←——— Mixins

    attr_accessor :string    ←——— Attribute (with
                                  both reader and
                                  writer methods)

    def each  ←——— Instance method
      string.split(" ").each do |word|
        yield word
      end
    end

end
```

Yield to a block. → (yield word)

Argument yielded to block

All of these details are then used in the generated documentation for the class: class name, superclass, mixins, attributes. There's an index of methods (with just the one entry). The full documentation for the method shows its arguments, and the fact that it takes a block.

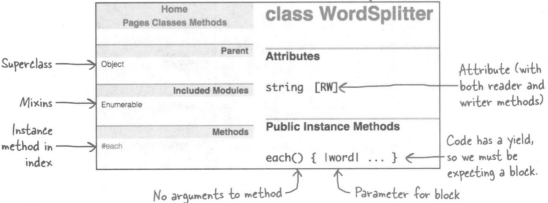

you are here ▸ 355

Adding your own documentation, with comments

A new user looking to learn about our `WordSplitter` class could just as easily look at the source code to learn these details, though. What we *really* need is a plain-English description of the class and its methods.

Thankfully, rdoc makes it really easy to add descriptions to the HTML documentation—with plain old Ruby comments in your source code! Not only does this keep the documentation near your code, where it's easy to update, it also helps out people who are reading the source instead of the HTML.

To add documentation for a class, simply add comments on the lines immediately before the `class` keyword. (If the comments span multiple lines, they'll be merged into one line in the docs.) Attributes can be documented with comments on the lines right before the attribute declaration. And class and instance methods can be documented on the lines before the `def` keyword for the method.

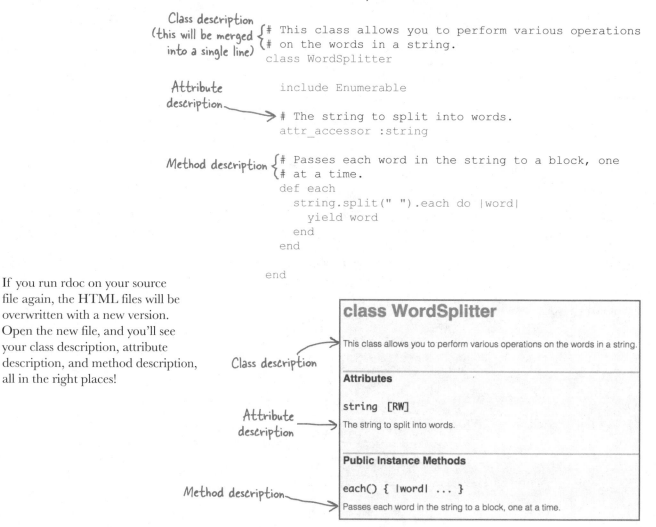

Class description (this will be merged into a single line)

```ruby
# This class allows you to perform various operations
# on the words in a string.
class WordSplitter

  include Enumerable

  # The string to split into words.
  attr_accessor :string

  # Passes each word in the string to a block, one
  # at a time.
  def each
    string.split(" ").each do |word|
      yield word
    end
  end

end
```

Attribute description

Method description

If you run rdoc on your source file again, the HTML files will be overwritten with a new version. Open the new file, and you'll see your class description, attribute description, and method description, all in the right places!

Class description

Attribute description

Method description

class WordSplitter

This class allows you to perform various operations on the words in a string.

Attributes

string [RW]

The string to split into words.

Public Instance Methods

each() { |word| ... }

Passes each word in the string to a block, one at a time.

The "initialize" instance method appears as the "new" class method

As you know, if you add an `initialize` method to a class, you don't call it directly. Instead, it's invoked via the `new` class method. This special case is also handled in the generated documentation. Let's try adding an `initialize` method to `WordSplitter`, along with a description, and see what happens...

```ruby
class WordSplitter
  ...
  # Creates a new instance with its string
  # attribute set to the given string.
  def initialize(string)
    self.string = string
  end
  ...
end
```

If we rerun rdoc and reload the HTML document, we'll see that instead of documenting an `initialize` instance method, rdoc added a `new` class method. (The rdoc formatter marks class methods with `::` in the method index.) Our description and the `string` argument are copied over to the `new` method as well.

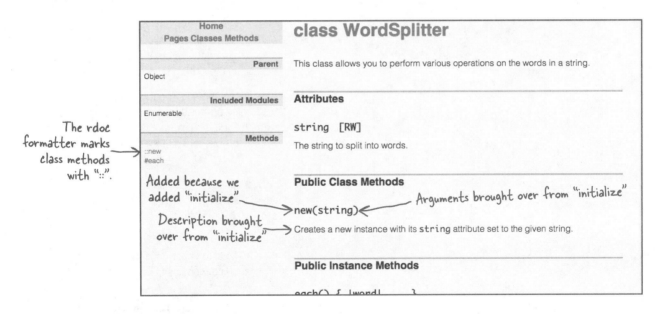

The rdoc formatter marks class methods with "::".

Added because we added "initialize"

Description brought over from "initialize"

Arguments brought over from "initialize"

That's it! Adding a few simple comments to your code is all that's required to generate easy-to-navigate, professional-looking HTML documentation for your classes, modules, and methods.

If you want others to find and use your code, great documentation is key. And Ruby makes it easy to add and maintain that documentation.

Your Ruby Toolbox

That's it for Chapter 11! You've added Ruby documentation to your toolbox.

Documentation

Type "ruby <classname>" or "ruby <modulename>" into any search engine to find HTML documentation for that class or module.

The "rdoc" command can be used to generate documentation from your Ruby source code.

Up Next...

What should your program do when things go wrong? You probably *could* detect and handle the problem using only the tools we've shown you so far, but your code would quickly get messy. In the next chapter, we'll show you a better way: *exceptions*.

BULLET POINTS

- Ruby's core classes and modules load automatically every time Ruby runs.

- A class's HTML documentation will include links to docs for its superclass, plus any modules it mixes in.

- HTML documentation will include indexes of all class and instance methods, with links to full documentation for the method.

- Instance methods are usually labeled with a hash mark (#). This notation can't be used in Ruby code; it's used only in documentation.

- Class methods are usually labeled with a dot operator (.) or scope resolution operator (::).

- Method documentation will include one or more call signatures, each of which demonstrates a different combination of arguments and blocks with which the method can be called.

- Different call signatures will sometimes result in different return values from the method. If so, this will be shown in the call signature.

- A class's documentation will not include methods that are inherited or mixed in, but it will include links to the documentation for its superclass and mixins so you can see the full set of methods available.

- Every Ruby installation includes the Ruby standard library: a collection of classes and modules that aren't loaded automatically, but can be loaded with a call to the `require` method.

- You can run `rdoc your_source_file.rb` from a terminal to generate HTML documentation for the classes and modules in your Ruby source file.

- If your class has an `initialize` instance method, it will appear in the documentation as the `new` class method (since that's how users will call it).

- You can add documentation for a class, module, attribute accessor, or method by placing comments immediately before its definition in your source code.

12 exceptions

Handling the Unexpected

I can't believe I lost my homework... But I can handle this. I'll just ask the teacher for an extension and do it again.

In the real world, the unexpected happens. Someone could delete the file your program is trying to load, or the server your program is trying to contact could go down. Your code could check for these exceptional situations, but those checks would be mixed in with the code that handles normal operation. (And that would be a big, unreadable mess.)

This chapter will teach you all about Ruby's exception handling, which lets you write code to handle the unexpected, and keep it separate from your regular code.

Don't use method return values for error messages

There's always a risk that users will make mistakes when calling methods in your code. Take this simple class to simulate an oven, for example. Users create a new instance, call its `turn_on` method, set its `contents` attribute to the dish they want to cook (we could only afford a small oven that holds one dish at a time), and then call the `bake` method to have their dish cooked to a nice golden brown.

```ruby
class SmallOven

  attr_accessor :contents

  def turn_on
    puts "Turning oven on."
    @state = "on"
  end
  def turn_off
    puts "Turning oven off."
    @state = "off"
  end

  def bake
    unless @state == "on"
      return "You need to turn the oven on first!"
    end
    if @contents == nil
      return "There's nothing in the oven!"
    end
    "golden-brown #{contents}"
  end

end
```

But users might forget to turn the oven on before calling `bake`. They could also call `bake` while the `contents` attribute is set to `nil`. So we've built in some error handling for both of those scenarios. Instead of returning the cooked food item, it will return an error string.

If the oven hasn't been turned on, warn the user.

If nothing is in the oven, warn the user.

If we remember to turn the oven on and place food inside, everything works great!

```ruby
dinner = ['turkey', 'casserole', 'pie']
oven = SmallOven.new
oven.turn_on
dinner.each do |item|          ← Process each menu item.
  oven.contents = item         ← Place the item in the oven.
  puts "Serving #{oven.bake}." ←
end                              Bake and serve
                                 the item.
```

```
Turning oven on.
Serving golden-brown turkey.
Serving golden-brown casserole.
Serving golden-brown pie.
```

But as we're about to see, it doesn't work so well when there's a problem. Using a method's return value to indicate an error (as in the code above) can cause *more* trouble…

Don't use method return values for error messages (continued)

So what happens if we forget to put food in the oven? If we accidentally set the oven's `contents` attribute to `nil`, our code will "serve" the warning message!

We forgot a course!

```ruby
dinner = ['turkey', nil, 'pie']
oven = SmallOven.new
oven.turn_on
dinner.each do |item|
  oven.contents = item
  puts "Serving #{oven.bake}."
end
```

That doesn't sound very tasty!

```
Turning oven on.
Serving golden-brown turkey.
Serving There's nothing in the oven!.
Serving golden-brown pie.
```

But that's just *one* course ruined. It's worse if we fail to turn the oven on—that could spoil our *entire meal*!

```ruby
dinner = ['turkey', 'casserole, 'pie']
oven = SmallOven.new
oven.turn_off  ←——— Accidentally switch the oven "off" instead of "on"!
dinner.each do |item|
  oven.contents = item
  puts "Serving #{oven.bake}."
end
```

Can we even eat these?

```
Turning oven off.
Serving You need to turn the oven on first!.
Serving You need to turn the oven on first!.
Serving You need to turn the oven on first!.
```

The real problem here is that when there's an error, our program keeps running as if nothing is wrong. Fortunately, we learned about a fix for this sort of thing back in Chapter 2…

Remember the `raise` method? It halts program execution with an error message when an error is encountered. And it seems a lot safer than method return values to communicate error messages…

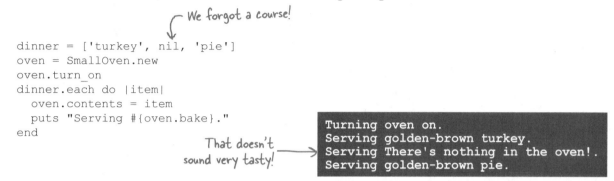

```ruby
class Dog

  attr_reader :name, :age

  def name=(value)
    if value == ""
      raise "Name can't be blank!"
    end
    @name = value
  end

end
```

If "value" is invalid...

...execution will halt here.

This statement won't be reached if "raise" is called.

Using "raise" to report errors

Let's try replacing the error return values in our `SmallOven` class with calls to `raise`:

```ruby
class SmallOven

  attr_accessor :contents

  def turn_on
    puts "Turning oven on."
    @state = "on"
  end
  def turn_off
    puts "Turning oven off."
    @state = "off"
  end

  def bake
    unless @state == "on"
      raise "You need to turn the oven on first!"
    end
    if @contents == nil
      raise "There's nothing in the oven!"
    end
    "golden-brown #{contents}"
  end

end
```

Raise an error if we attempt to bake while the oven is off.

Raise an error if we attempt to bake while the oven is empty.

This line won't be reached if an error is raised!

Now, if we try to bake something with the oven empty or turned off, instead of getting "served" an error message, we'll get an actual error...

```ruby
oven = SmallOven.new
oven.turn_off          ← Accidentally turn oven off.
oven.contents = 'turkey'
puts "Serving #{oven.bake}."
```

```
Turning oven off.
oven.rb:16:in `bake': You need to turn the oven on first! (RuntimeError)
        from oven.rb:29:in `<main>'
```

```ruby
oven = SmallOven.new
oven.turn_on
oven.contents = nil    ← Oven is empty.
puts "Serving #{oven.bake}."
```

```
Turning oven on.
oven.rb:19:in `bake': There's nothing in the oven! (RuntimeError)
        from oven.rb:29:in `<main>'
```

Using "raise" by itself creates new problems

Before, when we were using return values to report errors in the `bake` method, we would sometimes accidentally treat an error message as if it were food.

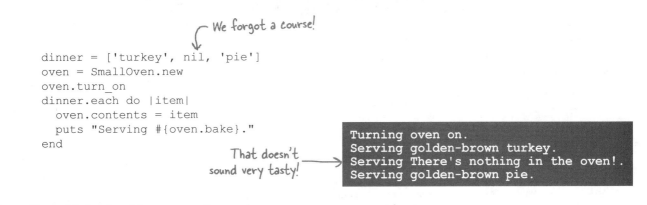

We forgot a course!

```
dinner = ['turkey', nil, 'pie']
oven = SmallOven.new
oven.turn_on
dinner.each do |item|
  oven.contents = item
  puts "Serving #{oven.bake}."
end
```

That doesn't sound very tasty!

```
Turning oven on.
Serving golden-brown turkey.
Serving There's nothing in the oven!.
Serving golden-brown pie.
```

But we'll say this for the old program: after serving us an error message, at least it went on to serve us the dessert course as well. Now that we're using `raise` to report errors in the `bake` method, our program exits the moment a problem is detected. No pie for us!

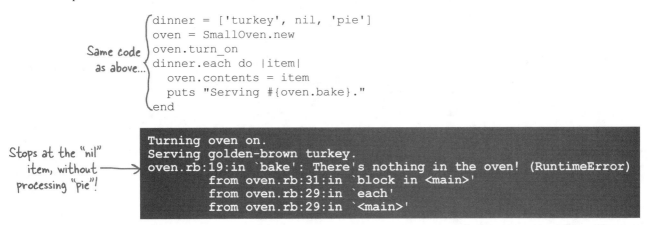

Same code as above...

```
dinner = ['turkey', nil, 'pie']
oven = SmallOven.new
oven.turn_on
dinner.each do |item|
  oven.contents = item
  puts "Serving #{oven.bake}."
end
```

Stops at the "nil" item, without processing "pie"!

```
Turning oven on.
Serving golden-brown turkey.
oven.rb:19:in `bake': There's nothing in the oven! (RuntimeError)
        from oven.rb:31:in `block in <main>'
        from oven.rb:29:in `each'
        from oven.rb:29:in `<main>'
```

And that error message is ugly, too. References to line numbers within your script might be useful to developers, but it will just confuse regular users.

If we're going to keep using `raise` within the `bake` method, we'll have to fix these problems. And to do that, we'll need to learn about *exceptions*…

Exceptions: When something's gone wrong

If we call `raise` all by itself in a script, we'll see output like this:

```
raise "oops!"
```

```
myscript.rb:1:in `<main>': oops! (RuntimeError)
```

The `raise` method is actually creating an **exception** object, an object that represents an error. If they're not dealt with, exceptions will stop your program cold.

Here's what's happening:

1 When you call `raise`, you're saying, "there's a problem, and we need to stop what we're doing *now*."

2 The `raise` method creates an exception object to represent the error.

3 If nothing is done about the error, your program will exit, and Ruby will report the error message.

```
myscript.rb:1:in `<main>':
oops! (RuntimeError)
```

But it's also possible to **rescue** an exception: to intercept the error. You can report the error message in a more user-friendly way, or sometimes even fix the problem.

An exception is an object that represents an error.

```
raise "oops!"
```

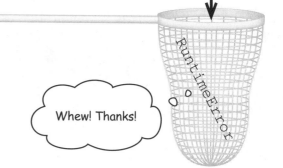

364   *Chapter 12*

Rescue clauses: A chance to fix the problem

If you have some code that you think might raise exceptions, you can surround it in a `begin`/`end` block, and add one or more `rescue` clauses that will run when an exception is encountered. A `rescue` clause may contain code to write an error message to a logfile, reattempt a network connection, or do whatever is needed to deal gracefully with the problem.

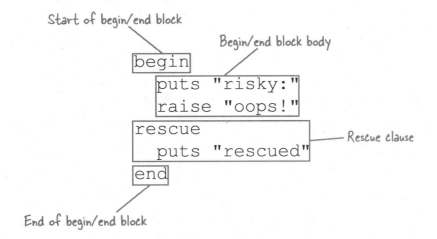

Start of begin/end block

Begin/end block body

```
begin
    puts "risky:"
    raise "oops!"
rescue
    puts "rescued"
end
```

Rescue clause

End of begin/end block

If any expression in the `begin` block body raises an exception, code execution will immediately move to the appropriate `rescue` clause if one is present.

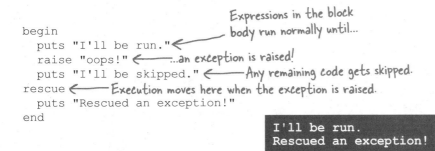

```
begin
  puts "I'll be run."
  raise "oops!"
  puts "I'll be skipped."
rescue
  puts "Rescued an exception!"
end
```

Expressions in the block body run normally until...

...an exception is raised!

Any remaining code gets skipped.

Execution moves here when the exception is raised.

```
I'll be run.
Rescued an exception!
```

Once the `rescue` clause finishes, code execution will continue normally following the `begin`/`end` block. Since you presumably handled the problem in the `rescue` clause, there's no need for your program to end.

Ruby's search for a rescue clause

You *can* raise an exception from your main program (outside of any method), but it's much more common for exceptions to be raised *inside* a method. If that happens, Ruby will first look for a rescue clause within the method. If it doesn't find one, the method will immediately exit (without a return value).

```ruby
def risky_method
  raise "oops!"              ← Immediately exits method
  puts "I'll be skipped."    ←
end                                 Never gets run

risky_method
```

If no rescue clause is found, the method immediately exits.

risky_method

```
myscript.rb:2:in `risky_method': oops! (RuntimeError)
        from myscript.rb:6:in `<main>'
```

RuntimeError

When the method exits, Ruby will also look for a rescue clause in the place the method was called. So if you're calling a method that you think might throw an exception, you can surround the call with a begin/end block and add a rescue clause.

```ruby
def risky_method
  raise "oops!"              ← Immediately exits method
  puts "I'll be skipped."    ←
end                                 Never gets run

begin
  risky_method     ← Throws an exception
rescue  ← Exception is rescued here!
  puts "Rescued an exception!"
end
```

```
Rescued an exception!
```

No rescue clause here... Exception falls through to the place method was called...

risky_method

...where it gets rescued.

main

RuntimeError

Ruby's search for a rescue clause (continued)

This can continue through multiple methods. If the method's caller doesn't have an appropriate `rescue` clause, Ruby will exit *that* method immediately, and look for a rescue clause in *its* caller. This continues through the chain of calls until an appropriate `rescue` clause is found. (If none is *ever* found, the program halts.)

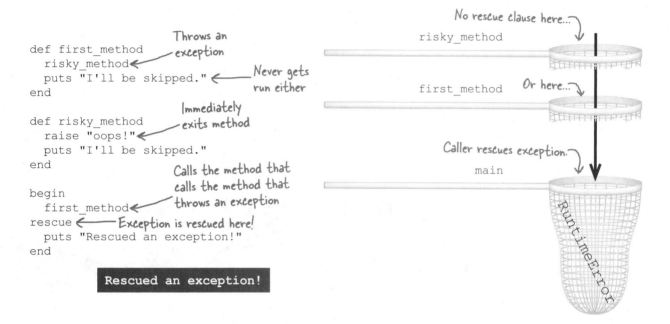

```
def first_method              Throws an
  risky_method ←───── exception
  puts "I'll be skipped." ←────── Never gets
end                                run either
                          Immediately
def risky_method      ── exits method
  raise "oops!" ←─────
  puts "I'll be skipped."
end                       Calls the method that
                          calls the method that
begin                 ──  throws an exception
  first_method ←───
rescue ←──────── Exception is rescued here!
  puts "Rescued an exception!"
end
```

```
Rescued an exception!
```

No rescue clause here...
risky_method

Or here...
first_method

Caller rescues exception.
main

RuntimeError

Ruby looks for a `rescue` clause in the method where the exception occurred. If none is found there, it looks in the calling method, then in **that** method's caller, and so on.

Using a rescue clause with our SmallOven class

Right now, if we call the `bake` instance method of our `SmallOven` class without setting the instance's `contents` attribute, we get a user-unfriendly error message. The program also stops immediately, without processing the remaining items in the array.

```ruby
class SmallOven
  ...
  def bake
    unless @state == "on"
      raise "You need to turn the oven on first!"
    end
    if @contents == nil
      raise "There's nothing in the oven!"
    end
    "golden-brown #{contents}"
  end

end

dinner = ['turkey', nil, 'pie']
oven = SmallOven.new
oven.turn_on
dinner.each do |item|
  oven.contents = item
  puts "Serving #{oven.bake}."
end
```

We forgot a course!

Stops at the "nil" item, without processing "pie"! →

```
Turning oven on.
Serving golden-brown turkey.
oven.rb:19:in `bake': There's nothing in the oven! (RuntimeError)
        from oven.rb:31:in `block in <main>'
        from oven.rb:29:in `each'
        from oven.rb:29:in `<main>'
```

Let's add a `rescue` clause to see if we can print a more user-friendly error.

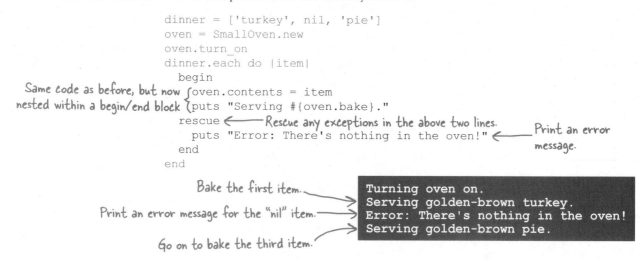

```ruby
dinner = ['turkey', nil, 'pie']
oven = SmallOven.new
oven.turn_on
dinner.each do |item|
  begin
    oven.contents = item
    puts "Serving #{oven.bake}."
  rescue
    puts "Error: There's nothing in the oven!"
  end
end
```

Same code as before, but now nested within a begin/end block

Rescue any exceptions in the above two lines.

Print an error message.

Bake the first item.

Print an error message for the "nil" item.

Go on to bake the third item.

```
Turning oven on.
Serving golden-brown turkey.
Error: There's nothing in the oven!
Serving golden-brown pie.
```

Much better! All the items in the array get processed, and we get a readable error message, all without the risks associated with returning an error string from the method!

We need a description of the problem from its source

When there's an error in the `bake` method, we pass a string
describing the problem to the `raise` method.

```ruby
class SmallOven
  ...
  def bake
    unless @state == "on"
      raise "You need to turn the oven on first!"
    end
    if @contents == nil
      raise "There's nothing in the oven!"
    end
    "golden-brown #{contents}"
  end

end
```

If the oven is off, we pass this message to "raise"...

We pass a different message when the oven is empty...

We're not really making use of those messages; instead, we have a
single string in the `rescue` clause that we always print, saying that
the oven is empty.

But if the oven is actually *off* instead of empty, we'll print an
inaccurate error message!

```ruby
dinner = ['turkey', 'casserole', 'pie']
oven = SmallOven.new
oven.turn_off
dinner.each do |item|
  begin
    oven.contents = item
    puts "Serving #{oven.bake}."
  rescue
    puts "Error: There's nothing in the oven!"
  end
end
```

If the oven is turned off...

...we ignore the messages passed to "raise" and use this one!

Wrong! The actual problem is that the oven is off!

```
Turning oven off.
Error: There's nothing in the oven!
Error: There's nothing in the oven!
Error: There's nothing in the oven!
```

We need a way to print the message that was passed to `raise` instead...

Exception messages

When you pass a string to the `raise` method, it uses that string to set the `message`
attribute of the exception it creates:

```ruby
unless @state == "on"
  raise "You need to turn the oven on first!"
end
if @contents == nil
  raise "There's nothing in the oven!"
end
```

Creates an exception object and sets its "message" attribute

Same here

All we need to do is remove our static error message, and print the `message` attribute of the
exception object in its place.

We can store the exception in a variable by adding `=>` to the `rescue` line, followed by any
variable we want. (The `=>` is the same symbol used in some hash literals, but in this context
it has nothing to do with hashes.) Once we have the exception object, we can print its
`message` attribute.

```ruby
begin
  raise "oops!"
rescue => my_exception
  puts my_exception.message
end
```

Create an exception with "oops!" as its message.

Store the exception in a variable.

Print the exception message.

```
oops!
```

Let's update our oven code to store
the exception in a variable, and
print its message:

```ruby
dinner = ['turkey', 'casserole', 'pie']
oven = SmallOven.new
oven.turn_off
dinner.each do |item|
  begin
    oven.contents = item
    puts "Serving #{oven.bake}."
  rescue => error
    puts "Error: #{error.message}"
  end
end
```

Oven is turned off.

Store the exception in a variable.

Print whatever message the exception contains.

The exception's message shows the actual problem.

```
Turning oven off.
Error: You need to turn the oven on first!
Error: You need to turn the oven on first!
Error: You need to turn the oven on first!
```

Problem solved. We can now display whatever exception message was
passed to the `raise` method.

Code Magnets

A Ruby program is all scrambled up on the fridge. Can you reconstruct the code snippets to make a working Ruby program that will produce the given output?

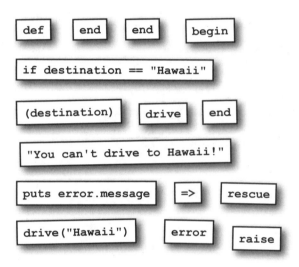

| def | end | end | begin |

| if destination == "Hawaii" |

| (destination) | drive | end |

| "You can't drive to Hawaii!" |

| puts error.message | => | rescue |

| drive("Hawaii") | error | raise |

Output:

```
File Edit Window Help
You can't drive to Hawaii!
```

Code Magnets Solution

A Ruby program is all scrambled up on the fridge. Can you reconstruct the code snippets to make a working Ruby program that will produce the given output?

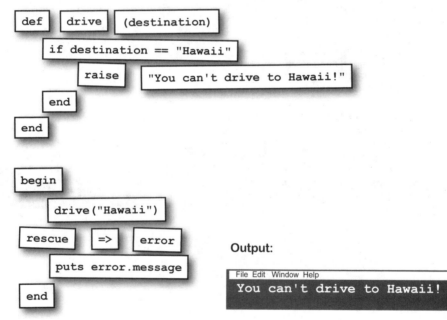

```ruby
def drive (destination)
  if destination == "Hawaii"
    raise "You can't drive to Hawaii!"
  end
end


begin
  drive("Hawaii")
rescue => error
  puts error.message
end
```

Output:

```
File Edit Window Help
You can't drive to Hawaii!
```

Our code so far...

We've covered a lot of ground since we started trying to improve the errors from our oven simulator code! Let's recap the changes we've made.

In the `SmallOven` class's `bake` method, we added `raise` statements that raise an exception when there's a problem. The exception object's `message` attribute is set differently depending on whether the oven is off or empty.

```ruby
class SmallOven

  attr_accessor :contents

  def turn_on
    puts "Turning oven on."
    @state = "on"
  end
  def turn_off
    puts "Turning oven off."
    @state = "off"
  end

  def bake
    unless @state == "on"
      raise "You need to turn the oven on first!"
    end
    if @contents == nil
      raise "There's nothing in the oven!"
    end
    "golden-brown #{contents}"
  end

end
```

Raise an error if we attempt to bake while the oven is off.

Raise an error if we attempt to bake while the oven is empty.

In our code that calls the `bake` method, we've set up our `rescue` clause to store the exception object in a variable named `error`. We then print the exception's `message` attribute to indicate exactly what went wrong.

```ruby
dinner = ['turkey', 'casserole', 'pie']
oven = SmallOven.new
oven.turn_on
dinner.each do |item|
  begin
    oven.contents = item
    puts "Serving #{oven.bake}."
  rescue => error
    puts "Error: #{error.message}"
  end
end
```

Store the exception in a variable.

Print whatever message the exception contains.

Our code so far... (continued)

So if our oven's `contents` attribute gets set to `nil`, we'll see one error message:

This will cause the oven's
contents to be set to "nil"!

```
dinner = ['turkey', nil, 'pie']
oven = SmallOven.new
oven.turn_on
dinner.each do |item|
  begin
    oven.contents = item
    puts "Serving #{oven.bake}."
  rescue => error
    puts "Error: #{error.message}"
  end
end
```

```
Turning oven on.
Serving golden-brown turkey.
Error: There's nothing in the oven!
Serving golden-brown pie.
```

There's the exception message.

...and if the oven is turned off, we'll see a different message.

```
dinner = ['turkey', 'casserole', 'pie']
oven = SmallOven.new
oven.turn_off                  Oven is turned off.
dinner.each do |item|
  begin
    oven.contents = item
    puts "Serving #{oven.bake}."
  rescue => error
    puts "Error: #{error.message}"
  end
end
```

Same exception,
raised three times

```
Turning oven off.
Error: You need to turn the oven on first!
Error: You need to turn the oven on first!
Error: You need to turn the oven on first!
```

Different rescue logic for different exceptions

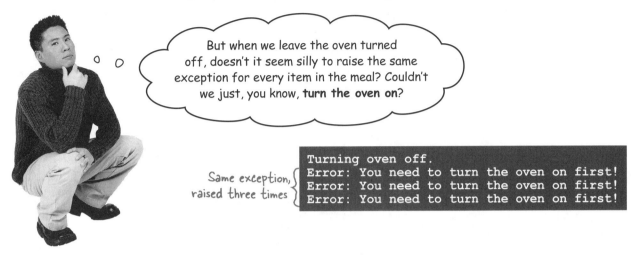

But when we leave the oven turned off, doesn't it seem silly to raise the same exception for every item in the meal? Couldn't we just, you know, **turn the oven on**?

Same exception, raised three times

```
Turning oven off.
Error: You need to turn the oven on first!
Error: You need to turn the oven on first!
Error: You need to turn the oven on first!
```

It *would* be nice if our program could detect the problem, switch the oven on, and then attempt to bake the item again.

But we can't just switch on the oven and try again for *any* exception we get. If the contents attribute is set to nil, there's no point in trying to bake *that* a second time!

```
class SmallOven
  ...
  def bake
    unless @state == "on"
      raise "You need to turn the oven on first!"
    end
    if @contents == nil
      raise "There's nothing in the oven!"
    end
    "golden-brown #{contents}"
  end

end
```

Turning on the oven and retrying would be a good way to handle this exception...

...but not this one!

We need a way to differentiate between the exceptions that the bake method can raise, so that we know to handle them differently. And we can do *that* using the exception's class…

Different rescue logic for different exceptions (continued)

We mentioned before that exceptions are objects. Well, all objects are instances of a class, right? You can specify what exception classes a particular `rescue` clause will handle. From then on, that `rescue` clause will ignore any exception that isn't an instance of the specified class (or one of its subclasses).

You can use this feature to route an exception to a `rescue` clause that is set up to handle it in the way you want.

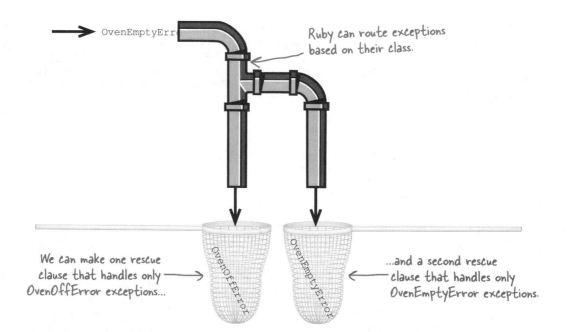

OvenEmptyError

Ruby can route exceptions based on their class.

We can make one rescue clause that handles only OvenOffError exceptions...

OvenOffError

OvenEmptyError

...and a second rescue clause that handles only OvenEmptyError exceptions.

But if we're going to handle different exception classes in different ways, we first need a way to specify what the class of an exception *is*…

Exception classes

When we call `raise`, it creates an exception object...and if nothing rescues the exception, you can see the class of that object when Ruby exits.

This exception object is an instance of the RuntimeError class.

```
raise "oops!"
```

```
myscript.rb:1:in `<main>': oops! (RuntimeError)
```

By default, `raise` creates an instance of the `RuntimeError` class. But you can specify another class for `raise` to use, if you want. Just pass the class name as the first argument, before the string you want to use as an exception message.

Specify a class.

```
raise ArgumentError, "This method takes a String!"
```

```
myscript.rb:1:in `<main>':
This method takes a String! (ArgumentError)
```

Specified class is raised!

Specify a class.

```
raise ZeroDivisionError, "Can't cut a pie into 0 portions!"
```

```
myscript.rb:1:in `<main>':
Can't cut a pie into 0 portions! (ZeroDivisionError)
```

Specified class is raised!

You can even create and raise your own exception classes. You'll get an error (and not the error you want) if you use just any old class, though:

```
class MyError      ←——This won't work!
end

raise MyError, "oops!"
```

```
myscript.rb:4:in `raise': exception
class/object expected (TypeError)
```

The "raise" method raised an exception of its own!

Exception classes (continued)

Only subclasses of Ruby's `Exception` class can be used to represent exceptions. Here's a partial hierarchy for the exception classes in Ruby's core library:

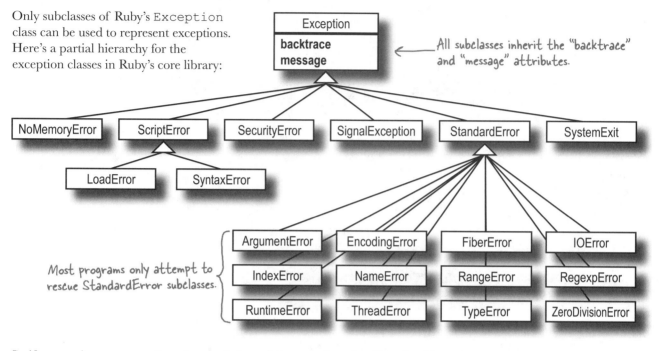

All subclasses inherit the "backtrace" and "message" attributes.

Most programs only attempt to rescue StandardError subclasses.

So if you make your exception class a subclass of `Exception`, it will work with `raise`...

```
class MyError < Exception
end
```
Must be a subclass of Exception

```
raise MyError, "oops!"
```
There's our exception!

```
myscript.rb:4:in `<main>': oops! (MyError)
```

...but notice that the majority of Ruby exception classes are subclasses of `StandardError`, not `Exception` directly. By convention, `StandardError` represents the type of errors that a typical program might be able to handle. Other subclasses of `Exception` represent problems that are outside of your program's control, like your system running out of memory or shutting down.

So while you *could* use `Exception` as the superclass for your custom exceptions, you should generally use `StandardError` instead.

```
class MyError < StandardError
end
```
Usually, you should subclass StandardError, not Exception.

```
raise MyError, "oops!"
```

```
myscript.rb:4:in `<main>': oops! (MyError)
```

Specifying exception class for a rescue clause

Now that we can create our own exception classes, we need to be able to rescue the *right* classes. You can include a class name right after the `rescue` keyword in a rescue clause, to specify that it should rescue only exceptions that are instances of that class (or one of its subclasses).

In this code, the raised exception (a `PorridgeError`) doesn't match the type specified in the `rescue` clause (`BeddingError`), so the exception isn't rescued:

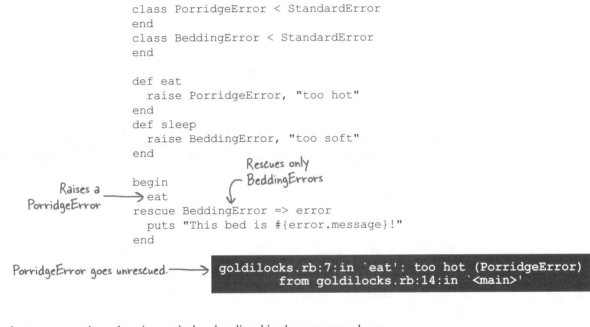

```
class PorridgeError < StandardError
end
class BeddingError < StandardError
end

def eat
  raise PorridgeError, "too hot"
end
def sleep
  raise BeddingError, "too soft"
end
```

Rescues only BeddingErrors

Raises a PorridgeError

```
begin
  eat
rescue BeddingError => error
  puts "This bed is #{error.message}!"
end
```

PorridgeError goes unrescued.

```
goldilocks.rb:7:in `eat': too hot (PorridgeError)
        from goldilocks.rb:14:in `<main>'
```

…but any exceptions that *do* match the class listed in the `rescue` clause *will* be rescued:

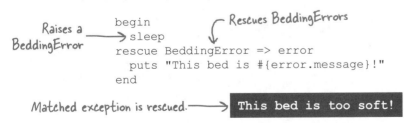

Raises a BeddingError

Rescues BeddingErrors

```
begin
  sleep
rescue BeddingError => error
  puts "This bed is #{error.message}!"
end
```

Matched exception is rescued.

```
This bed is too soft!
```

It's a good idea to always specify an exception type for your `rescue` clauses. That way, you'll only rescue exceptions that you actually know how to handle!

Multiple rescue clauses in one begin/end block

This code will rescue any instance of `BeddingError` that gets raised, but it ignores `PorridgeError`. We need to be able to rescue *both* exception types...

```ruby
class PorridgeError < StandardError
end
class BeddingError < StandardError
end

def eat
  raise PorridgeError, "too hot"
end
def sleep
  raise BeddingError, "too soft"
end
```

Raises a PorridgeError →

Rescues only BeddingErrors ↓

```ruby
begin
  eat
rescue BeddingError => error
  puts "This bed is #{error.message}!"
end
```

PorridgeError goes unrescued. →

```
goldilocks.rb:7:in `eat': too hot (PorridgeError)
        from goldilocks.rb:14:in `<main>'
```

You can add multiple `rescue` clauses to the same `begin`/`end` block, each specifying a different type of exception it should rescue.

```ruby
begin
  eat
rescue BeddingError => error        ← BeddingErrors routed here
  puts "This bed is #{error.message}!"
rescue PorridgeError => error       ← PorridgeErrors routed here
  puts "This porridge is #{error.message}!"
end
```

```
This porridge is too hot!
```

This allows you to run different recovery code depending on what type of exception was rescued.

```ruby
begin               ← Raises a BeddingError instead
  sleep
rescue BeddingError => error        ← Rescued here instead
  puts "This bed is #{error.message}!"
rescue PorridgeError => error
  puts "This porridge is #{error.message}!"
end
```

```
This bed is too soft!
```

Updating our oven code with custom exception classes

Now that we know how to raise our own exception classes, and how to handle different exception classes in different ways, let's try updating our oven simulator. If the oven is off, we need to turn it on, and if the oven is empty, we need to warn the user.

We'll create two new exception classes to represent the two types of exceptions that can occur, and make them subclasses of the `StandardError` class. Then we'll add `rescue` clauses for each exception class.

Define two new exception classes.
```ruby
class OvenOffError < StandardError
end
class OvenEmptyError < StandardError
end
```

```ruby
class SmallOven
  ...
  def bake
    unless @state == "on"
```
Raise one type of exception if the oven is off... →
```ruby
      raise OvenOffError, "You need to turn the oven on first!"
    end
    if @contents == nil
```
...and a different type if the oven is empty. →
```ruby
      raise OvenEmptyError, "There's nothing in the oven!"
    end
    "golden-brown #{contents}"
  end
end
```
We're missing a course again!
```ruby
dinner = ['turkey', nil, 'pie']
oven = SmallOven.new
oven.turn_off
```
← *We also turned the oven off again!*
```ruby
dinner.each do |item|
  begin
    oven.contents = item
    puts "Serving #{oven.bake}."
```
Rescue only OvenEmptyErrors →
```ruby
  rescue OvenEmptyError => error
    puts "Error: #{error.message}"
```
← *Print the exception message, like in our old code.*
Rescue only OvenOffErrors →
```ruby
  rescue OvenOffError => error
    oven.turn_on
```
← *The oven must be off, so turn it on.*
```ruby
  end
end
```

The OvenOffError rescue clause turns the oven on.

The OvenEmptyError rescue clause prints a warning.

```
Turning oven off.
Turning oven on.
Error: There's nothing in the oven!
Serving golden-brown pie.
```

It worked! When the cold oven raises an `OvenOffError`, the appropriate `rescue` clause is invoked, and the oven is turned on. And when the `nil` value raises an `OvenEmptyError`, the `rescue` clause for *that* exception prints a warning.

Trying again after an error with "retry"

We're missing something here… Our `rescue` clause for the `OvenOffError` turned the oven back on, and all the *remaining* items were baked successfully. But because the `OvenOffError` occurred while we were trying to bake the turkey, that part of our meal gets skipped! We need a way to go back and reattempt baking the turkey after the oven is turned on.

The rescue clause for the
OvenOffError turns the oven on.
But then we skip the turkey!

```
Turning oven off.
Turning oven on.
There's nothing in the oven!
Serving golden-brown pie.
```

The `retry` keyword should do just what we need. When you include `retry` in a `rescue` clause, execution returns to the start of the `begin`/`end` block, and statements there get rerun.

For example, if we encounter an exception because of an attempt to divide by zero, we can change the divisor and try again.

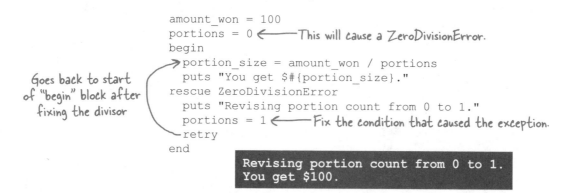

```
amount_won = 100
portions = 0          ←——This will cause a ZeroDivisionError.
begin
  portion_size = amount_won / portions
  puts "You get $#{portion_size}."
rescue ZeroDivisionError
  puts "Revising portion count from 0 to 1."
  portions = 1  ←—— Fix the condition that caused the exception.
  retry
end
```

Goes back to start
of "begin" block after
fixing the divisor

```
Revising portion count from 0 to 1.
You get $100.
```

Be cautious when using `retry`, however. If you don't succeed in fixing the issue that caused the exception (or there's a mistake in your `rescue` code), the exception will be raised again, retried again, and so on in an infinite loop! In this event, you'll need to press Ctrl-C to exit Ruby.

In the above code, if we had included `retry` but failed to actually fix the divisor, we'd get an infinite loop:

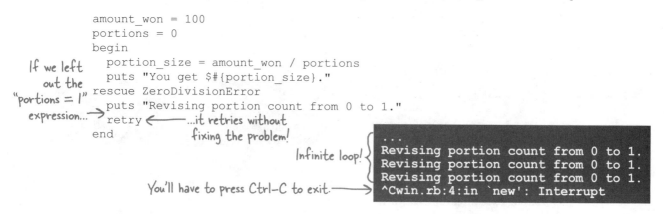

```
amount_won = 100
portions = 0
begin
  portion_size = amount_won / portions
  puts "You get $#{portion_size}."
rescue ZeroDivisionError
  puts "Revising portion count from 0 to 1."
  retry
end
```

If we left
out the
"portions = 1"
expression...

retry ←——...it retries without
fixing the problem!

Infinite loop!

You'll have to press Ctrl-C to exit.

```
...
Revising portion count from 0 to 1.
Revising portion count from 0 to 1.
Revising portion count from 0 to 1.
^Cwin.rb:4:in `new': Interrupt
```

Updating our oven code with "retry"

Let's try adding `retry` to our `rescue` clause after we turn the oven on, and see if the turkey gets processed this time:

```ruby
dinner = ['turkey', nil, 'pie']
oven = SmallOven.new
oven.turn_off
dinner.each do |item|
  begin
    oven.contents = item
    puts "Serving #{oven.bake}."
  rescue OvenEmptyError => error
    puts "Error: #{error.message}"
  rescue OvenOffError => error
    oven.turn_on
    retry   ←——— Restart the "begin" block
  end                 after turning the oven on.
end
```

The OvenOffError rescue clause turns the oven on.

The "begin" block is retried, and the turkey is cooked.

```
Turning oven off.
Turning oven on.
Serving golden-brown turkey.
Error: There's nothing in the oven!
Serving golden-brown pie.
```

We did it! Not only were we able to fix the issue that raised an exception, but the `retry` clause allowed us to process the item again (successfully this time)!

Exercise

Fill in the blanks in the code below so that it will produce the output shown.

```ruby
class _____ < StandardError
end

score = 52
begin
  if score > 60
    puts "passing grade"
  else
    _____ TestScoreError, "failing grade"
  end
rescue _____ => error
  puts "Received #{error._____}. Taking make-up exam..."
  score = 63
  _____
end
```

Output:

```
Received failing grade. Taking make-up exam...
passing grade
```

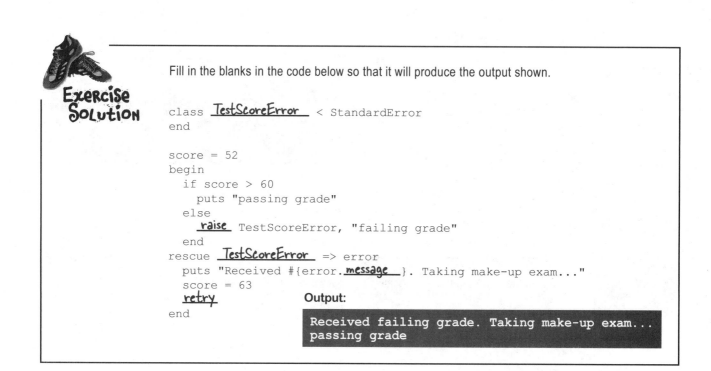

ExERCiSE
SoLuTioN

Fill in the blanks in the code below so that it will produce the output shown.

```ruby
class TestScoreError < StandardError
end

score = 52
begin
  if score > 60
    puts "passing grade"
  else
    raise TestScoreError, "failing grade"
  end
rescue TestScoreError => error
  puts "Received #{error.message}. Taking make-up exam..."
  score = 63
  retry
end
```

Output:

```
Received failing grade. Taking make-up exam...
passing grade
```

Things you want to do <u>no matter what</u>

We're just now realizing something about all the prior examples: we never turn the oven *off* when we're done.

It's not as simple as adding a single line of code to turn it off, though. This code will leave the oven on, because an exception is raised before `turn_off` can be called:

```
begin
  oven.turn_on
  oven.contents = nil
  puts "Serving #{oven.bake}."
  oven.turn_off
rescue OvenEmptyError => error
  puts "Error: #{error.message}"
end
```

Raises an exception

Never reached!

```
Turning oven on.
Error: There's nothing in the oven!
```

The oven never gets turned off!

No matter what, do NOT let me forget to turn off the oven! Last time I torched half the neighborhood.

We could add a call to `turn_off` in the `rescue` clause as well...

```
begin
  oven.turn_on
  oven.contents = nil
  puts "Serving #{oven.bake}."
  oven.turn_off
rescue OvenEmptyError => error
  puts "Error: #{error.message}"
  oven.turn_off
end
```

Copy the code from here...

...to the rescue clause.

```
Turning oven on.
Error: There's nothing in the oven!
Turning oven off.
```

The oven gets turned off despite the exception.

...but having to duplicate code like that isn't ideal, either.

The ensure clause

If you have some code that you need to run *regardless* of whether there's an exception, you can put it in an ensure clause. The ensure clause should appear in a begin/end block, after all the rescue clauses. Any statements between the ensure and end keywords are guaranteed to be run before the block exits.

The ensure clause will run if an exception is raised:

```
begin
  raise "oops!"
rescue
  puts "rescued an exception"
ensure
  puts "I run regardless"
end
```

The rescue clause runs...

...followed by the ensure clause.

```
rescued an exception
I run regardless
```

The ensure clause will run if an exception *isn't* raised:

```
begin
  puts "everything's fine"
rescue
  puts "rescued an exception"
ensure
  puts "I run regardless"
end
```

The "begin" block body runs...

...followed by the ensure clause.

```
everything's fine
I run regardless
```

Even if an exception isn't rescued, the ensure clause will still run before Ruby exits!

```
begin
  raise "oops!"
ensure
  puts "I run regardless"
end
```

The ensure clause runs...

...and only afterward does Ruby exit.

```
I run regardless
script.rb:2:in `<main>': oops! (RuntimeError)
```

Situations where you need to run some cleanup code whether an operation succeeds *or not* are pretty common in programming. Files need to be closed even if they're corrupted. Network connections need to be terminated even if you didn't get the data. And ovens need to be turned off even if the food's overcooked. An ensure clause is a great place to put this sort of code.

Ensuring the oven gets turned off

Let's try moving our call to `oven_off` to an `ensure` clause, and see how it works…

```
begin
  oven.turn_on
  oven.contents = 'turkey'
  puts "Serving #{oven.bake}."
rescue OvenEmptyError => error
  puts "Error: #{error.message}"
ensure
  oven.turn_off      We only need this in the
end                  ensure clause.
```

The "begin" block completes…

...followed by the ensure clause.

```
Turning oven on.
Serving golden-brown turkey.
Turning oven off.
```

It works! The `ensure` clause is called as soon as the `begin`/`end` block body finishes, and the oven is turned off.

Even if an exception is raised, the oven still gets turned off. The `rescue` clause runs first, followed by the `ensure` clause, which calls `turn_off`.

```
begin
  oven.turn_on
  oven.contents = nil
  puts "Serving #{oven.bake}."     Raises an exception
rescue OvenEmptyError => error
  puts "Error: #{error.message}"
ensure
  oven.turn_off      We only need this in the
end                  ensure clause.
```

The rescue clause runs…

...followed by the ensure clause.

```
Turning oven on.
Error: There's nothing in the oven!
Turning oven off.
```

In the real world, things don't always go according to plan, and that's why exceptions exist. It used to be that encountering an exception would bring your program to a screeching halt. But now that you know how to handle them, you'll find that exceptions are actually a powerful tool for keeping your code running smoothly!

Your Ruby Toolbox

That's it for Chapter 12! You've added exceptions to your toolbox.

Exceptions

When the "raise" method is called, your program stops executing code and creates an exception object representing an error.

You can handle the error (and prevent your program from exiting) by adding a "rescue" clause.

BULLET POINTS

- If you pass the name of an `Exception` subclass to the `raise` method, an exception of that class will be created.

- Instances of `Exception` and its subclasses have a `message` attribute that can be used to give more information about the problem.

- If you pass a string as a second argument to the `raise` method, it will be assigned to the `message` attribute of the exception object.

- You can add a `rescue` clause to a `begin/end` block. If the code following `begin` raises an exception, the code within the `rescue` clause will be run.

- After the code within a `rescue` clause runs, execution continues normally following the `begin/end` block.

- If an exception occurs within a method, and there is no `rescue` clause within that method, Ruby will exit the method and look for a `rescue` clause in the place the method was called.

- You can specify what exception classes a particular `rescue` clause will handle. Any exception that isn't an instance of the specified class (or one of its subclasses) will not be rescued.

- You can add multiple `rescue` clauses to a single `begin/end` block, each rescuing a different type of exception.

- You can define your own exception subclasses. Most exceptions that typical Ruby programs can handle will be subclasses of `StandardError`, which is itself a subclass of `Exception`.

- You can add the `retry` keyword within a `rescue` clause to rerun the code in the surrounding `begin/end` block.

- You can add an `ensure` clause at the end of a `begin/end` block. It will run before the `begin/end` block exits, whether or not an exception was raised.

Up Next...

Even programmers make mistakes, which is why testing your programs is so important. But testing everything by hand is time-consuming and, frankly, boring. In the next chapter, we'll show you a better way: *automated tests*.

13 unit testing

Code Quality Assurance

> I test all the equipment before every shift. That way, if there's a problem, we can fix it **before** we send out defective products!

Are you sure your software is working right now? Really sure?

Before you sent that new version to your users, you presumably tried out the new features to ensure they all worked. But did you try the *old* features to ensure you didn't break any of them? *All* the old features? If that question makes you worry, your program needs automated testing. Automated tests ensure your program's components work correctly, even after you change your code.

Unit tests are the most common, most important type of automated test. And Ruby includes **MiniTest**, a library devoted to unit testing. This chapter will teach you everything you need to know about it!

Automated tests find your bugs before someone else does

Developer A runs into Developer B at a restaurant they both frequent…

Developer A:

How's the new job going?

Ouch. How did *that* get onto your billing server?

Wow, that long ago… And your tests didn't catch it?

Your automated tests. They didn't fail when the bug got introduced?

What?!

Developer B:

Not so great. I have to head back into the office after dinner. We found a bug that's causing some customers to be billed twice as often as they should be.

We think it might have gotten introduced a couple of months ago. One of our devs made some changes to the billing code then.

Tests?

Um, we don't have any of those.

Your customers rely on your code. When it fails, it can be disastrous. Your company's reputation is damaged. And *you'll* have to put in overtime fixing the bugs.

That's why automated tests were invented. An **automated test** is a *separate program* that executes components of your *main program*, and *verifies* they behave as expected.

> I run my programs every time I add a new feature, to test it out. Isn't that enough?

Not unless you're going to test all the <u>old</u> features as well, to make sure your changes haven't broken anything. Automated tests save time over manual testing, and they're usually more thorough, too.

A program we <u>should</u> have had automated tests for

Let's look at an example of a bug that could be caught by automated tests. Here we have a simple class that joins an array of strings into a list that could be used in an English sentence. If there are two items, they'll be joined with the word *and* (as in "apple and orange"). If there are more than two items, commas will be added as appropriate (as in "apple, orange and pear").

```ruby
class ListWithCommas                          Set this to the array of items you want to join.
  attr_accessor :items
  def join                                     Add the word "and" before the last item.
    last_item = "and #{items.last}"
    other_items = items.slice(0, items.length - 1).join(', ')
    "#{other_items} #{last_item}"                Take the first through second-to-last
  end                    Return the whole       items, and join them with commas.
end                      thing as one string.
```

Within our `join` method, we take the last item in the array and add the word *and* to it. Then we use the array's `slice` instance method to get all the items *except* the last item.

We'd better take a moment to explain the `slice` method. It takes a "slice" of an array. It starts at the index you specify, and retrieves the number of elements you specify. It returns those elements as a new array.

Starting at the second element...   ...retrieve three elements.

```ruby
p ['a', 'b', 'c', 'd', 'e'].slice(1, 3)      ["b", "c", "d"]
```

Our goal is to get everything except the last item. So we ask for a slice beginning at index 0. We subtract 1 from the length of the array to get the slice length.

```ruby
array = ['a', 'b', 'c', 'd', 'e']
p array.slice(0, array.length - 1)           ["a", "b", "c", "d"]
```

Retrieve the first item...   ...through the second-to-last item.

Now that we know how our `join` method works, let's try the class out with a couple of lists:

```ruby
two_subjects = ListWithCommas.new
two_subjects.items = ['my parents', 'a rodeo clown']
puts "A photo of #{two_subjects.join}"
three_subjects = ListWithCommas.new
three_subjects.items = ['my parents', 'a rodeo clown', 'a prize bull']
puts "A photo of #{three_subjects.join}"
```

The `join` method seems to work! Until, that is, we make a change to it...

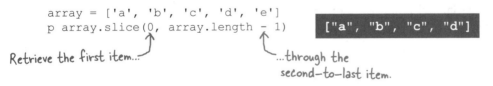

```
A photo of my parents and a rodeo clown
A photo of my parents, a rodeo clown and a prize bull
```

A program we **should** have had automated tests for (continued)

There's a small problem with this
output, though…

A photo of my parents, a rodeo clown and a prize bull

Maybe we're just immature, but we can imagine this leading to jokes that the parents *are* a rodeo
clown and a prize bull. And formatting lists in this way could cause other misunderstandings, too.

To resolve any confusion, let's update our code to place an additional comma before the *and* (as in
"apple, orange, and pear"). Then let's retest the `join` method with three items.

```ruby
class ListWithCommas
  attr_accessor :items
  def join
    last_item = "and #{items.last}"
    other_items = items.slice(0, items.length - 1).join(', ')
    "#{other_items}, #{last_item}"
  end
end
```
↑ Add a comma before the last item.

```ruby
three_subjects = ListWithCommas.new
three_subjects.items = ['my parents', 'a rodeo clown', 'a prize bull']
puts "A photo of #{three_subjects.join}"
```

There's the new comma.

A photo of my parents, a rodeo clown, and a prize bull

There! Now it should be clear that the parents were in the photo *with* the clown and the bull.

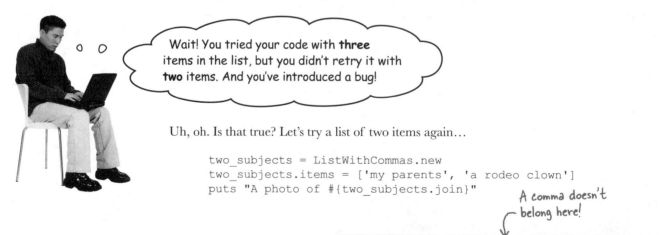

> Wait! You tried your code with **three** items in the list, but you didn't retry it with **two** items. And you've introduced a bug!

Uh, oh. Is that true? Let's try a list of two items again…

```ruby
two_subjects = ListWithCommas.new
two_subjects.items = ['my parents', 'a rodeo clown']
puts "A photo of #{two_subjects.join}"
```

A comma doesn't belong here!

A photo of my parents, and a rodeo clown

The `join` method used to return `"my parents and a rodeo clown"` for
this list of two items, but an extra comma got included here as well! We were so
focused on fixing the list of *three* items that we forgot to try other scenarios.

A program we <u>should</u> have had automated tests for (continued)

If we had automated tests for this class, this problem could have been avoided.

An automated test runs your code with a particular set of inputs, and looks for a particular result. As long as your code's output matches the expected value, the test will "pass."

But suppose that you accidentally introduced a bug in your code (like we did with the extra comma). Your code's output would no longer match the expected value, and the test would "fail." You'd know about the bug immediately.

Pass.

☑ If `items` is set to `['apple', 'orange', 'pear']`, then `join` should return `"apple, orange, and pear"`.

Fail!

☒ If `items` is set to `['apple', 'orange']`, then `join` should return `"apple and orange"`.

ListWithCommas
items
join

Having automated tests is like having your code inspected for bugs from top to bottom, automatically, every time you make a change!

Types of automated tests

There are actually many different types of automated tests in widespread use. Here are some of the most common:

*   *Performance tests* measure the speed of your program.

*   *Integration tests* run your entire program, to ensure that all its methods, classes, and other components integrate together successfully.

*   *Unit tests* run individual components (units) of your program, usually individual methods.

You can download libraries for writing all of these types of tests. But since Ruby comes with a library specifically intended for unit testing, that's what this chapter will focus on.

MiniTest: Ruby's standard unit-testing library

The Ruby standard library includes a unit-testing framework called **MiniTest**. (Ruby used to include a different library called **Test::Unit**. The new library is named MiniTest because it does many of the same things as Test::Unit, but with fewer total lines of code.)

Let's start by writing a simple test. This won't test anything practical; we need to show you how MiniTest works first. Then we'll move on to testing some actual Ruby code.

We start by requiring `'minitest/autorun'` from the standard library, which loads MiniTest and sets it up to run tests automatically when they load.

Now we can create our test. We create a new subclass of the `Minitest::Test` class, named whatever we want. Subclasses of `Minitest::Test` can be run as unit tests.

When a test runs, MiniTest goes through the test class, finds all the instance methods whose names begin with `test_`, and calls them. (You can add methods with other names, but they won't be treated as test methods.) We'll add two test methods to our class.

And within our two test methods, we'll make two calls to the `assert` method. The `assert` method is one of many methods inherited from `Minitest::Test`, and it's used to test whether your code is behaving as expected. Its behavior is very simple: if you pass it a true value, it passes, but if you pass it a false value, the whole test fails and stops immediately. Let's try passing `true` in one test, and `false` in the other.

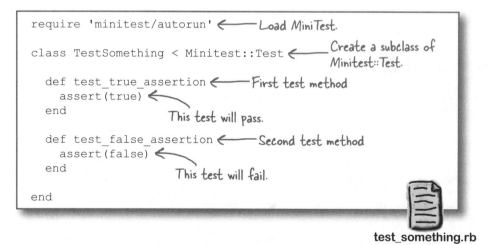

```
require 'minitest/autorun'          ← Load MiniTest.

class TestSomething < Minitest::Test  ← Create a subclass of
                                         Minitest::Test.
  def test_true_assertion    ← First test method
    assert(true)    ←
  end                          This test will pass.

  def test_false_assertion   ← Second test method
    assert(false)   ←
  end                          This test will fail.

end
```

test_something.rb

Let's save this code to a file, named *test_something.rb*. It's not much to look at, we admit. But let's try running it and see what happens!

Running a test

In your terminal, change to the directory where you saved *test_something.rb*.
Then run it with the command:

```
ruby test_something.rb
```

The tests will run automatically, and you'll see a summary of the results.

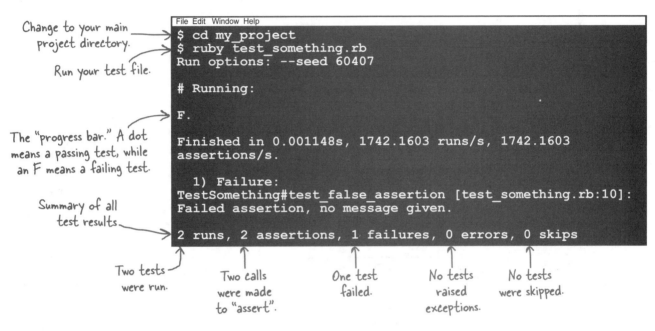

Change to your main project directory.

Run your test file.

The "progress bar." A dot means a passing test, while an F means a failing test.

Summary of all test results.

```
File Edit  Window Help
$ cd my_project
$ ruby test_something.rb
Run options: --seed 60407

# Running:

F.

Finished in 0.001148s, 1742.1603 runs/s, 1742.1603
assertions/s.

  1) Failure:
TestSomething#test_false_assertion [test_something.rb:10]:
Failed assertion, no message given.

2 runs, 2 assertions, 1 failures, 0 errors, 0 skips
```

Two tests were run.

Two calls were made to "assert".

One test failed.

No tests raised exceptions.

No tests were skipped.

Eventually, you'll have many tests, and they may take a while to run, so MiniTest prints a single character as each test runs, to form a "progress bar." It prints a dot if the current test passed, and an F if it failed.

When the tests complete, you'll see a report for each test that failed. It will include the name and line number of the test method, and the reason it failed. We'll look at these failures in more detail in a few pages.

The most important part of the output is the test summary. It lists the number of test methods that were run, the number of calls to assert and similar methods, the number of tests that failed, and the number that raised unrescued exceptions (errors). If there were zero failures and zero errors, it means your code is working properly. (Well, assuming you haven't made a mistake in your tests.)

Because we passed a false value to assert in one of our tests, the failure appears in the summary. Had this been an actual test, it would have been an indication that we needed to fix something in our code.

Testing a class

You've seen how to write and run a unit test in MiniTest. A test isn't very useful all by itself, though. Now that you understand the mechanics of MiniTest, we'll write a unit test for an actual Ruby class.

By convention (and to keep things neat), you should keep unit-test code in separate files from your main program code. So setting up and running this test will have a few extra steps...

 Save this simple class by itself in a file named *person.rb*.

```ruby
class Person
  attr_accessor :name
  def introduction
    "Hello, my name is #{name}!"
  end
end
```

person.rb

❷ In a separate file named *test_person.rb*, create and save this test class. (We'll talk about the details of this file's contents in a moment.)

```ruby
require 'minitest/autorun'
require 'person'

class TestPerson < Minitest::Test
  def test_introduction
    person = Person.new
    person.name = 'Bob'
    assert(person.introduction == 'Hello, my name is Bob!')
  end
end
```

test_person.rb

❸ Create two directories within your main project directory. By convention, one subdirectory should be called *lib*, and the other should be called *test*.

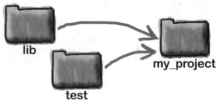

Testing a class (continued)

 Move the file with the class you want to test within the *lib* subdirectory, and move the test file into the *test* subdirectory.

person.rb → **lib**   **test_person.rb** → **test**

 In your terminal, change to your *main* project directory (the one that holds the *lib* and *test* directories). Then type this command:

```
ruby -I lib test/test_person.rb
```

The `-I lib` flag adds *lib* to the list of directories Ruby will search when you call `require`, allowing the *person.rb* file to be loaded. And specifying *test/test_person.rb* as the file to load will cause Ruby to look for a file named *test_person.rb* within the *test* subdirectory.

(For a way to automate this part, see the section on Rake in the appendix!)

Your unit tests will run and produce output similar to that shown here.

Change to your main project directory.

Run your test file in Ruby.

The dot means the test passed.

Summary of all test results

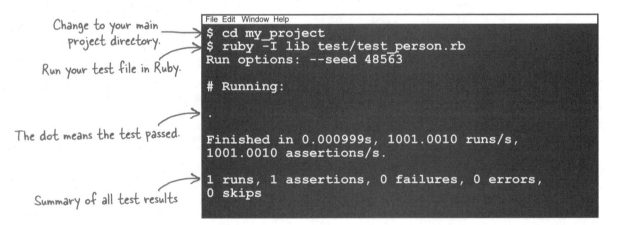

```
File Edit Window Help
$ cd my_project
$ ruby -I lib test/test_person.rb
Run options: --seed 48563

# Running:

.

Finished in 0.000999s, 1001.0010 runs/s,
1001.0010 assertions/s.

1 runs, 1 assertions, 0 failures, 0 errors,
0 skips
```

You can see in the summary at the bottom that there were zero failures and zero errors. Our test passed!

We'll take a more detailed look at the test code on the next page…

✳ Conventional Wisdom ✳

Create a directory named *lib* to hold files for your classes and modules. Create a separate directory named *test* to hold files for your unit tests.

A closer look at the test code

Now, let's take a closer look at that code for the unit test. In our *person.rb* file in the *lib* directory, we have a simple class that we want to test, with one attribute and one instance method.

```ruby
class Person
  attr_accessor :name
  def introduction
    "Hello, my name is #{name}!"
  end
end
```

lib/person.rb

And in our *test_person.rb* file in the *test* directory, we have our test code.

```ruby
require 'minitest/autorun'  ←——Load MiniTest.
require 'person'  ←——Load the class we're testing.

class TestPerson < Minitest::Test  ←——Define a test class.
  def test_introduction  ←——Define a test method.
    person = Person.new
    person.name = 'Bob'
    assert(person.introduction == 'Hello, my name is Bob!')
  end
end
```

test/test_person.rb

After loading MiniTest, we require the `'person'` file in order to load the `Person` class. The call to `require` works because when running the test, we added the `-I lib` flag to the command line. That adds the *lib* directory to the list of directories Ruby searches for files to load.

Once all the classes we need are loaded, we can define our test. We create a new subclass of the `Minitest::Test` class, named `TestPerson`, and add one test method to it (ensuring the method name starts with `test_`).

And it's within that test method that we finally determine whether our code is working correctly…

there are no
Dumb Questions

Q: The code never calls **TestPerson.new** or any of the test methods. How do the tests run by themselves?

A: When we `require` `'minitest/autorun'`, it sets up the test classes to run as soon as they load, automatically.

A closer look at the test code (continued)

Testing your code within a test method is very similar to making calls to it from a regular program.

If we were to create a `Person`, set its `name` attribute to `'Bob'`, and then do an equality comparison to see if the return value from its `introduction` method was `'Hello, my name is Bob!'`, the result of that comparison would of course be `true`:

```
person = Person.new
person.name = 'Bob'
puts person.introduction == 'Hello, my name is Bob!'
```
`true`

We perform exactly those steps within the `test_introduction` method. We create an ordinary `Person` instance, just like we would when using our class in an actual application. We assign a value to its `name` attribute, just like in an app. And we call its `introduction` method, just like we normally would.

The only difference is that we then compare the return value to the string we expect. If they are equal, the value `true` will be passed to `assert`, and the test will pass. If they're *not* equal, the value `false` will be passed to assert, and the test will fail. (And we'll know that we need to fix our code!)

```
                     def test_introduction
   Set up a Person  ⌠person = Person.new
      named "Bob".  ⌡person.name = 'Bob'
                         assert(person.introduction == 'Hello, my name is Bob!')
                     end
```

A Person named "Bob" should return this string.

Exercise

Fill in the blanks in the code below so that it will produce the output shown.

Output:

```
File  Edit  Window  Help
$ ruby test_math.rb
Run options: --seed 55914

# Running:

.F

Finished in 0.000863s, 2317.4971 runs/s,
2317.4971 assertions/s.

  1) Failure:
TestMath#test_fallacy [test_math.rb:8]:
Failed assertion, no message given.

2 runs, 2 assertions, 1 failures,
0 errors, 0 skips
```

```
require '_____/autorun'

class TestMath < _____
  def ____truth
    _____(2 + 2 == 4)
  end
  def ____fallacy
    _____(2 + 2 == 5)
  end
end
```

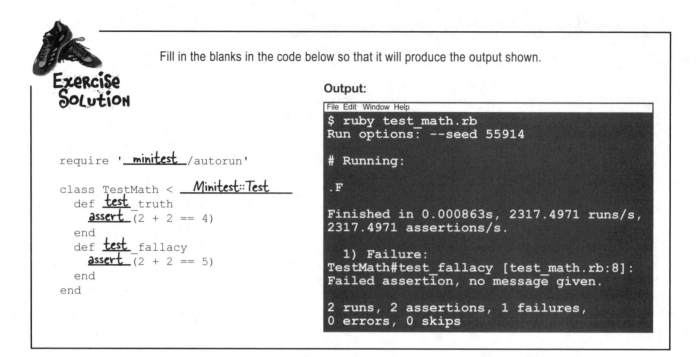

Exercise Solution

Fill in the blanks in the code below so that it will produce the output shown.

```ruby
require '_minitest_/autorun'

class TestMath < _Minitest::Test_
  def _test_truth
    _assert_(2 + 2 == 4)
  end
  def _test_fallacy
    _assert_(2 + 2 == 5)
  end
end
```

Output:

```
File  Edit  Window  Help
$ ruby test_math.rb
Run options: --seed 55914

# Running:

.F

Finished in 0.000863s, 2317.4971 runs/s,
2317.4971 assertions/s.

  1) Failure:
TestMath#test_fallacy [test_math.rb:8]:
Failed assertion, no message given.

2 runs, 2 assertions, 1 failures,
0 errors, 0 skips
```

Red, green, refactor

Once you have some experience with unit testing, you'll probably fall into a cycle that's commonly referred to as "red, green, refactor":

- **Red stage:** You write a test for the feature you *want*, even though it doesn't exist yet. Then you run the test to ensure that it *fails*.

- **Green stage:** You implement the feature in your main code. Don't worry about whether the code you're writing is sloppy or inefficient; your only goal is to get it working. Then you run the test to ensure that it *passes*.

- **Refactor stage:** Now, you're free to *refactor* the code, to change and improve it, however you please. You've watched the test *fail*, so you know it will fail again if your app code breaks. You've watched the test *pass*, so you know it will continue passing as long as your code is working correctly.

✗ **Red!**

✓ **Green!**

✓ **Refactor!**

This freedom to *change* your code without worrying about it breaking is the real reason you want unit tests. Anytime you see a way to make your code shorter or easier to read, you won't hesitate to do it. When you're finished, you can simply run your tests again, and you'll be confident that everything is still working.

Tests for ListWithCommas

Now that we know how to write and run a unit test with MiniTest, let's try writing a test to troubleshoot our `ListWithCommas` class.

`ListWithCommas` works just fine if we give it a list of *three* items to join:

```
three_subjects = ListWithCommas.new
three_subjects.items = ['my parents', 'a rodeo clown', 'a prize bull']
puts "A photo of #{three_subjects.join}"
```

> **A photo of my parents, a rodeo clown, and a prize bull**

But if we give it a list of just *two* items, we get an extra comma.

```
two_subjects = ListWithCommas.new
two_subjects.items = ['my parents', 'a rodeo clown']
puts "A photo of #{two_subjects.join}"
```

A comma doesn't belong here!

> **A photo of my parents, and a rodeo clown**

Let's write some tests that show what we *expect* from the `join` method, run them, and confirm that they're currently failing. Then, we'll alter the `ListWithCommas` class to make the tests pass. Once the tests are passing, we'll know our code is fixed!

We'll write two tests: one where we attempt to join two words, and one where we attempt to join three words. In each, we'll create a `ListWithCommas` instance and assign an array to its `items` attribute, just like we did in our actual program. Then, we'll call the `join` method and assert that its return value should equal our expected value.

```
require 'minitest/autorun'    ←—— Load MiniTest.
require 'list_with_commas'    ←—— Load the class we're testing.

class TestListWithCommas < Minitest::Test

  def test_it_joins_two_words_with_and   ←—— First test method
    list = ListWithCommas.new              ←—— Test "join" using two items.
    list.items = ['apple', 'orange']
    assert('apple and orange' == list.join)   ←—— The test will pass IF "join" returns the
  end                                              expected string.

  def test_it_joins_three_words_with_commas  ←—— Second test method
    list = ListWithCommas.new
    list.items = ['apple', 'orange', 'pear']    ←—— Test "join" using three items.
    assert('apple, orange, and pear' == list.join)   ←——
  end                                                  The test will pass IF "join"
                                                       returns the expected string.
end
```

Tests for ListWithCommas (continued)

We have our test class. Let's get set up to run it!

 Save the `ListWithCommas` class in a file named *list_with_commas.rb*.

```ruby
class ListWithCommas
  attr_accessor :items
  def join
    last_item = "and #{items.last}"
    other_items = items.slice(0, items.length - 1).join(', ')
    "#{other_items}, #{last_item}"
  end
end
```

list_with_commas.rb

 Save the `TestListWithCommas` class in a separate file named
test_list_with_commas.rb.

```ruby
require 'minitest/autorun'
require 'list_with_commas'

class TestListWithCommas < Minitest::Test

  def test_it_joins_two_words_with_and
    list = ListWithCommas.new
    list.items = ['apple', 'orange']
    assert('apple and orange' == list.join)
  end

  def test_it_joins_three_words_with_commas
    list = ListWithCommas.new
    list.items = ['apple', 'orange', 'pear']
    assert('apple, orange, and pear' == list.join)
  end

end
```

test_list_with_commas.rb

Tests for ListWithCommas (continued)

❸ As with the previous test, *list_with_commas.rb* should be saved in a directory named *lib*, and *test_list_with_commas.rb* should be saved in a directory named *test*. Those directories, in turn, should be placed within a single project directory.

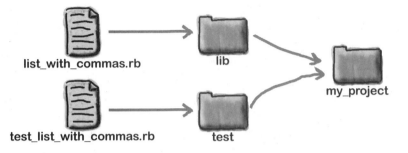

list_with_commas.rb   lib   my_project

test_list_with_commas.rb   test

❹ Once the files are in place, in your terminal, change to your main project directory. Then type this command:

```
ruby -I lib test/test_list_with_commas.rb
```

Your unit tests will run and produce output similar to that shown here.

Change to your main
project directory.

Run your test file in Ruby.

One test passes, and
the other test fails.

The failure appears
in the summary.

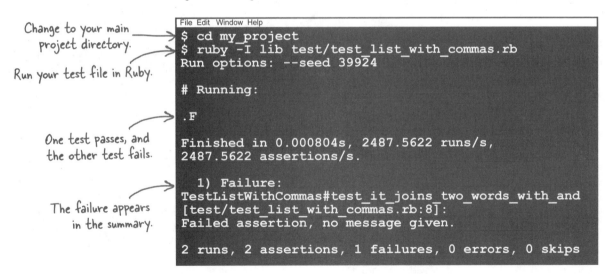

```
File Edit Window Help
$ cd my_project
$ ruby -I lib test/test_list_with_commas.rb
Run options: --seed 39924

# Running:

.F

Finished in 0.000804s, 2487.5622 runs/s,
2487.5622 assertions/s.

  1) Failure:
TestListWithCommas#test_it_joins_two_words_with_and
[test/test_list_with_commas.rb:8]:
Failed assertion, no message given.

2 runs, 2 assertions, 1 failures, 0 errors, 0 skips
```

The summary shows that the test with three items passes, but the test with two items fails. We've reached the "red" phase of the "red, green, refactor" cycle! With a working test, it should be really easy to fix the ListWithCommas class.

Pass. ☑   If items is set to ['apple', 'orange', 'pear'], then join should return "apple, orange, and pear".

Fail! ☒   If items is set to ['apple', 'orange'], then join should return "apple and orange".

Getting the test to pass

Right now we have two unit tests for our `ListWithCommas` class. The
test with *three* items in the list passes, but the test with *two* items fails:

```ruby
class ListWithCommas
  attr_accessor :items
  def join
    last_item = "and #{items.last}"
    other_items = items.slice(0, items.length - 1).join(', ')
    "#{other_items}, #{last_item}"
  end
end
```

Pass. ☑ If `items` is set to `['apple', 'orange', 'pear']`,
then `join` should return `"apple, orange, and pear"`.

Fail! ☒ If `items` is set to `['apple', 'orange']`, then `join`
should return `"apple and orange"`.

This is because the `ListWithCommas` `join` method includes an
extra comma when outputting a list of just two items.

```ruby
two_subjects = ListWithCommas.new
two_subjects.items = ['my parents', 'a rodeo clown']
puts "A photo of #{two_subjects.join}"
```

A comma doesn't belong here!

```
A photo of my parents, and a rodeo clown
```

Let's modify `join` so that when the list has just two items, it simply
joins them with the word *and*. We'll return the resulting string without
running any of the remaining code.

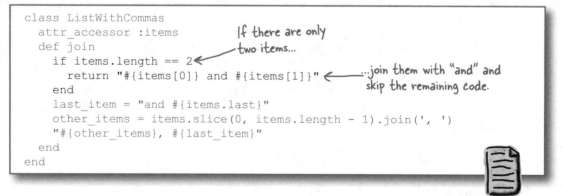

```ruby
class ListWithCommas
  attr_accessor :items
  def join
    if items.length == 2          # If there are only two items...
      return "#{items[0]} and #{items[1]}"   # ...join them with "and" and
    end                                       # skip the remaining code.
    last_item = "and #{items.last}"
    other_items = items.slice(0, items.length - 1).join(', ')
    "#{other_items}, #{last_item}"
  end
end
```

list_with_commas.rb

Getting the test to pass (continued)

We've updated our code, but is it working correctly? Our tests can tell us immediately! As before, type this in your terminal:

```
ruby -I lib test/test_list_with_commas.rb
```

We'll see that both tests are now passing!

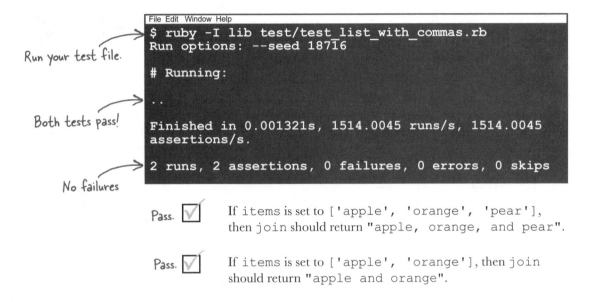

Run your test file.

Both tests pass!

No failures

```
File Edit Window Help
$ ruby -I lib test/test_list_with_commas.rb
Run options: --seed 18716

# Running:

..

Finished in 0.001321s, 1514.0045 runs/s, 1514.0045
assertions/s.

2 runs, 2 assertions, 0 failures, 0 errors, 0 skips
```

Pass. ☑ If items is set to ['apple', 'orange', 'pear'], then join should return "apple, orange, and pear".

Pass. ☑ If items is set to ['apple', 'orange'], then join should return "apple and orange".

Our tests are "green"! We can say with certainty that join works with a list of two items now, because the corresponding unit test now passes. And we don't need to worry about whether we broke any of the other code; we have a unit test assuring us that's fine, too.

We can resume using our class with confidence!

```
two_subjects = ListWithCommas.new
two_subjects.items = ['my parents', 'a rodeo clown']
puts "A photo of #{two_subjects.join}"
three_subjects = ListWithCommas.new
three_subjects.items = ['my parents', 'a rodeo clown', 'a prize bull']
puts "A photo of #{three_subjects.join}"
```

No extra comma when there are two items

Still works with three items ⟶

```
A photo of my parents and a rodeo clown
A photo of my parents, a rodeo clown, and a prize bull
```

Another bug to fix

It's conceivable that `ListWithCommas` could be set up with only a single item. But its `join` method doesn't behave very well at all in that case, treating that one item as if it appeared at the end of a list of items:

```
one_subject = ListWithCommas.new
one_subject.items = ['a rodeo clown']
puts "A photo of #{one_subject.join}"
```

Our class treats a single item as if it were at the end of a list!

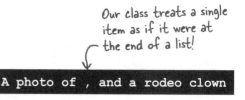

```
A photo of , and a rodeo clown
```

How *should* `join` behave in this case? If we have a list of one item, we don't really need commas, the word *and*, or anything at all. We could simply return that one item.

A photo of a rodeo clown

A list of one item should look like this.

Let's express this in a unit test. We'll create a `ListWithCommas` instance, and set its `items` attribute to an array with only one element. Then we'll add an assertion that its `join` method should return a string consisting of only that item.

```ruby
require 'minitest/autorun'
require 'list_with_commas'

class TestListWithCommas < Minitest::Test

  def test_it_prints_one_word_alone
    list = ListWithCommas.new          Set up a list with only a single item.
    list.items = ['apple']
    assert('apple' == list.join)       We should expect a string
  end                                  consisting of only that item.

  ...

end
```

test_list_with_commas.rb

Test failure messages

Let's try out our new test.

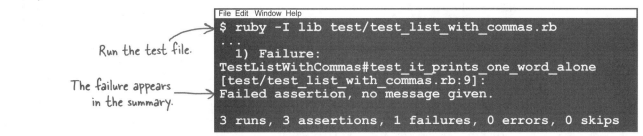

Run the test file.

The failure appears in the summary.

```
File Edit Window Help
$ ruby -I lib test/test_list_with_commas.rb
...
  1) Failure:
TestListWithCommas#test_it_prints_one_word_alone
[test/test_list_with_commas.rb:9]:
Failed assertion, no message given.

3 runs, 3 assertions, 1 failures, 0 errors, 0 skips
```

There's the failure!

It's unfortunate that this is the only feedback we're given regarding the problem, though:

> Failed assertion, no message given.

There are a couple of different ways we can get more information.

The first is to set up a test failure message. The `assert` method takes an optional second parameter with a message that should be displayed in the event the test fails. Let's try adding a message now:

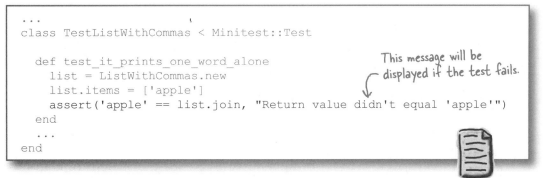

```
...
class TestListWithCommas < Minitest::Test

  def test_it_prints_one_word_alone
    list = ListWithCommas.new
    list.items = ['apple']
    assert('apple' == list.join, "Return value didn't equal 'apple'")
  end
  ...
end
```

This message will be displayed if the test fails.

test_list_with_commas.rb

If we try running the updated test, we'll see our custom error message in the failure summary.

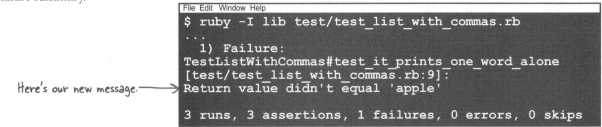

```
File Edit Window Help
$ ruby -I lib test/test_list_with_commas.rb
...
  1) Failure:
TestListWithCommas#test_it_prints_one_word_alone
[test/test_list_with_commas.rb:9]:
Return value didn't equal 'apple'

3 runs, 3 assertions, 1 failures, 0 errors, 0 skips
```

Here's our new message.

A better way to assert that two values are equal

Although our custom error message is more descriptive, it still doesn't show exactly *why* the test failed. It would help if the message showed what the `join` method *actually* returned, so that we could compare it to the *expected* value…

The second (and easier) way we can get a more descriptive failure message is to use a different assertion method. The `assert` method is just one of many methods that test classes inherit from `Minitest::Test`.

There's also the `assert_equal` method, which takes two arguments and checks that they are equal. If they're not, the test will fail, just as with `assert`. But more importantly, it will print the expected value and the actual value in the test summary, so that we can compare them easily.

Since all our calls to `assert` are doing equality comparisons, let's replace them all with calls to `assert_equal`. The first argument to `assert_equal` should be the value we expect, and the second argument should be the value our code actually returns.

```ruby
require 'minitest/autorun'
require 'list_with_commas'

class TestListWithCommas < Minitest::Test

  def test_it_prints_one_word_alone
    list = ListWithCommas.new
    list.items = ['apple']
    assert_equal('apple', list.join)      ←—— We should expect a string
  end                                            consisting of only that item.

  def test_it_joins_two_words_with_and
    list = ListWithCommas.new
    list.items = ['apple', 'orange']
    assert_equal('apple and orange', list.join)
  end

  def test_it_joins_three_words_with_commas
    list = ListWithCommas.new
    list.items = ['apple', 'orange', 'pear']
    assert_equal('apple, orange, and pear', list.join)
  end

end
```

test_list_with_commas.rb

A better way to assert that two values are equal (continued)

Let's try running our tests again, and see if the output is any more helpful.

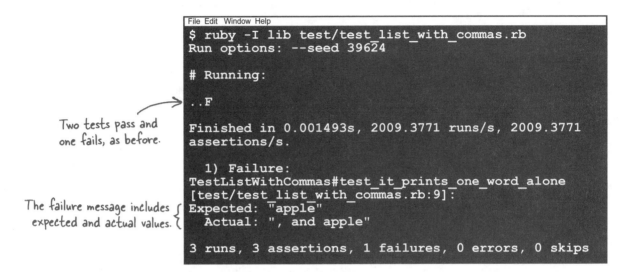

Two tests pass and one fails, as before.

The failure message includes expected and actual values.

```
File Edit Window Help
$ ruby -I lib test/test_list_with_commas.rb
Run options: --seed 39624

# Running:

..F

Finished in 0.001493s, 2009.3771 runs/s, 2009.3771
assertions/s.

  1) Failure:
TestListWithCommas#test_it_prints_one_word_alone
[test/test_list_with_commas.rb:9]:
Expected: "apple"
  Actual: ", and apple"

3 runs, 3 assertions, 1 failures, 0 errors, 0 skips
```

There they are in the output: the value we expected (`"apple"`), and the value we actually got (`", and apple"`)!

Now that it's clear what's wrong, it should be easy to fix the bug. We'll update our `ListWithCommas` code with another `if` clause. If there's only one item in the list, we'll simply return that item.

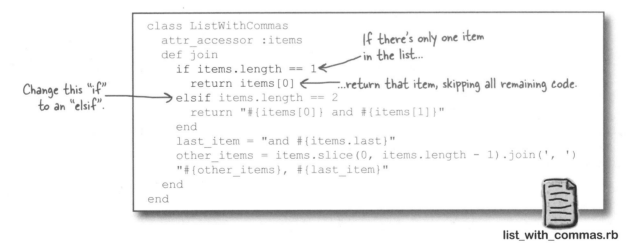

Change this "if" to an "elsif".

```ruby
class ListWithCommas
  attr_accessor :items
  def join
    if items.length == 1
      return items[0]
    elsif items.length == 2
      return "#{items[0]} and #{items[1]}"
    end
    last_item = "and #{items.last}"
    other_items = items.slice(0, items.length - 1).join(', ')
    "#{other_items}, #{last_item}"
  end
end
```

If there's only one item in the list...

...return that item, skipping all remaining code.

list_with_commas.rb

And if we rerun the tests, we'll see that everything's passing!

```
3 runs, 3 assertions, 0 failures, 0 errors, 0 skips
```

Some other assertion methods

As we mentioned, test classes inherit many assertion methods from `Minitest::Test`. You've already seen `assert`, which passes if it receives a true value, and fails if it receives a false value:

```
assert(true)        ← Passes
assert(false)       ← Fails!
```

And you've seen `assert_equal`, which takes two values, and fails if they are not equal:

```
assert_equal(1, 1)        ← Passes
assert_equal(1, 2)        ← Fails!
```

Let's take a brief look at some of the other assertion methods that are available…

The `assert_includes` method takes a collection as its first argument, and any object as its second argument. It fails if the collection does not include the given object.

```
assert_includes(['apple', 'orange'], 'apple')      ← Passes because the array includes "apple"
assert_includes(['apple', 'orange'], 'pretzel')    ← Fails because the array
                                                        doesn't include "pretzel"!
```

The `assert_instance_of` method takes a class as its first argument, and any object as its second argument. It fails if the object is not an instance of the given class.

```
assert_instance_of(String, 'apple')      ← Passes because "apple" is an instance of String
assert_instance_of(Fixnum, 'apple')      ← Fails because "apple" is NOT an instance of Fixnum!
```

And the `assert_raises` method takes one or more exception classes as arguments. It also takes a block. If the block does *not* raise an exception that matches one of the specified classes, it fails. (This is useful when you've written code that raises an error in certain circumstances, and need to test that it actually raises the error at the appropriate time.)

```
assert_raises(ArgumentError) do←      ← Passes because the block raises an ArgumentError
  raise ArgumentError, "That didn't work!"
end

assert_raises(ArgumentError) do      ← Fails because the block does NOT raise an ArgumentError
  "Everything's fine!"
end
```

Exercise

The code snippets below were all taken from MiniTest test methods.
Mark whether each assertion will pass or fail on the blank line next to it.

```
..........    assert_equal('apples', 'apples')


..........    assert_includes([1, 2, 3, 4, 5], 3)


..........    assert_instance_of(String, 42)


..........    assert_includes(['a', 'b', 'c'], 'd')


..........    assert_raises(RuntimeError) do
                raise "Oops!"
              end


..........    assert('apples' == 'oranges')


..........    assert_raises(StandardError) do
                raise ZeroDivisionError, "Oops!"
              end


..........    assert_instance_of(Hash, {})
```

Exercise Solution

The code snippets below were all taken from MiniTest test methods.
Mark whether each assertion will pass or fail on the blank line next to it.

Pass
....
```
assert_equal('apples', 'apples')
```

Pass
....
```
assert_includes([1, 2, 3, 4, 5], 3)
```

Fail
....
```
assert_instance_of(String, 42)
```

Fail
....
```
assert_includes(['a', 'b', 'c'], 'd')
```

Pass
....
```
assert_raises(RuntimeError) do
  raise "Oops!"
end
```
Remember, if you don't specify an exception class, a RuntimeError is raised by default.

Fail
....
```
assert('apples' == 'oranges')
```

Fail
....
```
assert_raises(StandardError) do
  raise ZeroDivisionError, "Oops!"
end
```
Raises a different type of exception than the test expects!

Pass
....
```
assert_instance_of(Hash, {})
```

Removing duplicated code from your tests

There's some repeated code among our various tests... Every test
starts with the creation of a `ListWithCommas` instance.

```ruby
require 'minitest/autorun'
require 'list_with_commas'

class TestListWithCommas < Minitest::Test

  def test_it_prints_one_word_alone
    list = ListWithCommas.new        ←——— Repeated
    list.items = ['apple']
    assert_equal('apple', list.join)
  end

  def test_it_joins_two_words_with_and
    list = ListWithCommas.new        ←——— Repeated
    list.items = ['apple', 'orange']
    assert_equal('apple and orange', list.join)
  end

  def test_it_joins_three_words_with_commas
    list = ListWithCommas.new        ←——— Repeated
    list.items = ['apple', 'orange', 'pear']
    assert_equal('apple, orange, and pear', list.join)
  end

end
```

test_list_with_commas.rb

When you're running multiple tests against the same type of object,
it's only natural that similar steps would be required to set each test up.
So MiniTest includes a way of avoiding that repeated code...

The "setup" method

MiniTest looks for an instance method named `setup` on your test class
and, if it's present, will run it before each test.

```ruby
require 'minitest/autorun'

class TestSetup < Minitest::Test
  def setup
    puts "In setup"
  end
  def test_one
    puts "In test_one"
  end
  def test_two
    puts "In test_two"
  end
end
```

The "setup" method runs before the first test. ———▶

The "setup" method runs again before the second test. ———▶

```
...
In setup
In test_one
In setup
In test_two
...
```

The `setup` method can be used to set up objects for your test.

```ruby
class TestSetup < Minitest::Test
  def setup
    @oven = SmallOven.new        ◀——— Set up an object for each test.
    @oven.turn_on
  end
  def test_bake
    @oven.contents = 'turkey'    ◀——— Use the object from "setup".
    assert_equal('golden-brown turkey', @oven.bake)
  end
  def test_empty_oven
    @oven.contents = nil         ◀——— Use the object from "setup".
    assert_raises(RuntimeError) { @oven.bake }
  end
end
```

Note that if you're going to use `setup`, it's important to store the
objects you create in *instance* variables. If you use *local* variables, they'll
be out of scope when your test method runs!

```ruby
class TestSetup < Minitest::Test
  def setup
    oven = SmallOven.new         ◀——— Don't use a local
    oven.turn_on                      variable like this!
  end
  def test_bake
    oven.contents = 'turkey'     ◀——— The "oven" variable is no
    assert_equal('golden-brown turkey', oven.bake)    longer in scope!
  end
end
```

Error ——▶ `undefined local variable or method 'oven'`

The "teardown" method

MiniTest also looks for a second instance method on your test class, named `teardown`. If it's present, it will be run *after* each test.

```ruby
require 'minitest/autorun'

class TestSetup < Minitest::Test
  def teardown
    puts "In teardown"
  end
  def test_one
    puts "In test_one"
  end
  def test_two
    puts "In test_two"
  end
end
```

The "teardown" method runs after the first test. ──→

The "teardown" method runs again after the second test. ──→

```
...
In test_one
In teardown
In test_two
In teardown
...
```

The `teardown` method is useful if you need to clean up after each test is run.

```ruby
class TestSetupAndTeardown < Minitest::Test
  def setup
    @oven = SmallOven.new
    @oven.turn_on
  end
  def teardown
    @oven.turn_off    ←──── Called after each test is run
  end
  def test_bake
    @oven.contents = 'turkey'
    assert_equal('golden-brown turkey', @oven.bake)
  end
  def test_empty_oven
    @oven.contents = nil
    assert_raises(RuntimeError) { @oven.bake }
  end
end
```

The `setup` and `teardown` methods run before and after *each* test, not just once. Even though there's only one copy of your setup code, you'll still have a fresh, clean object for each test you run. (It would quickly get messy if changes made to your object by a prior test could affect the result of the next test, after all.)

Up next, we'll take what we've learned and see if we can eliminate the duplicated code in the `ListWithCommas` tests...

Updating our code to use the "setup" method

Previously, we had code to set up a `ListWithCommas` instance in each test method. Let's move that duplicated code to a `setup` method. We'll store the object for each test in a `@list` instance variable, which we'll then reference from the test methods.

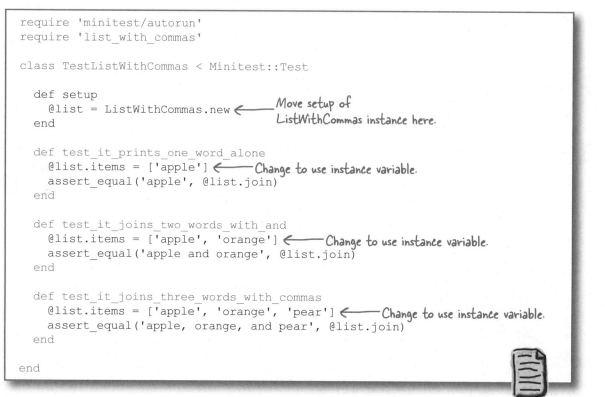

```ruby
require 'minitest/autorun'
require 'list_with_commas'

class TestListWithCommas < Minitest::Test

  def setup
    @list = ListWithCommas.new          ← Move setup of
  end                                      ListWithCommas instance here.

  def test_it_prints_one_word_alone
    @list.items = ['apple']             ← Change to use instance variable.
    assert_equal('apple', @list.join)
  end

  def test_it_joins_two_words_with_and
    @list.items = ['apple', 'orange']   ← Change to use instance variable.
    assert_equal('apple and orange', @list.join)
  end

  def test_it_joins_three_words_with_commas
    @list.items = ['apple', 'orange', 'pear']  ← Change to use instance variable.
    assert_equal('apple, orange, and pear', @list.join)
  end

end
```

test_list_with_commas.rb

Much cleaner! And if we run the tests, we'll see that everything passes as normal.

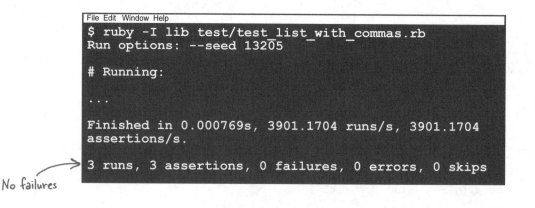

```
File  Edit  Window  Help
$ ruby -I lib test/test_list_with_commas.rb
Run options: --seed 13205

# Running:

...

Finished in 0.000769s, 3901.1704 runs/s, 3901.1704
assertions/s.

3 runs, 3 assertions, 0 failures, 0 errors, 0 skips
```

No failures

Pool Puzzle

Your **job** is to take code snippets from the pool and place them into the blank lines in the code. **Don't** use the same snippet more than once, and you won't need to use all the snippets. Your **goal** is to make code that will run and produce the output shown.

```ruby
_____ 'minitest/autorun'

class TestArray < _____

  def _____
    @array = ['a', 'b', 'c']
  end

  def test_length
    _____(3, _____.length)
  end

  def test_last
    assert_equal(____, @array.last)
  end

  def test_join
    _____('a-b-c', @array.join('-'))
  end

end
```

Output:

```
$ ruby test_setup.rb
Run options: --seed 60370

# Running:

...

Finished in 0.000752s, 3989.3617
runs/s, 3989.3617 assertions/s.

3 runs, 3 assertions, 0 failures,
0 errors, 0 skips
```

Note: each thing from the pool can only be used once!

```
                    first
        assert_equal        'c'        teardown
    assert                                          setup
            @array              Minitest::Test
    require              'a'              test        assert_equal
```

Pool Puzzle Solution

```ruby
require 'minitest/autorun'

class TestArray < Minitest::Test

  def setup
    @array = ['a', 'b', 'c']
  end

  def test_length
    assert_equal (3, @array.length)
  end

  def test_last
    assert_equal('c', @array.last)
  end

  def test_join
    assert_equal ('a-b-c', @array.join('-'))
  end

end
```

Output:

```
$ ruby test_setup.rb
Run options: --seed 60370

# Running:

...

Finished in 0.000752s, 3989.3617
runs/s, 3989.3617 assertions/s.

3 runs, 3 assertions, 0 failures,
0 errors, 0 skips
```

Your Ruby Toolbox

That's it for Chapter 13! You've added unit testing to your toolbox.

Unit Testing

A unit test executes components of your program, and verifies that they behave as expected.

MiniTest is a unit-testing framework that's included in the Ruby standard library.

Up Next...

We're getting close to the end of the book! It's time to put your Ruby skills to the test. Over the next two chapters, we're going to code a full web app. Don't be intimidated; we'll be showing you Sinatra, a library that will make the whole process easy!

BULLET POINTS

- Loading MiniTest with `require 'minitest/autorun'` will set it up to run tests automatically when they're loaded.

- To create a MiniTest unit test, you'll first need to define a subclass of `Minitest::Test`.

- MiniTest looks for instance methods of your test class that begin with `test_`, and runs them. Each such method comprises a unit test.

- Within your test methods, you can perform a test and pass its result to the `assert` method. If `assert` receives a false value, the test will fail. If `assert` receives a true value, the test will pass.

- By convention, your main program code should be placed in files within a subdirectory of your project named *lib*. Unit tests should be placed within a *test* subdirectory.

- When calling `assert`, you can pass an optional second argument with a failure message. If the test fails, that message will be displayed in the test results.

- The `assert_equal` method takes two arguments, and will fail the test unless they are equal.

- Many other assertion methods—such as `assert_includes`, `assert_raises`, and `assert_instance_of`—are inherited from `Minitest::Test`.

- If you add a `setup` instance method to your test class, it will be called *before* each test is run. It can be used to set up objects for use within your tests.

- If you add a `teardown` instance method to your test class, it will be called *after* each test is run. It can be used to run test cleanup code.

14 web apps

Serving HTML

This is the 21st century. Users want web apps. Ruby's got you covered there, too! Libraries are available to help you host your own web applications and make them accessible from any web browser. So we're going to spend these final two chapters of the book showing you how to build a full web app.

To get started, you're going to need **Sinatra**, a third-party library for writing web applications. But don't worry, we'll show you how to use the **RubyGems** tool (included with Ruby) to download and install libraries automatically! Then we'll show you just enough HTML to create your own web pages. And of course, we'll show you how to serve those pages to a browser!

Writing web apps in Ruby

An app that runs in your terminal is great—for your own use. But ordinary users have been spoiled by the Internet and the World Wide Web. They don't want to learn to use a terminal so they can use your app. They don't even want to install your app. They want it to be ready to use the moment they click a link in their browser.

It's time for your apps to say goodbye to the terminal...

```
File Edit Window Help
$ ruby hello.rb
Hello, world!
```

But don't worry! Ruby can help you write apps for the Web, too.

We won't lead you on—writing a full web app is not a small task, even using Ruby. This is going to require all of the skills you've learned so far, plus a few new ones. But Ruby has some excellent libraries available that will make the process as easy as possible!

...and say hello to the browser!

http://example.com/hello

Hello, web!

In these final two chapters of the book, we're going to build a simple online movie database. You'll be able to enter details about movies, which will be saved to a file. The website will provide a list of links to all movies that have been entered, and you'll be able to click on a movie's link to view details for that movie.

localhost:4567/movies

My Movies

- Jaws
- Alien
- Terminator 2

Add New Movie

List of movies

localhost:4567/movies/new

Add New Movie

Title: [Jaws]
Director: [Steven Spielberg]
Year Published: [ ]
[Submit]
Back to Index

Adding a new movie

localhost:4567/movies/6

Alien

Title: Alien
Director: Ridley Scott
Year Published: 1979
Back to Index

Details for a movie

Our task list

There's a lot to cover in the next two chapters, but don't worry—we'll be breaking this process down into little steps. Let's take a look at what will be involved…

This chapter will be focused on creating HTML pages and serving them in a browser. We'll get as far as creating a form for users to enter new movie data…

Then, in Chapter 15, we'll show you how to use that form data to set attributes of Ruby objects, and save those objects to a file. Once you've done that, you'll be able to load the data back in, and display it any way you want!

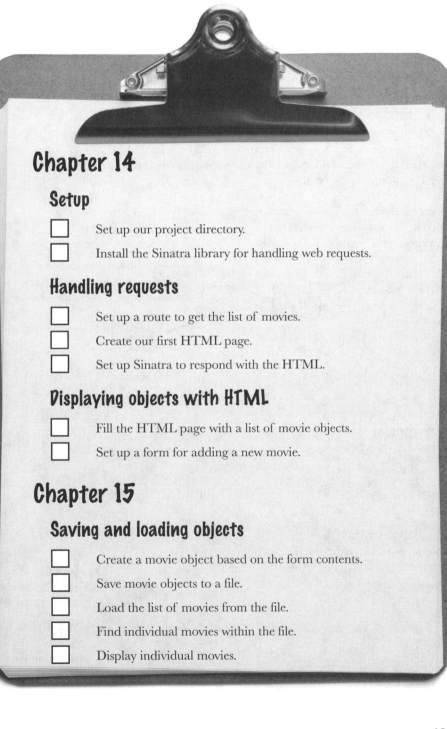

Chapter 14

Setup

☐ Set up our project directory.

☐ Install the Sinatra library for handling web requests.

Handling requests

☐ Set up a route to get the list of movies.

☐ Create our first HTML page.

☐ Set up Sinatra to respond with the HTML.

Displaying objects with HTML

☐ Fill the HTML page with a list of movie objects.

☐ Set up a form for adding a new movie.

Chapter 15

Saving and loading objects

☐ Create a movie object based on the form contents.

☐ Save movie objects to a file.

☐ Load the list of movies from the file.

☐ Find individual movies within the file.

☐ Display individual movies.

Project directory structure

By the end of Chapter 15, our project folder will look like this:

There are going to be several different files in our app before we're done. So we'll need a directory to hold the entire project. You can name it whatever you like, but we've chosen *movies*.

We'll also need two subdirectories to go inside the project directory. The first, *lib*, is going to hold Ruby source files (just like the *lib* directory we set up in Chapter 13).

We're also going to need a way to view our app's data. Since the app will be viewed in a web browser, that means we'll be using HTML files. We'll need a second subdirectory called *views* inside the project directory, alongside the *lib* directory.

So, create a directory named *movies*, and then place two directories inside it, named *lib* and *views*. (Don't worry about filling them with files right now; we'll create those as we go.)

```
movies
├── app.rb
├── movies.yml
├── lib
│   ├── movie.rb
│   └── movie_store.rb
└── views
    ├── index.erb
    ├── new.erb
    └── show.erb
```

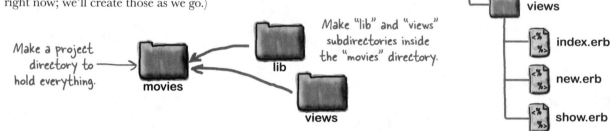

Make a project directory to hold everything.

Make "lib" and "views" subdirectories inside the "movies" directory.

movies   lib   views

That's all there is to it. Our first task is complete!

Setup

- ☑ Set up our project directory.
- ☐ Install the Sinatra library for handling web requests.

Next, we need to "install the Sinatra library for handling web requests." But what exactly is Sinatra? And what is a web request?

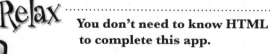

Relax

You don't need to know HTML to complete this app.

We'll explain just enough for you to understand the examples. If you're going to be doing more web development, though, we highly recommend picking up a copy of *Head First HTML and CSS* by Elisabeth Robson and Eric Freeman.

Browsers, requests, servers, and responses

When you type a URL into your browser, you're actually sending a *request* for a web page. That request goes to a *server*. A server's job is to get the appropriate page, and send it back to the browser in a *response*.

In the early days of the Web, the server usually read the contents of an HTML file on the server's hard drive, and sent that HTML back to the browser.

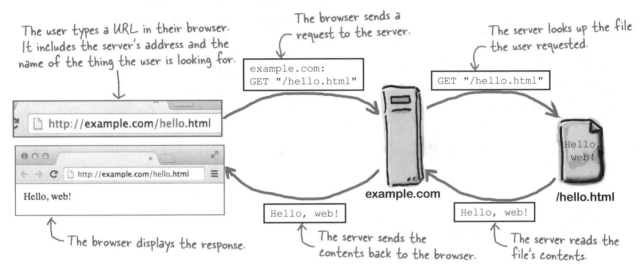

The user types a URL in their browser. It includes the server's address and the name of the thing the user is looking for.

The browser sends a request to the server.

The server looks up the file the user requested.

The browser displays the response.

The server sends the contents back to the browser.

The server reads the file's contents.

But today, it's much more common for the server to communicate with a *program* to fulfill the request, instead of reading from a file. And there's no reason that the program can't be written in Ruby!

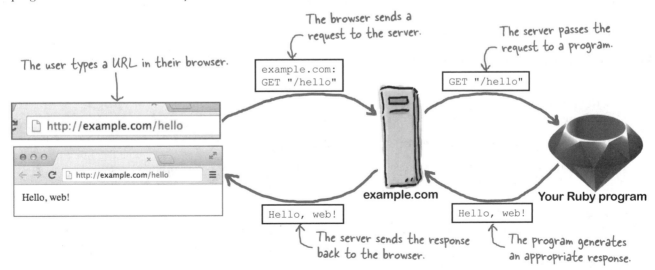

The user types a URL in their browser.

The browser sends a request to the server.

The server passes the request to a program.

The server sends the response back to the browser.

The program generates an appropriate response.

Sinatra takes requests

Handling a request from a browser is a lot of work. Fortunately, we don't have to do it all ourselves. We're going to rely on a library called Sinatra to receive the requests and return the responses. All *we* have to do is write the code that *generates* those responses.

But Sinatra isn't part of Ruby core (the classes and modules that are loaded every time you run Ruby). It's not even part of the Ruby standard library (the classes and libraries that are distributed with Ruby, but that have to be explicitly loaded by your program). Sinatra is an independently developed third-party library.

there are no Dumb Questions

Q: Don't you have to use Ruby on Rails to write web apps?

A: Many people have already heard of Ruby on Rails; it's the most popular web framework written in Ruby. But it's not the *only* framework. Sinatra is also very popular, in part because of its simplicity. Whereas a full Rails app spans dozens of classes and source code files, it's possible to write a Sinatra app in just a few lines of code. Many people find Sinatra apps easier to understand than Rails apps.

That's why we've chosen Sinatra for this introduction. But if you intend to go on to learn Rails next, don't worry. The skills you learn here will be relevant in Rails, too!

Downloading and installing libraries with RubyGems

When Ruby was a young language, users had to go through a lot before they could use a library like Sinatra:

- They had to find and download the source files.

- They had to decompress them.

- They had to figure out a good directory on their hard drive to put them in.

- They had to add that directory to the LOAD_PATH (the list of directories that Ruby searches in for files to load).

- If the library depended on *other* libraries, users had to perform the same steps for each of *those* libraries.

Needless to say, this was a pain. That's why Ruby is now distributed with the RubyGems tool, which manages all this complexity. With RubyGems, the process requires a lot less work on the user's part:

- A library author uses the RubyGems command-line tool to compress their source files together into a single, redistributable file, called a *gem*.

- The RubyGems tool uploads the gem to the central gem server, hosted at rubygems.org. (The site is free; it's supported by community donations.)

- Also using the RubyGems tool, users provide the name of a gem they want.

- RubyGems downloads the gem, decompresses it, installs it within a central directory of gems on the user's hard drive, and adds it to Ruby's LOAD_PATH. It then does the same for any other gems that the requested gem depends on.

The RubyGems tool is included with Ruby, so it's already installed on your system. And it makes a vast array of libraries available to you; a recent visit to rubygems.org showed that over 6,500 gems had been uploaded, and more are being added every week.

Installing the Sinatra gem

Let's try using RubyGems to install Sinatra now. You'll need an active Internet connection for this.

You invoke RubyGems using the gem command. In your terminal, type **gem install sinatra**. (It doesn't matter what directory you're in.) RubyGems will download and install several other gems that Sinatra depends on, then install Sinatra itself.

The command to install Sinatra →

RubyGems downloads and installs other gems that Sinatra depends on.

Downloading and installing Sinatra itself

```
File Edit Window Help
$ gem install sinatra
Fetching: rack-1.6.4.gem (100%)
Successfully installed rack-1.6.4
Fetching: rack-protection-1.5.3.gem (100%)
Successfully installed rack-protection-1.5.3
Fetching: tilt-2.0.1.gem (100%)
Successfully installed tilt-2.0.1
Fetching: sinatra-1.4.6.gem (100%)
Successfully installed sinatra-1.4.6
4 gems installed
$
```

Once the gem's installed, you can simply add require 'sinatra' to any Ruby program, and the Sinatra library will be loaded when that program runs!

Watch it!

Some operating systems might not let an ordinary user install files in the *gems* directory.

For security reasons, Mac OS X, Linux, and other Unix-based systems usually only let programs run by administrative users save files to the directory where gems are stored. If this is true for your OS, you may see an error message like this:

```
$ gem install sinatra
ERROR:  While executing gem ... (Gem::FilePermissionError)
    You don't have write permissions into the /var/lib/gems directory.
```

In such an event, try running the gem *command as an administrator by adding* sudo *(short for "super-user do" in front of it:* sudo gem install sinatra. *The OS may ask you for a password, and then the install should proceed normally.*

```
$ sudo gem install sinatra
[sudo] password for jay:
Fetching: rack-1.6.4.gem (100%)
Successfully installed rack-1.6.4
...
4 gems installed
```

A simple Sinatra app

We've installed the Sinatra gem, and our second task is complete.

We're ready to start handling requests from the browser!

We're still figuring out the basics of Sinatra, though. Before we dive into the movies app, let's take a few pages to demonstrate a simpler app as a warmup.

Setup

☑ Set up our project directory.

☑ Install the Sinatra library for handling web requests.

Handling requests

☐ Set up a route to get the list of movies.

☐ Create our first HTML page.

☐ Set up Sinatra to respond with the HTML.

Here's the code for a complete Sinatra app, which will deliver a short response to the browser. Save it to a file named *hello_web.rb*.

Save this to a file. →

```
require 'sinatra'

get('/hello') do
  'Hello, web!'
end
```

hello_web.rb

Pretty simple, right? Sinatra handles all the complexity of web requests for us. We'll describe the details in a couple of pages, but first let's try it out. In your terminal, change to the directory where you saved the file, and type:

```
ruby hello_web.rb
```

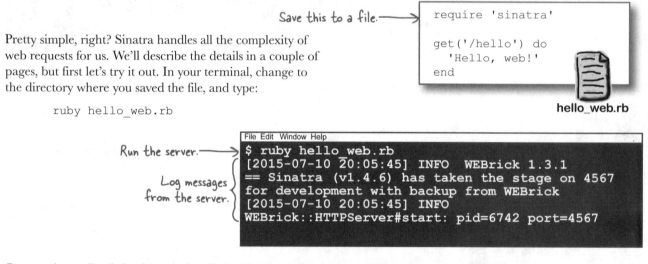

Run the server. →
```
$ ruby hello_web.rb
[2015-07-10 20:05:45] INFO  WEBrick 1.3.1
```
Log messages from the server.
```
== Sinatra (v1.4.6) has taken the stage on 4567
for development with backup from WEBrick
[2015-07-10 20:05:45] INFO
WEBrick::HTTPServer#start: pid=6742 port=4567
```

Our app immediately begins printing diagnostic messages to the console, to let us know that it's running. Now we just need to connect a web browser to it and test it out. Open your browser and type this URL into the address bar. (If the URL looks a little strange to you, don't worry: we'll explain what it means in a moment.)

```
http://localhost:4567/hello
```

The browser will send a request to the server, which will respond with `"Hello, web!"`. The request will also appear in the messages in your terminal. We've just sent our first data to the browser!

Sinatra will keep listening for requests until we stop it. When you're done with the page, press Ctrl-C in your terminal to signal Ruby to exit.

There's our app's response! → Hello, web!

`localhost:4567/hello`

Your computer is talking to itself

When we launched our little Sinatra app, it started its very own web server, right there on your computer, using a library called WEBrick (part of the Ruby standard library). Sinatra relies on a separate server like WEBrick for browsers to actually connect to. WEBrick forwards any requests it gets to Sinatra (or Rails, or whatever other web framework you're using).

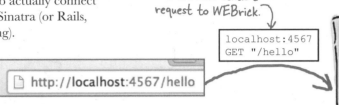

The browser sends a request to WEBrick.

```
localhost:4567
GET "/hello"
```

http://localhost:4567/hello

WEBrick
localhost:4567

Because the server program is running *on* your computer (and not somewhere out on the Internet), we use the special hostname `localhost` in the URL. This tells your browser that it needs to establish a connection *from* your computer *to* that same computer.

http://localhost:4567/hello
         Host   Port

We also need to specify a port as part of the URL. (A *port* is a numbered network communication channel that an application can listen for messages on.) From the log in the terminal, we can see that WEBrick is listening on port 4567, so we include that in the URL, following the hostname.

From the terminal log...

```
WEBrick::HTTPServer#start:
pid=6742 port=4567
```

Here's the port number.

there are no
Dumb Questions

Q: **I got an error saying the browser was unable to connect!**

A: Your server might not actually be running. Look for error messages in your terminal. Also check the hostname and port number in your browser; you might have mistyped them.

Q: **Why do I have to specify a port number in the URL? I don't have to do that with other websites!**

A: Most web servers listen on port 80, because that's the port that web browsers make requests to by default. But on many operating systems, you need special permissions to run a service that listens on port 80, for security reasons. That would be a pain for daily development work. So for apps that are still in development, Sinatra sets up WEBrick to listen on port 4567 instead.

Q: **My browser loaded a page saying, "Sinatra doesn't know this ditty."**

A: That's a response from the server, which is good, but it also means the resource you requested wasn't found. Check that your URL ends in */hello*, and ensure you haven't made a typo in *hello_web.rb*.

Q: **When I tried to run my app, I got a message saying "Someone is already performing on port 4567," and an "Address already in use" exception!**

A: Your Sinatra server is trying to listen on the same port as another program (which your OS won't allow). Have you run Sinatra more than once? If so, did you press Ctrl-C in the terminal to stop it when you were done? Be sure to stop the old server before running a new one. You can also specify a different port with the `-p` command-line option (so `sinatra myserver.rb -p 8080` would cause Sinatra to listen on port 8080).

Request type

So, thanks to the hostname and port in the URL, your browser's request got through to WEBrick. Now, WEBrick needs to pass along the request to Sinatra to generate a response.

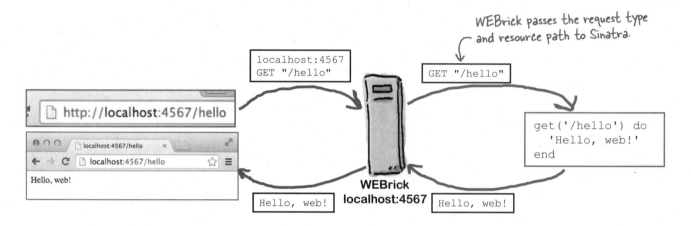

When forming a response, Sinatra needs to consider the request *type*. The request type specifies what *action* the browser wants to perform.

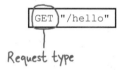

Browsers and servers communicate using HTTP, which stands for "**H**yper**T**ext **T**ransfer **P**rotocol." HTTP defines several *methods* (these aren't Ruby methods, but the meaning is similar) that a request can use. The most common methods are:

* GET: Used when your browser needs to *get* something from the server, usually because you entered a URL or clicked a link. This could be an HTML page, an image, or some other resource.

* POST: Used when your browser needs to *add* some data to the server, usually because you submitted a form with new data.

* PUT: Your browser needs to *change* some existing data on the server, usually because you submitted a form with modified data.

* DELETE: Your browser needs to *delete* some data from the server.

Our current request is a GET request. We entered a URL, and our browser knows that we want to *get* something in return. So it issued a request of the appropriate type.

Resource path

But *what* should we receive in response to our GET request? A server usually has lots of different resources that it can send to a browser, including HTML pages, images, and more.

The answer is there at the end of that URL we entered, following the hostname and port:

http://localhost:4567/hello

Path

That's the resource *path*. It tells the server which of its many resources you want to act on. Sinatra pulls the path off the end of the URL, and uses it when deciding how to respond to the request.

Resource path

So Sinatra is going to receive a GET request for the path '/hello'. How will it respond? That's up to *your* code!

Every HTTP request includes a request type (the method) and a resource path (the resource being accessed).

Sinatra routes

Sinatra uses *routes* to decide how to respond to a request. You specify the type of request that Sinatra should look for (GET, in this case), as well as a resource path. If an incoming request matches the given type and path, Sinatra will return the given response to the web server, which then passes it on to the browser.

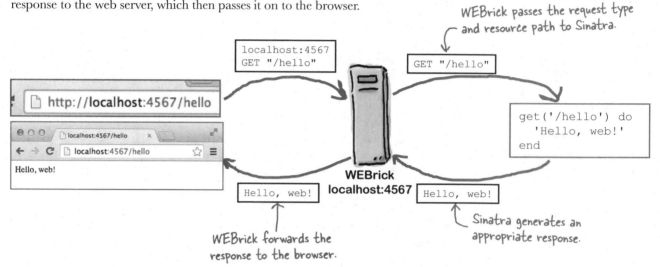

WEBrick passes the request type and resource path to Sinatra.

Sinatra generates an appropriate response.

WEBrick forwards the response to the browser.

Our script starts with `require 'sinatra'`, which loads the Sinatra library. This also defines several methods for setting up routes, including a method called `get`.

We make a single call to this `get` method, with the string `'/hello'` as an argument, and an associated block. This sets up a route for GET requests that have a path of `'/hello'`. Sinatra will save the block we provide, and call the block anytime it receives a GET request with a path of `'/hello'`.

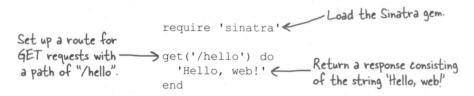

Load the Sinatra gem.

```
require 'sinatra'
get('/hello') do
  'Hello, web!'
end
```

Set up a route for GET requests with a path of "/hello".

Return a response consisting of the string 'Hello, web!'

Whatever value the block returns, Sinatra will return that value to the web server as its response. We set up this block to return the string `'Hello, web!'`, so that's what gets displayed in the browser!

There's our app's response!

Multiple routes in the same Sinatra app

Your app can't just respond `'Hello, web!'` to every request that comes in, though. You need to have it respond to different request paths in different ways.

You can accomplish this by setting up different routes for each path. Just call `get` once for each path, and provide a block that returns the appropriate response. Your app will then be able to respond to requests for any of those paths.

```ruby
require 'sinatra'

get('/hello') do
    'Hello, web!'
end

get('/salut') do
    'Salut web!'
end

get('/namaste') do
    'Namaste, web!'
end
```

Set up a route for GET requests with a path of "/hello". → `get('/hello') do`

Return a response consisting of the string 'Hello, web!'

Set up a route for GET requests with a path of "/salut". → `get('/salut') do`

Return a response consisting of the string 'Salut web!'

Set up a route for GET requests with a path of "/namaste". → `get('/namaste') do`

Return a response consisting of the string 'Namaste, web!'

```
● ● ●    localhost:4567/hello    ×
← → C    localhost:4567/hello

Hello, web!
```

```
● ● ●    localhost:4567/salut    ×
← → C    localhost:4567/salut

Salut web!
```

```
● ● ●    localhost:4567/namaste    ×
← → C    localhost:4567/namaste

Namaste, web!
```

Code Magnets

A Ruby program is all scrambled up on the fridge. Can you reconstruct the code snippets to make a Sinatra app that will accept GET requests for `'/sandwich'` and produce the response shown?

`'Make your own sandwich!'` `'sinatra'` `end` `get` `do` `require` `('/sandwich')`

Response:

```
● ● ●    localhost:4567/sandwich    ×
← → C    localhost:4567/sandwich    ☆    ≡

Make your own sandwich!
```

Code Magnets Solution

A Ruby program is all scrambled up on the fridge. Can you reconstruct the code snippets to make a Sinatra app that will accept GET requests for `'/sandwich'` and produce the response shown?

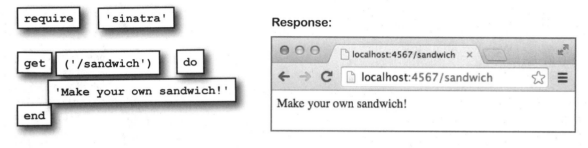

```
require   'sinatra'

get   ('/sandwich')   do
         'Make your own sandwich!'
end
```

Response:

A browser window showing localhost:4567/sandwich with the text "Make your own sandwich!"

A route for the list of movies

Now that we know how to create a Sinatra route, we're finally ready to set up a route for the list of movies! Save this code to a file named *app.rb*. Then move *app.rb* into your project directory, alongside the *lib* and *views* directories.

This will set up a route for GET requests to the `'/movies'` path. We'll just show some simple placeholder text for now.

You can run the app by changing to the directory it's saved to and entering **ruby app.rb**. Once Sinatra's running, visit `http://localhost:4567/movies` to view the page.

```ruby
require 'sinatra'

get('/movies') do
  'Coming Soon...'
end
```

movies / **app.rb**

Save this to app.rb in your project directory.

```
File  Edit  Window  Help
$ cd /tmp/movies
$ ruby app.rb
[2015-07-16 23:17:35] INFO
WEBrick 1.3.1
== Sinatra (v1.4.6) has taken
   the stage...
```

A browser window showing localhost:4567/movies with the text "Coming Soon..."

Our next task is done. Up next, we'll replace this placeholder text with some actual HTML!

Handling requests

☑ Set up a route to get the list of movies.

☐ Create our first HTML page.

☐ Set up Sinatra to respond with the HTML.

Making a movie list in HTML

So far, we've just been sending snippets of text to the browser. We need actual HTML, so that we can apply formatting to the page. HTML uses tags to apply formatting to text.

Don't worry if you haven't written HTML before; we'll be covering the basics as we go!

Before we try sending HTML from Sinatra, let's try making a plain HTML file in our text editor. Save the text below in a file named *index.html*.

Here are some noteworthy HTML tags used in this file:

- `<title>`: The page title to display in the browser tab.

- `<h1>`: A level-one heading. Usually shown in large, bold text.

- `<ul>`: An unordered list (usually shown as bullet points).

- `<li>`: A list item. Several of these are nested between the `<ul>` tags to form the list.

- `<a>`: Stands for "anchor." Creates a link.

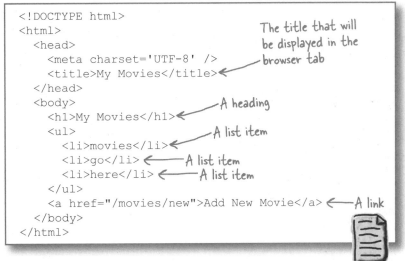

```html
<!DOCTYPE html>
<html>
  <head>
    <meta charset='UTF-8' />
    <title>My Movies</title>
  </head>
  <body>
    <h1>My Movies</h1>
    <ul>
      <li>movies</li>
      <li>go</li>
      <li>here</li>
    </ul>
    <a href="/movies/new">Add New Movie</a>
  </body>
</html>
```

The title that will be displayed in the browser tab

A heading

A list item
A list item
A list item

A link

index.html

Now, let's try viewing the HTML in a browser. Launch your favorite web browser, choose "Open File…" from the menu, and open the HTML file you just saved.

Notice how the elements on the page correspond with the HTML code…

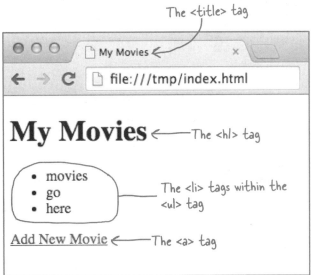

The `<title>` tag

My Movies ← The `<h1>` tag

The `<li>` tags within the `<ul>` tag

Add New Movie ← The `<a>` tag

You can click on the link if you want, but it will only produce a "page not found" error right now. We'll fix that later when we add a page for creating new movies.

Accessing the HTML from Sinatra

Our HTML file works great in the browser. That's another task complete!

No one *else* can see our HTML unless we make it available from our Sinatra app, though. Fortunately, there's an easy solution: Sinatra's `erb` method.

Handling requests

☑ Set up a route to get the list of movies.

☑ Create our first HTML page.

☐ Set up Sinatra to respond with the HTML.

The `erb` method reads the contents of a file within the app directory so that you can include those contents in Sinatra's response. It also uses the ERB library (part of the Ruby standard library) to let you embed Ruby code within the file, letting you customize the contents for each request. (ERB stands for "**e**mbedded **Rub**y.")

So all we have to do is place our HTML in a particular file, then call `erb` to include the HTML in Sinatra's response!

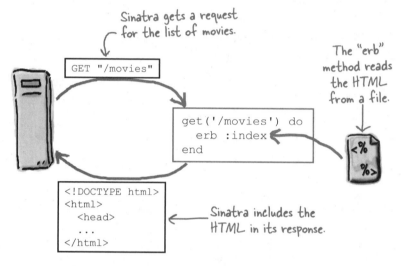

Sinatra gets a request for the list of movies.

```
GET "/movies"
```

```
get('/movies') do
  erb :index
end
```

The "erb" method reads the HTML from a file.

```
<!DOCTYPE html>
<html>
  <head>
  ...
</html>
```

Sinatra includes the HTML in its response.

The `erb` method takes a symbol as an argument, and converts that to a filename it should look for. By default, it looks for files in a subdirectory named *views* that have a filename ending in *.erb*. (These are known as ERB *templates*.)

If you call:	This template will be loaded:
`erb :index`	*movies/views/index.erb*
`erb :new`	*movies/views/new.erb*
`erb :show`	*movies/views/show.erb*

We want to be able to load our HTML with a call of `erb :index`. So you'll need to rename your *index.html* file to *index.erb*. Then move it into the *views* subdirectory within your project directory.

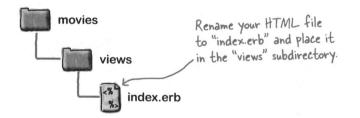

movies

views

index.erb

Rename your HTML file to "index.erb" and place it in the "views" subdirectory.

Accessing the HTML from Sinatra (continued)

We've got our HTML saved in the *index.erb* template within the *views* subdirectory:

```
<!DOCTYPE html>
<html>
  <head>
    <meta charset='UTF-8' />
    <title>My Movies</title>
  </head>
  <body>
    <h1>My Movies</h1>
    <ul>
      <li>movies</li>
      <li>go</li>
      <li>here</li>
    </ul>
    <a href="/movies/new">Add New Movie</a>
  </body>
</html>
```

views/index.erb

Now, let's set up our app to include the HTML in its response. Within the *app.rb* file you created before, replace the `'Coming soon...'` placeholder text with a call to `erb :index`.

The `erb` method returns the contents of the template as a string. Since the call to `erb` is the last expression in the block, that becomes the block's return value as well. And whatever the block returns becomes Sinatra's response to the web server.

```
require 'sinatra'

get('/movies') do          Responds to GET
                           requests for "/movies".
  erb :index          Load "views/index.erb".
end
```

app.rb

Let's see if it works. In your terminal, change to your project directory, and run the app with **ruby app.rb**. Then, in your browser, visit:

```
http://localhost:4567/movies
```

Sinatra will respond with the contents of our *index.erb* template!

Change to your project directory.

Run the app.

```
File Edit  Window Help
$ cd movies
$ ruby app.rb
[2015-07-10 20:05:45]
INFO  WEBrick 1.3.1
== Sinatra (v1.4.6) has
taken the stage on 4567
...
```

Sinatra responds with the contents of index.erb.

```
○ ○ ○     My Movies        ×
← → C   localhost:4567/movies

My Movies

  • movies
  • go
  • here

Add New Movie
```

A class to hold our movie data

ERB allows us to load our HTML page from Sinatra. That's another task complete.

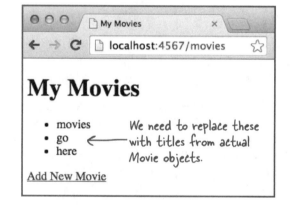

Handling requests

☑   Set up a route to get the list of movies.

☑   Create our first HTML page.

☑   Set up Sinatra to respond with the HTML.

Displaying objects with HTML

☐   Fill the HTML page with a list of movie objects.

☐   Set up a form for adding a new movie.

But the HTML we're displaying only has placeholder text where our movies are supposed to go. So our *next* task will be to create Ruby objects to hold our movie data, and then use those objects to fill in our HTML movie list.

My Movies

- movies
- go
- here

We need to replace these with titles from actual Movie objects.

Add New Movie

Of course, we can't create movie objects without a `Movie` class. Let's create one now. It'll be a very simple class, with three attributes: `title`, `director`, and `year`.

```ruby
class Movie
  attr_accessor :title, :director, :year
end
```

Mixing this class's code in with our Sinatra code would look rather messy, so let's save the `Movie` code in a separate file named *movie.rb* and place it in our *lib* directory.

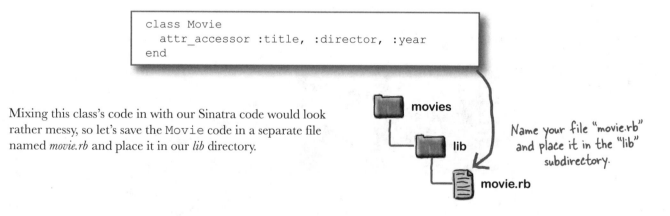

movies

lib

movie.rb

Name your file "movie.rb" and place it in the "lib" subdirectory.

Setting up a Movie object in the Sinatra app

Now let's create a `Movie` object within our Sinatra app.

In order to use the `Movie` class, we need to load the *movie.rb* file. We can do this with a call to `require` at the top of *app.rb*. (Remember, you can leave the *.rb* off; `require` will add it for you.)

With that done, we can create a new `Movie` instance within the block for the `get '/movies'` route. (We'll start with just one movie for now, and build up to a list later.) In a moment, we'll show you how to use the `Movie` object's data when generating the HTML page.

Notice that we're storing the `Movie` within an *instance* variable, not a local variable. We'll talk about the reason for this shortly.

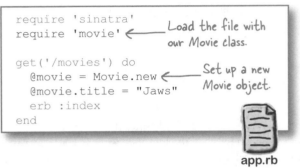

```ruby
require 'sinatra'
require 'movie'        ← Load the file with
                         our Movie class.

get('/movies') do          ← Set up a new
  @movie = Movie.new  ←       Movie object.
  @movie.title = "Jaws"
  erb :index
end
```

app.rb

Now that we're trying to `require` a file from the *lib* directory, we can't just run the app with `ruby app.rb` anymore. If we try, Ruby will report that it can't load *movie.rb*:

Can't find movie.rb! ——→

```
File Edit Window Help
$ cd movies
$ ruby app.rb
in `require': cannot load such file -- movie (LoadError)
$
```

As you may remember from Chapter 13, we need to add `-I lib` to the command line, to include the *lib* directory in the list of places that Ruby will search for files to load.

Add "lib" as a
directory that Ruby
can load files from. ——→
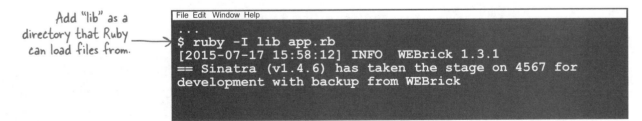

```
File Edit Window Help
...
$ ruby -I lib app.rb
[2015-07-17 15:58:12] INFO  WEBrick 1.3.1
== Sinatra (v1.4.6) has taken the stage on 4567 for
development with backup from WEBrick
```

We've got a movie object. How will we get it into the HTML page? We'll figure that part out next...

ERB embedding tags

Right now, our page consists of "static" (unchanging) HTML, with placeholder text where our movie titles should go. So how are we going to get our data into the page?

Remember that this isn't an ordinary HTML file; it's an "embedded Ruby" template. That means that we can stick Ruby code in the middle of it. When the `erb` method loads the template, it will evaluate the code. We can use Ruby code to embed the titles of our movies in the HTML!

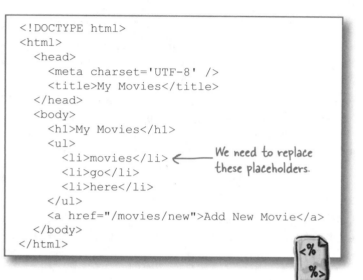

```
<!DOCTYPE html>
<html>
  <head>
    <meta charset='UTF-8' />
    <title>My Movies</title>
  </head>
  <body>
    <h1>My Movies</h1>
    <ul>
      <li>movies</li>    ←  We need to replace
      <li>go</li>           these placeholders.
      <li>here</li>
    </ul>
    <a href="/movies/new">Add New Movie</a>
  </body>
</html>
```

views/index.erb

But we can't just stick raw Ruby code into the middle of the file. The ERB parser wouldn't know which parts of the template were HTML, and which parts were Ruby. (If the Ruby interpreter tried to evaluate HTML, trust us, it wouldn't end well.)

```
<!DOCTYPE html>  ←  HTML code would
<html>              cause errors if it were
  <head>            treated as Ruby code!
    <meta charset='UTF-8' />
    <title>My Movies</title>
  </head>
  <body>
    <h1>My Movies</h1>
    <ul>
      <li>
        @movie.title  ←  We can't just stick Ruby
      </li>              code into the middle of
      <li>go</li>        the HTML!
      <li>here</li>
    </ul>
    <a href="/movies/new">Add New Movie</a>
  </body>
</html>
```

ERB lets you embed Ruby code within a plain-text template using embedding tags.

```
index.erb:1: syntax error, unexpected '<'
<!DOCTYPE html>
 ^
index.erb:2: syntax error, unexpected '<'
<html>
...
```

Instead, we need to embed our code within ERB *embedding tags*. These tags are used to mark Ruby code within an ERB template.

The ERB output embedding tag

One of the most commonly used ERB tags is <%= %>, the output embedding tag. Whenever ERB sees this tag, it will evaluate the Ruby code contained within the tag, convert the result to a string (if necessary), and insert that string into the surrounding text (in place of the tag).

Here's a modified version of our *index.erb* template with several output embedding tags:

```
<!DOCTYPE html>
<html>
  <body>
    <ul>
      <li><%= "A string" %></li>          Embed a plain string.
      <li><%= 15.0 / 6.0 %></li>          Embed the result of a math operation.
      <li><%= Time.now %></li>
    </ul>                                 Embed the current time.
  </body>
</html>
```

views/index.erb

Here's what that template looks like when converted to HTML:

```
<!DOCTYPE html>        The output embedding tags
<html>                 are each replaced with the
  <body>               result of their Ruby code.
    <ul>
      <li>A string</li>
      <li>2.5</li>
      <li>2015-07-18 12:35:38 -0700</li>
    </ul>
  </body>
</html>
```

And here's what that HTML looks like in the browser:

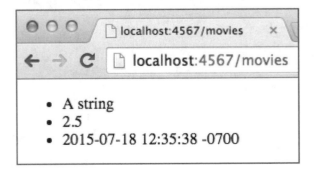

* A string
* 2.5
* 2015-07-18 12:35:38 -0700

Embedding a movie title in our HTML

In the route block, why did you store the `Movie` object in an **instance** variable instead of a local variable?

```ruby
require 'sinatra'
require 'movie'

get('/movies') do
  @movie = Movie.new
  @movie.title = "Jaws"
  erb :index
end
```

Sets up a new Movie object in an instance variable

app.rb

Instance variables defined within your Sinatra route blocks are also accessible within the ERB template. This allows your code in *app.rb* to work together with the code in your ERB template.

By storing our `Movie` object in the `@movie` instance variable within the Sinatra route block, we made it available for use within the ERB template! This will allow us to get data from the app into our HTML.

Let's change the placeholder text in *index.erb* to an output embedding tag with the `title` attribute of `@movie`. If we ensure the app is running and reload the page, we'll see our movie title!

Watch it!

Don't try to access local variables from your Sinatra route block in an ERB template!

Only instance variables from the main app will still be in scope within a template. (There is a way to set local variables in the template, but you'll have to consult the Sinatra documentation at http://sinatrarb.com for that.) If you try to access a variable that's local to the Sinatra route block, you'll get an error!

```html
<!DOCTYPE html>
<html>
  <head>
    <meta charset='UTF-8' />
    <title>My Movies</title>
  </head>
  <body>
    <h1>My Movies</h1>
    <ul>
      <li><%= @movie.title %></li>
    </ul>
    <a href="/movies/new">Add New Movie</a>
  </body>
</html>
```

Access the object that we defined in app.rb.

views/index.erb

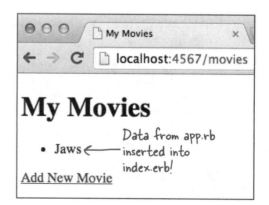

Data from app.rb inserted into index.erb!

Pool Puzzle

Your **job** is to take code snippets from the pool and place them into the blank lines in the three files below. **Don't** use the same snippet more than once, and you won't need to use all the snippets. Your **goal** is to make a Sinatra app that will run and produce the browser responses shown.

```
<!DOCTYPE html>
<html>
  <body>
    <%= @first %> plus
    <%= @second %> equals
    <%= _____ %>
  </body>
</html>
```
addition.erb

```
require _____

____('/addition') do
  @first = 3
  _____ = 5
  @result = _____ + @second
  erb _____
end

get(_____) do
  _____ = 2
  @second = 6
  _____ = @first * @second
  ____ :multiplication
end
```
app.rb

```
<!DOCTYPE html>
<html>
  <body>
    <%= @first %> times
    <%= _____ %> equals
    <%= @result %>
  </body>
</html>
```
multiplication.erb

Browser responses:

← → C localhost:4567/addition
3 plus 5 equals 8

← → C localhost:4567/multiplication
2 times 6 equals 12

Note: each thing from the pool can only be used once!

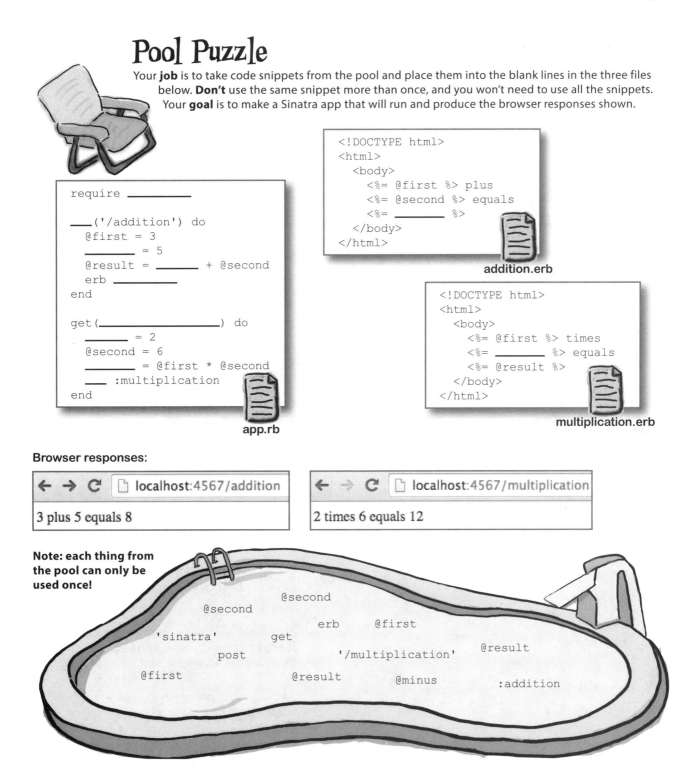

```
                    @second
@second
                        erb     @first
'sinatra'       get
        post            '/multiplication'      @result
@first          @result        @minus      :addition
```

Pool Puzzle Solution

Your **job** is to take code snippets from the pool and place them into the blank lines in the three files below. **Don't** use the same snippet more than once, and you won't need to use all the snippets. Your **goal** is to make a Sinatra app that will run and produce the browser responses shown.

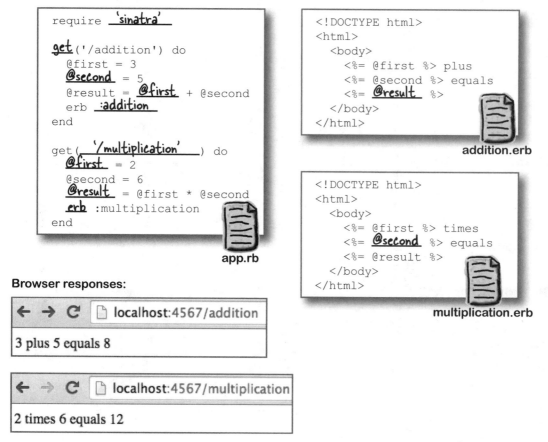

```ruby
require 'sinatra'

get('/addition') do
  @first = 3
  @second = 5
  @result = @first + @second
  erb :addition
end

get( '/multiplication' ) do
  @first = 2
  @second = 6
  @result = @first * @second
  erb :multiplication
end
```

app.rb

```html
<!DOCTYPE html>
<html>
  <body>
    <%= @first %> plus
    <%= @second %> equals
    <%= @result %>
  </body>
</html>
```

addition.erb

```html
<!DOCTYPE html>
<html>
  <body>
    <%= @first %> times
    <%= @second %> equals
    <%= @result %>
  </body>
</html>
```

multiplication.erb

Browser responses:

← → C localhost:4567/addition

3 plus 5 equals 8

← → C localhost:4567/multiplication

2 times 6 equals 12

there are no Dumb Questions

Q: I tried using `puts` inside an output embedding tag, like this: `<%= puts "hello" %>`. But I didn't get any output! Why?

A: The `puts` method may show the string `"hello"` in the *terminal*, but its *return value* is `nil`, and *that's* what ERB uses in your HTML (the `nil` gets converted to an empty string). So leave the `puts` off; that will most likely do what you want.

The regular embedding tag

The `<%= %>` output embedding tag allowed us to include *one* movie in our HTML. But we need to include a whole *list*. So we'll have to revise our ERB template.

A second commonly used ERB tag is `<% %>`, the regular embedding tag. (Unlike the output embedding tag, it doesn't have an equals sign.) It holds Ruby code that will be evaluated, but the results of which will not be directly inserted into the ERB output.

One common use of `<% %>` is to include certain HTML only if a condition is true, using `if` and `unless` statements. For example, if we used this code in *index.erb*, the first `<h1>` tag would be included in the output, but the second would be omitted:

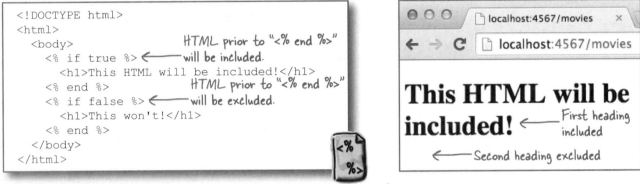

```
<!DOCTYPE html>
<html>
  <body>
    <% if true %>          HTML prior to "<% end %>"
      <h1>This HTML will be included!</h1>     will be included.
    <% end %>              HTML prior to "<% end %>"
    <% if false %>          will be excluded.
      <h1>This won't!</h1>
    <% end %>
  </body>
</html>
```

This HTML will be included! ← First heading included

← Second heading excluded

views/index.erb

Regular embedding tags are also often used with loops. If you embed a loop within an ERB template, any HTML or output embedding tags within the loop also get repeated.

If we used the below template in *index.erb*, it would loop over each item in the array, inserting a `<li>` HTML tag for each. And since the value for the `number` block parameter changes with each pass through the loop, the output embedding tag will insert a different number each time.

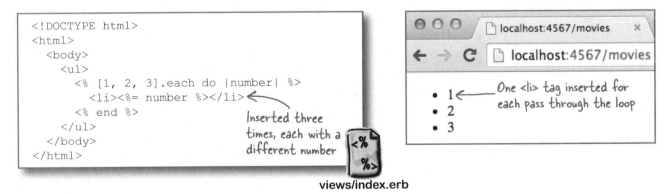

```
<!DOCTYPE html>
<html>
  <body>
    <ul>
      <% [1, 2, 3].each do |number| %>
        <li><%= number %></li>
      <% end %>
    </ul>
  </body>
</html>
```

Inserted three times, each with a different number

- 1 ← One `<li>` tag inserted for each pass through the loop
- 2
- 3

views/index.erb

Looping over several movie titles in our HTML

Now that we know how to use <% %> tags to add output for each item in an array, we're ready to process a whole array of Movie objects. So let's set up an array to process. (We'll "hardcode" it for now, to get us started. Later, we'll load in an array of movies from a file.)

Within the get('/movies') route block in *app.rb*, we'll replace the @movie instance variable with a @movies variable that holds an array. Then we'll add Movie objects to the array.

```ruby
require 'sinatra'
require 'movie'

get('/movies') do          Set up an
  @movies = []            array of movies.
  @movies[0] = Movie.new
  @movies[0].title = "Jaws"
  @movies[1] = Movie.new
  @movies[1].title = "Alien"
  @movies[2] = Movie.new
  @movies[2].title = "Terminator 2"
  erb :index
end
```

app.rb

Now we need to update our ERB template as well. In *index.erb*, we'll add <% %> tags that loop through each Movie in the array. Between the <% %> tags, we'll add an HTML <li> tag, and an ERB tag that outputs the current movie's title.

```erb
<!DOCTYPE html>
<html>
  <head>
    <meta charset='UTF-8' />
    <title>My Movies</title>
  </head>
  <body>
    <h1>My Movies</h1>
    <ul>
      <% @movies.each do |movie| %>
        <li><%= movie.title %></li>
      <% end %>
    </ul>
    <a href="/movies/new">Add New Movie</a>
  </body>
</html>
```

views/index.erb

If we restart Sinatra and reload the page, we'll see that an HTML <li> tag with a movie title has been inserted for each element in our @movies array!

localhost:4567/movies

My Movies

- Jaws
- Alien
- Terminator 2

One <li> for each item in @movies!

Add New Movie

Looping over several movie titles in our HTML (continued)

We've set up ERB embedding tags to display a list of movie titles in our HTML. That's another task complete!

Displaying objects with HTML

☑ Fill the HTML page with a list of movie objects.

☐ Set up a form for adding a new movie.

Exercise

Below is an ERB template. Determine what its result will be, then fill in the blanks in the output to the right.

(We've filled in the first one for you.)

```
<!DOCTYPE html>
<html>
  <body>
    <% [1, 2, 3, 4].each do |number| %>
      <% if number.even? %>
        <li><%= number %> is even.</li>
      <% else %>
        <li><%= number %> is odd.</li>
      <% end %>
    <% end %>
  </body>
</html>
```

Output:

```
<!DOCTYPE html>
<html>
  <body>
```
    <li>I is odd.</li>
    ....
    ....
    ....
```
  </body>
</html>
```

Exercise Solution

Below is an ERB template. Determine what its result will be, then fill in the blanks in the output to the right.

```
<!DOCTYPE html>
<html>
  <body>
    <% [1, 2, 3, 4].each do |number| %>
     <% if number.even? %>
       <li><%= number %> is even.</li>
     <% else %>
       <li><%= number %> is odd.</li>
     <% end %>
   <% end %>
  </body>
</html>
```

Output:

```
<!DOCTYPE html>
<html>
  <body>
```
       <li>1 is odd.</li>

       <li>2 is even.</li>

       <li>3 is odd.</li>

       <li>4 is even.</li>
```
  </body>
</html>
```

Letting users add data with HTML forms

Our app can display an HTML list of movies now, but it only has three movies. It's hard to imagine anyone bookmarking our site at this point. To make the app more compelling, we need to give users the ability to add their own movies.

What we have so far...

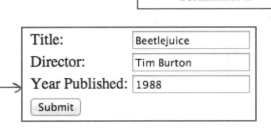

To allow users to add movies to our site, we're going to need HTML *forms*. A form usually provides one or more fields that a user can enter data into, and a submit button that allows them to send the data to the server.

We need an HTML form.

Below is HTML for a really simple form. There are some new tags here that we haven't seen before:

- `<form>`: This tag encloses all the other form components.

- `<label>`: A label for one of the form inputs. The value of its `for` attribute needs to match the `name` attribute of one of the `input` elements.

- `<input>` with a `type` attribute of `"text"`: A text field where the user can enter a string. Its `name` attribute will be used to label the field's value in the data sent to the server (kind of like a hash key).

- `<input>` with a `type` attribute of `"submit"`: Creates a button that the user can click to submit the form's data.

```
<!DOCTYPE html>
<html>
  <body>
    <form>
      <label for="food">Enter your favorite food:</label>
      <input type="text" name="food">
      <input type="submit">
    </form>
  </body>
</html>
```

This label is for the "food" input.

This label text will be shown within the page.

The "food" text input

A button that submits the form data

If we were to load this HTML in the browser, it would look like this:

```
new.html                    ×
←  →  C    file:///tmp/new.html                    ≡

Enter your favorite food: spaghetti|    Submit
```

The label

The text input

The submit button

Seems simple enough! Let's set up our app to load an HTML form for a movie's data and display it in the browser.

Getting an HTML form for adding a movie

When we visit `http://localhost:4567/movies` currently, our app calls `erb :index` and displays the HTML from the *index.erb* file in the *views* directory. Now we need to add a second page with the HTML form to add a new movie...

To do that, we'll need to add a second route to *app.rb*, right after the first. We'll set it up to handle GET requests for the `'/movies/new'` path. In the route's block, we'll add a call to `erb :new` so that it loads an ERB template from *new.erb* in the *views* directory.

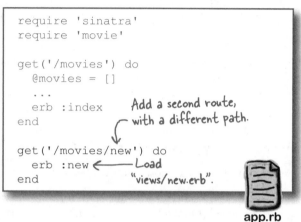

```ruby
require 'sinatra'
require 'movie'

get('/movies') do
  @movies = []
  ...
  erb :index          Add a second route,
end                   with a different path.

get('/movies/new') do
  erb :new  ←——Load
end           "views/new.erb".
```

app.rb

Now let's create the ERB template for our form. We don't need to embed any Ruby objects here, so this file will be pure HTML, without any ERB tags.

At the top of the page, we'll set an appropriate title using the `<title>` tag, and a heading using the `<h1>` tag.

Then we'll begin the form, using the `<form>` tag. Instead of having just one text input in this form, we'll have three: one for the movie's title, another for its director, and a third for the year it was released. Each `<input>` tag will have a different `name` attribute, to differentiate them. Each input will also have a corresponding `<label>`. As before, there will be a submit button at the end of the form.

Lastly, we include a link to the */movies* path at the bottom of the page, which the user can click to return to the movie list.

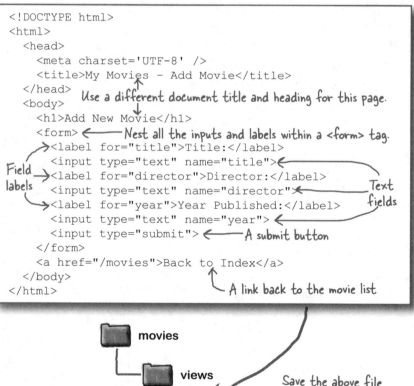

```html
<!DOCTYPE html>
<html>
  <head>
    <meta charset='UTF-8' />
    <title>My Movies - Add Movie</title>
  </head>
  <body>        Use a different document title and heading for this page.
    <h1>Add New Movie</h1>
    <form>  ←——Nest all the inputs and labels within a <form> tag.
      <label for="title">Title:</label>
      <input type="text" name="title">
      <label for="director">Director:</label>
      <input type="text" name="director">
      <label for="year">Year Published:</label>
      <input type="text" name="year">
      <input type="submit">  ←——A submit button
    </form>
    <a href="/movies">Back to Index</a>
  </body>
</html>
```

Field labels

Text fields

A link back to the movie list

As before, we need to save the template where the `erb` method will find it. Save it to a file named *new.erb*, within the *views* subdirectory.

movies → views → new.erb

Save the above file as "new.erb" within the "views" subdirectory.

HTML tables

Let's try out our new form! Restart your Sinatra app, and type the URL:

`http://localhost:4567/movies/new`

…into your address bar. (Or just click Add New Movie at the bottom of the index page; that link should work now that we've added a route for it.)

The form loads, but it's hard to read! The fields are all jumbled together. Let's take a moment to fix that, using tables.

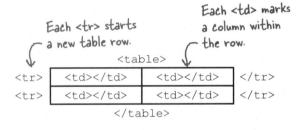

The form loads, but the fields aren't arranged neatly…

HTML tables can arrange your text, form fields, and other content into rows and columns. The most commonly used HTML tags for making tables are:

- `<table>`: This tag encloses all the other table components.

- `<tr>`: Stands for "table row." Each row contains data in one or more columns.

- `<td>`: Stands for "table data." There are usually several `<td>` elements nested within one `<tr>` element, each marking a column's worth of data.

Each `<tr>` starts a new table row.

Each `<td>` marks a column within the row.

```
                <table>
<tr>    <td></td>    <td></td>    </tr>
<tr>    <td></td>    <td></td>    </tr>
                </table>
```

Here's a simple HTML table, along with what it looks like in the browser. (Normally the table borders are invisible by default, but we've added them for clarity.)

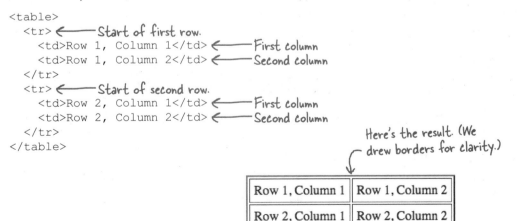

```
<table>
  <tr>              Start of first row.
    <td>Row 1, Column 1</td>        First column
    <td>Row 1, Column 2</td>        Second column
  </tr>
  <tr>              Start of second row.
    <td>Row 2, Column 1</td>        First column
    <td>Row 2, Column 2</td>        Second column
  </tr>
</table>
```

Here's the result. (We drew borders for clarity.)

| Row 1, Column 1 | Row 1, Column 2 |
| Row 2, Column 1 | Row 2, Column 2 |

Cleaning up our form with an HTML table

Let's clean up our form's crowded appearance using a table. Modify
new.erb as you see here:

```
<!DOCTYPE html>
<html>
  ...
  <body>
    <h1>Add New Movie</h1>
    <form>                ← Nest the HTML table inside the form.
      <table>←
        <tr>←         Start a new row for each label/input pair.         The label goes in
          <td><label for="title">Title:</label></td>←                    the first column.
          <td><input type="text" name="title"></td>←                     The input goes in
        </tr>                                                            the second column.
        <tr>←         A new row for the next input
          <td><label for="director">Director:</label></td>
          <td><input type="text" name="director"></td>
        </tr>
        <tr>←         A new row for the next input
          <td><label for="year">Year Published:</label></td>
          <td><input type="text" name="year"></td>
        </tr>
        <tr>←         The submit button gets a row to itself.
          <td><input type="submit"></td>←     There is no second column here.
        </tr>
      </table>←     End the table before
    </form>          ending the form.
    <a href="/movies">Back to Index</a>
  </body>
</html>
```

views/new.erb

If you visit the `'/movies/new'` path again, you'll see the form
arranged much more neatly!

A column for all the labels
A row for the title
A row for the director
A row for the year
The submit button gets a row to itself

Add New Movie

A column for all the text inputs

Title:
Director:
Year Published:
Submit
Back to Index

There's still more to do

The '/movies/new' route is responding with our HTML form. That's the last of our tasks for this chapter!

Displaying objects with HTML

☑ Fill the HTML page with a list of movie objects.

☑ Set up a form for adding a new movie.

Chapter 15

Saving and loading objects

☐ Create a movie object based on the form contents.

☐ Save movie objects to a file.

☐ Load the list of movies from the file.

☐ Find individual movies within the file.

☐ Display individual movies.

But...if you fill in that form and click Submit, not much happens! Our Sinatra app is set up to respond to HTTP GET requests to load the form, but there's no way for the form to post the data back to the server.

Nothing happens if you click Submit! ——→

Title:	Beetlejuice
Director:	Tim Burton
Year Published:	1988

[Submit]

Looks like we still have some work to do. Don't worry—we'll fix this (and more) in the next chapter!

Your Ruby Toolbox

That's it for Chapter 14! You've added Sinatra and ERB to your toolbox.

Sinatra

Sinatra is a "gem," a third-party library distributed separately from Ruby. Gems can be downloaded and installed automatically through the RubyGems tool.

Sinatra uses routes to determine how to handle each request from a web browser.

ERB

ERB stands for "embedded Ruby." It's a library that allows you to evaluate Ruby code and embed the results in a text template.

<% %> ERB tags are often used for conditional statements or loops.

<%= %> ERB tags are used to include a value in the output.

BULLET POINTS

- Typing a URL into a web browser or clicking a link causes the browser to send an HTTP GET request to the web server.

- GET requests include a resource path, which indicates which resource the browser needs to retrieve.

- Within a Sinatra app, to set up a route for GET requests, you call the `get` method with a resource path string and a block. From then on, GET requests for that path will be handled by the block you provided.

- If a route's block returns a string value, that string will be sent back to the browser in the response.

- Typically, Sinatra's response should be in HTML (HyperText Markup Language) format. HTML allows you to define the structure of a web page.

- The `erb` method loads a file from the *views* subdirectory with a name ending in *.erb*. It then evaluates any embedded Ruby code and returns the result as a string.

- ERB templates rendered by a Sinatra route's block can access instance variables from that block.

- An HTML form allows users to enter data into a web page.

- HTML tables format data in rows and columns.

Up Next...

This is it! The next chapter is the last. (Well, except for the appendix.) We've shown you how to present a form for users to enter data in their browser; we'll wrap things up by showing you how to *save* that data, and *load* it back in later.

15 saving and loading data

Keep It Around

> Whoops! You know, maybe I shouldn't throw this away. I'd better store it somewhere I can retrieve it later.

Your web app is just throwing users' data away. You've set up a form for users to *enter* data into. They're expecting that you'll *save* it, so that it can be *retrieved* and *displayed* to others later. But that's not happening right now! Anything they submit just *disappears*.

In this, our final chapter, we'll prepare your app to save user submissions. We'll show you how to set it up to accept form data. We'll show you how to convert that data to Ruby objects, how to save those objects to a file, and how to retrieve the right object again when a user wants to see it. Are you ready? Let's finish this app!

Saving and retrieving form data

In the last chapter, we learned how to use the Sinatra library to respond to HTTP GET requests from a browser. We built a `Movie` class and embedded movie data into an HTML page.

We even learned how to serve an HTML form so that users can enter new movie data.

But that's as far as HTTP GET requests can take us. We have no way to submit that form back to the server. And we wouldn't know how to save the form data if we got it.

In this chapter, we're going to fix all that! We'll learn how to take the user's form data and convert it to Ruby objects for easy storage. We'll also learn how to save those objects to a file and then retrieve them for display later. This chapter is going to bring your movie data full-circle!

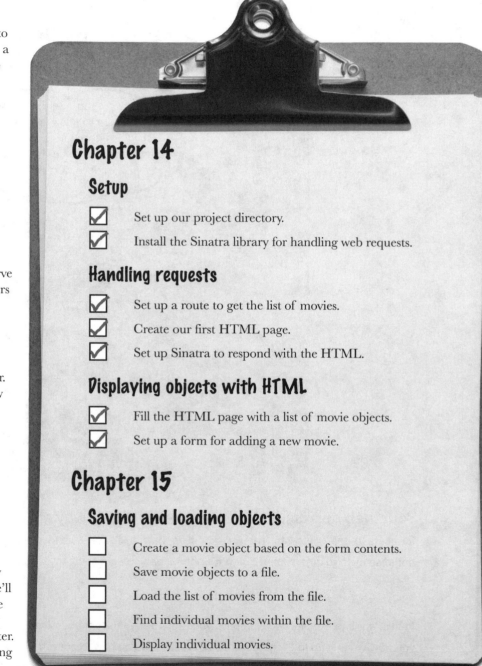

Chapter 14

Setup

- ☑ Set up our project directory.
- ☑ Install the Sinatra library for handling web requests.

Handling requests

- ☑ Set up a route to get the list of movies.
- ☑ Create our first HTML page.
- ☑ Set up Sinatra to respond with the HTML.

Displaying objects with HTML

- ☑ Fill the HTML page with a list of movie objects.
- ☑ Set up a form for adding a new movie.

Chapter 15

Saving and loading objects

- ☐ Create a movie object based on the form contents.
- ☐ Save movie objects to a file.
- ☐ Load the list of movies from the file.
- ☐ Find individual movies within the file.
- ☐ Display individual movies.

Saving and retrieving form data (continued)

Our users will be entering movie data into a form. We need a sensible format in which to store the data so that we can retrieve it later and display it. So we're going to convert the form data to `Movie` objects and assign each `Movie` a unique ID. Then, we'll save the `Movie` to a file.

Later, we'll be able to go through the file and create a set of links containing all the `Movie` IDs. When a user clicks a link, we'll get the ID from the link they clicked and retrieve the appropriate `Movie`.

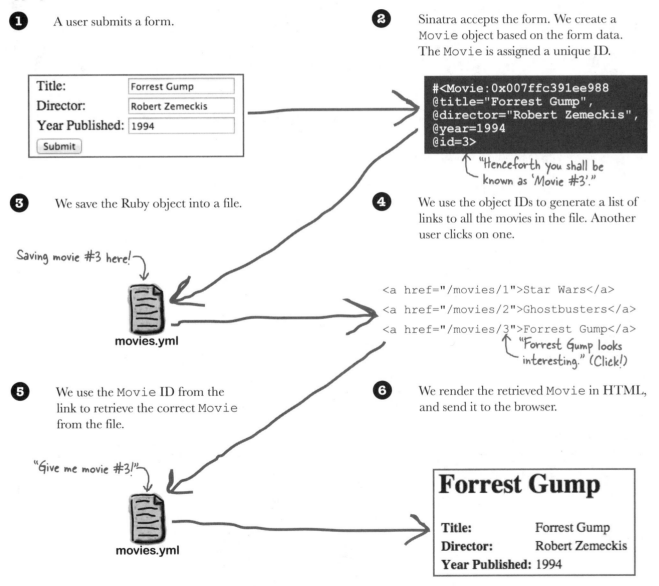

1 A user submits a form.

Title: Forrest Gump
Director: Robert Zemeckis
Year Published: 1994
Submit

2 Sinatra accepts the form. We create a `Movie` object based on the form data. The `Movie` is assigned a unique ID.

```
#<Movie:0x007ffc391ee988
@title="Forrest Gump",
@director="Robert Zemeckis",
@year=1994
@id=3>
```

"Henceforth you shall be known as 'Movie #3'."

3 We save the Ruby object into a file.

Saving movie #3 here!

movies.yml

4 We use the object IDs to generate a list of links to all the movies in the file. Another user clicks on one.

```
<a href="/movies/1">Star Wars</a>
<a href="/movies/2">Ghostbusters</a>
<a href="/movies/3">Forrest Gump</a>
```

"Forrest Gump looks interesting." (Click!)

5 We use the `Movie` ID from the link to retrieve the correct `Movie` from the file.

"Give me movie #3!"

movies.yml

6 We render the retrieved `Movie` in HTML, and send it to the browser.

Forrest Gump

Title: Forrest Gump
Director: Robert Zemeckis
Year Published: 1994

Our browser can GET the form...

When we left off last chapter, we had just added a form to our Sinatra app for movie data. The browser can submit a GET request for the `'/movies/new'` path, and Sinatra will respond with an HTML form. But nothing happens when the user clicks Submit!

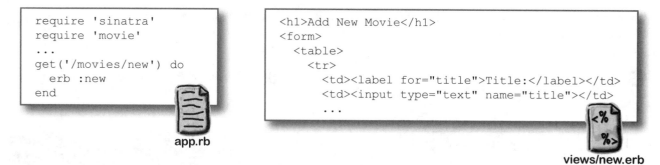

```
require 'sinatra'
require 'movie'
...
get('/movies/new') do
  erb :new
end
```
app.rb

```
<h1>Add New Movie</h1>
<form>
  <table>
    <tr>
      <td><label for="title">Title:</label></td>
      <td><input type="text" name="title"></td>
      ...
```
views/new.erb

Here's the problem: submitting an HTML form actually requires *two* requests to the server: one to *get* the form, and a second to *send* the user's entries back to the server.

We're already set up to handle the GET request for the form:

1. A user visits the `'/movies/new'` resource by typing a URL or clicking a link.

2. The browser sends an HTTP GET request for the `'/movies/new'` resource to the server (WEBrick).

3. The server forwards the GET request to Sinatra.

4. Sinatra invokes the block for its `get('/movies/new')` route.

5. The block responds with the form's HTML.

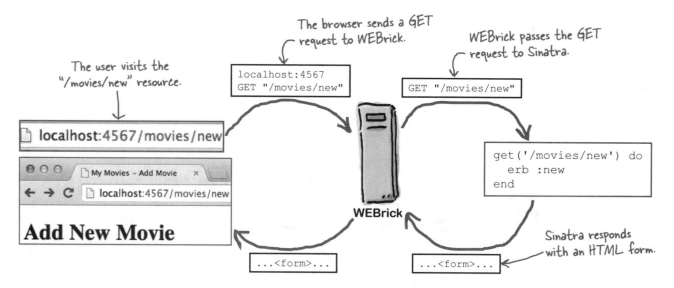

The user visits the "/movies/new" resource.

The browser sends a GET request to WEBrick.

WEBrick passes the GET request to Sinatra.

```
localhost:4567
GET "/movies/new"
```

```
GET "/movies/new"
```

localhost:4567/movies/new

My Movies – Add Movie

localhost:4567/movies/new

Add New Movie

```
get('/movies/new') do
  erb :new
end
```

WEBrick

Sinatra responds with an HTML form.

...<form>...   ...<form>...

...But it needs to POST the response

Now we need to set up Sinatra to handle an HTTP *POST* request, to process the form contents. Whereas GET requests *get data from* the server, POST requests *add data to* the server. (Why's it called "POST"? When you want to make a message available for others to read, you *post* it somewhere—same idea.)

The whole process goes like this:

1. The user fills in the form with a movie's data and clicks Submit.

2. The browser sends an HTTP POST request for the `'/movies/create'` resource to the server (WEBrick). The request includes all the form data.

3. The server forwards the POST request to Sinatra.

4. Sinatra invokes the block for its `post('/movies/create')` route.

5. The block gets the form data from the request and stores it.

6. The block responds with some HTML that indicates the data was received successfully.

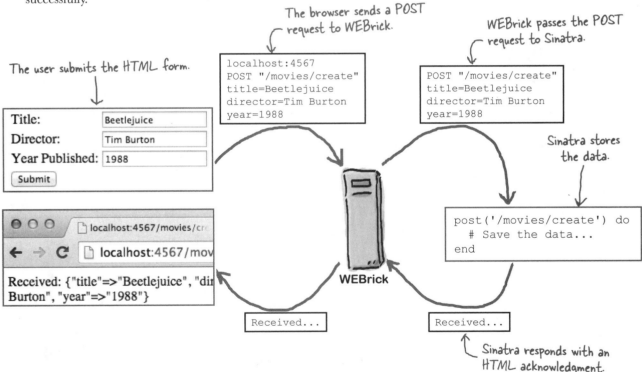

The user submits the HTML form.

The browser sends a POST request to WEBrick.

WEBrick passes the POST request to Sinatra.

Sinatra stores the data.

Sinatra responds with an HTML acknowledgment.

Setting the HTML form to send a POST request

The first step in processing form data is to ensure that the data reaches the server. And to do that, we need to configure the form to send a POST request. We'll need to add two attributes to the `<form>` tag in our HTML:

- `method`: The HTTP request method to use.

- `action`: A resource path for the request. This will be matched to a Sinatra route.

The user submits the HTML form.

Title: | Beetlejuice
Director: | Tim Burton
Year Published: | 1988

Submit

The browser sends a POST request.

```
localhost:4567
POST "/movies/create"
title=Beetlejuice
director=Tim Burton
year=1988
```

WEBrick

Let's modify the HTML in our *new.erb* file to add these attributes to the form. Since we want to use the POST method, we'll set the `method` attribute to `"post"`. Then we'll set the resource path in the `action` attribute to `"/movies/create"`.

```
<!DOCTYPE html>
<html>
  ...
  <body>
    <h1>Add New Movie</h1>
    <form method="post" action="/movies/create">
      <table>
        <tr>
          <td><label for="title">Title:</label></td>
          <td><input type="text" name="title"></td>
        </tr>
        ...
```

Submit this form by sending a POST request to "/movies/create".

views/new.erb

That sets up the form to *send* a POST request, but we don't have any way to *handle* the request yet. We'll take care of that next…

Setting up a Sinatra route for a POST request

We have the HTML form submitting POST requests to the '/movies/create' path. Now we need to set Sinatra up to process those requests.

To set up a Sinatra route for HTTP GET requests, you call the `get` method. And to set up a route for POST requests, you call—you guessed it—the `post` method. It works just like the `get` method; the method name represents the type of request it will look for, and it takes a string argument with the resource path to look for in the request. Like `get`, `post` also takes a block that will be called whenever a matching request is received.

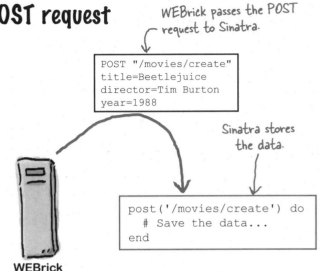

WEBrick passes the POST request to Sinatra.

```
POST "/movies/create"
title=Beetlejuice
director=Tim Burton
year=1988
```

Sinatra stores the data.

WEBrick

```
post('/movies/create') do
  # Save the data...
end
```

Within the block for a `post` route, you can call the `params` method to get a hash containing the form data from the request.

Let's set up a simple `post` route so that we can get a look at the form data. In the *app.rb* file, we'll call `post` with a resource path matching the one we set up in the form: '/movies/create'. We'll have the block simply return a string with the value of `params.inspect` to the browser.

```
require 'sinatra'
require 'movie'

get('/movies') do
  @movies = []
  ...
  erb :index
end

get('/movies/new') do
  erb :new
end

post('/movies/create') do
  "Received: #{params.inspect}"
end
```

Handle POST requests for '/movies/create'.

Send a string containing the form data back to the browser.

app.rb

Setting up a Sinatra route for a POST request (continued)

We've set our HTML form up
to send a POST request...

```
<form method="post" action="/movies/create">
   ...
</form>
```

And we've set up a corresponding route in our Sinatra app...

```
post('/movies/create') do
  "Received: #{params.inspect}"
end
```

Let's try out our new route. Restart the app and reload the
form page in your browser. Fill out the form using any movie
you'd like, and click Submit.

Fill out the form
and click Submit.

The form will submit a POST request to Sinatra,
which will respond with a plain-text string
representing the `params` hash.

There's the "params" hash,
with our form data!

Received: {"title"=>"Beetlejuice", "director"=>"Tim
Burton", "year"=>"1988"}

Lastly, let's create a `Movie` object based on the contents of the `params` hash.
We'll update the route block in *app.rb* to assign a new `Movie` object to an instance
variable. Then, we'll assign each of the hash values to an attribute of the `Movie`.

```
require 'sinatra'
require 'movie'
...
post('/movies/create') do
  @movie = Movie.new
  @movie.title = params['title']
  @movie.director = params['director']
  @movie.year = params['year']
end
```

Create a new
Movie instance.

Assign the
contents of the
form fields to
attributes of
the object.

app.rb

Setting up a Sinatra route for a POST request (continued)

We've written a Sinatra route that accepts the form data and uses it to populate the attributes of a new `Movie` object. That's another task complete!

We're not saving that `Movie` object anywhere right now, though. Fixing that will be our next task.

Saving and loading objects

- ☑ Create a movie object based on the form contents.
- ☐ Save movie objects to a file.
- ☐ Load the list of movies from the file.
- ☐ Find individual movies within the file.
- ☐ Display individual movies.

Exercise

Files for a Sinatra app and an ERB template are below. Fill in the blanks in both files so that the browser will display the form shown when the URL `http://localhost:4567/form` is requested, and display the result shown when the form is submitted.

```ruby
require 'sinatra'

get(_____) do
  erb _____
end

_____('/convert') do
  fahrenheit = _____['temperature'].to_f
  celsius = (fahrenheit - 32) / 1.8
  format("%0.1f degrees Fahrenheit is %0.1f degrees Celsius.", fahrenheit, celsius)
end
```

app.rb

```html
<!DOCTYPE html>
<html>
  <body>
    <form _____="post" action="_____">
      <label for="temperature">Degrees Fahrenheit:</label>
      <input type="text" name="_____">
      <input type="submit">
    </form>
  </body>
</html>
```

views/form.erb

Responses:

← → C localhost:4567/form ☆
Degrees Fahrenheit: 75   Submit

← → C localhost:4567/convert ☆
75.0 degrees Fahrenheit is 23.9 degrees Celsius.

Files for a Sinatra app and an ERB template are below. Fill in the blanks in both files so that the browser will display the form shown when the URL `http://localhost:4567/form` is requested, and display the result shown when the form is submitted.

```ruby
require 'sinatra'

get('/form') do
  erb :form
end

post('/convert') do
  fahrenheit = params['temperature'].to_f
  celsius = (fahrenheit - 32) / 1.8
  format("%0.1f degrees Fahrenheit is %0.1f degrees Celsius.", fahrenheit, celsius)
end
```

app.rb

```html
<!DOCTYPE html>
<html>
  <body>
    <form method="post" action="/convert">
      <label for="temperature">Degrees Fahrenheit:</label>
      <input type="text" name="temperature">
      <input type="submit">
    </form>
  </body>
</html>
```

views/form.erb

Responses:

← → C localhost:4567/form ☆
Degrees Fahrenheit: 75   Submit

← → C localhost:4567/convert ☆
75.0 degrees Fahrenheit is 23.9 degrees Celsius.

Converting objects to and from strings with YAML

We've added code to convert our HTML
form's data to a `Movie` object:

```
post('/movies/create') do
  @movie = Movie.new
  @movie.title = params['title']
  @movie.director = params['director']
  @movie.year = params['year']
end
```

But that object disappears as soon as we create it. We need to save it somewhere!

The `YAML` library, which comes with Ruby as part of its standard library, can help.
YAML stands for "YAML Ain't Markup Language," and it's a standard for representing
objects and other data in string form. Those strings can be saved to files, and converted
back to objects later. You can read more about the YAML standard on its website at:

> *http://yaml.org*

Before we try saving the YAML to a file, let's try converting some objects to strings, so we
can see what the YAML format looks like. Don't worry, you don't actually need to *know*
YAML. The YAML library will convert Ruby objects to and from YAML format for you!

The `YAML` module has a `dump` method that can convert almost any Ruby object to a
string representation. The code below creates a `Movie` object, then dumps it to a string:

```
require 'movie'   ← ─── Load the Movie class.
require 'yaml'    ← ─── Load the YAML module.
```

Create a Movie object.
```
movie = Movie.new
movie.title = "Fight Club"
movie.director = "David Fincher"
movie.year = 1999
```
─── The class of the object

```
puts YAML.dump(movie)
```

The object's attributes and their values

```
--- !ruby/object:Movie
title: Fight Club
director: David Fincher
year: 1999
```

The `YAML` module also has a `load` method that takes a string with YAML data and
converts it back to an object. This will help us load our saved objects back in later.

This code dumps the above `Movie` object to a YAML string, then converts
that string back to an object, with all the attribute values intact:

```
movie_yaml = YAML.dump(movie)   ← ─── Save the YAML string to a variable.
copy = YAML.load(movie_yaml)    ← ─── Convert the YAML string back into an object.
puts copy.title, copy.director, copy.year
```

All the old object's
attributes will be intact!

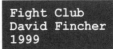
```
Fight Club
David Fincher
1999
```

Saving objects to a file with YAML::Store

Converting the objects to strings and back is only half of the solution, though—we still need to be able to save them for later. The YAML library includes a class named `YAML::Store`, which can save Ruby objects to disk and load them back in later.

The code for adding objects to a `YAML::Store` instance and retrieving them later looks very similar to the code for accessing a hash. You specify a key and a value you want to assign to that key. Later, you can access that same key and get the same value back.

The big difference, of course, is that `YAML::Store` saves the keys and values to a file. You can restart your program, or even access the file from a completely different program, and the keys and values will still be there.

To use `YAML::Store` within our Ruby code, we first need to load the library:

```ruby
require 'yaml/store'
```

Then, we can create a `YAML::Store` instance. The new method takes an argument with the name of the file the object should write to and/or read from. (A single store object can read from *and* write to the file.)

```ruby
store = YAML::Store.new('my_file.yml')
```
← Create a YAML::Store instance that writes to a file named my_file.yml.

Before we can add any objects to the store or read any objects from it, we have to call the `transaction` method. (`YAML::Store` is programmed to raise an error if we don't.) Why is this required? Well, if one program wrote to the file while another program was reading from it, we could get corrupted data back. The `transaction` method protects against this possibility.

So, to write some data to the file, we call the `transaction` method on the `YAML::Store` instance and pass it a block. Within the block, we assign the value we want to a key, just like we would with a hash.

Prevent other programs from writing to the file until the block exits.

```ruby
store.transaction do
  store["my key"] = "my value"
  store["key two"] = "value two"
end
```
Assign values to keys. These will be saved to the file!

It's the same process to read a value back out: make a call to `transaction`, and within the block, access the value you want.

We also need to call "transaction" before reading.

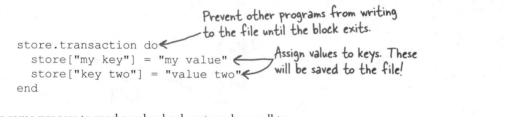

```ruby
store.transaction do
  puts store["my key"]
end
```
← Read the value from the file.

```
my value
```

Saving movies to a file with YAML::Store

In a few pages, we're going to make a class that will manage a YAML::Store instance for us, writing Movie objects to it and retrieving them again. But while we're getting the hang of this, let's write a simple script that uses a YAML::Store directly to save some movies to a file.

At the start of the script, we have to do some setup... Since the Movie and YAML::Store classes aren't available until we load them, we start with calls to require both 'movie' and 'yaml/store'. Then, we create a YAML::Store instance that reads and writes a file named *test.yml*. We create a couple of Movie instances and set all of their attributes.

Then comes the good part: we call the transaction method on the YAML::Store instance and pass it a block. Within the block, we do a couple of operations:

- We assign the movie objects to keys within the store.

- We retrieve the value for one of the keys we stored earlier, and print it.

```ruby
require 'movie'            ←——Load the Movie class.
require 'yaml/store'       ←——Load the YAML::Store class.

store = YAML::Store.new('test.yml')  ←—— Create a store that writes objects
                                          to a file named test.yml.

first_movie = Movie.new ←——Create a movie object.
first_movie.title = "Spirited Away"
first_movie.director = "Hayao Miyazaki"
first_movie.year = 2001

second_movie = Movie.new ←——Create a second movie.
second_movie.title = "Inception"
second_movie.director = "Christopher Nolan"
second_movie.year = 2010
                           ←—— Prevent other programs from writing to the file.
store.transaction do
  store["Spirited Away"] = first_movie   ←—┐
  store["Inception"] = second_movie      ←—┘ Store the two movies.

  p store["Inception"]   ←——Print one of the store's values.
end
```

Let's try this out! Save the script with a name of *yaml_test.rb*. Store it in your Sinatra project directory, alongside the *lib* directory, so that we can load the *movie.rb* file when we run it.

movies

yaml_test.rb

Save this file as "yaml_test.rb" within your project directory.

Saving movies to a file with YAML::Store (continued)

In your terminal, change to the project directory and run the
script with:

```
ruby -I lib yaml_test.rb
```

The script will create the *test.yml* file, and store the two movie
objects in it. Then it will access one of the movies and print a
debug string for it.

Change to your project directory.

Run the script.

One of the stored movies

```
File Edit Window Help
$ cd movies
$ ruby -I lib yaml_test.rb
#<Movie:0x007ffc391ee988 @title="Inception",
   @director="Christopher Nolan", @year=2010>
```

If you open the *test.yml* file in your text editor, you'll see our `Movie`
objects in YAML format, as well as the keys we saved them under.

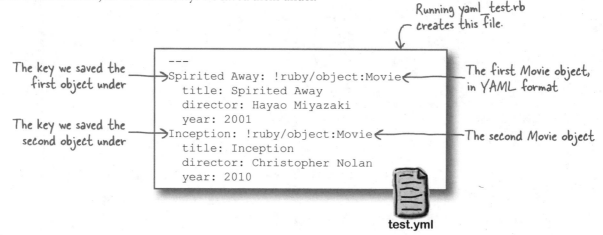

Running yaml_test.rb
creates this file.

The key we saved the
first object under

The key we saved the
second object under

```
---
Spirited Away: !ruby/object:Movie
  title: Spirited Away
  director: Hayao Miyazaki
  year: 2001
Inception: !ruby/object:Movie
  title: Inception
  director: Christopher Nolan
  year: 2010
```

The first Movie object,
in YAML format

The second Movie object

test.yml

Code Magnets

A Ruby program is all scrambled up on the fridge. Can you reconstruct the code snippets to make a working Ruby program? The program should create a file named *books.yml* that has the contents shown below.

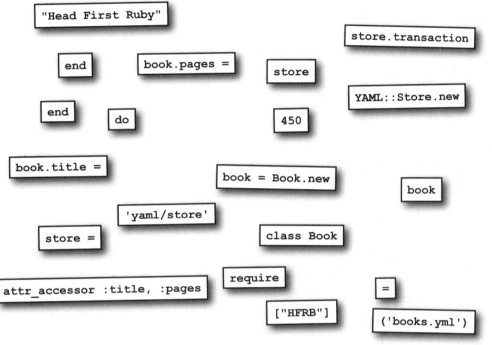

```
"Head First Ruby"

end        book.pages =        store        store.transaction

end    do        450        YAML::Store.new

book.title =        book = Book.new        book

        'yaml/store'

store =        class Book

attr_accessor :title, :pages        require

        ["HFRB"]        =

        ('books.yml')
```

Output:

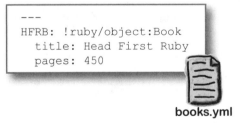

```
---
HFRB: !ruby/object:Book
  title: Head First Ruby
  pages: 450
```

books.yml

Code Magnets Solution

A Ruby program is all scrambled up on the fridge. Can you reconstruct the code snippets to make a working Ruby program? The program should create a file named *books.yml* that has the contents shown below.

```ruby
require 'yaml/store'

class Book
    attr_accessor :title, :pages
end

book = Book.new
book.title = "Head First Ruby"
book.pages = 450

store = YAML::Store.new ('books.yml')

store.transaction do
    store ["HFRB"] = book
end
```

Output:

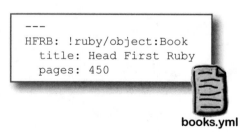

```
---
HFRB: !ruby/object:Book
  title: Head First Ruby
  pages: 450
```

books.yml

A system for finding Movies in the YAML::Store

We're about ready to start saving our `Movie` objects to a `YAML::Store`!

```
#<Movie:0x007ffc391ee988
@title="Forrest Gump",
@director="Robert Zemeckis",
@year=1994>
```

→ movies.yml

Before we do, though, it would be wise to ask ourselves a question: How will we get them back out again?

Later on, we're going to need to generate a list of links to all the movies in our database. When a user clicks that link, it will send a request to our app to get that movie. We need to be able to find a `Movie` object within the `YAML::Store` based solely on the information in that link.

```
<a href="/movies/????">Star Wars</a>
<a href="/movies/????">Ghostbusters</a>
<a href="/movies/????">Forrest Gump</a>
```

"Forrest Gump looks interesting." (Click!)

Find the movie with ID ????.

movies.yml

Forrest Gump	
Title:	Forrest Gump
Director:	Robert Zemeckis
Year Published:	1994

Render it as HTML.

So what do we use as an identifier for a movie? The `title` attribute might seem like an obvious choice. We were able to use titles as `YAML::Store` keys in our earlier script:

```
store["Spirited Away"] = first_movie
store["Inception"] = second_movie
```

Store the two movies.

But one problem with titles is that they often contain spaces, and space characters aren't allowed in URLs. You can use character encodings as a workaround, but that's really ugly:

```
<a href="/movies/Forrest%20Gump">Forrest Gump</a>
```

A character encoding representing a space

Titles aren't really unique identifiers, either. There was a movie named *Titanic* released in 1997, yes, but there was *also* a movie named *Titanic* released in 1953!

We're going to need something else to identify movies by…

Numeric IDs for Movies

For reasons like these, most web apps these days use simple numeric IDs to identify records within their databases. It's easier and more efficient. So, we're going to use numeric IDs as keys within our YAML::Store.

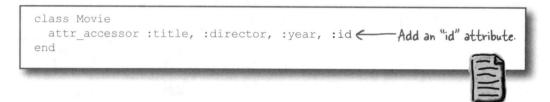

Numeric ID →
Numeric ID →

```
---
1: !ruby/object:Movie
   title: Star Wars
   director: George Lucas
   year: '1977'
   id: 1
2: !ruby/object:Movie
   title: Ghostbusters
   director: Ivan Reitman
   year: '1984'
   id: 2
```

To help us quickly link a Movie object with its YAML::Store key, let's open up the *movie.rb* file within the *lib* directory, and add an id attribute to the Movie class:

```
class Movie
  attr_accessor :title, :director, :year, :id    ← Add an "id" attribute.
end
```

lib/movie.rb

This will make it easier to do things like generate URLs later.

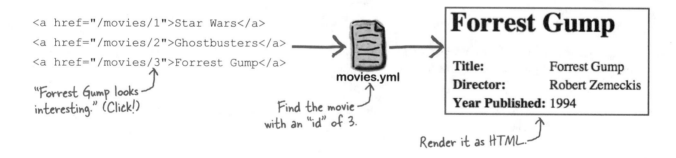

```
<a href="/movies/1">Star Wars</a>
<a href="/movies/2">Ghostbusters</a>
<a href="/movies/3">Forrest Gump</a>
```

"Forrest Gump looks interesting." (Click!)

movies.yml

Find the movie with an "id" of 3.

Forrest Gump

Title:	Forrest Gump
Director:	Robert Zemeckis
Year Published:	1994

Render it as HTML.

Finding the next available movie ID

Now, let's suppose that we've created a new `Movie` object based on the form contents, and it doesn't have an ID yet. What `YAML::Store` key should we assign it to? We'll need to go through the existing keys to find one that's available.

This object needs a → unique ID.

```
#<Movie:0x007ffc391ee988
@title="Beetlejuice",
@director="Tim Burton",
@year=1988
@id=nil>
```

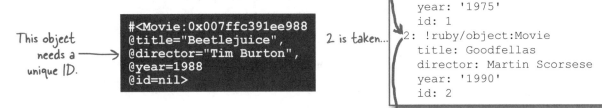

1 is taken...
```
---
1: !ruby/object:Movie
   title: Jaws
   director: Steven Spielberg
   year: '1975'
   id: 1
```
2 is taken...
```
2: !ruby/object:Movie
   title: Goodfellas
   director: Martin Scorsese
   year: '1990'
   id: 2
```

3 is available; we'll use 3.

To process the keys, we can use the `roots` instance method on a `YAML::Store`. The `roots` method returns all the keys in the store as an array:

```ruby
require 'yaml/store'

store = YAML::Store.new('numeric_keys.yml')
store.transaction do
  store[1] = 'Jaws'
  store[2] = 'Goodfellas'
  p store.roots
end
```

Assign to a couple of numeric keys.

Get the keys as an array.

```
[1, 2]
```
The YAML::Store's keys, in array form

Now we need to find the highest number in the array. Arrays have an instance method named `max` that will find the highest value in that array:

```ruby
p [1, 2, 9, 5].max
```
```
9
```
Highest value in the array

So we just call `roots` to get the array of keys, call `max` to get the highest number, and add 1 to the highest number to get our new ID.

```ruby
require 'yaml/store'

store = YAML::Store.new('numeric_keys.yml')
store.transaction do
  p store.roots.max + 1
end
```
Find the highest key in the store and add 1 to it.

```
3
```

Finding the next available movie ID (continued)

There's a catch, though. What if we're working with a `YAML::Store` that's empty? (And our store *will* be empty until we save our first movie…)

In that event, the `roots` method will return an empty array. Calling `max` on an empty array returns `nil`. And trying to add 1 to `nil` raises an error!

We haven't assigned to any keys in this file!

```ruby
require 'yaml/store'

store = YAML::Store.new('empty_store.yml')
store.transaction do
  p store.roots          ← Returns an empty array!
  p store.roots.max      ← Returns "nil"!
  p store.roots.max + 1  ← Raises an error!
end
```

```
[]
nil
undefined method `+' for nil:NilClass
```

To be safe, we'll need to check whether `max` returns `nil`, and use a value of 0 instead. And we can do this quickly and easily using the Boolean "or" operator (`||`). We saw this back in Chapter 9: if the value on the left side of `||` is `false` or `nil`, it will be ignored, and the value on the right side will be used instead. So we'll simply write:

```ruby
store.roots.max || 0
```

…and we'll get 0 if there are no keys in the store, or the highest existing key if there *are* keys.

This file is still empty.

```ruby
require 'yaml/store'

store = YAML::Store.new('empty_store.yml')
store.transaction do
  highest_id = store.roots.max || 0   ← If the "store.roots.max" expression returns "nil", we'll use 0 instead.
  p highest_id + 1
end
```

```
1
```

A class to manage our YAML::Store

We've figured out some reliable code to assign IDs to new movie objects in our YAML::Store. But we probably shouldn't add this code into the Sinatra app; there's enough clutter in there as it is. Instead, let's write a separate class to handle saving objects to a YAML::Store.

1 is taken...

2 is taken...

```
---
1: !ruby/object:Movie
   title: Jaws
   director: Steven Spielberg
   year: '1975'
   id: 1
2: !ruby/object:Movie
   title: Goodfellas
   director: Martin Scorsese
   year: '1990'
   id: 2
```

3 is available; we'll use 3.

Let's create a file named *movie_store.rb*, in our *lib* subdirectory. Within it, we'll define a class named MovieStore. We'll have its initialize method take a filename and create a YAML::Store that writes to that file. Then we'll add a save method that takes a Movie. If the Movie doesn't already have an assigned id, save will find the next available ID and assign that to the Movie. Once the Movie has an id, save will assign it to a key matching that ID within the store.

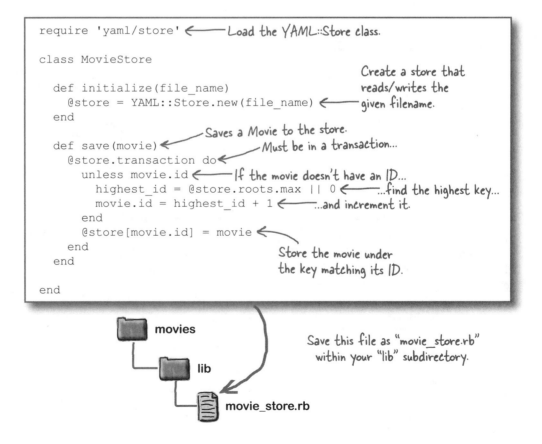

```ruby
require 'yaml/store'          ←——— Load the YAML::Store class.

class MovieStore
                                          Create a store that
  def initialize(file_name)               reads/writes the
    @store = YAML::Store.new(file_name)  ←——— given filename.
  end

  def save(movie)  ←——— Saves a Movie to the store.
    @store.transaction do  ←——— Must be in a transaction...
      unless movie.id  ←——— If the movie doesn't have an ID...
        highest_id = @store.roots.max || 0  ←——— ...find the highest key...
        movie.id = highest_id + 1  ←——— ...and increment it.
      end
      @store[movie.id] = movie  ←
    end
  end                       Store the movie under
end                         the key matching its ID.
```

Save this file as "movie_store.rb"
within your "lib" subdirectory.

movies

lib

movie_store.rb

Using our MovieStore class in the Sinatra app

We had to create a special class, `MovieStore`, to hold the code that works with `YAML::Store`. But now we reap the benefits: using `MovieStore` within our Sinatra app is super-simple!

At the top of *app.rb*, we need to `require 'movie_store'` in order to load the new class. We also create a new instance of `MovieStore`, and pass a filename of `'movies.yml'` to tell it which file to write to and read from.

Our block for the `post('/movies/create')` route is already set up to create a `Movie` object based on the data from the movie form. So we only need to pass the `Movie` to the `save` method on the `MovieStore`.

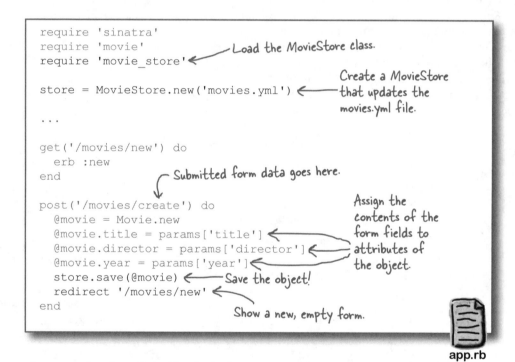

```ruby
require 'sinatra'
require 'movie'
require 'movie_store'          ← Load the MovieStore class.

store = MovieStore.new('movies.yml')  ← Create a MovieStore
                                         that updates the
                                         movies.yml file.
...

get('/movies/new') do
  erb :new
end                        ← Submitted form data goes here.

post('/movies/create') do
  @movie = Movie.new
  @movie.title = params['title']      ← Assign the
  @movie.director = params['director'] ← contents of the
  @movie.year = params['year']        ← form fields to
  store.save(@movie)   ← Save the object!  attributes of
  redirect '/movies/new'  ←              the object.
end

         ← Show a new, empty form.
```

app.rb

After we save the movie, we need to show something in the browser, so we make a call to a Sinatra method that we haven't used before: `redirect`. The `redirect` method takes a string with a resource path (or an entire URL if need be) and sends a response to the browser directing it to load that resource. We use a path of `'/movies/new'` to direct the browser to load the new movie form again.

Testing the MovieStore

You know the routine by now: go to your project directory in your terminal and restart the app. Then visit the page to add a new movie:

        http://localhost:4567/movies/new

Enter a movie in the form and click Submit. All you'll see in the browser is that the form clears (because the redirect response tells the browser to load the form page again)...

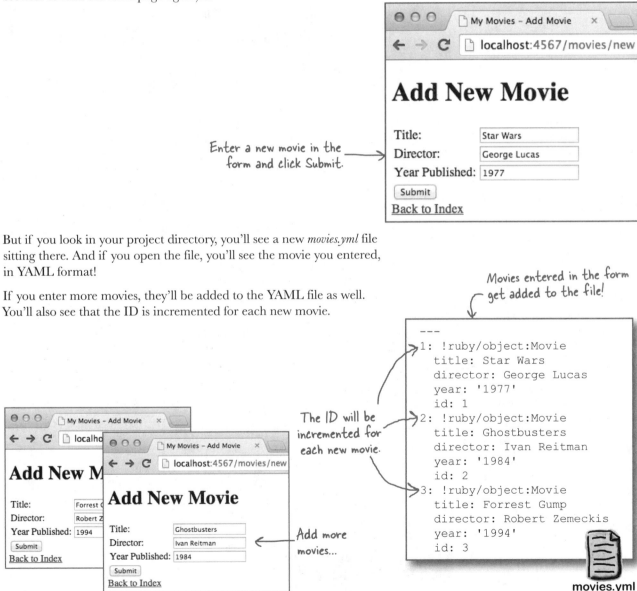

Enter a new movie in the form and click Submit.

But if you look in your project directory, you'll see a new *movies.yml* file sitting there. And if you open the file, you'll see the movie you entered, in YAML format!

If you enter more movies, they'll be added to the YAML file as well. You'll also see that the ID is incremented for each new movie.

Movies entered in the form get added to the file!

The ID will be incremented for each new movie.

Add more movies...

movies.yml

Loading all movies from the MovieStore

It took some work, but we're finally able to save movie objects to the `YAML::Store`. Another task is complete!

Our next task is to get all those movies back out and display them on the movie index.

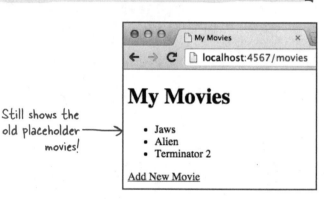

Saving and loading objects

- ☑ Create a movie object based on the form contents.
- ☑ Save movie objects to a file.
- ☐ Load the list of movies from the file.
- ☐ Find individual movies within the file.
- ☐ Display individual movies.

Right now, if you visit the index page:

```
http://localhost:4567/movies
```

…you'll see the placeholder movies we created earlier, instead of our saved movies. They're still hardcoded into the `get('/movies')` route block in *app.rb*.

Still shows the old placeholder movies! →

We'll need to load our saved movies in from the file instead, if we want them to appear in the index…

We need to add a method to `MovieStore` that returns an array of all the values in the `YAML::Store`. But while the `roots` method can give us an array of all the *keys*, there's no single method that can give us all the values…

That's okay, though! Since `roots` returns an array, we can simply use the `map` method on it. As you probably remember from Chapter 6, `map` passes each element of an array to a block, and returns a new array with all the block's return values. So we can simply pass a block to `map` that returns the value of each key in the store.

Here's a simple script that demonstrates this in action on our *numeric_keys.yml* store from earlier:

```ruby
require 'yaml/store'

store = YAML::Store.new('numeric_keys.yml')
store.transaction do
  store[1] = 'Jaws'
  store[2] = 'Goodfellas'
  p store.roots           ←——— Print all the keys.
  p store.roots.map { |key| store[key] }   ←——— Create a new array with
end                                              the values for each key.
```

```
[1, 2]
["Jaws", "Goodfellas"]
```

Loading all movies from the MovieStore (continued)

Now let's use the same idea in our `MovieStore`. We'll create a new method named `all`, which returns every `Movie` object in the store. We'll use `map` on the array returned by `roots` to get the `Movie` stored under each key.

```
require 'yaml/store'

class MovieStore

  def initialize(file_name)
    @store = YAML::Store.new(file_name)
  end

  def all
    @store.transaction do
      @store.roots.map { |id| @store[id] }
    end
  end

  ...

end
```

Retrieves all movies in the store → `def all`

Accessing the store requires a transaction. → `@store.transaction do`

Create an array with the values for each key. → `@store.roots.map { |id| @store[id] }`

lib/movie_store.rb

there are no Dumb Questions

Q: How is the array of `Movie` objects getting returned from the `all` method?

A: The `map` method returns an array of `Movie` objects. The `transaction` *block* returns that array. The `transaction` *method* returns whatever its *block* returns. And the return value of the `transaction` method becomes the return value of the `all` method.

Here's a more explicit equivalent of the above code:

```
def all
  transaction_return_value = @store.transaction do
    block_return_value = @store.roots.map { |id| @store[id] }
    block_return_value
  end
  transaction_return_value
end
```

block_return_value is returned from the "transaction" method.

Movies get returned from the block.

Returns an array of Movies

The "transaction" return value becomes the return value of the "all" method.

But really, we find thinking through all these steps tiresome. We prefer to ignore the call to `transaction`— to pretend it isn't even there. You'll generally find that your code works the same regardless!

Loading all movies in the Sinatra app

Now that we've added a method to retrieve all the movies from our `MovieStore`, we don't have to change much in the Sinatra app.

Previously, we had a set of hardcoded placeholder movies that we stored in the `@movies` instance variable, for use in the *index.erb* HTML template. All we have to do is replace those `Movie` objects with a call to `store.all`.

```
get('/movies') do
  @movies = []
  @movies[0] = Movie.new
  @movies[0].title = "Jaws"
  @movies[1] = Movie.new
  @movies[1].title = "Alien"
  @movies[2] = Movie.new
  @movies[2].title = "Terminator 2"
  erb :index
end
```

Replace this...

```
require 'sinatra'
require 'movie'
require 'movie_store'

store = MovieStore.new('movies.yml')

get('/movies') do
  @movies = store.all
  erb :index
end
```

...with this!

```
get('/movies/new') do
  erb :new
end

post('/movies/create') do
  @movie = Movie.new
  @movie.title = params['title']
  @movie.director = params['director']
  @movie.year = params['year']
  store.save(@movie)
  redirect '/movies/new'
end
```

app.rb

The `Movie` objects saved in our `YAML::Store` will be loaded into the `@movies` instance variable, ready for use in our HTML index!

After you make the change above, restart your app in the terminal. The old placeholder movie titles will be replaced with the movies from your *movies.yml* file!

The movie titles will be loaded from movies.yml!

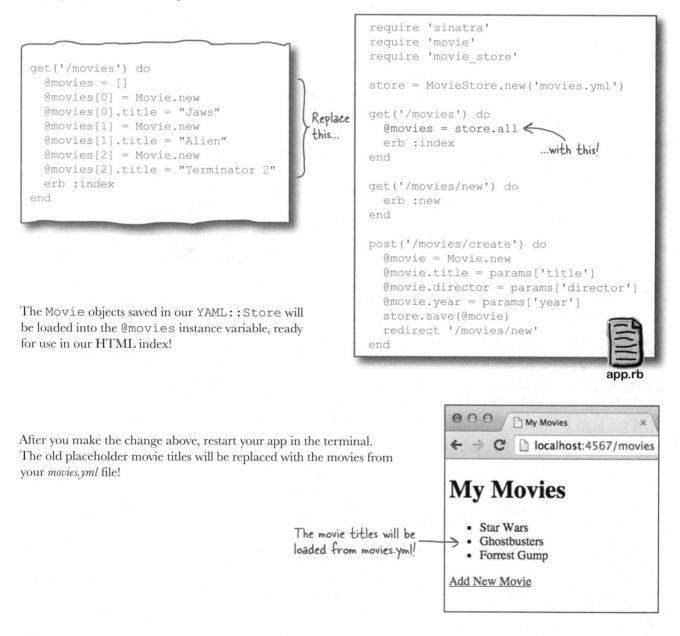

My Movies

- Star Wars
- Ghostbusters
- Forrest Gump

Add New Movie

Building HTML links to individual movies

Listing all the movies in the file was relatively easy. Next, we need the ability to create links to individual movies.

Our movie index page shows the `title` attribute for each `Movie` object. But we've been filling in `director` and `year` attributes too. We should really display those somewhere as well...

So, we'll make a page where we can show an individual movie's data. We'll present all of the `Movie` object's attributes, in table form.

A movie's individual page should show the movie's full details.

We also need a way to find the individual pages for each movie... On the movie index page, let's convert each movie title to a clickable link that takes us to that movie's specific page.

Each of these should be a clickable link to a movie's individual page.

Building HTML links to individual movies (continued)

In order for a link to a movie's detail page to work, its path needs to contain enough information for us to find the resource (the `Movie` object) it links to.

Every HTML link contains a resource path it needs to retrieve, in its `href` attribute. When you click a link, it sends a GET request for that resource path to the server (just like when you enter a URL in the address bar).

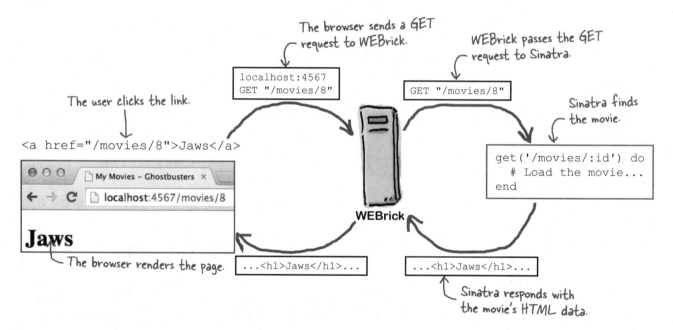

Sinatra needs to be able to find a `Movie` in our `YAML::Store`, based *entirely* off that resource path in the link.

So what information can we include to help identify the right `Movie`? How about its `id` attribute?

We can embed the `id` in the links we create… Later, when a user clicks those links, the ID will be part of the resource path sent to the server. We simply look up that key in our `YAML::Store`, and use the `Movie` object it returns to generate an HTML page!

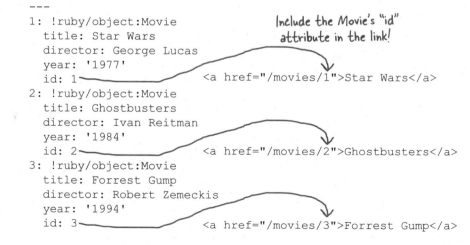

Building HTML links to individual movies (continued)

Let's update the HTML for our movie index page to add unique links to the individual movie pages. Open the *index.erb* file in the *views* subdirectory. Within the `each` block that processes each `Movie` object, add an `<a>` tag surrounding the movie title. Using an ERB `<%= %>` tag, set the `href` attribute to refer to the current `Movie` object's `id` attribute.

```html
<!DOCTYPE html>
<html>
  <head>
    <meta charset='UTF-8' />
    <title>My Movies</title>
  </head>
  <body>
    <h1>My Movies</h1>
    <ul>
      <% @movies.each do |movie| %>
        <li>
          <a href="/movies/<%= movie.id %>"><%= movie.title %></a>
        </li>
      <% end %>
    </ul>
    <a href="/movies/new">Add New Movie</a>
  </body>
</html>
```

Within the loop that processes each movie...

...add a link to a path containing the movie's ID...

...with the movie title as the displayed text.

views/index.erb

If you visit `http://localhost:4567/movies` in your browser, the updated HTML for the movie list will look something like this:

Movie IDs in the resource path

Movie titles as the link text

```html
<ul>
  <li>
    <a href="/movies/1">Star Wars</a>
  </li>
  <li>
    <a href="/movies/2">Ghostbusters</a>
  </li>
  <li>
    <a href="/movies/3">Forrest Gump</a>
  </li>
</ul>
```

The titles will be converted to (nonworking) links.

```
● ● ●      □ My Movies         ×
←  →  C    □ localhost:4567/movies

My Movies

 • Star Wars
 • Ghostbusters
 • Forrest Gump

Add New Movie
```

...and the movie titles will be converted to clickable links. Those links won't lead anywhere for now, but we'll fix that next!

Named parameters in Sinatra routes

We had to add a route in our Sinatra app to handle requests for the movie index:

```
get('/movies') do
  @movies = store.all
  erb :index
end
```

And we had to add another route to handle requests for the form to add a movie:

```
get('/movies/new') do
  erb :new
end
```

So it shouldn't surprise you to learn that we'll need a route for the individual movie pages as well. But, of course, it's not practical to add a route for *each* movie:

```
get('/movies/1') do
  # Load movie 1
end
get('/movies/2') do
  # Load movie 2
end
get('/movies/3') do
  # Load movie 3
end
```

Sinatra allows you to create a single route that can handle requests for multiple resources by using a *named parameter* in the resource path. Following any slash (/) in the path string, you can put a colon (:) followed by a name to indicate a named parameter. The route will process requests for any path that matches the route's pattern, and will record the segments of the path that match the named parameter in the params hash for your code to access.

It's probably simpler just to see it in action. If you were to run Sinatra code like this:

```
require 'sinatra'

get('/zipcodes/:state') do
  "Postal codes for #{params['state']}..."
end
```

A route with a parameter named "state"

Respond with a string that includes the "state" parameter.

...then you could access this URL:

> http://localhost:4567/zipcodes/Nebraska

...and Sinatra would respond with the string "Postal codes for Nebraska...". You could also access:

> http://localhost:4567/zipcodes/Ohio

...and Sinatra would respond with "Postal codes for Ohio...". Whatever string follows '/zipcodes/' in the URL will be stored under the 'state' key in the params hash.

Postal codes for Nebraska...

Postal codes for Ohio...

Using a named parameter to get a movie's ID

So, we need Sinatra to respond to
any URL in a format like this:

```
http://localhost:4567/movies/1
http://localhost:4567/movies/2
http://localhost:4567/movies/3
```

...but we *don't* want to write code
like this:

```
get('/movies/1') do
  # Load movie 1
end
get('/movies/2') do
  # Load movie 2
end
...
```

Let's try adding a single route that uses a named parameter, `'id'`, in its request path.
It will handle any request whose URL matches the format above. It will also capture
the ID from the path, so we'll be able to use it in looking up a `Movie` object.

Define a new `get` route with a
path of `'/movies/:id'` at
the <u>bottom</u> of the *app.rb* file. (It's
important that this route appear
after the other routes; we'll talk
about why in a moment.)

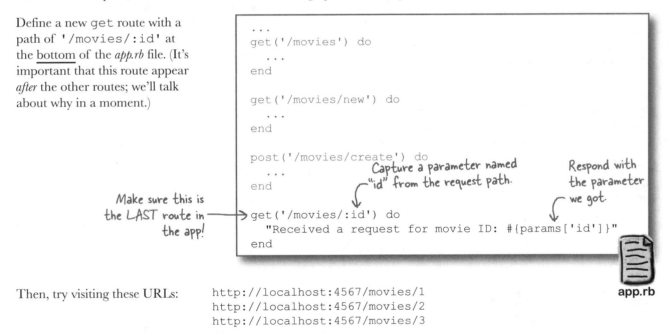

```
...
get('/movies') do
  ...
end

get('/movies/new') do
  ...
end

post('/movies/create') do
  ...
end

get('/movies/:id') do
  "Received a request for movie ID: #{params['id']}"
end
```

Make sure this is
the LAST route in
the app!

Capture a parameter named
"id" from the request path.

Respond with
the parameter
we got.

app.rb

Then, try visiting these URLs:

```
http://localhost:4567/movies/1
http://localhost:4567/movies/2
http://localhost:4567/movies/3
```

...or any other ID you like. Sinatra will respond to all of them, and will
include the `'id'` parameter in its response.

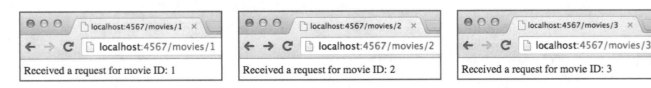

Defining routes in order of priority

We mentioned that it was important to define the `get('/movies/:id')` route *after* the other routes in your Sinatra app. Here's why: the *first* Sinatra route to match a request is the one that gets to process it. All later routes get ignored.

Suppose we had an order processing app. It has a route to request a form for a new order, and another route with a parameter named `'part'` to view all existing orders that include a particular part. And suppose that we define the route with the named parameter *before* the other route...

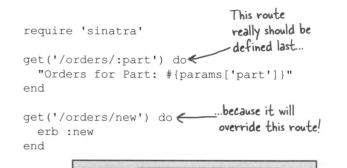

```
require 'sinatra'

get('/orders/:part') do
  "Orders for Part: #{params['part']}"
end

get('/orders/new') do
  erb :new
end
```

This route really should be defined last...

...because it will override this route!

If we tried to access the new order form at:

>   http://localhost:4567/orders/new

...the first route defined would take priority, and Sinatra would try to present us orders for a part with an `'id'` of `'new'`!

```
● ● ●          localhost:4567/orders/nev ×
← → C      localhost:4567/orders/new
Orders for Part: new
```

"new" gets treated like an ID!

In our movies app, if we had defined the `get('/movies/:id')` route *before* the `get('/movies/new')` route, we would have faced the same problem. Any attempt to load the new movie form at:

>   http://localhost:4567/movies/new

...would be treated as a request to show details for a movie with an `'id'` of `'new'`.

```
...
get('/movies/:id') do
  "Received a request for movie ID: #{params['id']}"
end

get('/movies/new') do
  ...
end
...
```

Requests for this route would be overridden by the previous route!

```
● ● ●          localhost:4567/movies/ne ×
← → C      localhost:4567/movies/new
Received a request for movie ID: new
```

The lesson here is that more specific Sinatra routes should be defined first, and less specific ones later. If one of your routes has named parameters, it should probably be among the last routes you define.

This Sinatra app isn't working quite right. Match the three URLs below with the response this app would give. (You won't use one of the responses.)

```ruby
require 'sinatra'

get('/hello') do
  "Hi there!"
end

get('/:greeting') do
  greeting = params['greeting']
  "Sinatra says #{greeting}!"
end

get('/goodbye') do
  "See you later!"
end
```

...... `http://localhost:4567/hello`

...... `http://localhost:4567/ciao`

...... `http://localhost:4567/goodbye`

A | See you later!

B | Sinatra says ciao!

C | Sinatra says goodbye!

D | Hi there!

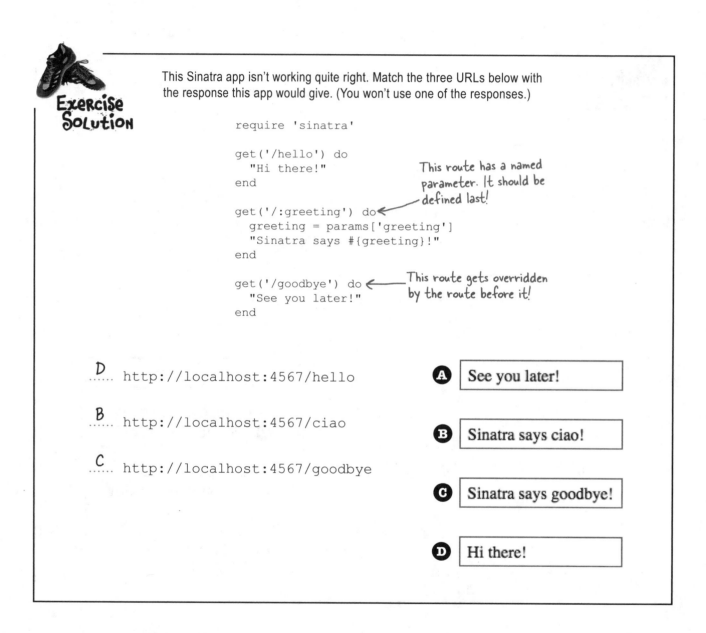

This Sinatra app isn't working quite right. Match the three URLs below with the response this app would give. (You won't use one of the responses.)

Exercise Solution

```ruby
require 'sinatra'

get('/hello') do
  "Hi there!"
end

get('/:greeting') do
  greeting = params['greeting']
  "Sinatra says #{greeting}!"
end

get('/goodbye') do
  "See you later!"
end
```

This route has a named parameter. It should be defined last!

This route gets overridden by the route before it!

D ...... `http://localhost:4567/hello`

B ...... `http://localhost:4567/ciao`

C ...... `http://localhost:4567/goodbye`

A | See you later!

B | Sinatra says ciao!

C | Sinatra says goodbye!

D | Hi there!

Finding a Movie in the YAML::Store

We've got our movie IDs embedded in the links on our site, and we're set up to capture a parameter with the ID from the HTTP GET request. Now it's time to use that ID to look up a `Movie` object.

Movie IDs

```
<a href="/movies/1">Star Wars</a>
<a href="/movies/2">Ghostbusters</a>
<a href="/movies/3">Forrest Gump</a>
```

Our movies are all saved in the `YAML::Store` using their ID as a key. Retrieving them should be simple!

Each Movie's "id" attribute matches the key it's saved under in the YAML::Store.

```
---
1: !ruby/object:Movie
  title: Star Wars
  director: George Lucas
  year: '1977'
  id: 1
2: !ruby/object:Movie
  title: Ghostbusters
  director: Ivan Reitman
  year: '1984'
  id: 2
```

movies.yml

Add a `find` instance method to the `MovieStore` class. It should take an ID for use as a key, and return the value (the `Movie` object) under that key in the `YAML::Store`.

As with all other `YAML::Store` operations, this will need to take place within a `transaction` method block.

```
require 'yaml/store'

class MovieStore

  def initialize(file_name)
    @store = YAML::Store.new(file_name)
  end

  def find(id)                    ← Take an ID to use as a key.
    @store.transaction do         ← Needs to be in a
      @store[id]                       transaction...
    end
  end                             ← Return the Movie object
                                     stored under this key.
  def all
    @store.transaction do
      @store.roots.map { |id| @store[id] }
    end
  end

  ...

end
```

movie_store.rb

That's it! We're now set up to find movies that we've saved.

An ERB template for an individual movie

Our `MovieStore` class has a new `find` method, ready to return an individual movie's data. All that remains is to utilize `find` in the Sinatra app and add HTML for displaying a movie. We're almost done!

 Load the list of movies from the file.

 Find individual movies within the file.

☐ Display individual movies.

We're set up to load an individual `Movie` so we can display its attributes, but we still need an HTML template to display it within. Let's create a *show.erb* file within the *views* subdirectory, and add this HTML to it.

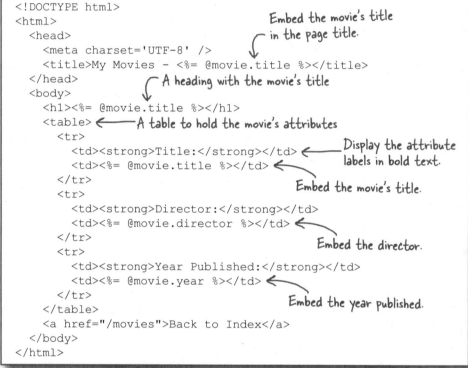

```html
<!DOCTYPE html>
<html>
  <head>
    <meta charset='UTF-8' />
    <title>My Movies - <%= @movie.title %></title>
  </head>
  <body>
    <h1><%= @movie.title %></h1>
    <table>
      <tr>
        <td><strong>Title:</strong></td>
        <td><%= @movie.title %></td>
      </tr>
      <tr>
        <td><strong>Director:</strong></td>
        <td><%= @movie.director %></td>
      </tr>
      <tr>
        <td><strong>Year Published:</strong></td>
        <td><%= @movie.year %></td>
      </tr>
    </table>
    <a href="/movies">Back to Index</a>
  </body>
</html>
```

Embed the movie's title in the page title.

A heading with the movie's title

A table to hold the movie's attributes

Display the attribute labels in bold text.

Embed the movie's title.

Embed the director.

Embed the year published.

There's not much new about this page. We access a `Movie` object that's stored within the `@movie` instance variable (which we'll set up in the Sinatra route in a moment). We use `<%= %>` ERB tags to embed the movie's attributes within the HTML.

An HTML `<table>` tag displays the movie's attributes in rows. The first column of each row is a label for the attribute. The HTML `<strong>` tag (which we haven't used thus far) simply displays the text in **bold**. The second column holds the attribute's value.

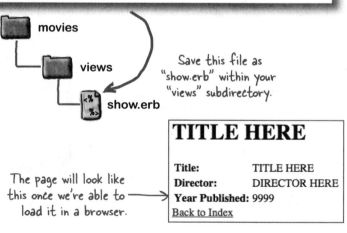

Save this file as "show.erb" within your "views" subdirectory.

The page will look like this once we're able to load it in a browser.

TITLE HERE

Title:	TITLE HERE
Director:	DIRECTOR HERE
Year Published:	9999

Back to Index

Finishing the Sinatra route for individual movies

We've added a `find` method to the `MovieStore` that can load a `Movie` based on its `id` attribute, and a *show.erb* file to display the `Movie`. It's time to link those two together. In our Sinatra app, let's modify our `get('/movies/:id')` route to load a movie and render it in HTML.

```ruby
require 'sinatra'
require 'movie'
require 'movie_store'

store = MovieStore.new('movies.yml')

get('/movies') do
  @movies = store.all
  erb :index
end

get('/movies/new') do
  erb :new
end

post('/movies/create') do
  @movie = Movie.new
  @movie.title = params['title']
  @movie.director = params['director']
  @movie.year = params['year']
  store.save(@movie)
  redirect '/movies/new'
end

get('/movies/:id') do
  id = params['id'].to_i
  @movie = store.find(id)
  erb :show
end
```

We need to take the `'id'` parameter from the resource path so we can load the `Movie` from the `MovieStore`. The parameter will be a string, though, and the `MovieStore`'s keys are all integers. So the first thing we do in the route block is convert the string to an integer using the `to_i` method.

Once we have the ID as an integer, we can pass it to the `find` method on the `MovieStore`. We'll get a `Movie` object back, which we store in the `@movie` instance variable (for use by the ERB template).

Convert the 'id' parameter from a string to an integer.

Use the ID to load the movie from the store.

Embed the movie in the HTML from show.erb and return it to the browser.

app.rb

Lastly, we call `erb :show`, which will load the *show.erb* template from the *views* directory, embed the @movie object's attributes into it, and return the resulting HTML to the browser.

After all that hard work setting up movie data, wiring it into the app was pretty easy. Our Sinatra app is complete!

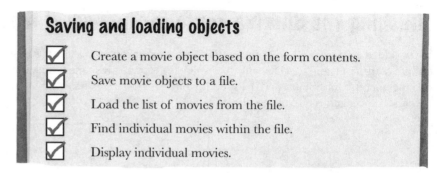

Let's try it all out!

Are you ready? We've done a lot of work to get this far, so this is the big moment…

Restart your app from the terminal, and visit `http://localhost:4567/movies` in your browser. Click on the link to any of the movies.

The app will get the movie ID from the URL, load the `Movie` instance from the `YAML::Store`, embed its attributes in the *show.erb* template, and send the resulting HTML to your browser.

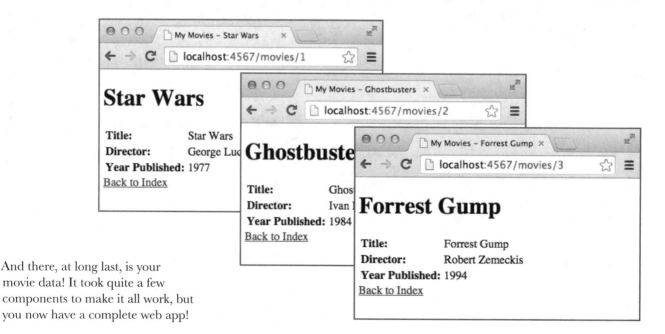

And there, at long last, is your movie data! It took quite a few components to make it all work, but you now have a complete web app!

Our complete app code

Here's the project directory structure for our complete app:

- 📁 **movies**
  - 📄 **app.rb**
  - 📄 **movies.yml**
  - 📁 **lib**
    - 📄 **movie.rb**
    - 📄 **movie_store.rb**
  - 📁 **views**
    - 📄 **index.erb**
    - 📄 **new.erb**
    - 📄 **show.erb**

The *app.rb* file is the core of the app. It holds all our Sinatra routes.

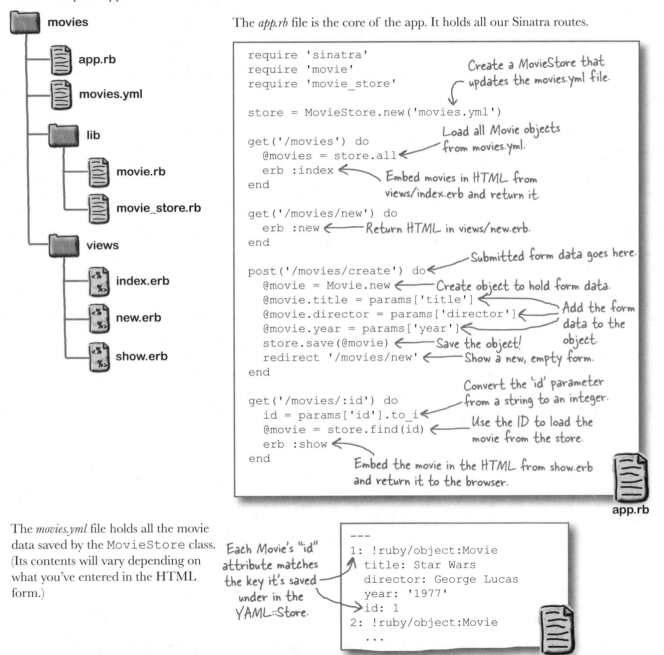

```ruby
require 'sinatra'
require 'movie'
require 'movie_store'

store = MovieStore.new('movies.yml')

get('/movies') do
  @movies = store.all
  erb :index
end

get('/movies/new') do
  erb :new
end

post('/movies/create') do
  @movie = Movie.new
  @movie.title = params['title']
  @movie.director = params['director']
  @movie.year = params['year']
  store.save(@movie)
  redirect '/movies/new'
end

get('/movies/:id') do
  id = params['id'].to_i
  @movie = store.find(id)
  erb :show
end
```

Create a MovieStore that updates the movies.yml file.

Load all Movie objects from movies.yml.

Embed movies in HTML from views/index.erb and return it.

Return HTML in views/new.erb.

Submitted form data goes here.

Create object to hold form data.

Add the form data to the object.

Save the object!

Show a new, empty form.

Convert the 'id' parameter from a string to an integer.

Use the ID to load the movie from the store.

Embed the movie in the HTML from show.erb and return it to the browser.

app.rb

The *movies.yml* file holds all the movie data saved by the `MovieStore` class. (Its contents will vary depending on what you've entered in the HTML form.)

Each Movie's "id" attribute matches the key it's saved under in the YAML::Store.

```yaml
---
1: !ruby/object:Movie
  title: Star Wars
  director: George Lucas
  year: '1977'
  id: 1
2: !ruby/object:Movie
  ...
```

movies.yml

Our complete app code (continued)

Our `Movie` class simply specifies a few attributes for each object.

```ruby
class Movie
  attr_accessor :title, :director, :year, :id
end
```

lib/movie.rb

The `MovieStore` class is responsible for saving `Movie` objects to the
YAML file and retrieving them later.

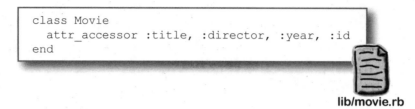

```ruby
require 'yaml/store'          ←——— Load the YAML::Store class.

class MovieStore
                                              Create a store that
  def initialize(file_name)                   reads/writes the
    @store = YAML::Store.new(file_name) ←——— given filename.
  end
                      ←—— Find the Movie with this ID.
  def find(id)  ←
    @store.transaction do ←——— Accessing the store requires a transaction.
      @store[id] ←——— Return the Movie object stored under this key.
    end
  end             Retrieves all movies
                  —— in the store      Must be in a
  def all ←                            transaction...
    @store.transaction do ←
      @store.roots.map { |id| @store[id] } ←    Create an array
    end                                         with the values
  end                                           for each key.

                   —— Saves a Movie to the store
  def save(movie) ←    —— Must be in a transaction...
    @store.transaction do ←
      unless movie.id ←——— If the movie doesn't have an ID...
        highest_id = @store.roots.max || 0 ←———...find the highest key...
        movie.id = highest_id + 1 ←———...and increment it.
      end
      @store[movie.id] = movie ←
    end                           Store the movie under
  end                             the key matching its ID.

end
```

lib/movie_store.rb

Our complete app code (continued)

In the *views* subdirectory, the *show.erb* file contains an ERB template with HTML to embed a single movie's data within.

```
<!DOCTYPE html>
<html>
  <head>
    <meta charset='UTF-8' />
    <title>My Movies - <%= @movie.title %></title>
  </head>
  <body>
    <h1><%= @movie.title %></h1>
    <table>
      <tr>
        <td><strong>Title:</strong></td>
        <td><%= @movie.title %></td>
      </tr>
      <tr>
        <td><strong>Director:</strong></td>
        <td><%= @movie.director %></td>
      </tr>
      <tr>
        <td><strong>Year Published:</strong></td>
        <td><%= @movie.year %></td>
      </tr>
    </table>
    <a href="/movies">Back to Index</a>
  </body>
</html>
```

Embed the movie's title in the page title.

A heading with the movie's title

Embed the movie's title.

Embed the director.

Embed the year published.

views/show.erb

And the *index.erb* file contains a template that creates a link to each of the individual movies.

```
<!DOCTYPE html>
<html>
  <head>
    <meta charset='UTF-8' />
    <title>My Movies</title>
  </head>
  <body>
    <h1>My Movies</h1>
    <ul>
      <% @movies.each do |movie| %>
        <li>
          <a href="/movies/<%= movie.id %>"><%= movie.title %></a>
        </li>
      <% end %>
    </ul>
    <a href="/movies/new">Add New Movie</a>
  </body>
</html>
```

Process each movie...

...add a link to a path containing the movie's ID...

...with the movie title as the displayed text.

views/index.erb

Our complete app code (continued)

Lastly, the *new.erb* file contains an HTML form for entering a new movie's data. When the form is submitted, it sends the movie data in an HTTP POST request to the `'/movies/create'` path. A Sinatra route in *app.rb* uses the data to create a new `Movie` object, and saves it using the `MovieStore`.

```html
<!DOCTYPE html>
<html>
  <head>
    <meta charset='UTF-8' />
    <title>My Movies - Add Movie</title>
  </head>
  <body>
    <h1>Add New Movie</h1>
    <form method="post" action="/movies/create">
      <table>
        <tr>
          <td><label for="title">Title:</label></td>
          <td><input type="text" name="title"></td>
        </tr>
        <tr>
          <td><label for="director">Director:</label></td>
          <td><input type="text" name="director"></td>
        </tr>
        <tr>
          <td><label for="year">Year Published:</label></td>
          <td><input type="text" name="year"></td>
        </tr>
        <tr>
          <td><input type="submit"></td>
        </tr>
      </table>
    </form>
    <a href="/movies">Back to Index</a>
  </body>
</html>
```

Submit this form by sending a POST request to "/movies/create".

Field label

Text field

Field label

Text field

Field label

Text field

Submit button for form

views/new.erb

And that's it—a complete web app that can store user-submitted data and retrieve it again later.

Writing web apps can be a complex process, but Sinatra leverages the power of Ruby to make it as simple as possible for you!

Your Ruby Toolbox

That's it for Chapter 15! You've added YAML::Store to your toolbox.

Sinatra
ERB
YAML::Store

YAML::Store relies on the YAML library to convert Ruby objects to a string format, which it then writes to a file.

A YAML::Store instance is used similarly to a hash, allowing you to store a value under a key and then access it later using the same key.

BULLET POINTS

- When the `method` attribute of an HTML form has been set to `"post"`, and the user submits it, the browser sends the form data to the server in an HTTP POST request.

- A form also has an `action` attribute that specifies a resource path. That path gets included in the POST request, just like with GET requests.

- Sinatra has a `post` method that is used to define routes for POST requests.

- Within the block for a `post` route, you can call the `params` method to get a hash with the form data from the request.

- The `YAML::Store.new` method takes a string with the name of a file it should read from and/or write to.

- `YAML::Store` instances have a `transaction` method that prevents other programs from writing to the file. The `transaction` method takes a block, where you can call whatever other methods you need on the `YAML::Store`.

- The `roots` instance method on a `YAML::Store` returns an array containing all the keys in the store.

- Sinatra lets you include named parameters in the path for a route. The section of the request path that's in the same position as the named parameter will be captured and made available as part of the `params` hash.

- If more than one Sinatra route matches the same request, the route that was defined first will be the one to handle it.

- Routes with named parameters should usually be defined last, so that they don't accidentally override other routes.

Up Next...

We're not done! There's a lot we didn't have room to cover in this book, so we've added an appendix with the most important items, plus some resources to help you plan your *next* Ruby project. Read on!

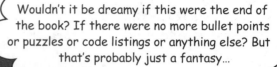

Wouldn't it be dreamy if this were the end of the book? If there were no more bullet points or puzzles or code listings or anything else? But that's probably just a fantasy...

Congratulations!
You made it to the end.

Of course, there's still an appendix.
And the index.
And then there's the website...
There's no escape, really.

The top ten topics (we didn't cover)

Whoo! For a minute I thought you were going to end the book without mentioning private methods! Or regular expressions! Don't scare me like that!

We've covered a lot of ground, and you're almost finished with this book. We'll miss you, but before we let you go, we wouldn't feel right about sending you out into the world without a *little* more preparation. We can't possibly fit everything you'll need to know about Ruby into these few pages... (Actually, we *did* include everything originally, by reducing the type point size to .00004. It all fit, but nobody could read it. So we threw most of it away.) But we've kept all the best bits for this Top Ten appendix.

This really *is* the end of the book. Except for the index, of course. (A must-read!)

#1 Other cool libraries

Ruby on Rails

Sinatra (which we covered in Chapters 14 and 15) is a great way to build simple web apps. But all apps need new features, and so they grow over time. Eventually you'll need more than just a place to put your ERB templates. You'll also need a place to put database configuration, a place to put JavaScript code and CSS styles, a place to put code to tie all this together, and more.

And that's where Ruby on Rails excels: giving you standardized places to put things.

It starts with the fundamental architecture of every Rails app, which follows the popular *Model, View, Controller* (MVC) pattern:

- The *model* is where you put data for your app. Rails can automatically save model objects to a database for you and retrieve them again later. (This is similar to the `Movie` and `MovieStore` classes we created for our Sinatra app.)

- The *view* is where you put code to display model data to users. By default, Rails uses ERB templates to render HTML (or JSON, or XML) views. (Again, just like we did in our Sinatra app.)

- The *controller* is where you put code to respond to browser requests. Controllers take a request, call on the model to get the appropriate data, call on the view to render an appropriate response, and send the response back to the browser.

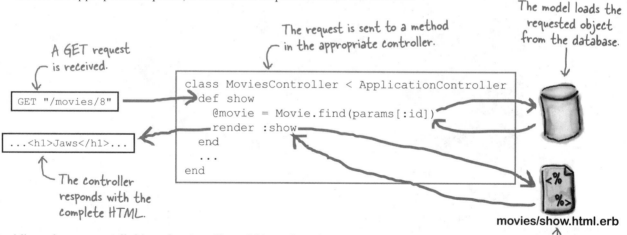

The request is sent to a method in the appropriate controller.

A GET request is received.

The model loads the requested object from the database.

```
GET "/movies/8"
```

```
class MoviesController < ApplicationController
  def show
    @movie = Movie.find(params[:id])
    render :show
  end
  ...
end
```

```
...<h1>Jaws</h1>...
```

The controller responds with the complete HTML.

movies/show.html.erb

The view embeds the object's data in an HTML template.

Deciding where to put all this code yourself would be a daunting task. Configuring Ruby to know where to look for it all would be worse. That's why Rails promotes "convention over configuration." If you put code for your model, view, and controller in the standard places Rails looks, you don't have to configure any of this. It's all handled for you. And that's why Rails is such a powerful (and popular) web framework!

Visit *http://rubyonrails.org/* to learn more about Rails.

#1 Other cool libraries (continued)

dRuby

dRuby, part of the Ruby standard library, is a great example of Ruby's power. It stands for "distributed Ruby," and it allows you to make *any* Ruby object network-accessible. You just create the object and tell dRuby to offer it up as a service. Then you can call methods on that object from Ruby scripts running *on a completely different computer*.

You don't have to write special service code. You hardly have to write *anything*. It just works, because Ruby is uniquely suited to forward method calls from one object to another. (We'll talk about that more in a bit).

Here's a short script that makes an ordinary array available over the network. You just give dRuby the array, and specify the URL (including a port number) at which it should be made available. We've also added some code to repeatedly print the array, so you can watch as client programs modify it.

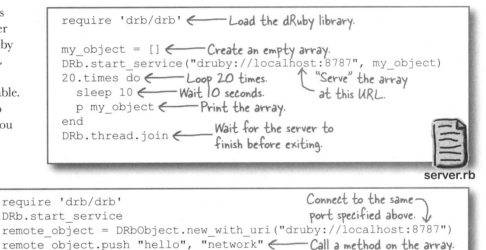

```
require 'drb/drb'          Load the dRuby library.

my_object = []             Create an empty array.
DRb.start_service("druby://localhost:8787", my_object)
20.times do                Loop 20 times.        "Serve" the array
  sleep 10                 Wait 10 seconds.      at this URL.
  p my_object              Print the array.
end
DRb.thread.join            Wait for the server to
                           finish before exiting.
```
server.rb

Now, here's a separate script that acts as a client. It connects to the server script over the network, and gets an object that acts as a *proxy* to the remote object.

```
require 'drb/drb'
DRb.start_service                                    Connect to the same
remote_object = DRbObject.new_with_uri("druby://localhost:8787")   port specified above.
remote_object.push "hello", "network"    Call a method on the array.
p remote_object.last    Call another method on the array.
```
client.rb

Any method you call on the proxy is sent over the network, and called on the remote object. Any return values are sent back over the network, and returned from the proxy.

To try this out, open a terminal window and run **server.rb**. It will start printing the contents of the array in my_object every 10 seconds.

Now, in a *different* terminal window, run **client.rb**. If you switch back to the first terminal, you'll see that the client has added new values to the array!

Are there security concerns with this? You bet. Make sure you're behind a firewall when using dRuby. For more information (and more cool ideas), look up dRuby in the Ruby standard library documentation.

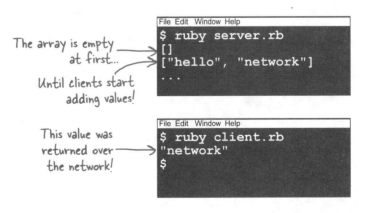

The array is empty at first... Until clients start adding values!

```
File Edit Window Help
$ ruby server.rb
[]
["hello", "network"]
...
```

This value was returned over the network!

```
File Edit Window Help
$ ruby client.rb
"network"
$
```

#1 Other cool libraries (continued)

CSV

If you've ever had an office job, you've probably had to work with data in spreadsheets, either yours or someone else's. And while spreadsheets offer formulas, the syntax is limiting (and a pain to remember).

Most spreadsheet programs can export CSV format (short for **C**omma-**S**eparated **V**alues), a plain-text format where rows are separated into text lines and columns are separated by commas.

A CSV file

```
Associate,Sale Count,Sales Total
"Boone, Agnes",127,1710.26
"Howell, Marvin",196,2245.19
"Rodgers, Tonya",400,3032.48
```

sales.csv

Ruby offers the CSV library as part of its standard library, to make processing CSV files more convenient. This short script uses CSV to print just the associate names and sales totals from the above file. It skips printing the header row, and instead lets you use the headers as keys to access column values, as if each row of the CSV file were a hash.

Load the library.

Treat the first line as a set of column headers.

Process each line of the file.

```
require 'csv'
CSV.foreach("sales.csv", headers: true) do |row|
    puts "#{row['Associate']}: #{row['Sales Total']}"
end
```

Access column data using the headers as keys.

```
Boone, Agnes: 1710.26
Howell, Marvin: 2245.19
Rodgers, Tonya: 3032.48
```

We only had room to mention these three libraries in this appendix. Look for "Ruby standard library" in a search engine to learn about the dozens of options in the standard library. And for *thousands* more gems, visit *http://rubygems.org*.

#2 Inline if and unless

We've said all along that Ruby helps you do more with less code. This principle is built right into the language. One example of this is inline conditionals.

You've already seen the regular forms of `if` and `unless`, of course:

```
if true                          unless true
   puts "I'll be printed!"          puts "I won't!"
end                              end
```

But if the code within your conditional is only one line long, you have the option to move the conditional to the end of that line. These expressions work just like the ones above:

```
puts "I'll be printed!" if true

puts "I won't!" unless true
```

#3 Private methods

When you first create a class, you'll probably be the only one using it. But that (hopefully) won't always be the case. Other developers will find your class and realize it solves their problems, too. But their problems are not always the same as your problems, and perhaps they will use your class in ways you didn't foresee. That's fine, *until* you need to make changes to your class.

Suppose you need to add a 15% surcharge on any amount your customers are billed for. You could create an `Invoice` class that allows you to set a `subtotal` attribute. You could have a `total` method that calculates the total amount for the bill. And to keep the `total` method from getting too complex, you might break the calculation of fees out into a separate `fees` method, which `total` calls.

```
class Invoice
  attr_accessor :subtotal          Add a 15% surcharge to
  def total                        the subtotal.
    subtotal + fees(subtotal, 0.15)
  end
  def fees(amount, percentage)       Multiply the amount by the fee rate.
    amount * percentage
  end
end


invoice = Invoice.new
invoice.subtotal = 500.00
p invoice.total
```

```
575.0
```

But then you learn that your department intends to add a flat $25 fee to all invoices as well. So you add a `flat_rate` parameter to your `fees` method to account for that...

```
class Invoice
  attr_accessor :subtotal                Add a $25 flat fee.
  def total
    subtotal + fees(subtotal, 0.15, 25.00)
  end                                      Add a parameter to the
  def fees(amount, percentage, flat_rate)   "fees" method.
    amount * percentage + flat_rate
  end
end
```

This works great, until you get a call from another department, who want to know why your class broke their code. Evidently they started using your `fees` method to calculate their own 8% surcharge. But their code is still written with the assumption that `fees` requires *two* parameters, even though it's been updated to require *three*!

```
fee = Invoice.new.fees(300, 0.08)
p fee
```

```
in 'fees': wrong number of arguments (2 for 3)
```

#3 Private methods (continued)

The problem here is that other developers are calling your `fees` method from *outside* your class, when you really only intended for it to be called *inside* your class. Now you have a choice: figure out how to make the `fees` method work for both you *and* the other developers who are using it, or change it back and then never modify it again.

There's a way to avoid this situation, though. If you know a method will only be used from inside your class, you can mark it as `private`. **Private methods** can only be called from within the class on which they're defined. Here's an updated version of the `Invoice` class, with the `fees` method marked private:

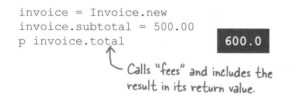

```
class Invoice
  attr_accessor :subtotal
  def total
    subtotal + fees(subtotal, 0.15, 25.00)
  end
private
  def fees(amount, percentage, flat_rate)
    amount * percentage + flat_rate
  end
end
```

You can still call the private method from other Invoice methods.

All methods defined after this will be marked private to the Invoice class.

Now, code that tries to call the `fees` method from outside the `Invoice` class will receive an error indicating that the method being called is private.

```
fee = Invoice.new.fees(300, 0.08)
```

```
private method `fees' called for #<Invoice:0x007f97bb02ba20>
```

But your `total` method (which is an instance method on the same class as `fees`) can still call it.

```
invoice = Invoice.new
invoice.subtotal = 500.00
p invoice.total
```

```
600.0
```

Calls "fees" and includes the result in its return value.

The other department will have to find a different way to calculate their fees, it's true. But future misunderstandings of this sort will be averted. And you'll be free to make any changes to the `fees` method you need! Private methods can help keep your code clean and easy to update.

#4 Command-line arguments

We like to "quote" emails that we reply to by marking them with a > character before each line of text. That way, the recipient will know what we're talking about.

Here's a quick script that will read in the contents of a text file and insert "> " before each line:

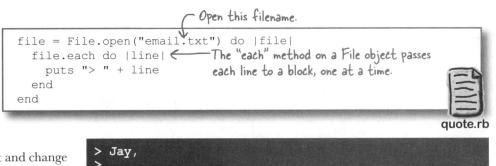

Open this filename.

```
file = File.open("email.txt") do |file|
  file.each do |line|
    puts "> " + line
  end
end
```

The "each" method on a File object passes each line to a block, one at a time.

quote.rb

We have to go into the script and change the filename every time we want to use a new input file, though. It would be nice if we had a way to specify the filename *outside* of our script.

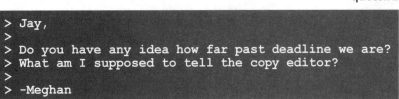

```
> Jay,
>
> Do you have any idea how far past deadline we are?
> What am I supposed to tell the copy editor?
>
> -Meghan
```

And we can! We just need to use *command-line arguments*. Programs that run in your terminal often allow you to specify arguments after the program name, much like arguments to a method call, and Ruby scripts are no exception. You can access the arguments your script was called with through the ARGV array, which is set up every time a Ruby program runs. The first argument is at ARGV[0], the second at ARGV[1], and so forth.

The two-line *args_test.rb* script below demonstrates this. If we run it in a terminal, whatever we type in the terminal after the script name will be printed when the script runs.

```
p ARGV[0]
p ARGV[1]
```

args_test.rb

File Edit Window Help
```
$ ruby args_test.rb hello terminal
"hello"
"terminal"
```

We can use ARGV in *quote.rb* to allow us to specify any input file we want, each time we run it. We just need to replace the hardcoded filename with ARGV[0]. From then on, when we run *quote.rb* in the terminal, we can simply specify an input filename after the script name!

Use the string in the first command-line argument as the name of the file to open.

Now, you can supply a filename as an argument to the script!

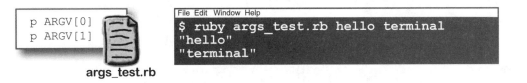

```
file = File.open(ARGV[0]) do |file|
  file.each do |line|
    puts "> " + line
  end
end
```

quote.rb

File Edit Window Help
```
$ ruby quote.rb reply.txt
> Tell them I'm really sorry!
> Just ONE more week!
>
> -Jay
```

#5 Regular expressions

Regular expressions are a way of looking for *patterns* within text. Many programming languages offer regular expressions, but they're especially easy to work with in Ruby.

If you're looking for an email address within some text, you can use a regular expression to say, "Find me some letters, followed by an @ symbol, then more letters, then a period, then more letters."

`/\w+@\w+\.\w+/` ⟵———A regular expression to find an email address

If you're looking for the end of a sentence, you can use a regular expression to say, "Find me a period, question mark, or exclamation point, followed by a space."

`/[.?!]\s/` ⟵———A regular expression to find the end of a sentence

Regular expressions are insanely powerful, but they can also be complex and hard to read. Even if you only learn their most basic features, though, you'll still find them quite useful. Our goal here is to give you a sample of what they can do for you, and give you a couple of resources where you can learn more on your own.

Suppose you have a string, and you need to find a phone number within it:

`"Tel: 555-0199"`

You can create a regular expression to find it for you. Regular expression literals start and end with a forward slash (/) character.

`/555-0199/` ⟵———A regular expression literal.

A regular expression by itself doesn't do anything, though. You can use the `=~` operator in a conditional to test whether the regular expression matches your string:

Tests whether the regular expression on the right matches the string on the left.

```
if "Tel: 555-0199" =~ /555-0199/
  puts "Found phone number."
end
```

```
Found phone number.
```

Relax

....
You don't have to know regular expressions to program in Ruby.

They're powerful, but they're also very complex, so they're not used all the time. But even if you only learn the basics, they can be a big help if you're working with a lot of strings!
....

#5 Regular expressions (continued)

Right now, our regular expression can only match one phone number: 555–0199. To match other numbers as well, we can use the \d *character class*, which will match any digit from 0 through 9. (Other character classes include \w for characters from words, and \s for whitespace.)

```ruby
if "Tel: 555-0148" =~ /\d\d\d-\d\d\d\d/    ←——— Match any digits.
  puts "Found phone number."
end
```

> **Found phone number.**

Instead of typing \d repeatedly like the code above, we can use a single \d followed by +, which looks for one *or more* of the preceding match.

```ruby
if "Tel: 555-0148" =~ /\d+-\d+/    ←——— Match one or more digits.
  puts "Found phone number."
end
```

> **Found phone number.**

Better yet, we can use a number inside of curly braces, which indicates you expect the preceding match to occur *that number of times*.

```ruby
if "Tel: 555-0148" =~ /\d{3}-\d{4}/    ←——— Match three digits, then a dash, then four digits.
  puts "Found phone number."
end
```

> **Found phone number.**

You can record the text that your regular expression matched by using a *capture group*. If you place parentheses around part of your regular expression, then that part of the match will be recorded in a special variable named $1. You can print the value in $1 to see what was matched.

```ruby
if "Tel: 555-0148" =~ /(\d{3}-\d{4})/    ←——— The matched part of the string gets stored in "$1".
  puts "Found phone number: #{$1}"
end
```

> **Found phone number: 555-0148**

A regular expression is just another object in Ruby, so you can pass them as arguments to methods. Strings have a sub method that will look for a regular expression within a string, and substitute a new string in place of the match. This call to sub will blank out any phone numbers within the string:

```ruby
puts "Tel: 555-0148".sub(/\d{3}-\d{4}/, '***-****')
```

> **Tel: ***-******

This has been just a *tiny* taste of what regular expressions can do. There's lots more functionality that we don't have room to cover here, and you could go your entire programming career without ever fully mastering regular expressions. But if you learn the basics, they can save you a lot of time and coding!

If you want to learn more, check out the chapter on regular expressions in *Programming Ruby* by Dave Thomas, Chad Fowler, and Andy Hunt. (We'll talk about that book more in a bit.) Or look up the Regexp class in the Ruby core documentation.

#6 Singleton methods

Most object-oriented languages let you define instance methods that are available on *all* instances of a class. But Ruby is one of the few that let you define instance methods on a *single* instance. Such methods are known as **singleton methods**.

Here we have a `Person` class, with one instance method, `speak`. When you first create an instance of `Person`, it only has the `speak` instance method available.

```
class Person
  def speak
    puts "Hello, there!"
  end
end

person = Person.new
person.speak
```

```
Hello, there!
```

But in Ruby, it's possible to define an instance method that is available on one single object. Following the `def` keyword, you include a reference to the object, a dot operator, and the name of the singleton method you want to define.

This code will define a `fly` method on the object in the `superhero` variable. The `fly` method can be called like any other instance method, but it will be available *only* on `superhero`.

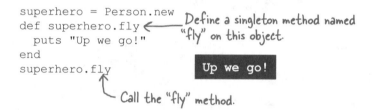

```
superhero = Person.new
def superhero.fly          Define a singleton method named
  puts "Up we go!"         "fly" on this object.
end
superhero.fly
```

```
Up we go!
```

Call the "fly" method.

It's also possible to override methods defined by the class with singleton methods. This code overrides the `speak` instance method from the `Person` class with a version unique to the `superhero`:

Override the "speak" method from the Person class.

```
def superhero.speak
  puts "Off to fight crime!"
end
superhero.speak
```

```
Off to fight crime!
```

Call the overridden method.

This ability can be quite useful in unit tests, where you sometimes need an object's method *not* to behave the way it usually does. For example, if an object always creates files to store output, and you don't want it littering your hard drive with files each time you run a test, you can override the file creation method on the instance in your tests.

Singleton methods are surprisingly handy, and just one more example of Ruby's flexibility!

#7 Call any method, even undefined ones

When you call an instance method that *hasn't* been defined on an object, Ruby calls a method named `method_missing` on that object. The version of `method_missing` that all objects inherit from the `Object` class simply raises an exception:

```
object = Object.new
object.win
```

```
undefined method `win' for #<Object:0x007fa87a8311f0> (NoMethodError)
```

But if you override `method_missing` in a class, you can create instances of it and call undefined methods on them, and you won't get an exception. Not only that, you can do interesting things with these "phantom methods"…

Ruby always passes at least one argument to `method_missing`: the name of the method that was called, in the form of a symbol. Also, whatever `method_missing` returns will be treated as the return value of the phantom method. So here's a class that will return a string with the name of any undefined method you call on it.

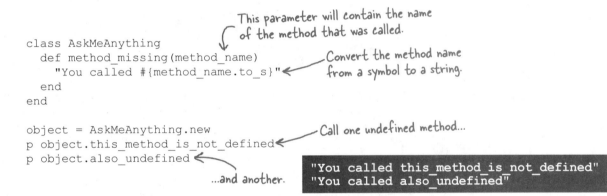

This parameter will contain the name of the method that was called.

```
class AskMeAnything
  def method_missing(method_name)
    "You called #{method_name.to_s}"
  end
end
```

Convert the method name from a symbol to a string.

```
object = AskMeAnything.new
p object.this_method_is_not_defined
p object.also_undefined
```

Call one undefined method…

…and another.

```
"You called this_method_is_not_defined"
"You called also_undefined"
```

Any arguments passed to the undefined method get forwarded on to `method_missing`, so we can return arguments to the phantom method as well…

First argument forwarded here ⌐   ⌐ Second argument forwarded here

```
class AskMeAnything
  def method_missing(method_name, arg1, arg2)
    "You called #{method_name.to_s} with #{arg1} and #{arg2}."
  end
end

object = AskMeAnything.new
p object.with_args(127.6, "hello")
```

```
"You called with_args with 127.6 and hello."
```

#7 Call any method, even undefined ones (continued)

Here's a `Politician` class whose instances will promise to do anything you ask them to. You can call any undefined method and pass it an argument, and `method_missing` will print both the method name and argument.

```ruby
class Politician
  def method_missing(method_name, argument)
    puts "I promise to #{method_name.to_s} #{argument}!"
  end
end
```

Convert from symbol to string.

```ruby
politician = Politician.new
politician.lower("taxes")
politician.improve("education")
```

```
I promise to lower taxes!
I promise to improve education!
```

It gets even better, though… Remember our dRuby code from a few pages ago, which created a proxy object that called methods on another object *over the network*?

```ruby
require 'drb/drb'
DRb.start_service
remote_object = DRbObject.new_with_uri("druby://localhost:8787")
remote_object.push "hello", "network"
p remote_object.last
```

Connect to remote server, and get a proxy for an array.

Call a method on the array.

Call another method on the array.

Proxy objects in dRuby allow you to call *any method* on them. Since the proxy defines almost no methods of its own, those calls get forwarded to the proxy's `method_missing` method. There, the name of the method you called and any arguments you provided are passed over the network to the server.

The server then calls the method on the *actual* object and sends any return value back over the network, where it's returned from the *proxy* object's `method_missing`.

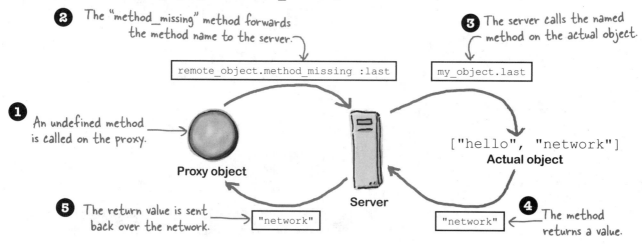

2 The "method_missing" method forwards the method name to the server.

```
remote_object.method_missing :last
```

3 The server calls the named method on the actual object.

```
my_object.last
```

1 An undefined method is called on the proxy.

Proxy object

Server

```
["hello", "network"]
```
Actual object

5 The return value is sent back over the network.

```
"network"
```

```
"network"
```

4 The method returns a value.

The process is complex, but `method_missing` makes it as easy as calling a method on the proxy!

#8 Automating tasks with Rake

Remember back in Chapter 13, when we wanted to run unit tests on classes in our *lib* subdirectory, we had to add -I lib to the command line? We also had to specify the file containing the tests we wanted to run…

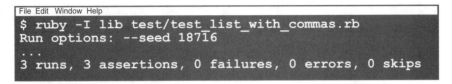

```
File Edit Window Help
$ ruby -I lib test/test_list_with_commas.rb
Run options: --seed 18716
...
3 runs, 3 assertions, 0 failures, 0 errors, 0 skips
```

It's a bit of a pain now, but what if our project grew and we had dozens of test files? Running them one at a time would get pretty unmanageable. And testing is just one of the tasks we have to perform on a regular basis. Eventually, we'll need the ability to build documentation, package our project as a gem, and more.

Ruby comes with a tool called Rake that can simplify all of this for us. You can run the rake command from your terminal, and it will look for a file called "Rakefile" (with no filename extension) in your project directory. This file should contain Ruby code that sets up one or more *tasks* that Rake can perform for us.

Here's a Rakefile that sets up a task to run all of our tests for us. It uses the class Rake::TestTask, which comes with Rake and is specialized for running tests. This TestTask is set to load files from the *lib* directory (no more need for -I lib), and to run every test file in the *test* directory (no need to specify test files one at a time).

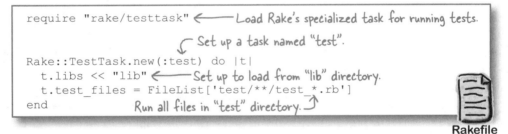

```
require "rake/testtask"        ←—— Load Rake's specialized task for running tests.
                         ┌ Set up a task named "test".
Rake::TestTask.new(:test) do |t|
    t.libs << "lib"  ←——Set up to load from "lib" directory.
    t.test_files = FileList['test/**/test_*.rb']
end              Run all files in "test" directory. ⌐
```

Rakefile

Once a Rakefile is saved in your project directory, you can change to that directory in your terminal and run the command rake, followed by the name of the task you want to run. For our example, there's only one task, test, so we'll run that.

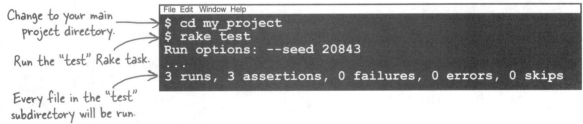

Change to your main project directory.
Run the "test" Rake task.
Every file in the "test" subdirectory will be run.

```
File Edit Window Help
$ cd my_project
$ rake test
Run options: --seed 20843
...
3 runs, 3 assertions, 0 failures, 0 errors, 0 skips
```

With that one simple command, Rake will find and run all the files in our *test* subdirectory!

Rake can help with more than just tests, though. There are also generic tasks that you can use to run any other sort of command you might need. Look up Rake in Ruby's standard library documentation to learn more.

#9 Bundler

At the start of Chapter 14, we ran `gem install sinatra` in the terminal to download and install the Sinatra gem. That was simple enough, since we only needed one gem.

But suppose we also needed the *i18n* gem to help with internationalization (translation to other written languages), and the *erubis* gem for better ERB support. Suppose that we need to make sure we're using an *older* version of i18n, because our code relies on a method that has been removed in the latest version. Suddenly installing gems doesn't seem so simple anymore.

But as usual, there's a tool available that can help: Bundler. Bundler allows each application on your system to have its own set of gems. It also helps you maintain those gems, ensuring the proper version of each is downloaded and installed, and preventing multiple versions of the same gem from conflicting with each other.

Bundler is *not* installed with Ruby; it's distributed as a gem itself. So we first need to install it by typing **gem install bundler** (or **sudo gem install bundler**, if your system requires it) in the terminal. This will install the Bundler library, as well as a `bundle` command that you can run from your terminal.

Install Bundler. ———→

```
File Edit Window Help
$ gem install bundler
Fetching: bundler-1.10.6.gem (100%)
Successfully installed bundler-1.10.6
...
```

Bundler gets the names of gems to install from a file named "Gemfile" (note the similarity to "Rakefile") in your project folder. So, we'll create a Gemfile now.

A Gemfile contains Ruby code just like a Rakefile does, but this file calls methods from the Bundler library. We start with a call to the method `source`, with the URL of the server we want to download gems from. Unless your company is running its own gem server, you'll want to use the Ruby community's server: `'https://rubygems.org'`. Next, we call the method `gem` for each gem we want to install, and provide the gem name and version we want as arguments.

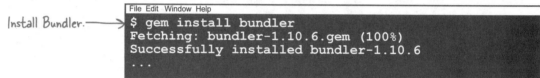

```
source 'https://rubygems.org'   ←——— Download these gems from rubygems.org.

gem "sinatra", "1.4.6"   ←——— Use version 1.4.6 of the Sinatra gem.
gem "i18n", "0.6.11"   ←——— Use version 0.6.11 of the i18n gem.
gem "erubis", "2.7.0"   ←——— Use version 2.7.0 of the Erubis gem.
```

Gemfile

Once your Gemfile has been saved, change to your project directory in your terminal and run **bundle install**. Bundler will automatically download and install the particular versions of the gems that your Gemfile references.

Change to the project directory.

Run the "bundle install" command.

Bundler will install the gems listed in your Gemfile.

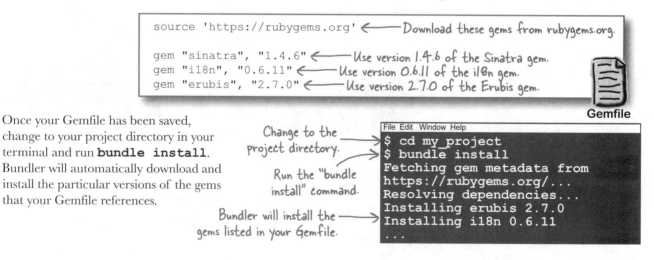

```
File Edit Window Help
$ cd my_project
$ bundle install
Fetching gem metadata from
https://rubygems.org/...
Resolving dependencies...
Installing erubis 2.7.0
Installing i18n 0.6.11
...
```

#9 Bundler (continued)

After Bundler installs the gems in your Gemfile, you can proceed to reference them in your code just as if you'd installed them yourself. You need to make a little change when *running* your app, though: always be sure to prefix the command in your terminal with the `bundle exec` command.

Here's why: if you *don't* use the `bundle` command to run your app, then it's running outside Bundler's control. Even then, everything might seem fine. But part of Bundler's job is to ensure that other gem versions on your system don't conflict with the gems that Bundler installed. It can't do that unless it's running.

So, to be safe, when using Bundler, always type `bundle exec` when running your app (or read up on other ways to ensure your app runs within the Bundler environment). You'll save yourself some trouble someday!

You can learn more about Bundler at: *http://bundler.io/*

Add "bundle exec" before your usual run command.

Your app will run normally, but using only the gems Bundler provides.

```
File Edit  Window Help
$ bundle exec ruby -I lib app.rb
[2015-08-05 22:33:16] INFO
WEBrick 1.3.1
== Sinatra (v1.4.6) has taken
the stage on 4567
...
```

#10 Other books

This is the end of *this* Ruby book, but it's just the start of your Ruby journey. We want to recommend a couple of excellent books that will help you along the road.

Programming Ruby 1.9 & 2.0 (Fourth Edition)
By Dave Thomas, with Chad Fowler and Andy Hunt

The Ruby community has nicknamed this book the "Pickaxe" due to the picture of a pickaxe on its cover. It's well known and widely used.

There are two kinds of technical books out there: tutorial books (like the one you're holding) and reference books (like *Programming Ruby*). And the Pickaxe is a great reference: it covers all the topics we didn't have room for in this book. At the back, it has documentation on all the important classes and modules from Ruby's core and the standard library. (So you won't need the HTML documentation if you have this.)

The Well-Grounded Rubyist (Second Edition)
By David A. Black

If you want insight into the simple elegance of Ruby's inner workings, this is the place to get it. Did you know there's actually no such thing as a class method in Ruby? (So-called class methods are actually just singleton methods on a class object.) Did you know classes are just modules that allow instance variables? David A. Black takes language behavior that sometimes seems complex and inconsistent, and reveals the underlying rules that will make it all click.

Index

Symbols

& (ampersand), denoting block parameter to method 168, 192

&& (and) operator 27

* (asterisk), multiplication operator 6, 122

\ (backslash), in escape sequences 19

\\ (double backslashes) 19

: (colon)
    denoting Sinatra named parameter 484
    replacing hash rocket (=>) with 245
    symbol references using 62

: : (double colon) scope resolution operator, marking class methods 347–348, 357

, (commas)
    joining strings with 391
    separating arguments by 15
    separating array elements 156
    separating parameters by 38, 173

{ } curly braces
    denoting blocks 175
    hash literals 228, 237–238, 245
    using for string interpolation 16

. (dot)
    denoting class methods in documentation 347
    Float vs. Fixnum literals 112–113
    operator, calling methods using 8, 14, 37, 131–136

" (double quotes). *See also* ' (single quotes)
    in double-quoted string 19
    #{...} notation inside 16, 24
    specifying strings using 6

= (equals) sign
    assigning variables using 7
    in naming methods 38

= = (equality) operator 6, 313, 322

! (exclamation mark)
    in naming methods 38
    != (not equal to) operator 27

** (exponentiation) operator 6

/ (forward slash)
    denoting regular expression literals 506
    division operator 6, 112–113, 122
    in Sinatra route paths 484

>= (greater than or equal to operator) 27
    as method 313, 322

> (greater than) sign
    as method 313–315, 322
    calling as method 314
    comparison operator 6

(hash) mark
    at start of method names in documentation 339
    making comments using 14

=> (hash rocket) 245

=> in rescue clause 370

< (less than) sign
    as method 313, 322
    comparison operator 6
    indicating inheritance 81

<= (less than or equal to operator) 27
    as method 312, 322

<< operator, inserting elements into arrays using 158

- (minus sign), subtraction operator 6, 122

| | (or) operator 27, 305–306, 310, 474

( ) parentheses
    using with parameters 36
    with method calls 15

% (percent) sign, format sequences 116–118

B

backslash (\), in escape sequences 19

between? method 313, 322

Black, David A., The Well-Grounded Rubyist (2nd edition) 513

blocks

    about 155, 167

    accessing during method call 185, 192

    adding rescue clause to begin/end 366, 380–381

    building arrays based on return value in 217–219

    creating 169

    declaring &block parameter 174

    each method with

        about 179

        getting rid of repeated code 181–183

        using 180, 202

    find_all method

        passing array elements 203–204, 209–212, 223

        passing words 328–329

    finding array elements using 201–202

    formats for

        curly brace { } 175

        do...end 169, 175

    hash default

        about 272–273

        assigning to hash 274

        block return value 275–276

        hash default objects vs. 280

        matching values assigned to hash 275

        rules for using 283

    include? method in 202–203

    in documentation 342

    map method

        passing array elements into blocks 216–219

        passing words 328–329

    methods

        associating with 176

        calling block multiple times 172–173

        defining methods that take blocks 168

        flow of control between blocks and 170

        passing many blocks into single method 171

        similarities with 204

    parameters in 173–174, 206, 211, 213

    passing hashes to 240

    processing files using 197

    reject method

        passing array elements 212–213

        passing words 328–329

    return keyword within 206

    return values

        about 204–206

        complete code for 220

        find_all method with 210–211

        finding index of array element 215

        hash 275–276

        map method with 216–219

        methods using 209

        opening and closing files 196–197

        processing collections 194–195

        reject method with 212–213

        split method with 214

    split method with 214

    understanding values and 206

    using ampersand (&) to accept 168, 192

    using yield keyword with 174, 192

    variables and 184–185, 198

Boolean values

    methods named with ? returning 202, 223

    operators 26–27

    truthy and falsy values 234–235

    using or (| |) operator for assignment 305–306, 310

Bundler 512–513

C

call method 168, 173

call signatures in documentation 341–342, 358

chomp method 20

classes

    about 21, 46

    Array, documentation on methods in 344

    as superclasses 105

E

each method
    about 179
    Enumerable methods calling 327–329
    hashes and 240
    using 180–183, 186–187
else statement 26
    avoiding use with unless statements 29
Employee class
    adding initialize method to 124–126, 142–143
    creating instances of 110
    defining 108–109
    fixing rounding errors in 114
    implementing pay stubs for hourly employees through
        inheritance 137–139
    setting object attributes 120–123
    using self keyword 131–133
    validation of accessor methods 129–134
encapsulation 58–60
end keyword 26, 36, 48, 169, 291
ensure clause 386–387
Enumerable
    about 311, 326–327, 329, 343
    Comparable vs. 326
    documentation on 343–344
    methods 325
    methods calling each method 327–329
    mixing into classes 327–328
Enumerator class 342
equals (=) sign
    assigning variables using 7
    in naming methods 38
equality (= =) operator 6, 313, 322
ERB
    defined 436
    embedding tags 440
    output embedding tag (<%= %>) 441–442, 483, 490
    regular embedding tag (<% %>) 445–446
ERB library 436

erb method 436–437
ERB templates
    accessing instance variables within 442
    creating for HTML form 450
    displaying objects 490
    setting local variables in 442
error messages, using raise method to report errors
    362–364
escape sequences, in strings 19
Exception classes 375–381, 388
exceptions
    about 364
    differentiating between 375–381
    ensure clause 386–387
    messages 370
    rescue clauses
        about 366–367, 388
        handling exceptions 365
        retry keyword in 382–383
        specifying exception classes for 379
        using 368–369
    using raise method to report errors 362–364
    ZeroDivisionError 412
exclamation mark (!)
    in naming methods 38
    != (not equal to) operator 27
exercises
    on arrays and blocks 189–190, 221–222
    on assertions in testing 411–412, 417
    on Comparable 323–324
    on constructing blocks 207–208
    on creating
        classes 51–52
        instances 65–66
        program using modules and classes 295–296
        Sinatra route 433–434
    on defining Sinatra routes 487–488
    on definitions connected with inheritance 89–90
    on Enumerable 330–331
    on ERB tags 443–444
    on expressions 9–10
    on File class and blocks 199–200

G

GET method for HTTP requests

    about 430

    handling requests 432, 458

    HTML links sending requests 482

    request paths 433

gets method 15, 20

greater than or equal to operator (>=) 27

    as method 313–315, 322

greater than (>) sign

    as method 313–314, 322

    calling as method 314

    comparison operator 6

H

<h1> HTML tag 435

hash default blocks

    about 272–273

    assigning to hash 274

    block return value 275–276

    hash default objects vs. 280

    rules for using 283

hash default objects

    detailed look at 270

    leaving off hash keys and 244

    modifying 269

    problems with 267–268

    references to 279

    rules for using 281–283

    using immutable objects as 281, 284

    using numbers as default for 237, 280

    values returned from unassigned keys and 255, 272

hashes

    about 228–229, 231

    arrays vs. 229, 241, 255

    as method parameters 242–245

    as objects 230

    assigning values to 270, 274–275

    creating new 237, 255, 270

    default object 237, 255

    each method and 240

    Enumerable module and 326

    initialize methods using 244–246

    instance methods of 230

    making optional as parameters 245

    method arguments and 242–243

    nil values 233–234, 246

    regular parameters vs. hash parameters 243

    returning values not nil 236–237

    similarities between arrays and 229

    typos in arguments 248

    using keyword arguments 248–252

    yielding two-element arrays 240

hash keys

    assigning values to 270, 274–275

    checking using if/else statements 236–237

    leaving off in method arguments 244, 246

    normalizing 238–239

    objects used as 229

    referencing hash default object 272

    referring same object 268

    unassigned 267

    using nil with 244

    using square brackets [ ] 228, 237–238

    using symbols as parameter keys 243

hash literals

    omitting curly braces { } for method arguments 245

    using curly braces { } 228, 237–238

hash (#) mark

    at start of method names in documentation 339

    making comments using 14

hash rocket (=>) 245

Head First HTML and CSS (Robson and Freeman) 424

heap 259

href attribute 482–483

HTML documentation 336, 344, 357, 358

K

keyword arguments
    hash parameters and 249–252
    in methods 255
keywords
    and 391, 404
    class 48
    def 36
    do 169
    end 26, 36, 48, 169, 291
    retry 382–383
    return 43, 149, 206
    self 131–136, 138, 154, 179
    super 96–98
        about 96–97
        initialize and 142–144
        omitting parentheses with 97
        return value of 105
        using 98
    yield 174, 179, 192

L

<label> HTML tag 449–450
length method
    on arrays 161, 192
    on hashes 230
less than (<) sign
    as method 313, 322
    comparison operator 6
    indicating inheritance 81
less than or equal to operator (<=) 27
    as method 312, 322
lib directory 397, 419, 424, 439
libraries
    CSV 502
    dRuby 501
    ERB 436
    MiniTest. *See* MiniTest library
    Ruby standard 350–352, 502
    WEBrick 429, 432, 458–459, 482
    YAML 465

<li> HTML tag 435
ListWithCommas class 401–409
literals
    array 229
    Float vs. Fixnum 112–113
    for numbers 52, 120, 154
    hash
        leaving off curly braces { } 245
        using curly braces { } 228, 237–238
    regular expression 506
load method 465
LOAD_PATH 426
local variables, methods and 55
loops
    about 34
    arrays and 161–164, 180–183, 186–187
    until 30–31
    while 30–31, 161, 180–183, 186–187

M

map method
    documentation on 344
    on Enumerable 311, 325
    using 217–219, 328–329, 478–479
math operators
    about 6
    addition operator (+) 6, 122
    as methods 122
    division (/) 6, 112–113, 122–123
    exponentiation (**) 6
    multiplication (*) 6, 122
    subtraction (-) 6, 122
Matsumoto, Yukihiro "Matz," developer of Ruby 2
max method 474
method arguments
    about 15, 38–40
    hashes and 242–243
method attribute of <form> HTML tag 460
method body 36, 38
method calls
    arguments passing with 39
    on objects 8

Y

Z

Have it your way.

Get even more for your money.

Join the O'Reilly Community, and register the O'Reilly books you own. It's free, and you'll get:

- $4.99 ebook upgrade offer
- 40% upgrade offer on O'Reilly print books
- Membership discounts on books and events
- Free lifetime updates to ebooks and videos
- Multiple ebook formats, DRM FREE
- Participation in the O'Reilly community
- Newsletters
- Account management
- 100% Satisfaction Guarantee

Signing up is easy:

1. Go to: oreilly.com/go/register
2. Create an O'Reilly login.
3. Provide your address.
4. Register your books.

Note: English-language books only

To order books online:
oreilly.com/store

For questions about products or an order:
orders@oreilly.com

To sign up to get topic-specific email announcements and/or news about upcoming books, conferences, special offers, and new technologies:
elists@oreilly.com

For technical questions about book content:
booktech@oreilly.com

To submit new book proposals to our editors:
proposals@oreilly.com

O'Reilly books are available in multiple DRM-free ebook formats. For more information:
oreilly.com/ebooks